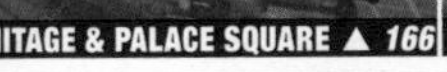

...MITAGE & PALACE SQUARE ▲ 166

SUMMER GARDEN ▲ 186

A VISTA OF BRIDGES ▲ 194

...TS SQUARE ▲ 224

A. NEVSKY MONASTERY ▲ 253

PETERHOF ▲ 256

show that attracts many devotees.

THEATER SQUARE
The Mariinsky Theater has made this square the city's artistic hub.

KOLOMNA DISTRICT
The four islands, nine embankments and twenty bridges of this 19th-century district can be explored by boat.

NEVSKY PROSPEKT
The city's main thoroughfare is lined with shops, churches and various palaces. Malaya Sadovaya Street is especially worth a visit.

ARTS SQUARE
Three museums, two theaters, the Philharmonia, and the crafts market nearby make up this historic area.

NEVSKY MONASTERY
It contains the Artists' Necropolis, where great Russian artists are buried.

PETERHOF
This great Baroque palace and its parks are the venue for popular festivities.

ST PETERSBURG

KNOPF GUIDES

● Encyclopedia section

■ **NATURE** The natural heritage: species and habitats characteristic to the area covered by the guide, annotated and illustrated by naturalist authors and artists.
HISTORY The impact of international historical events on local history, from the arrival of the first inhabitants to the present day, with key dates appearing in a timeline above the text.
ARTS AND TRADITIONS The region's local customs and traditions and their continuing role in contemporary life.
ARCHITECTURE The architectural heritage, focusing on style and topology, a look at rural and urban buildings, major civil, religious and military monuments.
AS SEEN BY PAINTERS A selection of paintings of the city or country by different artists and schools, arranged chronologically or thematically.
AS SEEN BY WRITERS An anthology of texts focusing on the city or country, taken from works of all periods and countries, arranged thematically.

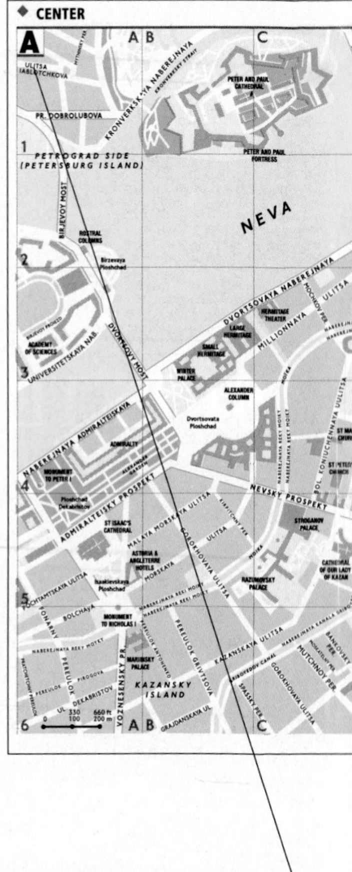

▲ Itineraries

Each itinerary begins with a map of the area to be explored.
✪ **SPECIAL INTEREST** These sites are not to be missed. They are highlighted in gray boxes in the margins.
★ **EDITOR'S CHOICE** Sites singled out by the editor for special attention.
INSETS On richly illustrated double pages, these insets turn the spotlight on subjects deserving more in-depth treatment.

◆ CENTER
A
A B
ULITSA IABLOTCHKOVA
MYTNINSKY PER.
PR. DOBROLUBOVA
KRONVERKSKAYA NABEREJNAYA

Each map in the map section is designated by a letter. In the practical information, each place can be pinpointed on the map (for example: ◆ **A** B1).

◆ Practical information

All the travel information you will need before you go and when you get there.
USEFUL ADDRESSES A selection of the best hotels and restaurants compiled by an expert.
PLACES TO VISIT A handy table of addresses and opening hours.
APPENDICES Bibliography, list of illustrations and general index.
MAP SECTION Maps of all the areas covered by the guide, preceded by a street index; these maps are marked out with letters and figures making it easy for the reader to pinpoint a town, region or site.

The itinerary map shows the main sites of interest.

■ ● ▲ ◆ The above symbols within the text provide cross-references to a place or a theme discussed elsewhere in the guide.

★ The star symbol signifies sites singled out by the editor for special attention.

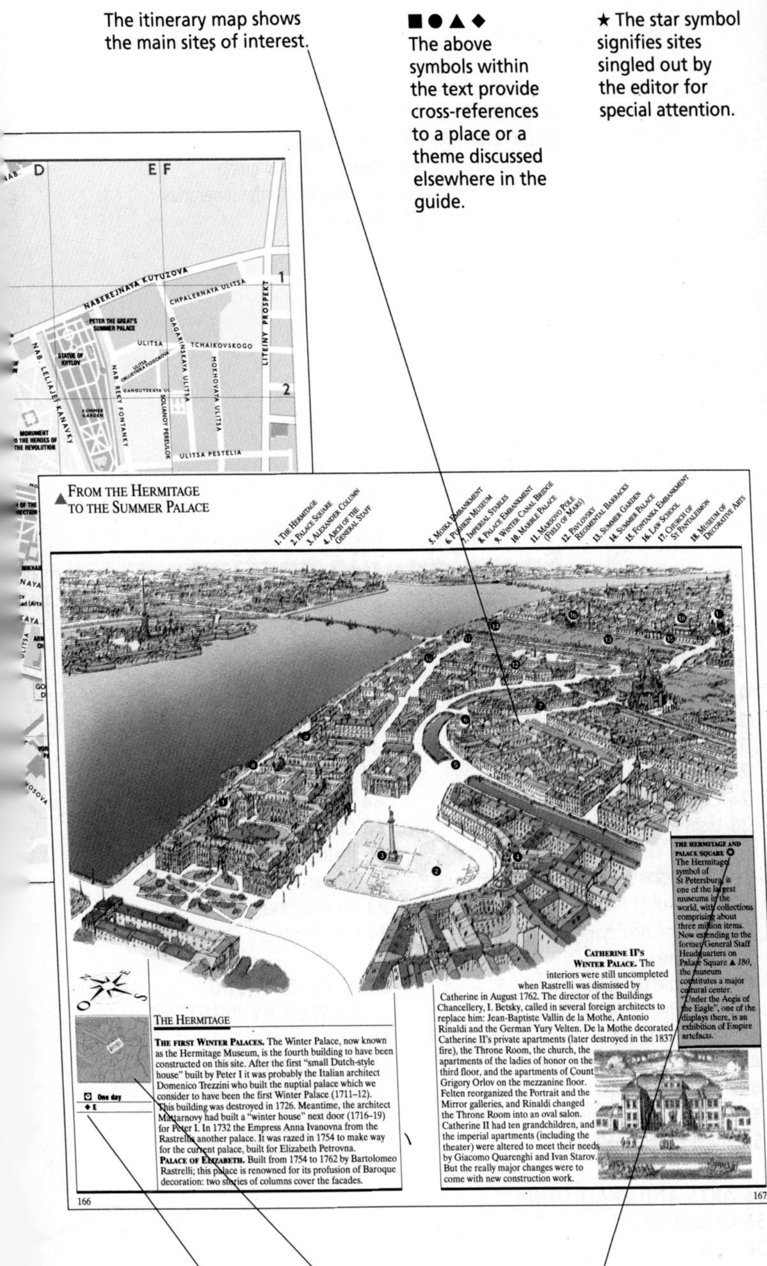

NABEREJNAYA KUTUZOVA
CHPALERNAYA ULITSA
PETER THE GREAT'S SUMMER PALACE
ULITSA TCHAIKOVSKOGO
STATUE OF KRYLOV
NAB. LELIAJEF KANAVKY
NAB. REKY FONTANKY
GAGARINSKAYA ULITSA
MOKHOVAYA ULITSA
LITEINY PROSPEKT
SOLIANOY PERELOK
ULITSA PESTELIA
MONUMENT TO THE HEROES OF THE REVOLUTION
▲ FROM THE HERMITAGE TO THE SUMMER PALACE
1. THE HERMITAGE
2. PALACE SQUARE
3. ALEXANDER COLUMN
4. ARCH OF THE GENERAL STAFF
5. MOIKA EMBANKMENT
6. PUSHKIN MUSEUM
7. IMPERIAL STABLES
8. PALACE EMBANKMENT
9. WINTER CANAL BRIDGE
10. MARBLE PALACE
11. MARSOVO POLE (FIELD OF MARS)
12. PAVLOVSKY REGIMENTAL BARRACKS
13. SUMMER GARDEN
14. SUMMER PALACE
15. FONTANKA EMBANKMENT
16. LAW SCHOOL
17. CHURCH OF ST PANTALEIMON
18. MUSEUM OF DECORATIVE ARTS
One day
◆ E
THE HERMITAGE
THE FIRST WINTER PALACES. The Winter Palace, now known as the Hermitage Museum, is the fourth building to have been constructed on this site. After the first "small Dutch-style house" built by Peter I it was probably the Italian architect Domenico Trezzini who built the nuptial palace which we consider to have been the first Winter Palace (1711–12). This building was destroyed in 1726. Meantime, the architect Mattarnovy had built a "winter house" next door (1716–19) for Peter I. In 1732 the Empress Anna Ivanovna from the Rastrelli another palace. It was razed in 1754 to make way for the current palace, built for Elizabeth Petrovna.
PALACE OF ELIZABETH. Built from 1754 to 1762 by Bartolomeo Rastrelli; this palace is renowned for its profusion of Baroque decoration: two stories of columns cover the facades.
166
CATHERINE II'S WINTER PALACE. The interiors were still uncompleted when Rastrelli was dismissed by Catherine in August 1762. The director of the Buildings Chancellery, I. Betsky, called in several foreign architects to replace him: Jean-Baptiste Vallin de la Mothe, Antonio Rinaldi and the German Yury Velten. De la Mothe decorated Catherine II's private apartments (later destroyed in the 1837 fire), the Throne Room, the church, the apartments of the ladies of honor on the third floor, and the apartments of Count Grigory Orlov on the mezzanine floor. Felten reorganized the Portrait and the Mirror galleries, and Rinaldi changed the Throne Room into an oval salon. Catherine II had ten grandchildren, and the imperial apartments (including the theater) were altered to meet their needs by Giacomo Quarenghi and Ivan Starov. But the really major changes were to come with new construction work.
THE HERMITAGE AND PALACE SQUARE ✪
The Hermitage, symbol of St Petersburg, is one of the largest museums in the world, with collections comprising about three million items. Now extending to the former General Staff Headquarters on Palace Square ▲ 180, the museum constitutes a major cultural center. "Under the Aegis of the Eagle", one of the displays there, is an exhibition of Empire artefacts.
167

At the beginning of each itinerary, the time it will take to cover the area is indicated beneath the mini-map, as are the grid references to the map section

The mini-map pinpoints the itinerary within the wider area covered by the guide.

✪ This symbol indicates places of special interest.

Encyclopedia section

▲ Itineraries in St Petersburg

◆ Practical information

FROM THE FORTRESS TO THE ISLANDS OF THE DELTA ▲ 143

A historic place from which to explore the city, the Fortress contains the Peter and Paul Cathedral, the History Museum and the Old Arsenal. The Petrograd Side, a district on the right bank of the Neva, has buildings in the Art Nouveau style. To the west lie the islands of the delta, which, with their parks and gardens, are a favorite place of relaxation for St Petersburgers.

VASILYEVSKY ISLAND ▲ 155

The part of the island known as the Point (Strelka) has a large population of students and academics, and many monuments, museums, colleges and research institutes connected to the university or the Russian Navy. Menshikov Palace, with splendid apartments, and the Kunstkammer, Peter the Great's gallery of curiosities, both on University Embankment, are open to visitors.

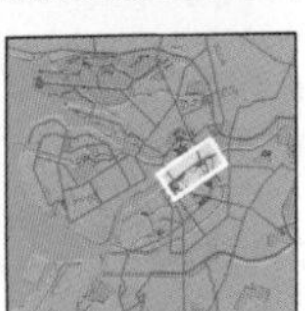

FROM THE HERMITAGE TO THE SUMMER PALACE ▲ 165

Oppposite the Fortress, on the left bank of the Neva, stand palaces, gardens and major monuments, all of them examples of the Peter-the-Great style. They include the Hermitage, one of the largest museums in the world, Palace Square and, between the Marble Palace and the Summer Palace, the huge Field of Mars. Fine 18th-century statues grace the Summer Garden.

FROM THE ADMIRALTY TO THE HAYMARKET ▲ 189

Highlights include the Admiralty and New Holland districts, built on the site of former shipyards; the beautiful St Isaac's Cathedral, the largest church in St Petersburg; Theater Square, hub of the city's artistic life and home of the acclaimed Mariinsky Theater; St Nicholas' Cathedral, a fine example of Baroque elegance in blue, white and gold; and the 19th-century Dostoevsky District.

AROUND NEVSKY PROSPEKT ▲ 211

Nevsky Prospekt is the city's main thoroughfare and its finest commercial street. On Arts Square and Ostrovsky Square stand major artistic institutions: among them are the Russian Museum in Mikhail Palace, Engineers' Castle, the Shostakovich Philarmonia and the Alexandrinsky Theater. The Church of the Resurrection, with its famous twisted onion domes, is also not to be missed.

FROM THE FONTANKA TO INSURRECTION SQUARE ▲ 235

Running from Fountains House to the Rimsky-Korsakov Museum and Dostoevsky Museum, and taking in the Samoilov Museum and Pushkin Street, this literary and musical itinerary follows in the footsteps of great Russian writers and composers. An additional highlight is Beloselsky-Belozersky Palace, now used as a cultural center that also features a waxworks museum.

FROM SMOLNY TO ALEXANDER NEVSKY MONASTERY ▲ 245

Smolny Monastery and Cathedral, masterpieces of Russian Baroque architecture, contrast with the restrained style of the Smolny Institute , which played a prominent role in the 1917 Revolution. This historical itinerary takes in Kikin Palace, Tauride Palace and the Alexander Nevsky Monastery, where major figures in Russian intellectual life are buried.

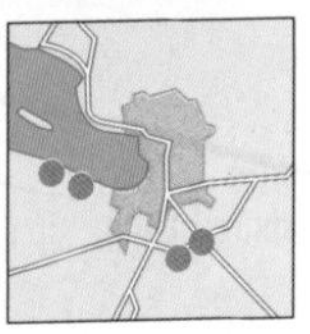

PALACES ON THE OUTSKIRTS OF ST PETERSBURG ▲ 255

Major festivities takes place at Peterhof, a palace set in grounds with elaborate fountains. Oranienbaum, which has been open to visitors for several years now, contains some remarkable examples of marquetry. Also open to the public are Tsarskoe Selo, whose well-known façade is 985 feet wide, and Pavlovsk, by far the most sophisticated of all Russian summer palaces.

Numerous specialists and academics have contributed to this guide. All the information that it contains has been approved by them.

• Encyclopedia section

NATURE
Vladimir Leftchenko,
Alexey Nekrassov, Jean-Pierre Verdet,
Philippe Dubois
LANGUAGE
Annette Lefebvre
HISTORY
Tamara Kondratieva
ARTS AND TRADITIONS
Antoine Nivière, Alexandra Schouwaloff,
Emmanuel Ducamp, Béatrice Picon-Vallin,
Natalia Metelitsa, Igor Dimitriev,
Prascovie de Saint-Hippolyte
ARCHITECTURE
Brigitte de Montclos, Ewa Bérard,
Andrey Punin, Vladimir Rivline
ST PETERSBURG AS SEEN BY PAINTERS
Alexandra Schouwaloff
THE RUSSIAN AVANT-GARDE
Andrey Nakov
ST PETERSBURG AS SEEN BY WRITERS
Lucinda Gane
ALEXANDER PUSHKIN
Anne Klimoff

▲ Itineraries in St Petersburg

Anne Nercessian, Alexander Noskov,
Brigitte de Montclos, Natalya Brodskaya,
Vera Biron, Vitaly Sychev, Natalya Metelitsa,
Vladimir Leon, Alexandra Schouwaloff,
Tamara Kondratieva, Emmanuel Ducamp

◆ Practical information

Olga Yartseva
Hotels and restaurants: Olga Yartseva,
Robert Cottrell of the *Financial Times*
and Catherine Sharpe

KNOPF GUIDES

This is a Borzoi Book published by Alfred A. Knopf

Completely revised and updated in 2003

Published in the United States by Alfred A. Knopf, a division of Random House, Inc., New York, and simultaneously in Canada by Random House of Canada Limited, Toronto. Distributed by Random House, Inc., New York.

Knopf, Borzoi Books, and the colophon are registered trademarks of Random House, Inc

www.aaknopf.com

ISBN 0-375-71025-6

Originally published in France by Nouveaux-Loisirs, a subsidiary of Editions Gallimard, Paris, 1994. Copyright © 1994 by Editions Nouveaux-Loisirs

Translated by
Anthony Roberts
and Yvonne Worth (Practical section)

Edited and typeset by
Book Creation Services, London

Printed and bound in Italy by
Editoriale Lloyd

ST PETERSBURG

EDITORS
Sophie Mastelinck and Agnès Baubault, with Odile Simon (Nature)
LAYOUT
Yann Le Duc assisted by Annie Civard and Carole Gaborit
PICTURE RESEARCH
Catherine Boncenne
UPDATE
Olga Yartseva and Sophie Besançon (editing)

ILLUSTRATIONS
Nature: Jean Chevallier, François Desbordes, Claire Felloni, Catherine Lachaux, Dominique Mansion, Pascale Robin, John Wilkinson
Architecture: Michel Aubois, Jean-François Binet, Vincent Brunot, François Desbordes, Jean-Marie Guillou, Jean-Michel Kacedan, Maurice Pommier, Sylvain Roueri, Amato Soro, Catherine Totems
Itineraries: Jean-Michel Kacedan, Maurice Pommier, Laure Massin (coloring), Jean-Philippe Chabot, Frédéric Bony
Maps: Vincent Brunot, Éric Gillion, Marc Lagarde (coloring)
Computer graphics: Édigraphie, Paul Coulbois, Xavier Garnerin (Latitude), Patrick Merienne

PHOTOGRAPHY
V. Baranovsky, V. Buss, Roger Gain, Koncharov, V. Savik, V. Terebenin

WITH SPECIAL THANKS TO
Anne Nercessian, Vera Biron (Dostoevsky Museum, St Petersburg), Véronique Schiltz, Galina Vassiliev (Historic Archives of St Petersburg), Georges Willembachov (Hermitage Museum), Martine Kahane (Opéra Garnier-Bastille), Alexandre Illinsky, Vladimir Terebebin, Helena Asséeva, Isabelle Haas and Stéphanie François

Encyclopedia section

"The quays of St Petersburg are among the loveliest things in Europe: why? Because they embody both luxury and solidity."
Astolphe de Custine

Photograph: bicentary celebrations of the founding of St Petersburg, May 1900

"The aspect of St Petersburg is more conducive of astonishment than admiration . . . if it is not quite perfectly beautiful, it is none the less completely strange."
Olympe Audovard

Photograph: The Fontanka from Anichkov Bridge, 1900

"On the left was a little black canal, which lay against the colossus of the Admiralty . . . gilded at every edge, and adorned by a glinting statue of Fame, all in gold . . ."
Louis-Ferdinand Céline

Photograph: entrance to the Admiralty, c. 1900

"There is nothing finer than Nevsky Prospekt, not in St Petersburg at any rate; for in St Petersburg it is everything. And, indeed, is there anything more gay, more brilliant, more resplendent than this beautiful street of our capital?"

Nikolai Gogol

Photograph: Nevsky Prospekt, 1906

Nature

THE SITE

The St Petersburg region extends 280 miles west to east and between 65 and 200 miles north to south. Its southeast extremity is washed by the waters of the Gulf of Finland; and to the north of it is Lake Ladoga. The region lies to the northwest of the Russian plateau, the substratum of which is crystalline rock. The various ice ages produced morainic elevations and lakes, which in general give the land its undulating aspect. The climate is one of strong contrasts, being conditioned on the one hand by the movement of air masses off the Atlantic and on the other by polar continental air, which is dry and very cold in winter.
St Petersburg itself is situated more or less where the northern and temperate climatic regions meet.

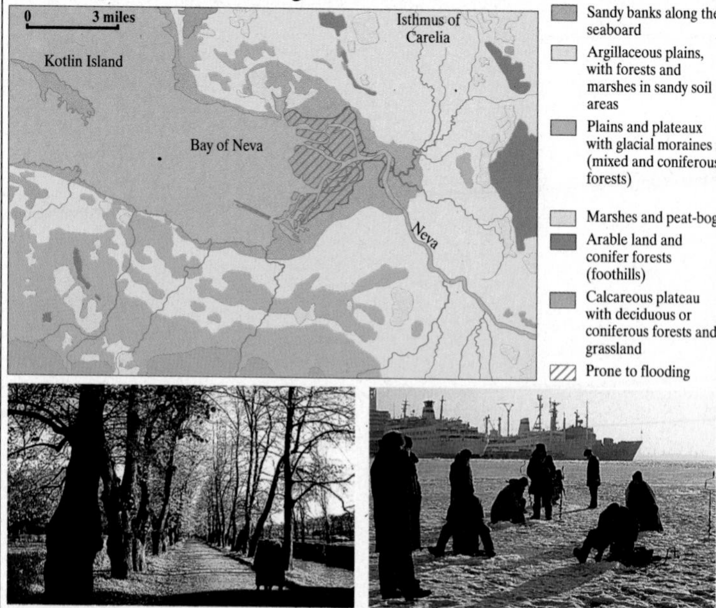

Autumn weather is characterized by frequent depressions, with strong winds causing occasional floods.

In December Atlantic depressions bring rain and snow; in January and February the arrival of dry air from the Arctic makes for cloudless skies.

The black tern lives in noisy colonies among the marshes skirting the Bay of the Neva.

On the island of Kotlin the construction of a dyke was begun in the 1980's as a measure to protect the city from flooding. The dyke is still unfinished, because it has been shown to disturb the Neva estuary's ecosystem.

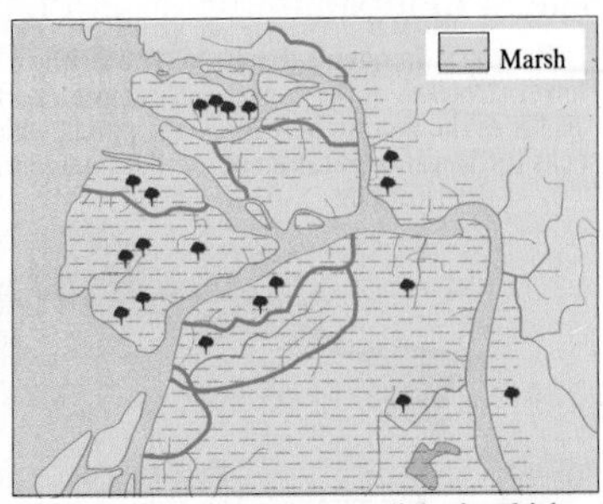

The marshy, island-strewn delta in which Peter the Great chose to build his capital ● *78* benefits from Atlantic weather, without which the region would probably be icebound for much of the year.

Average temperatures at ground level (°c)

— 16 — July isotherm (61°F)

— -8 — January isotherm (18°F)

33 Maximum temperatures (91°F)

-40 Minimum temperatures (-40°F)

Average precipitation (mm)

less — more

Isohyet

Prevailing winds

July

January

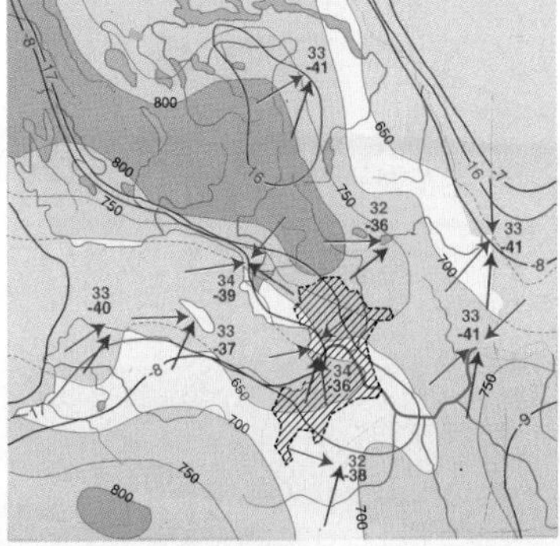

In the spring the weather changes frequently on account of the continual confrontation of air masses.

In July the average temperature is 67°F. July is also a season of thunderstorms; cloudbursts can be very violent.

SPARLING
Between March and May this deep-sea fish runs up the Neva to Lake Ladoga, where it spawns. At this time of year hundreds of fishermen stand on the Neva bridges, waiting for the *koriuchka* to come up river.

The Neva flows out of Lake Ladoga, then crosses the isthmus of Carelia to form a delta at its junction with the Gulf of Finland. The river's entire length is less than 50 miles, but it is some 500 yards across at its widest point and about 80 feet deep. The Neva's vast volume of water makes it the sixth largest river in Europe.

ROACH
The roach frequents the lower stretches of the Neva, as far as the mouth; here it seeks the sandy substratum of the river bed.

PERCH
The strong currents of the Neva are a perfect habitat for the perch, which lays its eggs on aquatic plants.

BREAM
Well-adapted to the Neva's waters, bream tend to frequent the muddier parts of the river bed.

PIKE PERCH
This voracious fish, very common in Eastern Europe, prefers still waters but may also be found where the current flows strongly.

RUFFE
A bottom-dwelling fish confined to lakes and big rivers, the ruff habitually moves in shoals.

SWIFT AND HOUSE MARTIN
These birds nest on the great riverfront buildings of St Petersburg, notably the Hermitage ▲ *168*. They feed on insects, skimming close to the water's surface.

During the winter the Neva may be impassable for a period varying between two and five months. In the winter of 1941–2 ● *50* the Neva was covered by ice over 3 feet thick. The river's powerful current sometimes brings very high water.

The worst flooding on record took place in 1824 ● *35*. Dykes have been constructed in the bay of the Neva to protect the city.

Following the thaw the Neva may still remain impassable to ships for over a month. Every spring great blocks of ice sweep down the river from Lake Ladoga to the open sea.

BLACK-HEADED GULL
Present on the river all year round, this half-tame gull will often eat from the hand during the winter.

The Summer Garden ▲ *186* is a combination of rigorous landscaping and exuberant animal life.

The building of the city of St Petersburg led inevitably to a significant change in the vegetation of the surrounding region. The new artificial plantations brought with them a number of foreign exotic plant species to live alongside the indigenous varieties. Nowadays St Petersburg still remains a "green city", with historic spaces – such as the Summer Garden and the enormous parks of Krestovsky and Elagin islands – which serve as urban reminders of the great forests that lie further afield.

RED SQUIRREL
The shy, agile rodent is widespread throughout the parks and cemeteries of St Petersburg.

PINE MARTEN
A carnivorous member of the weasel family, which habitually feeds on birds as well as small mammals, beetles and carrion.

HOODED CROW
Omnipresent in the city, this crow is especially numerous in the smaller parks and around the Alexander Nevsky Monastery ▲ *253*.

Male

Female

SISKIN
The siskin is common in the mountain and forest regions of Europe – and in the parks of St Petersburg.

SCARLET ROSEFINCH
This oriental species is currently expanding its range deep into Western Europe.

FIELDFARE
The fieldfare nests in noisy colonies, especially in the Summer Garden.

THRUSH NIGHTINGALE
A legendary songbird, the eastern European version of our common nightingale.

Tourists may be surprised by the sight of men scything the grass by hand in Elagin Park ▲ *154*.

ALDER
The berries of this small tree, which favors cool, humid soils, attracts birds like the siskin during the winter months.

LIME TREE
The lime is very common in and around St Petersburg. In June and July the gardens are richly scented with its blooms.

HORNBEAM
Hornbeams, widely planted in Russia during the 19th century, supply generous shade and easily worked wood.

WILLOW WARBLER
This long-distance migrant nests in large numbers in the woods around St Petersburg, where willows, rowans and birches predominate.

The forests of the St Petersburg region straddle a transitional zone between the northern taiga, where conifers proliferate, and the mixed woodlands of the temperate regions. The latter, a blend of deciduous trees and conifers, seem to have receded southward following a very cold, wet period over four thousand years ago. In the Carelian forest there are fewer deciduous trees, and rowans predominate. Numerous lakes, interspersed with marshes and heather-covered peat bogs, give this area a charm that is properly more Scandinavian than Russian, yet this is the quintessential "Russian forest" described by novelists.

CHAFFINCH
Large numbers of chaffinches populate the St Petersburg region in summer, migrating to southern Europe in the winter.

NORWAY PINE
Abundant on the sandy soils around the northern rim of the Gulf of the Neva.

BIRCH
One of the principal hardwood trees in the St Petersburg region; it often grows with conifers.

SPRUCE
Typical of the Carelian forest. Its fruits are a rich source of food for woodland birdlife.

BEARBERRY
The *toloknyanka* is very similar to the bilberry and is widely used in pharmacology.

MILITARY ORCHID
The military orchid flowers in May and June on calcareous sunny banks and along the margins of woods.

SWAMP-BERRY
The deep blue fruit of the swamp-berry is a common sight in marshy areas during the autumn.

COTTON GRASS
In June, when the *puchitsa* is in flower, its fluffy seedballs cover the ground like newly-fallen snow.

ELK (MOOSE)
In the 1970's elk were still present in large numbers up to the edge of the city. Stocks have declined steeply in recent years.

GRAY WOLF
A small wolf population survives around St Petersburg, but is now under severe threat from hunters.

Desbordes

SPOTTED FLYCATCHER
A migrant bird with dull plumage, the spotted flycatcher favors the upper branches of trees; often the only sign of its presence is a high-pitched "tsic" call.

The cemeteries of St Petersburg come as a surprise to most visitors to the city. From the outside they appear impenetrable, but those who persevere will be rewarded with the sight of an unkempt riot of graves, bushes and sprawling wild plants. During the Soviet era the cemeteries were not maintained, with the result that the growth of lush vegetation remained unchecked; this in turn attracted abundant wild creatures which took advantage of the near-natural conditions that prevailed there.

The tangle of plants and ruined tombstones offers a quiet refuge from the din of the surrounding city.

RED FOX
The parks and cemeteries of St Petersburg have made it possible for the red fox to survive in the heart of the city. Foxes may often be glimpsed by daylight, hunting for mice, rats and voles.

Pied flycatcher
Very numerous in temperate woodlands, this migrant nests in older trees.

Robin
Unlike robins in western Europe, those in Russia migrate southward in winter.

Blackcap
This warbler arrives in St Petersburg in May, migrating south in August.

Tree sparrow
Very common in the open green spaces of St Petersburg, it is seldom seen in the built-up areas, unlike its cousin the house sparrow.

Poplar
In the early summer the cotton-like seeds of the catkin carpet the surrounding vegetation in white.

Russian elm
These elms are especially common in St Petersburg's cemeteries; they seem less vulnerable to disease than the western European variety.

Ivy
Most of the older graves in the cemeteries are completely obscured by ivy.

Raspberries
In the autumn wild raspberries are a delight to strollers and birds alike.

Norway maple
St Petersburg lies roughly at the northernmost limit of the Norway maple.

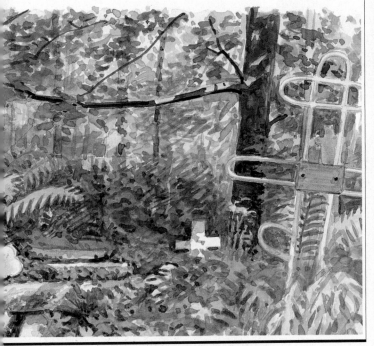

LIGHT AT MIDNIGHT

> "Across the sky, gilded
> By the sun's perpetual rays
> Dawn hurries to relieve
> The unconsummated dusk
> And night endures for barely an hour."
> Pushkin, *The Bronze Horseman*

As St Petersburg is not within the Arctic Circle, there is no midnight sun, but its latitude is sufficiently high (almost 60°N) to bring some light throughout the night. The sun only just dips below the horizon and the earth's atmosphere continues to diffuse its beams. Most plants are in full bloom at this time of year.

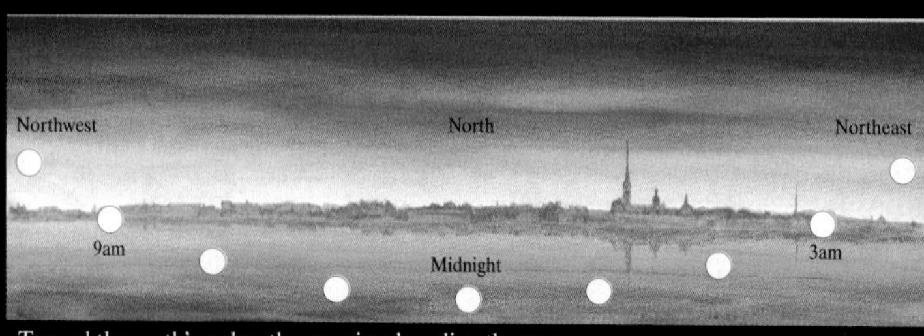

Toward the earth's poles, the sun rises less directly over the horizon, and the more the days vary in length over the year.

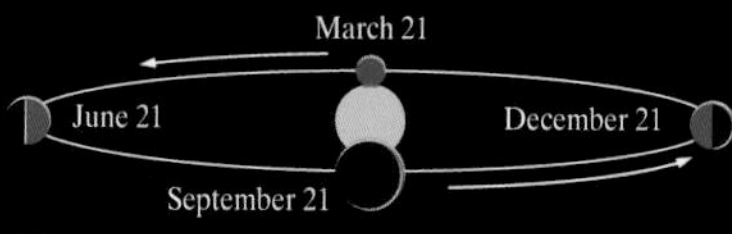

The earth describes its elliptical orbit around the sun in 365 days and 6 hours. During this revolution the inclination of the earth varies in relation to the sun, determining the lengths of the days and seasons.

▼ SUMMER SOLSTICE

On June 21 the night, or rather twilight, lasts only five hours at St Petersburg. At midnight the sun lies only 6° beneath the horizon. In London at the same time of year the night lasts for seven hours and the sun drops 23° below the horizon. In New York the night lasts for nine hours and twenty minutes and the sun drops 25° below the horizon.

▲ WINTER SOLSTICE

On December 21 at noon the sun stands at slightly over 6° above St Petersburg. In London it is at 26° and in New York at 27°. From mid-afternoon onward the Gulf of Finland is under cover of night.

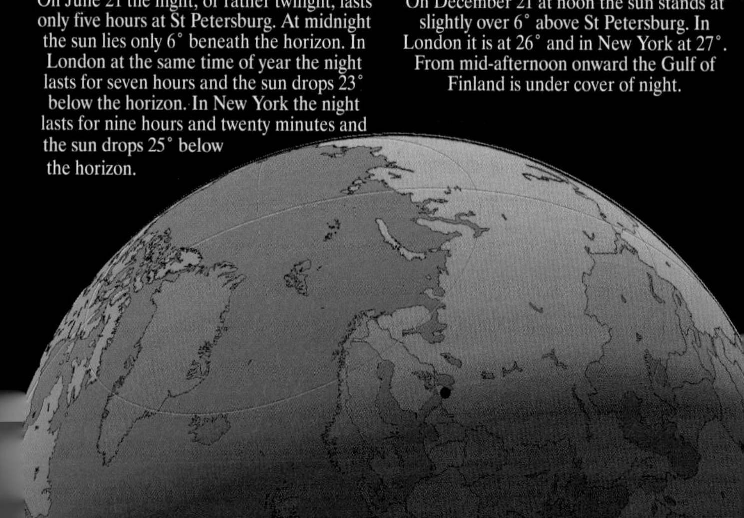

History and language

1700 | 1750

1682–1725
Reign of Peter the Great, who proclaimed himself Emperor

1700–21
Northern War: the Russians annex Estonia, Latvia and Carelia

1703–25 "A WINDOW ON EUROPE"

A NEW ETERNAL CITY

On May 16, 1703 a village by the Neva, recently abandoned by its Finnish inhabitants, began to resound to the din of saws and axes. On June 29, the Feast of Saint Peter and Saint Paul, the foundations of a church were laid within the precinct of the future fortress of the same name: Sankt-Piter-Bourkh (pronounced in the Dutch manner) identified the Czar with the names of the two saints. In doing so, Peter the Great sought to endow Russia with an imperial, messianic destiny, of which Rome was the paramount model.

The arms of the city of St Petersburg borrow from the emblems of Rome and the Vatican: thus the crossed anchors refer both to the papal keys, which symbolize faith, and to the fleet created by Peter the Great, which could also "open the gates of Paradise". From the first years of its construction, the city of St Petersburg was known to Russians as "paradise".

THE CONQUEST OF NATURE FOR REASONS OF STATE

Peter's city gradually grew out of the marshes. In September 1703 the wooden fortress was completed, along with the Czar's house. But soon stone was brought in as the principal construction material. The richest families were obliged by law to build their mansions of stone, and were heavily fined if they failed to do so. According to an *ukaze* (edict) of 1714, which remained in force for sixty-five years, every boat, vessel or waggon entering the city had to bring with it a certain amount of cut stone. On the building sites labored vast numbers of convicts and serfs (40,000 on average between 1709 and 1716), adventurers, soldiers, Russian craftsmen and foreign specialists. The foreigners came in the hope of gain and were sometimes detained by force. Hunger and cold killed nearly 100,000 people during the first years of building, sacrificed to the will and ambition of the Czar. Strategic and commercial considerations justified the choice of his apparently unpromising site. By May 1703 Peter was promising substantial grants to the first three merchant vessels to drop anchor in the new port.

1795
Third partition of Poland between Austria, Prussia and Russia

1800

1809
Annexation of Finland

1812
Napoleon in Moscow

June 18, 1815
Battle of Waterloo

September 26, 1815
Foundation of the Holy Alliance

1853–6:
Crimean War

THE "PALMYRA OF THE NORTH"

In a letter dated September 28, 1704, Czar Peter referred to the city under construction as his "new capital". The inauguration took place in 1712, at which time the Russian court, the Senate and the foreign embassies all moved to St Petersburg from Moscow; Peter was subsequently married there, to a Lithuanian peasant girl. The first museums, a library, a theater, an observatory and the Academy of Sciences were quickly opened. In the vicinity of St Petersburg were built the palaces of Oranienbaum and Peterhof, while a road was built to Tsarskoe Selo, the future summer residence of the Czars.

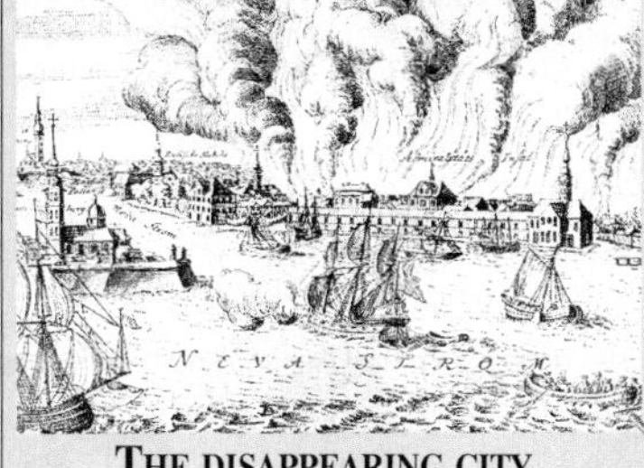

THE DISAPPEARING CITY

After the death of Peter the Great, half the Russian court and at least half of the population of St Petersburg fled the city. The *ukaze* of 1729, which threatened fugitives with exile and the confiscation of their property, had little effect. New, harsher measures sparked a revolt, and in 1737 the city was burned down. Nevertheless the Empress Elizabeth I (right), Peter the Great's daughter, pressed on with the construction of the Winter and Anichkov palaces and the Gostiny Dvor, so realizing her father's dream. Catherine II ● *40* lifted the restrictions, enticed the population back with perquisites, and initiated major construction projects such as the Tauride Palace and Marble Palace, the Hermitage, the Smolny Institute, the bridges and the granite river embankment. Toward the mid-19th century, thanks to the talents of both Russian and foreign-born artists, St Petersburg "... became distinct from the other cities of Europe, precisely because it so nearly resembled each one of them". Travelers called it the "London", "Venice", "Rome", "Berlin" or "Paris" of Russia, as it struck them. But the city's new attractions obliged its inhabitants to adapt: some social groups to luxury and extravagance, the rest to the behavior of their superiors in the hierarchy. Poets and writers, meanwhile, became intrigued by the mystery of this seductive but far from traditional city.

February 19, 1861
Abolition of serfdom in Russia

December 1865
Abolition of slavery in the USA

1889–92
Counter-reforms

1861 **1880**

1863–5
Liberal reforms of Alexander II

1864–76
Marx and Engels: the First International

March 1, 1881
Assassination of Czar Alexander

1883
Marxist propaganda appears in Russia

THE INDUSTRIAL CENTER OF THE EMPIRE

The first steamships and the Moscow–St Petersburg railway line (1851) opened a new era in the city's history. By 1868 the Putilov factory was already a major producer of rails, locomotives and carriages. In 1900, 13,000 workers were employed there, with about a hundred more metallurgical factories developing in related sectors. Other factories, using modern British and German equipment (Nobel, Nevsky, Lessner) built ships and typographical machines and (in competition with Obukhov) supplied the needs of the Army. There was also a number of textile mills in and around St Petersburg. A new port, constructed in 1885, was added to that of Kronstadt, expanding the city's potential for international trade: corn and wood were exported in vast quantities, balancing imports of steel and machine tools. Banks, many of whose shareholders were foreigners, proliferated during the boom of the 1890's.

THE ST PETERSBURG CIVIL SERVANT

According to the poet Grigoriev, Russian civil servants – whose uniforms varied from one ministry to the next – were the "alpha and omega" of St Petersburg. Schoolboys, university students, soldiers, sailors, policemen and ecclesiastics completed the picture. Right from the time of its foundation, St Petersburg was a heavily regulated city: the aspect of the roofs and chimneys, the construction materials, the color and height of all buildings (which might on no account be taller than the Winter Palace), the width of the streets, the hours by which the gates had to be closed, and the arrangements for street cleaning were all carefully ordained by bureaucratic rules.

A CENTER FOR FREE THOUGHT

Paradoxically, it was in this tightly controlled environment that free thought blossomed – thanks to the culture of an intellectual elite, naturally, but also thanks to the special receptiveness of St Petersburgers. Seventy percent of the workers in the capital knew how to read and write, as opposed to an average of 21 percent in the rest of the Russian Empire. St Petersburgers spread the word on avant-garde art, along with technical innovation (airplanes) and new diversions (cinema, football).

1904–5 Russo-Japanese War

1912–13 Balkan Wars

June 28, 1914 Assassination of Franz-Ferdinand of Austria at Sarajevo

1924 England, France, Sweden and other European nations recognize the USSR

1900 1920

12 March 1918 Moscow replaces St Petersburg as capital

1918–20 Civil War and foreign intervention

March 2–6, 1919 First Congress of the Third International (Komintern) in Moscow

December 30, 1922 The USSR is officially inaugurated

THE COMING OF THE REVOLUTION

On July 20, 1914, from a balcony of the Winter Palace, Nicholas II read the declaration which brought Russia into the Great War. On August 18 the German name of the capital was changed to the more Russian-sounding Petrograd – much closer to "Pieter", as ordinary people had always called it. For the writer Solzhenitsyn, who described the war years practically from day to day (*The Red Wheel*, 4,000 pages), the declaration of war was the beginning of the greatest drama of the century, whilst for Lenin it represented a great gift offered by the Czar to the nascent Revolution. According to Lenin, in an underdeveloped nation revolution could come about only as a consequence of war: while Karl Marx thought revolution improbable anywhere but within the most advanced capitalist systems. History began to prove Lenin right in February 1917.

On the night of October 24–5, 1917 insurgents attacked the Winter Palace, seat of the provisional government. With a roar that drowned the stutter of machine-gun fire, a wave of humanity swirled around the great building. The October Revolution was under way.

THE DESTRUCTION OF ST PETERSBURG

The October Revolution – so glorified for seventy-six years thereafter – led to many irreparable losses for St Petersburgers. The city was transformed in two ways. On the edge of the central area quantities of dilapidated buildings in which tens of thousands of workers lived were emptied and destroyed. Meantime the historic capital began to fall apart from the very first months of Soviet supremacy. Spacious apartments were divided up among working families, and the original décor, of two-headed eagles, crowns and statues, removed; a decree abolishing private ownership deprived houses and shops, fountains and gardens of ordinary maintenance; and railings, stained glass, stair carpets, bas-reliefs and weathercocks simply vanished. The campaigns against religion brought about the destruction or conversion into offices of a large number of churches. Much-needed capital was raised by the sale of works of art abroad. At the same time the names of streets and squares were altered, short-circuiting the collective memory: about 500 names were changed, including that of the Nevsky Prospekt, which became Avenue 25 October. About 400 names vanished altogether, along with the things they referred to. Finally, on Lenin's death in January 1924, the Soviet Congress, "at the request of the workers", abolished the name of the capital altogether.

1938
Munich Agreements (September)

1939
The Russo-German Pact (August). Partition of Poland (September)

1940
Pact with Finland (March)
Annexation of the Baltic States and Bessarabia (June)

1941
The Germans invade Russ (June). They are halted ou Moscow (December)

1924 — **1940**

1929
First attempts at collectivization

1936
The Anti-Komintern Pact (Germany and Russia)

April 8–11, 1940
Massacre of 1,400 Polish prisoners at Katyn by Russian security services

1949
Creation of NATO (April)

1924–91: Leningrad, glory and calamity

A new image of the city

The houses of one and a half million emigrants and victims of war and revolution were occupied by workers and peasants fleeing collectivization (1928–33). These people became city workers and were distinct from the native St Petersburgers in their language and way of life. The atmosphere of the city, in which before the revolution the cream of the aristocracy and the intelligentsia had flourished, became envenomed as Leningrad found itself increasingly sidelined and provincialized. Nevertheless, the Soviet government in Moscow continued to regard Leningrad as a free-thinking potential rival. The Party's purges and wholesale arrests uprooted many recently arrived families, adding to the prevailing loss of identity in the city.

A new image was to emerge later, in consequence of the heroic resistance during the siege of Leningrad (1941–4), although the city's troubles did not come to an end until the 1960's and 1970's, with the stabilization of the population and an improvement in living conditions.

The opening of Leningrad to tourism

The work of restoration which had continued ever since the end of the siege had taken on a different character by the end of the 1970's, the purpose of which was to recreate the city's former charm. After the opening of an initial underground railway in 1955, new lines were built on a regular basis; the length of the Neva embankment was tripled (nearly 100 miles of it were reinforced with granite); park space in the city was increased to 22,500 acres, and the number of bridges was increased to 310 by 1989. Meantime cheap high-rise housing began to make its mark on the various islands (42 new projects were completed in 1970). Soviet tourists arrived to visit the "glorious city", and with the new policy of detente toward the West even foreign visitors began to appear.

March 5, 1953 Death of Stalin

August 1, 1975 Helsinki conference. Signature of the final act on Human Rights

November 1989 Fall of the Berlin Wall

1993 September 21: Supreme Soviet is dissolved. December 12: Election of the first Russian Duma; a new constitution is drawn up by referendum

1960 — 1980 — 1990 — 2005

February 1956 Khrushchev denounces Stalin's personality cult

March 11, 1985 Gorbachev is elected First Secretary of the Soviet Communist Party

1991 June 12: First democratic election in Russia: Yeltsin elected President. December 25: The USSR becomes the Commonwealth of Independent States

The palaces around Leningrad

The environs of Leningrad suffered terribly from the German occupation, and after the Allied victory in World War Two the towns in the region were so badly damaged that they had to be reconstructed rather than restored. With their 18th-century palaces and parks, these museum-towns are very much a part of Leningrad and are well worth visiting. They are also highly functional: Petrodvorets, with its university campus, is populated by students; Tsarskoe Selo trains farmers from all over the country at its Agricultural Institute; Gatchina is a scientific research center with a number of different institutes. Oranienbaum, Pavlosk and the isthmus of Carelia are now popular summer resorts. The latter is well-known for its beach, Duny; it has become an upmarket resort for the people of St Petersburg. A sports complex is also being built there.

St Petersburg since 1991

Rebirth of the city

On June 12, 1991, 54 percent of the city's inhabitants voted to restore its historic name. "St Petersburg" has come back, but with more difficulty than the Kirov Ballet experienced in readopting the name of Mariinsky, or the University in jettisoning the name of Zhdanov. Russian and foreign sponsors support the ongoing embellishment projects for the city: the houses along the Nevsky Prospekt have been repainted, the streets remetalled, and foreign cafés are opening apace. But the real sign of a renaissance, foreshadowing St Petersburg's tricentenary, has been the resumption of literary work on and about it: the appearance of a first major collection entitled *The Petersburg Metaphysic* has confirmed this trend.

A solution to the problem of flooding

On several buildings in the city are plaques indicating the levels of the worst floods among the 253 which have afflicted St Petersburg since 1703. One of these recalls the catastrophe of November 7, 1824, when the water rose 12 feet. Today, the reformist administrators of St Petersburg and their Finnish neighbors are committed to renewing the city's flood protection facilities, while respecting the ecology of the region.

GEDENKE
DES HOHEN WASSERS
AM 7 NOVEMBER
1824

Czar Alexander I presents his army to Napoleon.

MIKHAIL FYODOROVICH (1613–45)*. The first of the Romanov Czars, son of Fyodor Nikitich, better known as Filaret, patriarch of Tuchino and descendant of the Riurik family (founder of the Kiev state, the first state of Russia).

ALEXEI I (1645–76)*. The son of Mikhail Fyodorovich. In the early years of his reign, the state was run by his tutor, the boyar B. Morozov. This reign was marked by a major social crisis and ecclesiastical reforms initiated by the Patriarch of Moscow, Nikon.

SOPHIA (1682–9)*. In 1689 Sophia Alexeyevna was assigned to the monastery of Novodyvichy (Moscow) and the regency passed to Natasha Naryshkin (second wife of Alexei I and mother of Peter I).

FYODOR III (1676–82)*. The son of Alexei I and Maria Ilinychna, Fyodor was bored by affairs of state and allowed his advisors to run the country. He died at 21.

CATHERINE (1691–1733)

ANNA YOANNOVNA (1730–40)*. Niece of Peter I, Anna was chosen by the supreme council (over her daughters Anna and Elizabeth) to succeed Peter II. Hers was an arbitrary regime.

ALEXEI (1690–1718). After joining the conspiracy against his father, Alexei was condemned by the Czar imprisoned and tortured.

PETER II (1727–30)*. Grandson of Peter I. Peter's brief reign was marked by the return of the court to Moscow and the eviction of Prince Menshikov.

IVAN VI (1740–1)* Regency of Anna.

ALEXANDER I (1801–25)* (left). The adored grandson of Catherine II. Russia in his reign joined the coalition against Napoleon; later, Alexander instigated major reforms and founded many new institutions.

ALEXANDER III (1881–94)*. Son of Alexander The assassination of his father led him to bring a halt to the reform movement and re-establish conservative regime.

NICHOLAS II ● *44* **(1894–1917)*.** Son of Alexander III. The dynasty's last emperor. His reign ended in the upheaval of the Revolution in 1917, which cost Nicholas and his family their lives (July 17, 1918).

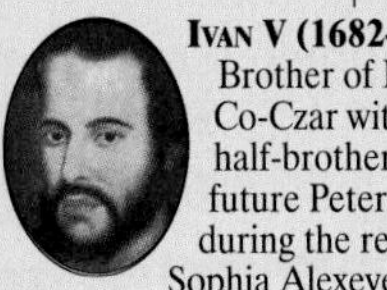

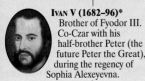

Ivan V (1682–96)*
Brother of Fyodor III. Co-Czar with his half-brother Peter (the future Peter the Great), during the regency of Sophia Alexeyevna.

Peter I (1682–1725)*. ● *38*. On the death of his mother, Peter the Great seized the reins of power. His second wife, **Catherine I (1725–7)*** was a Lithuanian peasant girl. On his death, she became the first Empress of Russia.

Anna (1708–28)

Elizabeth Petrovna ● *31* **(1741–61)***
Daughter of Peter the Great, she organized a coup d'etat in 1741, deposing Ivan IV, great-nephew of Anna Ivanovna.

Peter III (1761–2)*. Son of the Duke of Holstein-Gottorp. In 1745 he married Sophia of Anhalt-Zerbst (the future Catherine II).

Catherine II ● *40* **(1762–96)***
Took power in a 1762 coup d'etat, supported by the officers who had assassinated her husband.

Paul I (1796–1801)*. Son of Peter III and Catherine II, whom he loathed. Assassinated in the Engineer's Castle.

Nicholas I (1825–55)*. Brother of Alexander I. His reign was marked by the Decembrist uprising and the Crimean War.

Alexander II (1855–81)*
Son of Nicholas I. From the end of the Crimean War, he undertook a reform program (abolition of serfdom in 1861) but was assassinated by terrorists.

* Dates of reign.

Rasputin ▲ *202* **(1872–1916)**
Born a peasant (his real name was Grigor Novykh), Rasputin was introduced into the court of Nicholas II on account of his healing powers. Very quickly he gained huge influence over the Czar's political decisions. On December 16, 1916 he was assassinated by Prince Yusupov.

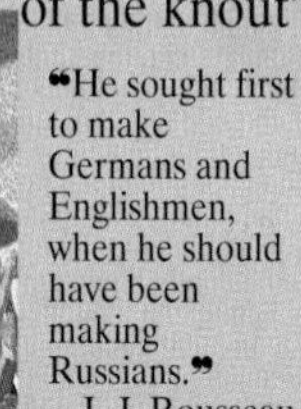

By inviting Western technicians and military officers to Russia, Peter the Great was able to form a regular Army and Navy capable of defending his country's interests. As Czar, his principal objective was to make Russia a great military power, not to transplant European civilization into it. But a century after his death, Russian intelligentsia was divided between the Slavophiles, who wished to eradicate Peter from Russian history, and the Occidentalists, who recognized his openness to progress while acknowledging that civilization was beaten into Russia "by blows of the knout".

"He sought first to make Germans and Englishmen, when he should have been making Russians."
J.-J. Rousseau

SAILOR, SOLDIER AND CRAFTSMAN . . .
At the age of ten, and on his own initiative, Peter formed an army. This "child's game" led to the founding of the three elite regiments which later spearheaded Russia's victory over Napoleon. The Czar grew up far from the sea but was forever dreaming of it. An abandoned English ship in one of his grandfather's dry-docks sparked his longing for a great Russian fleet. He learnt about naval construction at Saardam, in 1697: the first frigate of Russia's fleet was partly built by his hands.

A "NOBLE SAVAGE"
In the European vogue, Peter had an African prince called Ibrahim brought to his court. The man who organized the kidnapping was an ancestor of Tolstoy's. Ibrahim became a general (Hannibal) in the Russian Army, and was the great-grandfather of the poet Pushkin ● *114*.

The founder of the Kunstkammer
A passionate collector, Peter was as interested in objects like this Scythian gold panther as in human foetuses, which horrified the Russians ▲ *160*. He was reduced to giving free meals as an enticement to whomever among his subjects would come and see his collections.

Eccentric values
Culturally, Peter was an innovator; but many of his changes were frankly viewed as sacrilege. Beards had to be shaved; clothes were "teutonized" in styles that had formerly been regarded in Russia as carnival costumes. The Czar also instituted a Council of Drunkenness as a parody of the Ecclesiastical Council, and arranged elaborate marriages and funerals for dwarves, whom he pilloried to amuse his court. Russian culture somehow remained in place, but with its values knocked topsy-turvy.

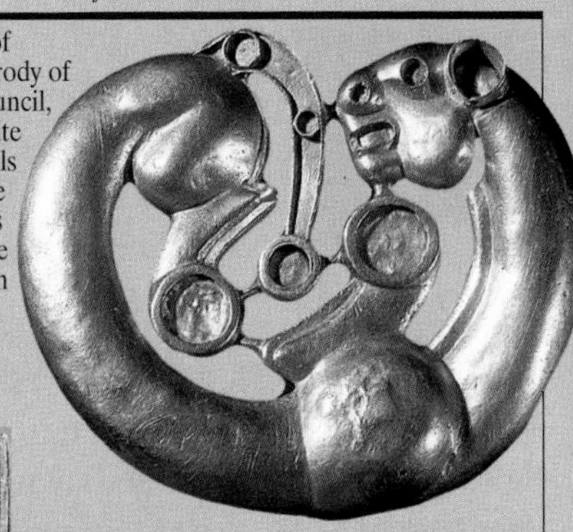

The despot
Peter, as Czar, pitied no man and respected nothing. During his reign the nobles were forced to educate themselves; if they did not, they were forbidden to marry. They also had to "divert themselves": in other words, frequent cafés and drink vodka, and serve vodka on all occasions, on pain of forfeiting all their possessions. The Czar's son Alexei ▲ *147* was accused of plotting against him, arrested, condemned to death – and tortured by Peter's own hand.

Bronze grotesque▲ *148*
In 1991 Chemiakin, a Russian-French-American sculptor, offered to the city of St Petersburg a symbol of the fallen empire, in the form of a statue of Peter fixed in his chair. The head, sculpted after a mask done by Rastrelli in 1719, is completely disproportionate to the body.

On her arrival in Russia Sophia of Anhalt-Zerbst, Princess of Pomerania and fiancée of Peter III, noted in her journal: "I will reign alone over Russia." Shortly after, while Russophobia and disdain for the orthodoxy of her husband were causing outrage in St Petersburg, she converted to the Orthodox religion. In 1762 she acceded to the throne as Catherine II, supported by the officers who had assassinated her husband.

A CIVILIZING INFLUENCE

When Catherine acceded, the state of academic faculties in the city was such that there might be only one student per class; police had to recruit pupils on the day schools opened.

A PHILOSOPHER ON THE THRONE

Catherine wished her reforms to answer the desires and interests of her subjects. Quoting Montesquieu, Quesnay and Beccaria, she put forward her ideas in a treatise, the *Nakaz*, whose triumph is depicted in the allegory at right. In 1767 Catherine formed a legislative committee, but came up against deputies who were ignorant of both government and the mechanics of the modern state, and unanimously defended the right to possess serfs.

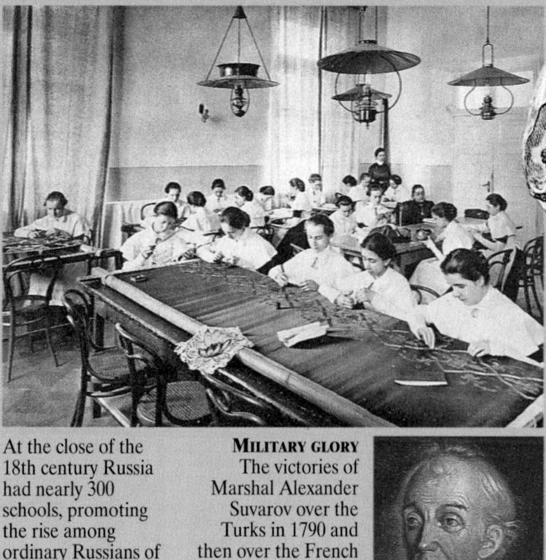

At the close of the 18th century Russia had nearly 300 schools, promoting the rise among ordinary Russians of an intelligentsia. The nobility was educated at home, but 200 of its daughters were taught at the Smolny Institute, which opened in 1764 ▲ *250*.

MILITARY GLORY

The victories of Marshal Alexander Suvarov over the Turks in 1790 and then over the French Army in the Alps in 1799 not only earned him the title of Prince of Italy but also gave Russia a decisive role on the European scene.

Pugachov's revolt
In 1774, Pugachov, an illiterate cossack calling himself Peter III, threatened the throne of Catherine II.

People from the Volga regions, peasants working in the factories of the Urals and serfs flocked to Pugachov's banner.

"A worse rebel than Pugachov"
This was Catherine's note on Radishchev's book *A Journey from St Petersburg to Moscow* (1790). Its author, a Russian noble who had studied at the University of Leipzig, was influenced by "half-baked scholars like Rousseau and Raynal". Observing the wretched state of the serfs in the two capitals, Radishchev condemned the regime of the "enthroned philosopher", who according to him was " . . . a deformed monster, impudent, obese, with a hundred yapping heads".

The notes of Catherine II
Kurakin, the Czar's best friend, secretly collected the only copy of the notes of Catherine II, sealed by Paul I. These notes did not appear until 1858, when they were published in French, in London, on the initiative of the revolutionary Herzen – who also published Radishchev.

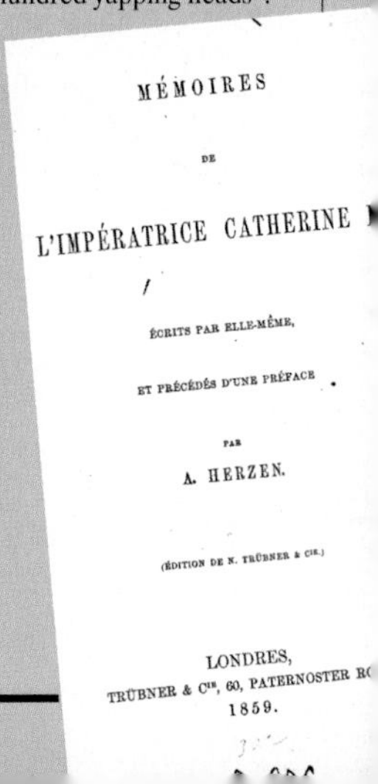

MÉMOIRES

DE

L'IMPÉRATRICE CATHERINE

ÉCRITS PAR ELLE-MÊME,

ET PRÉCÉDÉS D'UNE PRÉFACE

PAR

A. HERZEN.

(ÉDITION DE N. TRÜBNER & Cie.)

LONDRES,
TRÜBNER & Cie, 60, PATERNOSTER RO
1859.

During the military campaigns against Napoleon (1813–14) aristocratic Russian officers, educated from an early age by foreign tutors and (later) professors, saw at first hand constitutional regimes which had rid themselves of serfdom, and whose masses were moved by revolutionary ideals. On their return to Russia they formed secret societies with the aim of transforming their own country along the same lines. From 1822 onward these societies had polarized into two opposing groups, the Northern and the Southern.

Constitutional monarchy or republic?
Lively debates pitted Pestel, republican leader of the Southern Society, against Nikita Muraviev, the Northern leader, who proposed a constitutional monarchy. Some of the conspirators saw Pestel as a new Robespierre.

The Senate Square
The conspirators decided to act on December 14, 1825, when the regiments of St Petersburg were scheduled to swear their oath of loyalty to Nicholas I. While some caused a diversion among the soldiers drawn up on the Senate Square ▲ *194*, others (including Prince Trubetskoy, the instigator of the coup) hesitated so long that the Czar's troops were able to foil the revolt, killing 1,271 people.

Hanged rebels
The five leaders of the Decembrist insurrection were led to the gallows on July 14, 1826, with signs reading "Assassins of the Czar" hung around their necks. Three of the ropes broke, and the hangings had to be carried out again.

"The public is right; in Russian writers it sees its only guides, its only defenders, and its only saviors against their country's autocracy, against orthodoxy, and against official nationalism."

Bielinsky, Letter to Gogol, 1847

Women of courage

"We, heroines? We are only such in the works of poets, for all we have done is follow our husbands . . ." wrote Alexandra Davidoff, wife of one of the Decembrist rebels condemned to exile in Siberia. With Alexandra went twenty-two other women, among them the princesses Trubetskoy, Volkonsky, and Shakhovskoy. All abandoned their children to go into voluntary exile.

For posterity

Lost in the crowd, the fourteen-year-old Alexander Herzen witnessed the religious service ordered by Nicholas I at the Kremlin following the hanging of the Decembrists, which impressed him with a lasting horror. In 1855 the five martyrs featured on the cover of the review *Pole Star*, which Herzen published in London and which was aimed at the Russian intelligentsia.

The exile of the Decembrists

The women and their servants found lodgings in the vicinity of the prisons where their husbands were detained. The 120 men were condemned to hard labor in the salt mines. Their shackles were removed in 1830, and rings made out of them for the men's wives to wear. Discussion, correspondence and clandestine visits helped the months to pass. Between 1832 and 1839, their sentences served, the Decembrists installed themselves in Siberia, where they contributed to cultural renewal and political debate.

THE 1905 REVOLUTION

Following a wave of political reforms, after 1890 the Russian economy had to cope with the industrial revolution and the expansion of the cities, in which only 13 percent of the population lived. The agrarian sector remained stagnant: the peasants, who made up 85 percent of the Russian population, were kept in a state of abject serfdom by local aristocrats, despite their official enfranchisement. Two percent of the population owned nearly all of Russia's land, and the autocratic government proved incapable of changing a steadily worsening situation for the better. Finally, a disastrous war with Japan revealed the depth of the crisis.

BLOODY SUNDAY
On January 9, 1905, 140,000 demonstrators stood before the Winter Palace, brandishing icons and chanting their grievances. The response of the imperial troops was to open fire. The nationwide wave of outrage at the massacre turned into full-blown revolution.

THE BATTLESHIP POTEMKIN
In the summer of 1905 a spoiled meat broth served to the seamen aboard the battleship *Potemkin*, docked in a Black Sea port, provoked a violent uprising which left Odessa in ruins.

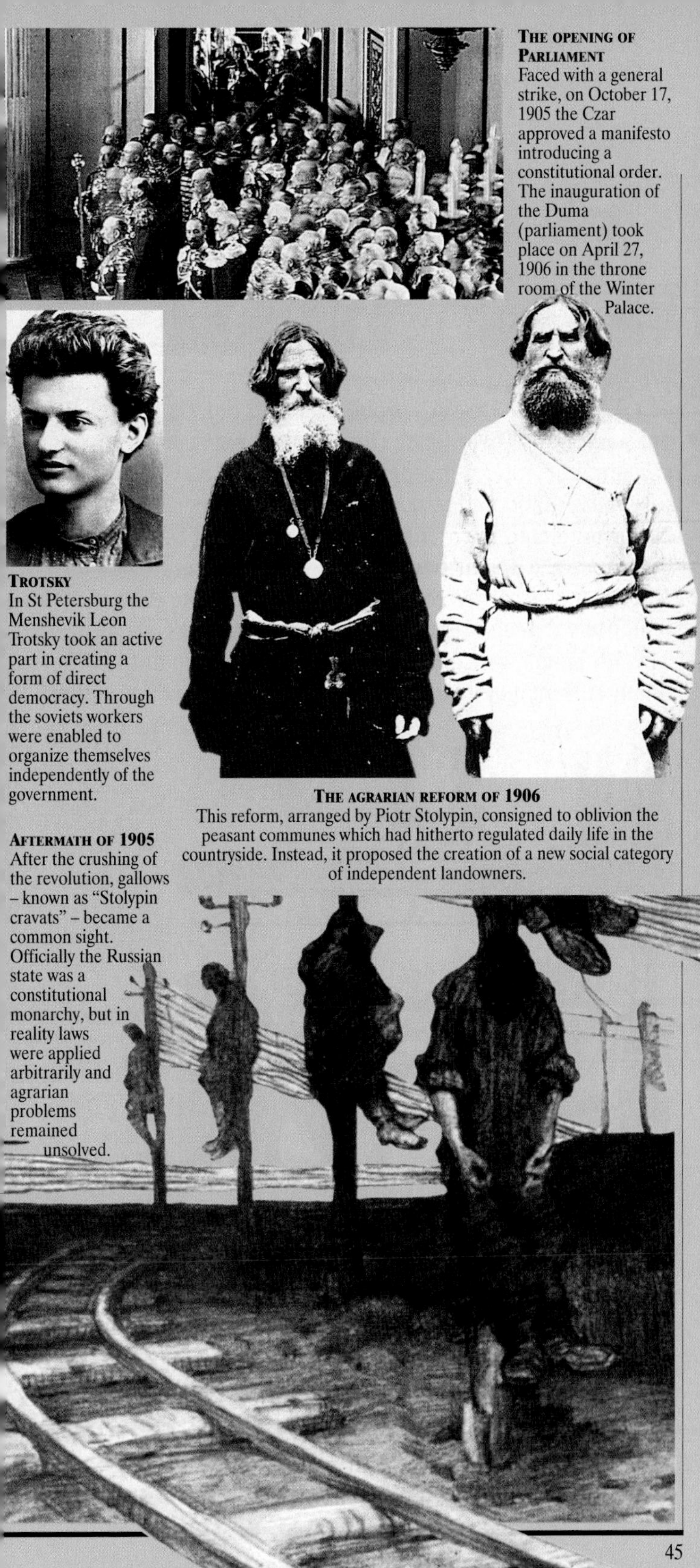

The opening of Parliament
Faced with a general strike, on October 17, 1905 the Czar approved a manifesto introducing a constitutional order. The inauguration of the Duma (parliament) took place on April 27, 1906 in the throne room of the Winter Palace.

Trotsky
In St Petersburg the Menshevik Leon Trotsky took an active part in creating a form of direct democracy. Through the soviets workers were enabled to organize themselves independently of the government.

The agrarian reform of 1906
This reform, arranged by Piotr Stolypin, consigned to oblivion the peasant communes which had hitherto regulated daily life in the countryside. Instead, it proposed the creation of a new social category of independent landowners.

Aftermath of 1905
After the crushing of the revolution, gallows – known as "Stolypin cravats" – became a common sight. Officially the Russian state was a constitutional monarchy, but in reality laws were applied arbitrarily and agrarian problems remained unsolved.

The 1917 Revolution

Nicholas II and his family, prisoners at Tsarskoe Selo.

Russia's problems were compounded by World War One. The economy was unable to accelerate its rate of production to meet the new needs. Prices rose and inflation attained alarming proportions. Nicholas II was no longer a credible monarch, being perceived as the protector of Rasputin, a debauched charlatan who had cured his son Alexei; and as he was commander-in-chief of the Army a series of military defeats were sufficient to destroy the Czar altogether. The 4th Duma, which had remained loyal to him until 1915, finally stiffened in its opposition and resolved to depose him.

The fall of the Czarist system
The Czarist regime collapsed in five days, between February 23 and 27. Two plots, one in the Czar's immediate entourage, the other fomented by deputies in the Duma, projected the Czar's replacement by his brother. But the conspirators were forestalled by a spontaneous uprising by workers and soldiers in Petrograd, who seized the Arsenal and proclaimed a republic.

Two powers
A power struggle ensued between the members of the provisional government, led by Prince Lvov, who wished to install a parliamentary regime and thereafter maintain the status quo, and the Petrograd Soviet, which advocated radical change.

Fraternity
While the streets of Petrograd resounded to the strains of the "Varsovienne" in honor of the martyrs of international revolution, the April Crisis suddenly struck. The Soviet offered the allies a "peace without annexations or reparations", which the provisional government affected to ignore.

SOCIALIST POWER
The socialist Kerensky, who became Prime Minister in July, was unable to control the radicalization of the masses.

"ALL POWER TO THE SOVIETS"
From April onward this was the rallying cry of the Bolsheviks. Their role in crushing a *putsch* led by General Kornilov, a monarchist rival of Kerensky, enabled them to attract both revolutionary socialists and Mensheviks to their cause during August. The bolshevization of the soviets was then quickly accomplished.

THE BOLSHEVIK TRIUMPH
This poster, which has since become an icon, was at first little understood. The failure of the Kornilov *putsch* drew Western attention away from Russia. In France and England the fall of Kerensky and the October Revolution ▲ *248* were passed over almost without comment, even in well-informed socialist circles. The bolshevization of the soviets likewise went unnoticed.

The Terror, or Purge, is often explained in terms of the personal motivations of Stalin himself, who was bent on revenge against the older Bolsheviks and on gaining absolute power. In fact, Stalin's ambitions were quickly outstripped by the sheer enormity of the phenomenon he had instigated. After the assassination of Kirov the Purge reached a paroxysm, with over two million political prisoners between 1934 and 1938. The State-Party system never succeeded in overcoming the socio-economic difficulties stemming from violent collectivization and accelerated industrialization. Confronted with social tensions, officials at every level of Soviet society promoted the fear of Stalin, along with his virtual deification.

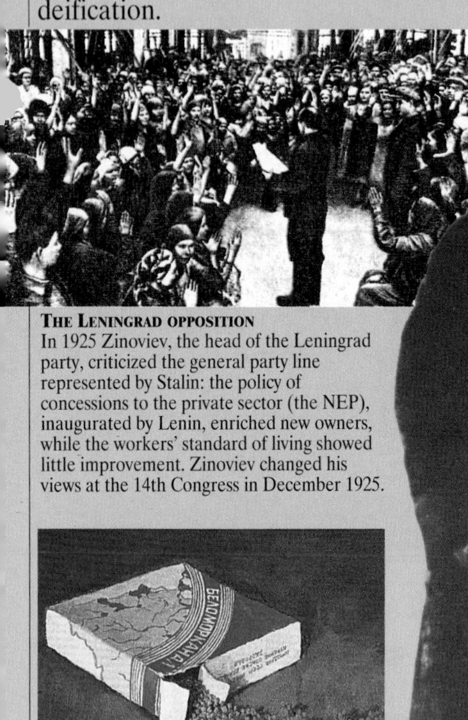

THE LENINGRAD OPPOSITION
In 1925 Zinoviev, the head of the Leningrad party, criticized the general party line represented by Stalin: the policy of concessions to the private sector (the NEP), inaugurated by Lenin, enriched new owners, while the workers' standard of living showed little improvement. Zinoviev changed his views at the 14th Congress in December 1925.

THE WHITE SEA–LAKE ONEGA CANAL
The canal linking the White Sea with Lake Onega, a giant construction project 140 miles long, was completed as part of the first Five Year Plan (1928–32). Mostly built by political prisoners, the canal gave its name to the tobacco brand Belomorkanal. The painting above illustrates the tribute in human lives which the Soviets had to pay to Stalin's planners.

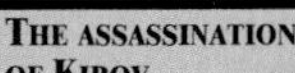

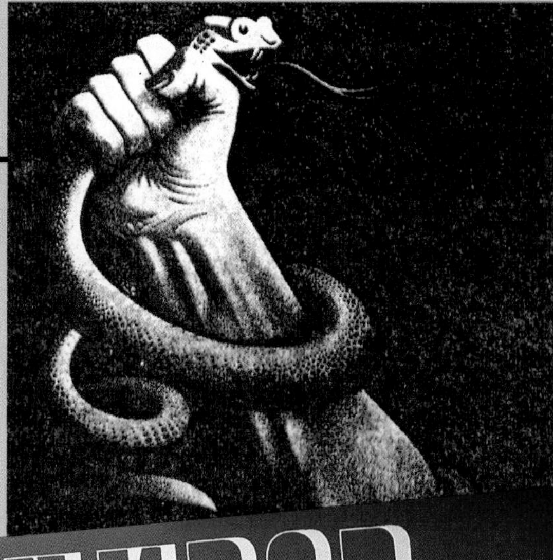
М. КИРОВ
ИСКОРЕНИМ
ШПИОНОВ и ДИВЕРСАНТОВ!

THE ASSASSINATION OF KIROV
Kirov (below), the party chief, was very popular in Leningrad on account of his attempts to raise the workers' standard of living. On December 1, 1934 Kirov's assassination allowed those responsible for Russia's economic chaos to direct the popular fury against "spies", "saboteurs" and other "turncoats".

"NIGHT TERROR"
The great show trials held in Moscow unleashed a widespread sense of insecurity, the "night terror". Arrests were invariably carried out at dawn.

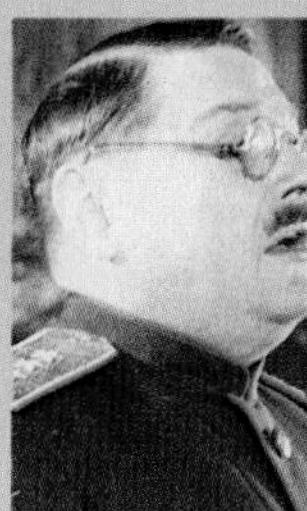

THE PURGE OF COSMOPOLITANS
Leningrad artists and intellectuals were the first victims of a campaign led by Zhdanov, the ideological head of the Central Committee, who demanded "proletarian science and art".

1948: THE LENINGRAD AFFAIR
Popov, the party chief (below), was shot along with a number of other officials on a charge of seeking to turn Leningrad into the capital of a federal Russia.

The siege of Leningrad

Condemned to death
The three million inhabitants under siege by the Wehrmacht had fuel and provisions for only two months: their water and electricity supplies were cut by the bombardments. Only a quarter of the sixty-eight armaments factories supplying the defenders of Leningrad were operational.

Soviet agents and diplomats rapidly informed Stalin of alarming German troop movements along the frontier. Having underestimated the threat, Stalin found himself obliged to intervene personally when Nazi troops flooded into the USSR. The ensuing battle, as sudden as it was catastrophic, took a huge toll in Russian lives. The siege of Leningrad, which was to last nine hundred days, was one of the most tragic consequences of Stalin's giant error. On September 8, 1941 the front had come within 4 miles of the city's southwestern edge, and Leningrad was linked to the rest of the country only by air and by way of the frozen waters of Lake Ladoga.

Famine in Leningrad
Famine took hold from the autumn of 1941 onward, and was sharpened by the loss by fire of most of the warehouses containing the city's meager reserves of food. By December over 53,000 people had died, and the daily bread ration was down to 9 oz for workers and 4½ oz for the unemployed and for children. During the siege over 800,000 people died of hunger, 17,000 were killed, and 35,000 were wounded in the fighting.

The lifeline
One of the few ways out of besieged Leningrad lay across the frozen waters of Lake Ladoga. From November 1942 a track was made across the ice which allowed the city to be supplied with bread. In the summer a network of pipes and cables running across the bed of the lake carried electricity and gasoline to the beleaguered citizens.

“We have no fear of bullets
Nor do we grieve for our houses,
But we are resolved to preserve our mother tongue
In all its truth and force.” Anna Akhmatova, Feb. 23, 1942

Hope returns
By the end of 1942 Leningrad was gradually coming back to life: factories reopened and the nightmare of famine faded. In January 1943 the Red Army succeeded in breaking the German blockade along the lake shore: a railway was constructed via Schlisselburg, known as the “Victory Line”.

A symbol of life
The composer Dmitry Shostakovich, who volunteered for military service, was assigned for his own safety to sentry duty on the roof of the Conservatoire and ordered to compose a special work for the People’s Theater. Evacuated from Moscow at the age of 35, he completed his work in the Urals: the *7th (“Leningrad”) Symphony* ▲ *228* was performed at Kubichev and Leningrad in 1942.

Imperishable glory
The celebratory fireworks of January 27, 1944 clothed the city in a lasting aura of heroism. After the war a million citizens were decorated for their part in the siege. At the coming of *perestroika*, the Museum of the Defense of Leningrad (instituted 1946–9), reopened its doors; an association of survivors was founded, and September 8 was declared a day of national mourning.

Russian belongs to the Eastern Slavic family of languages. This family is further subdivided into three main groups: the Occidental Slavic languages (Sorb, Czech and Slovak), the southern Slavic languages (Serbian, Macedonian and Bulgarian), and the oriental Slavic languages (Ukrainian, Byelorussian and Russian). The second and third groups are all written with the cyrillic alphabet, with very slight variations.

THE CYRILLIC ALPHABET

The monk Cyril and his brother Methodus perfected the glagolitic alphabet in 863. This alphabet was soon supplanted by a simplified equivalent, the cyrillic. The cyrillic alphabet includes several characters taken from both the Greek and Roman alphabets. In 1710 Peter the Great, with his *grajdnka* (civil alphabet), suppressed the graphic survivals of nasal vowels, and simplified the forms of certain letters. The orthographic reform of 1917 replaced the Ѣ by e, and almost did away with the use of the hard sign Ъ. The cyrillic alphabet in its present form contains thirty-two letters.

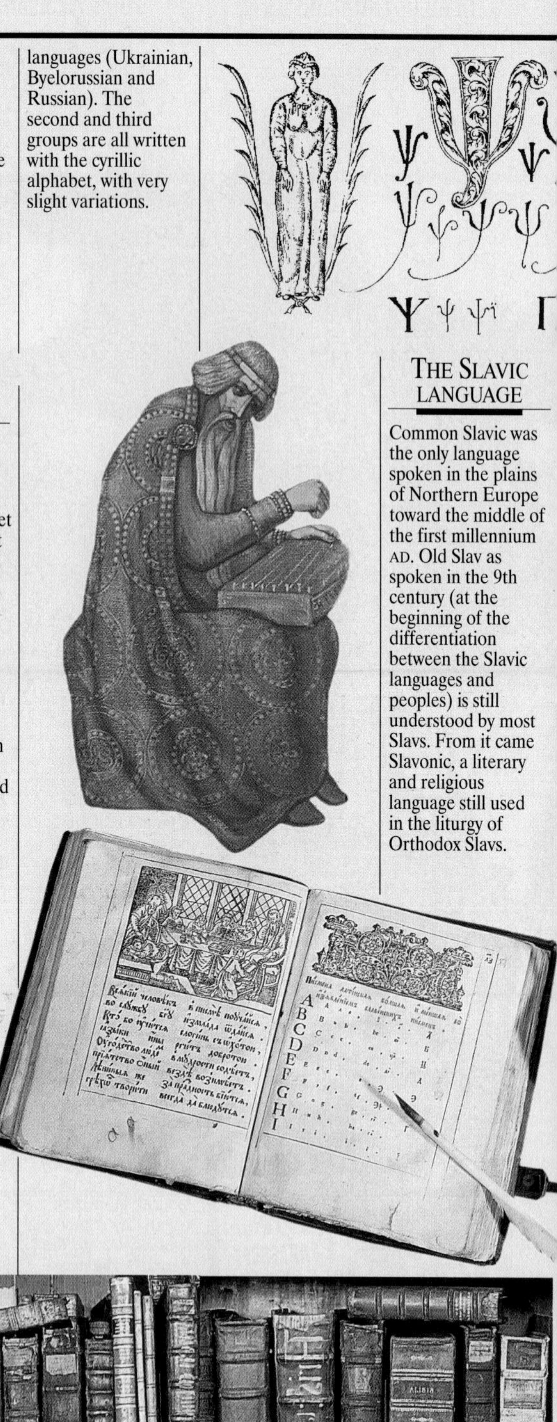

THE SLAVIC LANGUAGE

Common Slavic was the only language spoken in the plains of Northern Europe toward the middle of the first millennium AD. Old Slav as spoken in the 9th century (at the beginning of the differentiation between the Slavic languages and peoples) is still understood by most Slavs. From it came Slavonic, a literary and religious language still used in the liturgy of Orthodox Slavs.

FOREIGN CONTRIBUTIONS

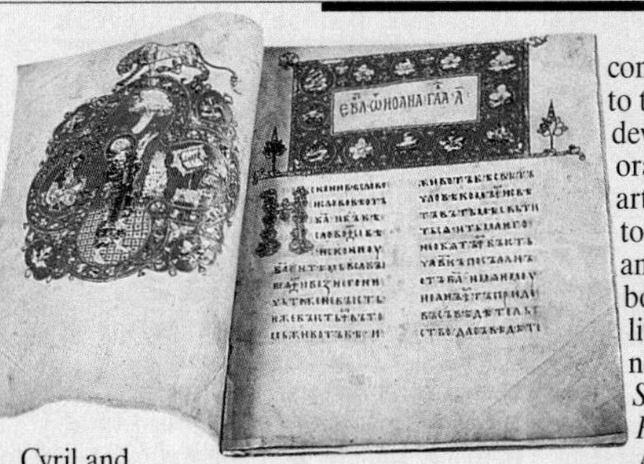

Cyril and Methodus were sent to Moravia by the Byzantine Emperor Michael III to evangelize the Slavs. Their new alphabet allowed them to translate the New Testament into the old Slav language. For centuries thereafter the Psalter was to be the principal reading matter of Russians. Their many contacts with Byzantium, both peaceful and belligerent, eventually led to the conversion of the Kiev prince Vladimir in 988, followed by that of his people; this event marked the entry of the pagan Slavs into Christendom. Later Western influences contributed to the development of oral and folk art, in addition to an original and precocious body of literature, notably *The Sayings of Prince Igor*.

After the 11th century, old Russian texts, such as the Ostromir New Testament, were written in a mixture of authentic Russian and Slavonic, the proportions of which varied from period to period and genre to genre. The interraction of these two languages eventually determined the form of what we know as literary Russian.

THE AWAKENING NATION

The Mongol invasion (13th century) and the domination of the "Golden Horde" (Tartar state) condemned the Russian language to centuries of isolation, which was eventually shaken off by a new religious and national awareness. This turning inward, at first forced but later deliberate, was generally damaging, but after a period of difficulty, in 1613 the Romanovs took over: intellectual inquiry again appeared along with literature. The Slavonic, Greek and Latin Academy, founded in Moscow in 1682, used a ponderous, artificial, heavily russified Slavonic language which stifled poetic creativity; yet it laid the groundwork for the blossoming of Russian literature in the following century, by bringing *belles-lettres* to the forefront of Russian life.

LOMONOSOV

In his *Russian Grammar* (1755) Lomonosov, a brilliant self-taught scholar, historian and philologist, purged the written language of obsolete Slavonic expressions, then reordered the lexicon into three categories: Slavonic, mixed and Russian terms. Three styles emerged from the combination of these elements: low, medium and high. This rigid classification had the merit of giving spoken Russian the place it deserved in literature (including song, epigram, private correspondence, comedy), the Slavonic terms being relegated to a more abstract, elevated linguistic register.

LITERATURE AND THE RUSSIAN LANGUAGE

THE LANGUAGE OF POETS

Even more than grammarians, writers like Sumarokov, Derzhavin and Karamzin (left) were the architects of the modern Russian language. At the turn of the 18th into the 19th century they prepared the ground for the great works of Pushkin. Under Catherine the Great intellectual and artistic life intensified in richness and was marked by a desire to imitate French classicism as well as scrupulously to respect the hierarchy of genres and styles established by Lomonosov. Karamzin rejected all distinctions between the spoken language and the written one: his ambition was to elevate spoken Russian to the status of a literary language.

MODERN RUSSIAN

Thus modern literary Russian emerged by stages, enriched by the language spoken by ordinary people. Russian songs and *bylines* (song epics) passed into print and, thanks to the discovery of *The Sayings of Prince Igor*, the master story-writer Ivan Krylov was able to contribute to a synthesis between popular and academic Russian. Nevertheless, it was Alexander Pushkin who perfected literary expression in the Russian language, with his motto: "When things are simple, say them simply."

THE SPREAD OF THE RUSSIAN LANGUAGE

With the creation of the Soviet Union and its fifteen republics, twelve of which were non-Slav, Russian became the official language of the Federation. Learning the language was made compulsory, not only for Soviet youth but also for the youth of the other Eastern countries. Many Africans, Asians and Latin Americans went to study in the Soviet Union and learned to speak fluent Russian. Under the cultural influence of the West the language has borrowed heavily (and sometimes inelegantly) from foreign tongues, absorbing words which have often supplanted Russian ones. Yet Russian is also acquiring new home-grown terms to describe the political, economic, social and moral upheavals of the era.

Today Russian is one of the five official languages of the United Nations, even though Russia's current difficulties impede its spread.

Arts and traditions

Today, as in the past, foreign visitors to Russia are amazed by the magnificence of the Orthodox liturgy, the gold of its icons and its polyphonic choral music. The Russians themselves cherish the beauty and symbolism of their Byzantine rite; a beauty which, according to the old chronicles, originally motivated their conversion to Christianity. Beyond their esthetic value these rites embody theological and spiritual teachings which remain unaltered since the 17th-century schism of the traditionalist "Old Believers". The Orthodox liturgy was the sole vehicle of faith permitted by the Soviet regime.

The liturgy
The length and the sheer splendor of Orthodox services tend to reinforce the idea of eternity and holiness, while its informality seems to welcome all comers.

The Orthodox year, with its round of feasts and fasts, is extremely rich and varied. The Russian Church still observes the Julian Calendar, which is thirteen days out of step with the Gregorian Calendar. The linchpin of church life is the Sunday Eucharist, during which clergy and congregation, including young children, take Communion.

Russian clergy
Parish priests (often married men) form the "white" clergy, while the "black" clergy are monks who have taken vows. Formerly the color of their vestments showed the difference between them. The bishops are appointed from among the monks and celibate or widowed priests; the principal of these bishops, the Patriarch of Moscow, is the titular head of the Russian Orthodox Church.

The iconostasis
Covered with five rows of icons ● *58* and topped by a cross, the iconostasis is a central element in every Russian Orthodox church. It depicts the prophets, the feasts of the liturgical year and the dëesis (prayer) of the saints in company with Christ. The larger lower row is made up of the icons of Christ, the Virgin and the various saints. It has three doors, used by the clergy: the central one (the "royal door"), reserved for the most solemn rites of the Orthodox Church, symbolizes the entrance to the kingdom of God.

Orthodox churches
As the meeting point of God and mankind, the church signifies heaven on earth. Orthodox churches can be square cruciform, and have a ntral dome; important churches have five domes, symbolizing Christ and the four Evangelists.

The seven sacraments
The Orthodox rite of baptism is followed by Chrismation (or Confirmation). The other sacraments are the Eucharist, marriage, ordination of the clergy, penitence, and the anointing of the sick.

Orthodox Easter
Called the "feast of feasts", Easter is the climax of the Orthodox year. After the forty-day Lenten fast and the ceremonies of Holy Week, the celebration rite begins with a candlelit procession, followed by the announcement of Christ's Resurrection. At Matins the victory of life over death is exalted; later, friends and relatives gather round the Easter table, with its Easter eggs and cakes blessed at church.

The Orthodox Church, which rejected the charge of idolatry made during the iconoclastic controversy in Byzantium (8th century), defines the icon as bearing witness to divine revelation, and thus justifiable in terms of the dogma of incarnation (God may not be represented in a picture but Christ, who was made man, can be). The icon is neither a work of art nor a pious image: it has a clear liturgical function, as well as a teaching role.

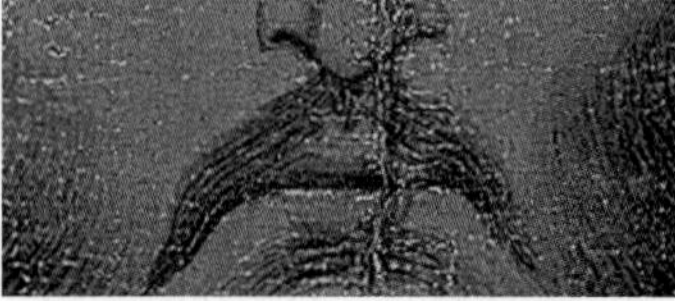

THE ORIGINS
Icons, which came to Russia with Christianity from Byzantium, reached a degree of perfection following the iconoclastic crisis. The Greek mosaic artists who decorated the churches of Kiev in the 11th century trained the first Russian iconographers. In the *Head of Christ* below the influence of mosaic is clearly discernible, notably in the golden lines traced through the hair.

A PAINTED SCRIPT
The technique of icon-making has not changed for centuries. It employs only natural materials. The wooden panel is first covered with a fine layer of plaster, and the image is painted on the wet surface; the powdered mineral colors are blended with an egg-based emulsion. The painting is then embellished with gold leaf and varnished, and the title is inscribed in vermilion lettering. In the Slavonic language a single word is used for the functions of writing and painting; therefore the artist does not merely paint his icon but he "writes" it too. Above: *Life of Saint Serge of Radonega* (16th century).

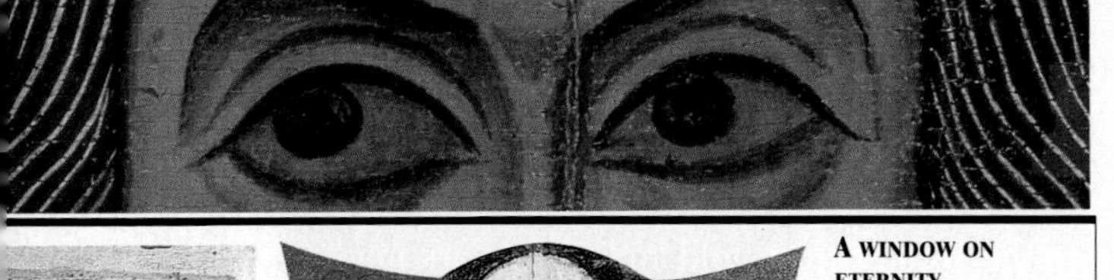

A WINDOW ON ETERNITY

This *Christ in Majesty* (16th century) shows all the symbolism and sanctity of the icon, through the use of concentric circles and inverted perspective to express a relationship between time and space which is very different to that of the world in which we live. In this way the icon becomes a kind of window on eternity. Such rules were codified in manuals, which also laid out guidelines for icon composition, the ordering of themes and use of color.

ANONYMOUS WORKS

Novgorod, Pskov, Suzdal and later Moscow succeeded one another as schools of iconography, each with its own tradition. The icon was never signed by an individual, but the fine rendering of the *Presentation of Christ* (right) is probably the work of Andrei Rublev, the great Muscovite icon-painter of the 15th century.

DECADENCE

From the 17th century onward the art of the icon was affected by excessive symbolism and borrowings from the West. The detailed and naturalistic *Trinity* (1671) by Simeon Ushakov, the official Kremlin painter, differs greatly from the icon by Rublev which inspired it.

REDISCOVERY OF THE ICON

In the 16th century a tradition arose of covering almost the entire work with precious metals. In the *Virgin of Kazan* (above, late 19th century) only the faces are visible. In the early 20th century the icon regained its original esthetic and theological aspects.

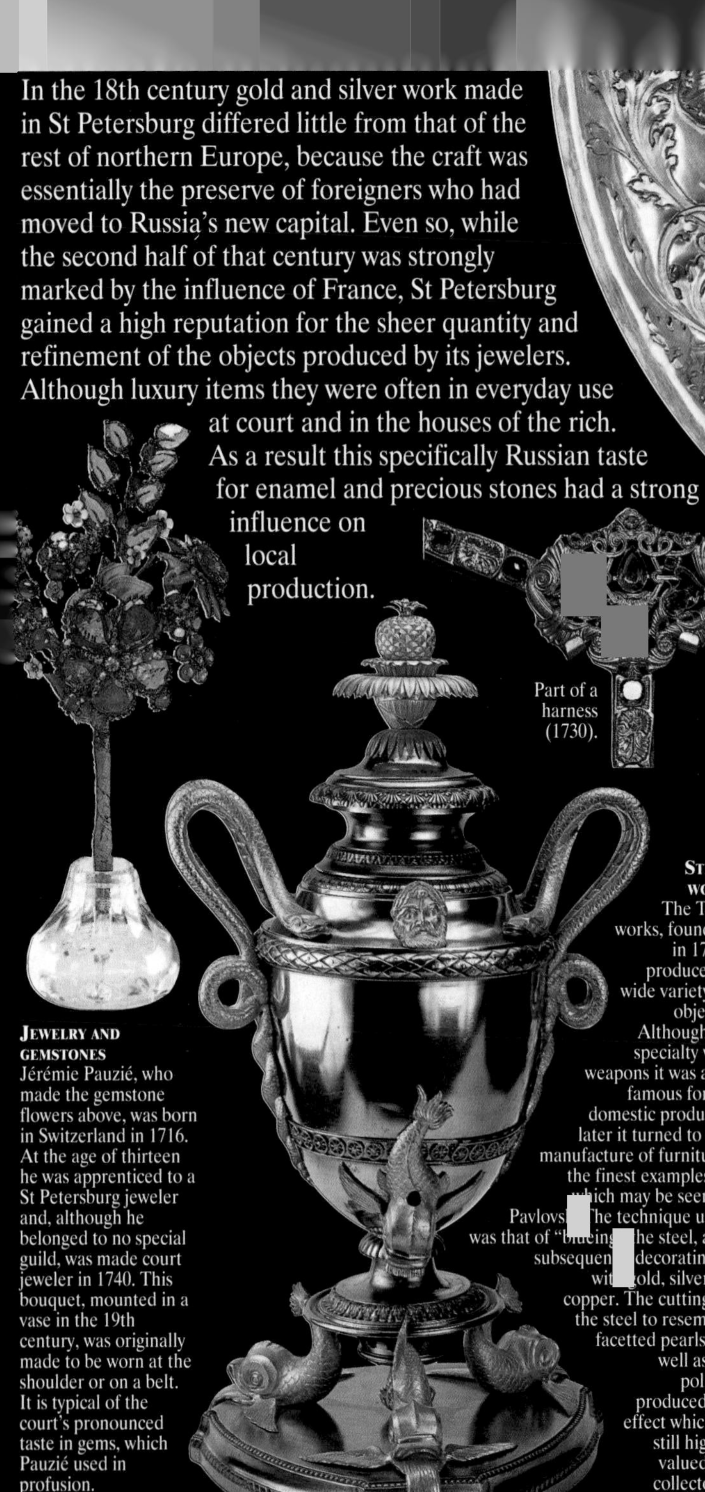

In the 18th century gold and silver work made in St Petersburg differed little from that of the rest of northern Europe, because the craft was essentially the preserve of foreigners who had moved to Russia's new capital. Even so, while the second half of that century was strongly marked by the influence of France, St Petersburg gained a high reputation for the sheer quantity and refinement of the objects produced by its jewelers. Although luxury items they were often in everyday use at court and in the houses of the rich. As a result this specifically Russian taste for enamel and precious stones had a strong influence on local production.

Part of a harness (1730).

STÉEL WORK
The Tula works, founded in 1712 produced wide variety o objects Although it specialty wa weapons it was also famous for it domestic products later it turned to the manufacture of furniture the finest examples o hich may be seen a Pavlovs he technique used was that of "b ing he steel, and subsequen decorating i wi old, silver o copper. The cutting o the steel to resemble facetted pearls, a well as it polish produced ar effect which i still highl valued b collectors

JEWELRY AND GEMSTONES
Jérémie Pauzié, who made the gemstone flowers above, was born in Switzerland in 1716. At the age of thirteen he was apprenticed to a St Petersburg jeweler and, although he belonged to no special guild, was made court jeweler in 1740. This bouquet, mounted in a vase in the 19th century, was originally made to be worn at the shoulder or on a belt. It is typical of the court's pronounced taste in gems, which Pauzié used in profusion.

MASTERWORKS
This gilded silver platter, decorated by the *repoussé* technique, resembles the work being done at the same period in Germany. There is no hallmark on the piece but the dedication to Peter the Great dates it to between 1721 and 1725.

Chessmen, Tula, late 18th century.

TOBACCO BOX
Tobacco boxes of this type were very much the fashion at the Russian court; they were frequently presented by monarchs as diplomatic gifts, and were also given as lovers' pledges. Pauzié made scores of them for the Empress Elizabeth I.

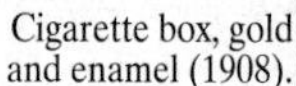

Cigarette box, gold and enamel (1908).

"If you compare my creations to those of Tiffany, Boucheron and Cartier you will conclude that they are of lesser value . . . but what, in fact, are these companies? They are sellers of jewelry, they are not artists. Hugely valuable objects interest me little, if their value resides in nothing more than an infinity of diamonds and pearls." This remark by Fabergé neatly expresses the spirit of his world-famous firm.

CARL FABERGÉ
Born in St Petersburg in 1846, the son of a modest jeweler of Huguenot stock, Peter Carl Fabergé took over the family business in 1870 and began by producing jewelry to conform with the prevailing taste for all things French. The arrival of his brother Agathon, an imaginative artist, contributed to the blossoming of the business after 1882.

THE FLOWERS
Fabergé's naturalist compositions are executed with astonishing skill: oatgrass and cornflowers on golden stalks rise from a translucent vase of rock crystal.

THE EGGS
Fabergé's eggs are marvels of inventiveness and delicacy. They are still copied today.

ENAMELS
Worked in *champlevé* or applied in successive layers on a checkered background, enamelwork was produced in over a hundred different hues.

PRECIOUS METALS
Fabergé's metals were also very finely worked: up to four shades of gold might be blended to produce the desired effect. Silver was deliberately left in its original state.

IMPERIAL COMMISSIONS
Under the aegis of the master Mikhail Perkhin, in the 1890's Fabergé's workshops produced large quantities of objects and gems, many of them commissioned by the Czar's family. Fabergé Easter eggs were given by Nicholas II to his mother and his wife.

SEMI-PRECIOUS STONES
Pink and black rhodonite, mouse-gray Kalkan jasper and pale green nephrite (mined in the Urals) gave Fabergé's designers all the imaginative scope they needed to create their confectionery dishes, figurines and quaint animal sculptures.

Peter the Great had tried to reproduce Delft and Meissen "porcelain" (in fact it was faience) in Russia, without success. It was not until the appearance of Dmitry Vinogradov (1720–58), a friend of the famous savant Lomonosov, that the technique was achieved with any degree of success. Later, in the reign of Elizabeth I, the process of manufacture was perfected, a fact mentioned in a contemporary publication. The first imperial porcelain works on the banks of the Neva produced buttons, cane tops and knife handles (1745–50). Then, as technical skills improved, complete table services were manufactured for the court, along with statuettes whose imperfections were often masked by lavish gilding.

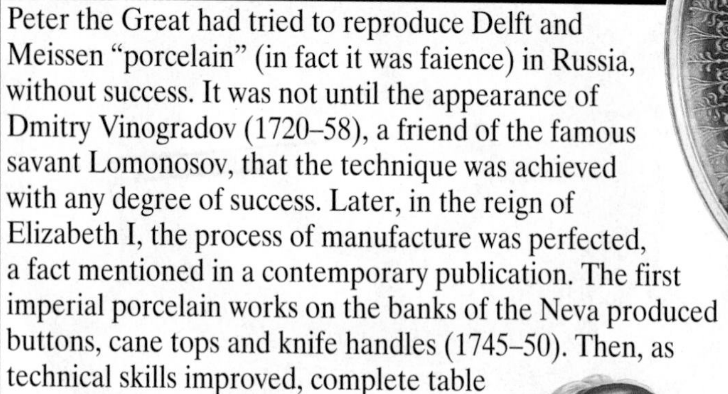

MADE-TO-ORDER TABLE SERVICES
Private factories soon made their appearance, competing directly with the imperial works; they created made-to-order table services, some commissioned by Catherine II. These services, which might include up to a thousand pieces, reflect the growing luxury of the imperial table, particularly in the 19th century.

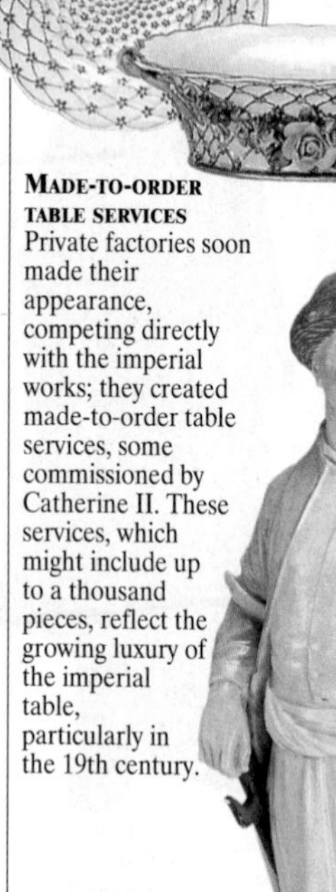

FIGURINES
The production of figurines, typically Russian, has never ceased in St Petersburg. The only changes brought to it by the Revolution were in the types of figures portrayed.

From revived styles to Art Nouveau
Following its approximation to the Sèvres style in the late 18th century, Russian porcelain went through a historicist period in the first quarter of the 19th century. Later it regressed into a multicolored, richly gilded Rococo style. At the close of the 19th century the imperial porcelain works came under the influence of Copenhagen, adopting modern simplified forms and new colors and designs in the Art Nouveau style.

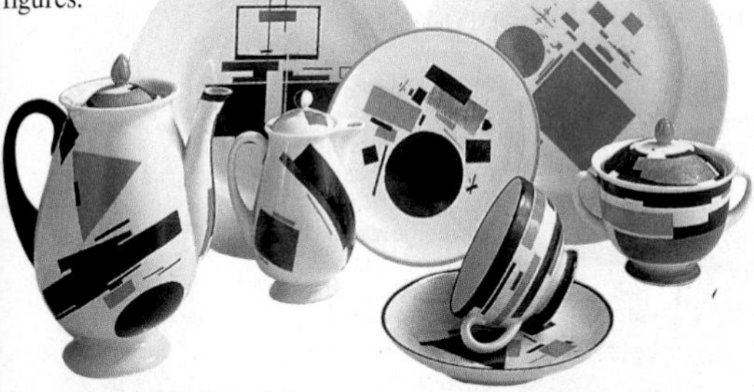

Gureev Table Service (1807)
This service bears the name of the head of Alexander I's Imperial Cabinet. The various pieces are remarkably diverse, with beautifully defined figures.

Constructivist porcelain
Porcelain manufacture was a domain in which the modernization of designs and ideas could immediately be applied. This meant that propaganda themes coexisted with Constructivist work, often produced by such renowned artists as Malevich and Kandinsky, who in no way disdained this unusual medium. Above, a tea-service in porcelain designed by Malevich; the link with his paintings ● *109*, *110* is evident.

As a rule the palaces of St Petersburg were decorated with furniture designed on French, English and German models, when these pieces were not directly imported from Western Europe. Furniture made in Russia remained simple and massive until the reign of Peter I, but its quality developed rapidly throughout the second half of the 18th century. The extensive building projects of Catherine II and her court stimulated a marked increase in demand, which eventually could be satisfied only by locally made products.

In the time of Peter the Great, the furniture trade specialized in marquetry as well as carved, painted and gilded pieces.

FREEDOM OF MOVEMENT
In the 18th century the work of cabinet-making in Russia was shared between the master-craftsmen of St Petersburg and trained serfs on aristocratic estates. Their virtuosity proved the innate skills of Russian woodworkers: the materials they used were many and varied, and they did not hesitate to blend indigenous wood species, which had an undeserved reputation for poor quality, with more exotic ones.

CARELIAN BIRCHWOOD
In the early 19th century new types of furniture – tiered consoles, serpent-shaped elbow rests and claw-foot armchairs – were introduced. Between 1820 and 1840 the use of natural woods became generalized, emphasizing the ornate aspect of Carelian birchwood.

New materials
An instinct for variety in materials is characteristic of this aspect of Russian decorative art. Already in the reigns of Elizabeth I and Catherine II steel-based furniture manufactured at the Tula works had made its appearance ● *60* near Moscow.

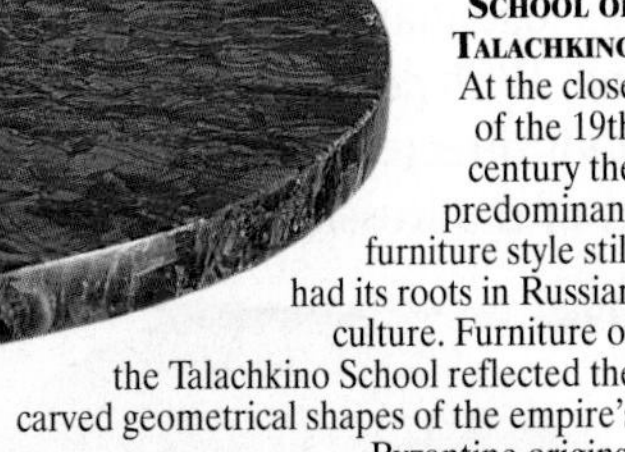

School of Talachkino
At the close of the 19th century the predominant furniture style still had its roots in Russian culture. Furniture of the Talachkino School reflected the carved geometrical shapes of the empire's Byzantine origins.

"Russian Jacob"
Another exclusive style of the late 18th century was "Russian Jacob" (strips of brass inlaid in mahogany, in geometrical patterns).

Gilt and semi-precious stones
In the 19th century Russia produced remarkable pieces of furniture (such as tables and monumental candelabra) incorporating colored crystal and stones mined in the Urals, which added to the exoticism of the new Italianate palaces then being built.

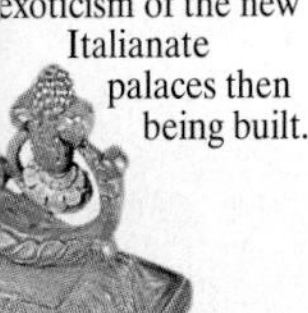

In their own way the theaters of St Petersburg bear witness to Russian political history, since their names invariably changed tc reflect the party in power. As the custodians of Russia's great dramatic, lyrical and choreographical works the imperial Mariinsky and Alexandrinsky theaters mounted the masquerade of the early 20th century, which are evoked in Anna Akhmatova "Poem without a Hero". These illustrated the dreams of a societ in crisis; they included Lermontov's legendary *Masked Ball*, with lavish décor by Alexander Golovine. With *perestroika*, new theat emerged; and innovative productions directed by Lev Dodin hav demonstrated the enduring vitality of the Russian theater.

ALEXANDRINSKY THEATER ▲ *230*. As the Academy of Drama in 1920, renamed the Pushkin Theater in 1937, the Alexandrinsky was, along with the Maly Theater in Moscow, one of the two great centers of 19th-century Russian culture. Between 1908 and 1918 it was profoundly influenced by the work of the great reformer Vsevolod Meyerhold (below).

MARIINSKY THEATER ▲ *202*
This great institution was inaugurated in 186 with the purpose of presenting the classical repertoire. Renamed the Kirov Theater in 19 it later became the mecca of the Russian Bal ▲ *200*. It reverted to its original name in 199

LITTLE THEATER OF OPERA AND BALLET ▲ *225*
Also known as the Maly or Mussorgsky Theater, at one time this was named the Mikhailovsky Theater. As the third of the former imperial playhouses it was the home of a French company from 1879 to 1917. Renamed the Little (*maly*) Theater, it was one of the few experimental institutions for opera and ballet in Russia during the 1930's.

БЕЗПЛАТНО.

18 95

Au Théâtre-Michel

LE MATIN

Hymne national:

„БОЖЕ, ЦАРЯ ХРАНИ!"

par les artistes, choristes et orchestre du Théâtre Impérial Français.

LES JOBARDS

LE GENDRE DU COLONEL

ORDRE DU SPECTACLE

On commencera à 12 heures

BDT (Tovstonogov Theater)
"Theater of tragedy, romantic drama and high comedy" – or so its original purpose was described.

The theater was known as the Gorky Theater between 1932 and 1993. For thirty years it mounted the classic plays of G.A. Tovstonogov (below right, during a rehearsal), after whom it was renamed in 1993.

BDT poster for Shakespeare's Henry IV (right)

В. Шекспир

Король Генрих IV

Theater of Musical Comedy (1929)
The director and satirical artist Nicholas Akimov (left) worked here from 1930 to 1950. This theater is known for its original repertoire.

Little (Maly) Dramatic Theater ▲ *238*
This repertory theater, founded in 1944, acquired a wider reputation in the 1980's under its director Lev Dodin. The Maly Theater Company gained worldwide fame with new plays like *Brothers and Sisters* (1985, from a novel by F. Abramov) and *Gaudeamus* (1990, by Sergei Kaledin, left). In 1998 the Maly Theater won the accolade of Theater of Europe, the third to do so after the Odeon in Paris and the Piccolo Teatro in Milan.

St Petersburg, where the first school of Russian dance opened in 1738, well in advance of Moscow, is the cradle of ballet. The entire history of classical dance is marked by Russian emotion and poetry, which enriched a technique originally imported from Europe. This enabled Russian dancers, while mastering both Italian virtuosity and French academic rigor, to apply themselves to the expression of the inner life of their roles. From the *divertissements* and interludes devised by 18th-century ballet masters such as Landé and Fossano to the worldwide phenomenon of the Diaghilev ballets, Russia has raised this particular art to the highest level of her cultural heritage.

BALLETS RUSSES (1908–29)
The success of the Ballets Russes gave a new stimulus to European ballet, as dance in Russia became the focus of a wide variety of artistic movements and interests. The research of the choreographer Fokine and the painters Bakst and Benois resurrected images of antiquity, the Orient, Old Russia and traditional festivals.

LEON BAKST (1866–1924)
As a scene-painter and decorator working for Serge Diaghilev, Leon Bakst moved to Paris in 1909. Above, a costume design for *Narcisse*, Saisons Russes, Paris 1911.
Baskt's sketches are on show at the Theater Museum, Ostrovsky Square ▲ *231*.

SERGE DIAGHILEV (1872–1929)
As the founder of the World of Art association Diaghilev masterminded the successful Saisons Russes tours abroad. He brought together the most brilliant and innovative artistic talents of his time: Bakst and Picasso, Fokine and Nijinsky, Karsavina and Pavlova, Rimsky-Korsakov, Stravinsky, Prokofiev and many more.

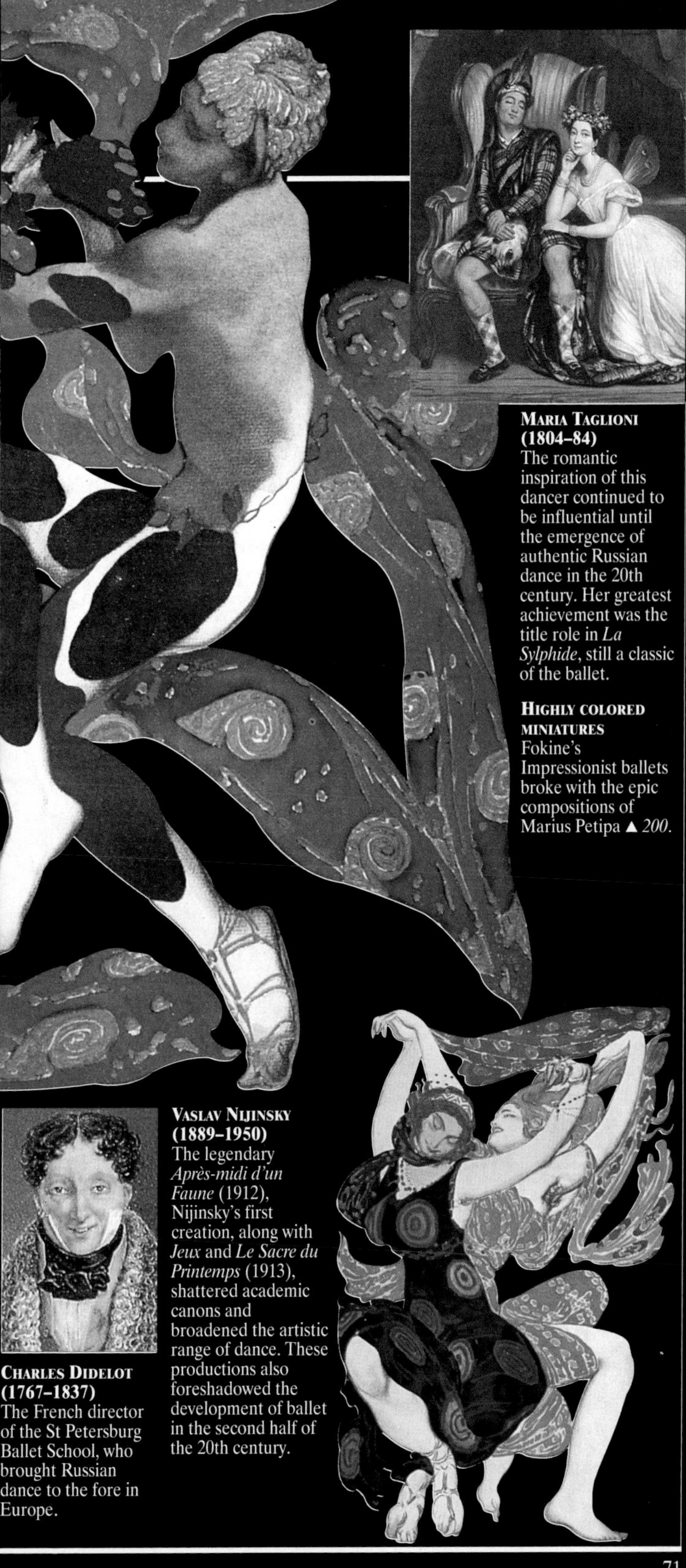

Maria Taglioni (1804–84)
The romantic inspiration of this dancer continued to be influential until the emergence of authentic Russian dance in the 20th century. Her greatest achievement was the title role in *La Sylphide*, still a classic of the ballet.

Highly colored miniatures
Fokine's Impressionist ballets broke with the epic compositions of Marius Petipa ▲ *200*.

Charles Didelot (1767–1837)
The French director of the St Petersburg Ballet School, who brought Russian dance to the fore in Europe.

Vaslav Nijinsky (1889–1950)
The legendary *Après-midi d'un Faune* (1912), Nijinsky's first creation, along with *Jeux* and *Le Sacre du Printemps* (1913), shattered academic canons and broadened the artistic range of dance. These productions also foreshadowed the development of ballet in the second half of the 20th century.

The Capella, the Conservatoire and the Philharmonia, as the centers of St Petersburg's musical establishment, made it their business to encourage artistic creativity and the expression of musical talent. In the 20th century the musical traditions of the St Petersburg School are associated with the esthetic of the Group of Five, which included the composers Balakirev, Borodin, Cui, Mussorgsky and Rimsky-Korsakov. While the historic past and folktales of Russia were the main sources of inspiration, the music itself remained thoroughly European.

The Capella
Founded in 1479 in the reign of Ivan III, the original purpose of the Capella was to train church choirs. In the 18th century, at St Petersburg, it became an imperial chapel, with the most talented musicians serving as its directors. Later it offered a wide variety of musical training, from directing of choirs (1846) to folk music (1918). In 1920 the Capella introduced women's voices into Russian choirs for the first time.

The Conservatoire
The fame of the Conservatoire, founded in 1862, rests on the extraordinary creative activity which at one time was centered upon it. The musicologist and art historian Stasov was the catalyst for the Group of Five composers, who were inspired by folktales and historical legends such as Boris Godunov; these were very different from the Moscow School, represented by Tchaikovsky and Rachmaninov, whose musical inspiration was more European in style.

HE PHILHARMONIA
ıis institution
ıs named after
ıostakovich in 1974.
mitry Shostakovich
906–75), although
quasi-official
viet composer,
l out of favor
th the authorities
1947. Encouraged
Zhdanov, he
longed to the
adition of Bach
d Mussorgsky. His
ork includes fifteen
mphonies, among
em the famous
h (*"Leningrad"*)
mphony ● *51*.

SERGEI PROKOFIEV (1891–1953)
Trained as a pianist and composer at the St Petersburg Conservatoire, Prokofiev began his career as a concert artist. Between 1918 and 1932 he lived outside Russia; on his return to the Soviet Union he suffered political persecution. His work sums up the finest achievements of Russian music, from Glinka through to Rachmaninov (*Romeo and Juliet*, 1938).

OR TRAVINSKY 882–1971)
pupil of
imsky-Korsakov,
travinsky lived in
ussia until 1914.
e was later a
ermanent
ember of the
aisons Russes in
aris, where his
allets *The*
rebird (1910),
etrushka (1911)
nd *The Rite of*
pring (1913) were
erformed. The
emes of these
allets were
spired by
ussian folklore.

● Recipe: "Blinis"

Blinis, made from one of the oldest of flour-based recipes, were originally eaten "in communion" with the souls of deceased loved ones in Russia: at Christmas with *koutia* (broth made with cracked wheat), at funerals and during Carnival. Following the 1917 Revolution *blinis* became everyday fare in Russia, unconnected with the Orthodox calendar.

Preparing the mixture

Ingredients
(for six people):
2lb 3 oz/10 cups flour
1½ oz yeast
½ tsp salt
1 tsp caster sugar
10 fl. oz lukewarm water
1 pint lukewarm milk
3 tbsp oil
3 eggs

1. Prepare in advance: in a warm bowl dissolve the yeast, salt and sugar in the lukewarm water. Pour the mixture into a mixing bowl.

2. Mixing well with a whisk, add the flour, milk and egg yolks, working till smooth.

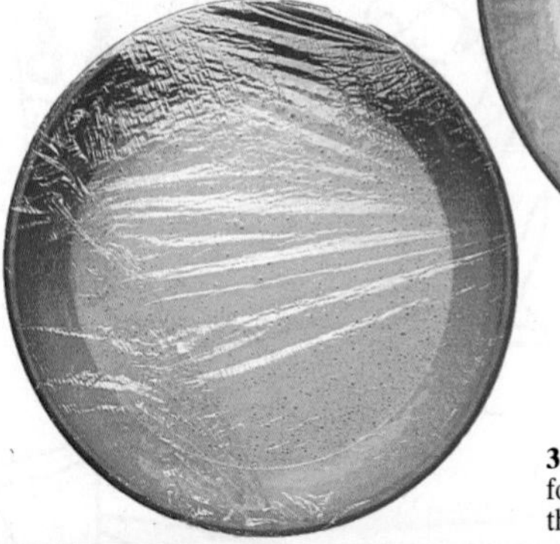

3. Allow the mixture to rise in a warm place for 40 minutes. Cover the bowl. Then whip the egg whites until stiff.

ЖАЛУI ПОДI ПРОЧЪ ОТЪМЕНА МНЕ ДЕЛА НЕТ ДАТЕБА
ИШЕЛЪ ЅАЖЕПУ ХВАТАЕШЪ БЛИНОВЪ ПЕЧЬ МЕШАЕШЪ
АЖЕПУ ХВАТАТЬ НЕВЕЛАТЪ ДЛАТОГО ЧТО БЛИНЫ
ДГОРАТЪ АТОТЪ ЧАСЪ РЕЅОНЪ СЫШУ СКОВОРОДНЕМЪ ХВ
Ю МНЕ ХОТА КТЫДНО АТЕ БУДЕТЪ УЖЕ ОБИДНО А ВИТЬ

4. Gently fold the egg whites into the mixture with a spatula.

5. Lightly grease a 5-inch frying pan with a half-potato dipped in melted butter.

6. Pour a little of the mixture into the heated frying pan, turning the pan to make the mixture spread as thinly as possible.

7. Cook at medium heat, as with pancakes (the first is often a disaster).

8. The *blinis* are then covered with melted butter and thick cream (*smetana*), and eaten with *zakuski* (hors d'oeuvres): smoked salmon, tarama, herring, salmon eggs, or similar tasty accompaniments. Traditionally, Russians serve *blinis* with an assortment of chilled red and black caviar and ice-cold vodka.

Russian Specialties

Shawls
Light and warm, Russian shawls come in many colors, usually with bright flower patterns. They are available in most department stores in St Petersburg.

Zefirs
Sweets resembling meringues coated in chocolate.

Russian Vodka
The best place to buy good-quality vodka is in shops specializing in the national drink. The most highly recommended brands are Sankt Petersburg, Diplomat, Piatizvezdnaya, and Sinopskaya.

Russian Vodka Museum
The displays here trace the history of distilling in Russia from the 10th century. Guided visits include the opportunity to taste some of the best vodkas, along with a suitable selection of zakouski.

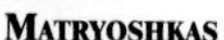

Matryoshkas
These little dolls, usually made by Muscovite craftsmen, are very popular with tourists. The quality of the painted design may vary considerably.

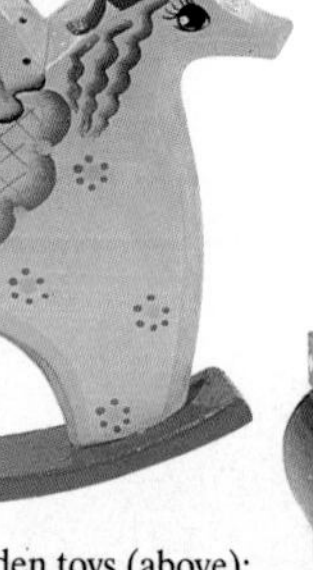

Crafts
Handpainted wooden toys (above); objects made of amber or semi-precious stones (green malachite box, far right); lacquered Palekh boxes (right) echo the art of this former school of iconography.

Architecture

THE TOWN PLAN: THE FOUNDING OF ST PETERSBURG

PETER I'S SKETCH FOR PETERHOF (1712)
This "Trident" design, copied from Versailles, was used on the left bank of the Neva, the Admiralty supplying the point of convergence of the three avenues.

In May 1703 Peter I, then at war with the Swedes, captured a stronghold at the mouth of the Neva river. To consolidate his victory he began building a new fortress 4 miles downstream dedicated to saints Peter and Paul, later adding the Admiralty and shipyards on the left bank. The site was unhealthy and ill-protected; nevertheless, by 1712 the Czar was determined to build his new capital there. St Petersburg, ". . . the window through which Russia looked out on Europe", evolved into a huge experiment, whereby patterns borrowed from Western cities were assimilated into Russian tradition.

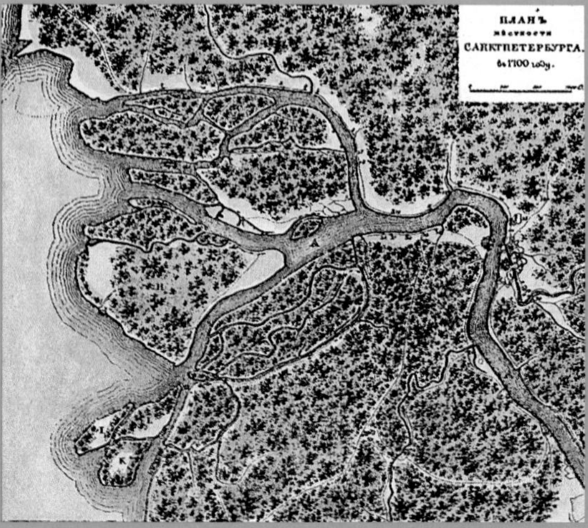

HISTORY AND LEGEND
The legend of this city, which was born of the will of a single man, has left an indelible mark on history. Buil "on the corpses o thousands of men" popular tradition has i that St Petersburg wil one day return to the waves from which i rose.

THE MOUTH OF THE NEVA IN 1698
Apart from one or two settlements of Carelians, the flat, sea-level islands of St Petersburg were uninhabited and clothed with forest. They were subject to floods made even more fearsome by the current flowing out of Lake Ladoga where it meets the powerful waves of the Gulf of Finland.

THE PETER AND PAUL FORTRESS (1703)
A symbol of autocratic military power, the Peter and Paul Fortress stands directly opposite the Imperial Palace. The gilded spires of the Peter and Paul Cathedral, the Admiralty and Mikhail Palace add bright verticals to the flat, gray urban landscape.

THE DEVELOPMENT OF THE CITY
The plans drawn up by Jean-Baptiste Leblond, the chief architect for St Petersburg, were remarkable for a system of Dutch-style canals, supposed to absorb the flood waters and facilitate communications. Other features were an arrangement of the various districts to suit different sections of the population, and an attempt (eventually abandoned) to surround the city with ramparts.

St Petersburg in 1725

Although in 1725 St Petersburg was far from completed, the planning options governing its later construction were already fixed. There were two fortresses to guard the mouth of the Neva (Peter and Paul on the right bank and the Admiralty on the left); the Menshikov Palace and the Kunstkammer endowed Vasilyevsky Island with its first architectural features; the Summer Palace and the gardens bounded the city to eastward; the river's tributaries had been channeled; and the Nevsky Prospekt had been laid out.

Warehouses The first constructions in the city were of wood, always abundant in Russia.

Standard houses

In the interest of stylistic unity, the Italian architect Domenico Trezzini designed standard houses ". . . adapted to every class of society". With its Corinthian pilasters and central flight of steps, the House of the Ambassadors (above, 1710) was the most elegant building in St Petersburg, although it was constructed of wood and puddled clay. At left, the standard "economy" house.

In his haste to jettison Muscovite traditions Peter the Great engaged foreigners to build his modern city, naval installations and cultural center. Dutch engineers and Italian and German architects succeeded one another, until the arrival in 1716 of the French master builder Leblond. Leblond and his team were commissioned both to build, and to train the Russians in contemporary Western architectural concepts. "Naryshkin Baroque", characteristic of late 17th-century Moscow, gave way to Dutch pediments cheek by jowl with Italianate superimposed orders, German staircases and French curb-roofing.

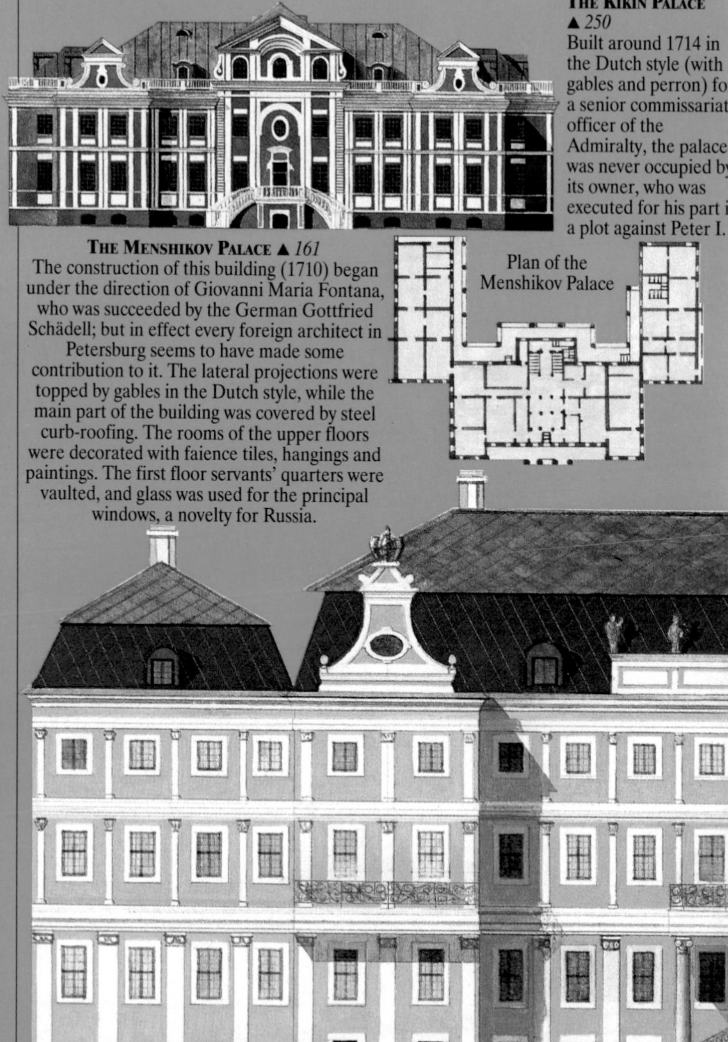

THE KIKIN PALACE
▲ *250*
Built around 1714 in the Dutch style (with gables and perron) for a senior commissariat officer of the Admiralty, the palace was never occupied by its owner, who was executed for his part i a plot against Peter I.

THE MENSHIKOV PALACE ▲ *161*
The construction of this building (1710) began under the direction of Giovanni Maria Fontana, who was succeeded by the German Gottfried Schädell; but in effect every foreign architect in Petersburg seems to have made some contribution to it. The lateral projections were topped by gables in the Dutch style, while the main part of the building was covered by steel curb-roofing. The rooms of the upper floors were decorated with faience tiles, hangings and paintings. The first floor servants' quarters were vaulted, and glass was used for the principal windows, a novelty for Russia.

Plan of the Menshikov Palace

The Summer Palace
Built in 1710 by Trezzini along the lines of the "standard" St Petersburg house for "notables", the Summer Palace was enlarged and redecorated by Andreas Schlüter in 1714.

European-style window, Summer Palace
Light is admitted to the palace by two levels of rectangular windows. Between these levels, exactly aligned with the windows, are terracotta reliefs illustrating Russian naval triumphs.

Cabin of Peter the Great ▲ *151*
The last surviving example of the first period of construction at St Petersburg, this little building is in the classic form of the *isba*. It comprises two small rooms on either side of an entryway. The wooden walls are painted red in imitation of brick on the outside, and hung with fabric on the inside. The window-panes are of mica.

Born in Paris in 1700, Bartolomeo Rastrelli arrived in St Petersburg in 1716 with his father, a sculptor. He had a strong influence on the city's architecture during the thirty years spanning the reigns of Anna Yoannovna and Elizabeth I. As the designer of the imperial palaces, from 1734 onward he introduced Rococo into the Summer Palace, becoming Empress Elizabeth's court architect. The blossoming of Baroque art was also favored by Peter the Great, who paid for Russian students to be trained in Western Europe: in this sense, the assimilation of Western models led to an authentically creative result.

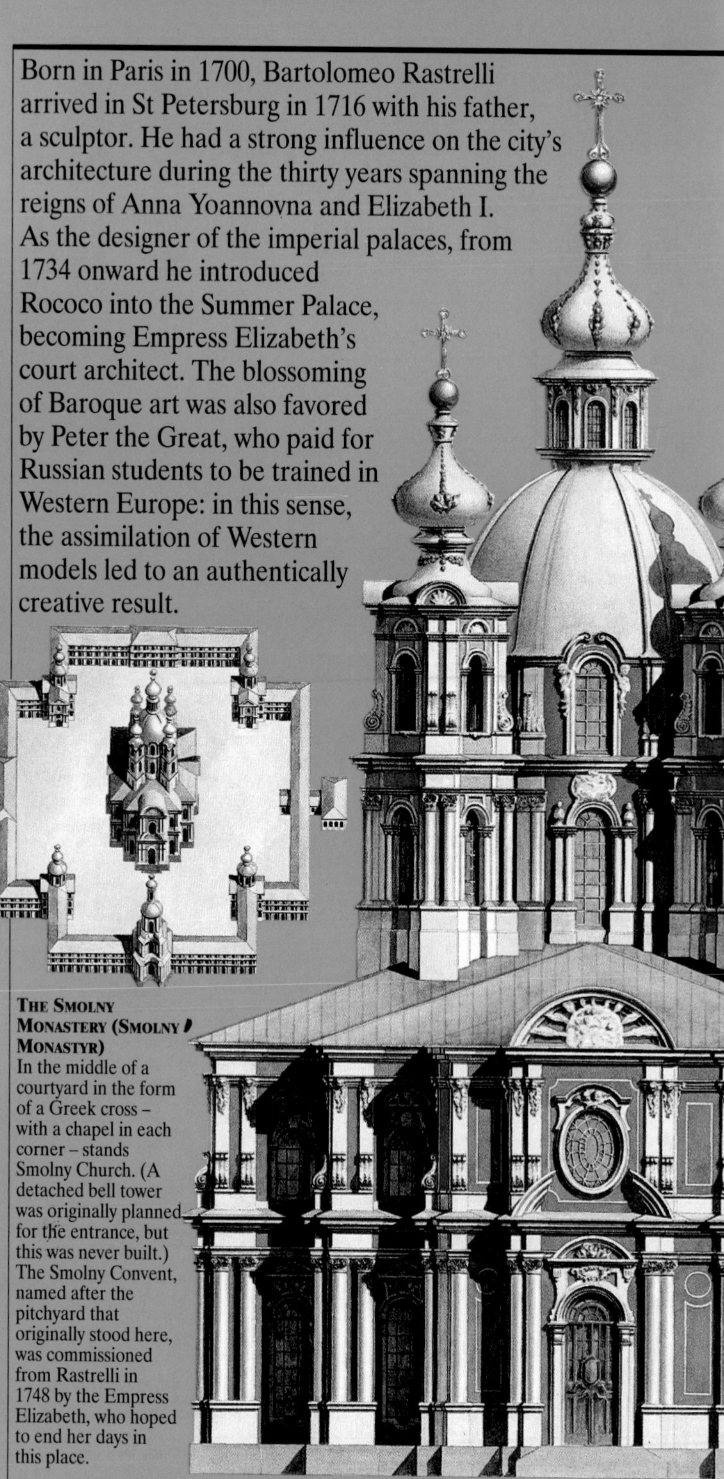

THE SMOLNY MONASTERY (SMOLNY MONASTYR)
In the middle of a courtyard in the form of a Greek cross – with a chapel in each corner – stands Smolny Church. (A detached bell tower was originally planned for the entrance, but this was never built.) The Smolny Convent, named after the pitchyard that originally stood here, was commissioned from Rastrelli in 1748 by the Empress Elizabeth, who hoped to end her days in this place.

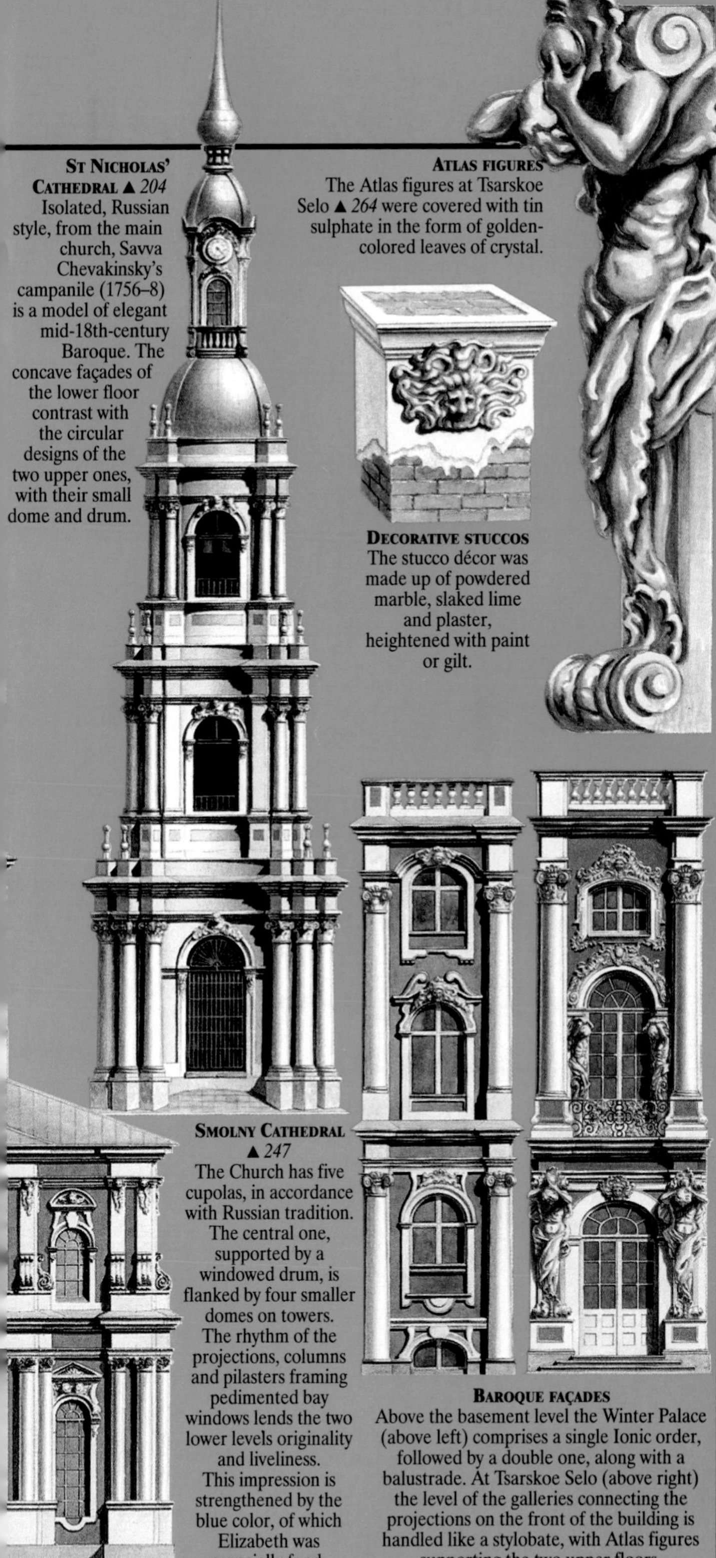

ST NICHOLAS' CATHEDRAL ▲ *204*
Isolated, Russian style, from the main church, Savva Chevakinsky's campanile (1756–8) is a model of elegant mid-18th-century Baroque. The concave façades of the lower floor contrast with the circular designs of the two upper ones, with their small dome and drum.

ATLAS FIGURES
The Atlas figures at Tsarskoe Selo ▲ *264* were covered with tin sulphate in the form of golden-colored leaves of crystal.

DECORATIVE STUCCOS
The stucco décor was made up of powdered marble, slaked lime and plaster, heightened with paint or gilt.

SMOLNY CATHEDRAL ▲ *247*
The Church has five cupolas, in accordance with Russian tradition. The central one, supported by a windowed drum, is flanked by four smaller domes on towers. The rhythm of the projections, columns and pilasters framing pedimented bay windows lends the two lower levels originality and liveliness. This impression is strengthened by the blue color, of which Elizabeth was especially fond.

BAROQUE FAÇADES
Above the basement level the Winter Palace (above left) comprises a single Ionic order, followed by a double one, along with a balustrade. At Tsarskoe Selo (above right) the level of the galleries connecting the projections on the front of the building is handled like a stylobate, with Atlas figures supporting the two upper floors.

The New Holland Arch

On the accession of Catherine II, Bartolomeo Rastrelli was no longer in favor. The Czarina, w[illegible] preferred sober lines, imposed a return to the canons of antiquity and the 17th century, surrounding herself wit[illegible] European architects such as Vallin de la Mothe, Antonio Rinald[illegible] the Scottish court architect Charles Cameron, Yuri Velten and Giacomo Quarenghi. Later, Alexander I brought the Empire sty[illegible] to St Petersburg (known in Russia, as the "classic" style), as a statement of imperial power. After the accession of Nicholas I i[illegible] 1825 the major town planning review of the capital was entruste[illegible] to the Italian Carlo Rossi. It was Rossi who conceived the great colonnaded squares, so strong a feature of the city today.

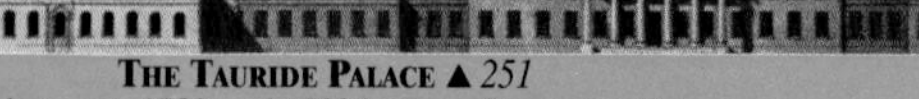

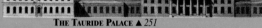

THE TAURIDE PALACE ▲ *251*
Built between 1783 and 1789 by Ivan Starov for Prince Potemkin, the Tauride Palace is austere to a fault, with smooth walls, rectangular unadorned bays, an upper level topped by a frieze of alternating triglyphs and bare metopes, and a Doric portico.

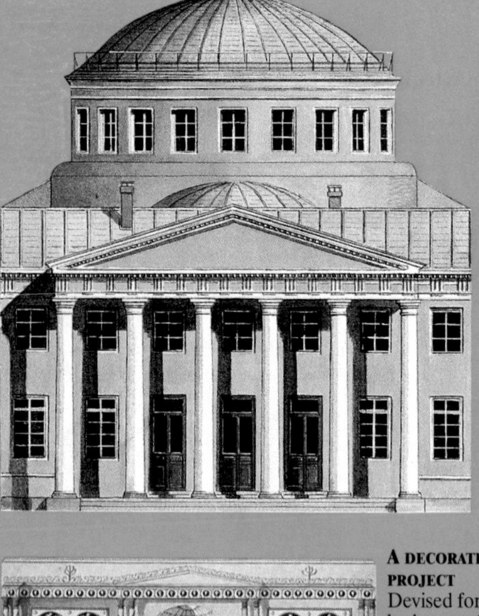

PLAN OF THE TAURIDE PALACE
The central axis leading to the main gallery is flanked by pavilions linked to the main body of the building by wings; one of these contains the theater, the other the private apartments.

A DECORATIVE PROJECT
Devised for the state bedroom of the Grand Duchess Maria Fyodorovna, the wife of the future Paul I, in the Catherine Palace of Tsarskoe Selo ▲ *264*. The designer was Charles Cameron.

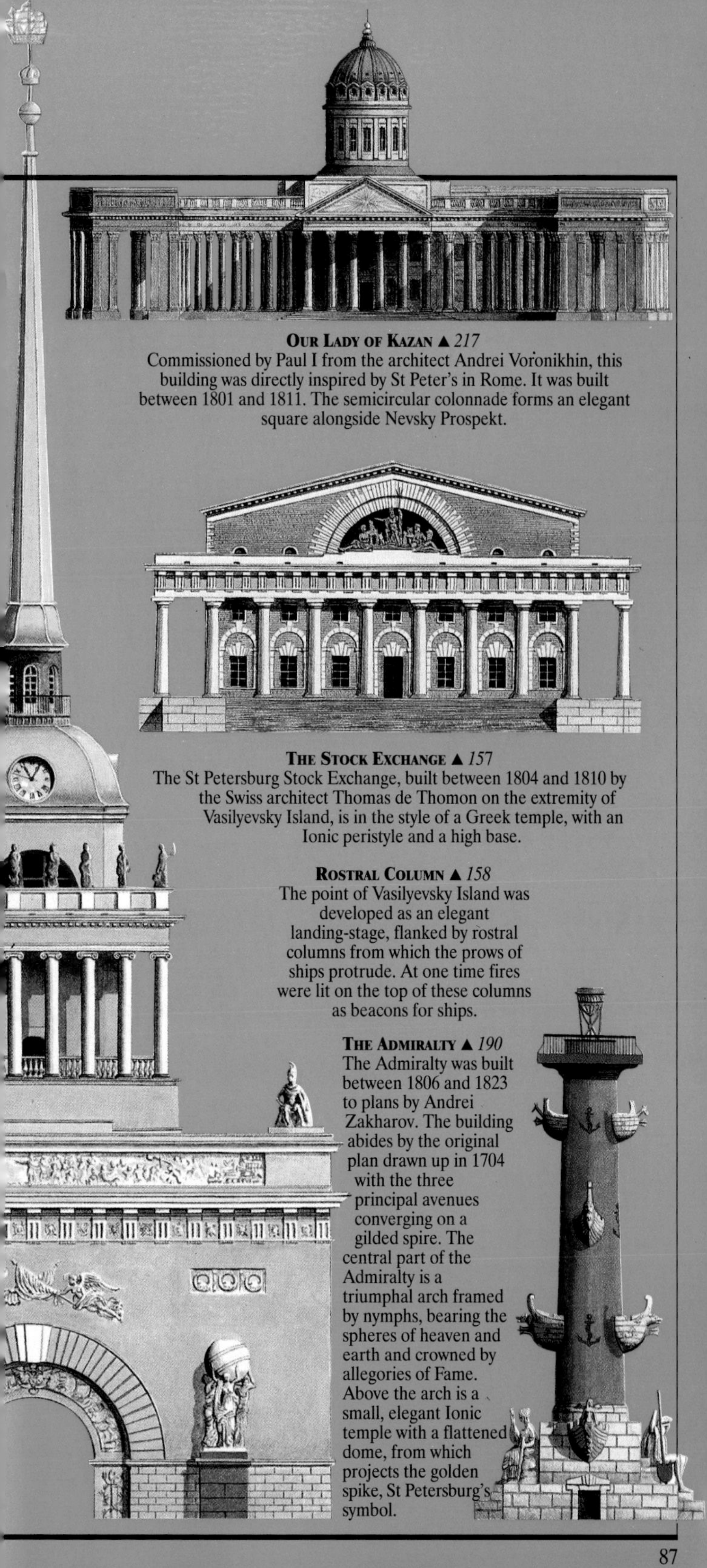

Our Lady of Kazan ▲ *217*
Commissioned by Paul I from the architect Andrei Voronikhin, this building was directly inspired by St Peter's in Rome. It was built between 1801 and 1811. The semicircular colonnade forms an elegant square alongside Nevsky Prospekt.

The Stock Exchange ▲ *157*
The St Petersburg Stock Exchange, built between 1804 and 1810 by the Swiss architect Thomas de Thomon on the extremity of Vasilyevsky Island, is in the style of a Greek temple, with an Ionic peristyle and a high base.

Rostral Column ▲ *158*
The point of Vasilyevsky Island was developed as an elegant landing-stage, flanked by rostral columns from which the prows of ships protrude. At one time fires were lit on the top of these columns as beacons for ships.

The Admiralty ▲ *190*
The Admiralty was built between 1806 and 1823 to plans by Andrei Zakharov. The building abides by the original plan drawn up in 1704 with the three principal avenues converging on a gilded spire. The central part of the Admiralty is a triumphal arch framed by nymphs, bearing the spheres of heaven and earth and crowned by allegories of Fame. Above the arch is a small, elegant Ionic temple with a flattened dome, from which projects the golden spike, St Petersburg's symbol.

Western Europe's fascination with the past was reflected in St Petersburg, where neo-Baroque, neoclassicism, neo-Gothic and neo-Renaissance vied for precedence. The architecture of St Isaac's Cathedral is reminiscent of St Paul's in London, while the lavish décor of its interior borrows from every conceivable style. The Church of the Resurrection (also known as the Church of the Redeemer, or the Church of the Spilt Blood) is an example of a specifically Russian form of historicism, which had its origin in Moscow. It was built on the spot where Alexander II was assassinated, and has magnificent mosaics.

ATLAS AT THE BELOSELSKY-BELOZERSKY PALACE
This was the first palace in St Petersburg built with specific reference to the Russian Baroque style created by Rastrelli a century earlier.

THE CHESME CHURCH
Built between 1777 and 1780 by Yuri Velten, in honor of Orlov's 1770 naval victory against the Turks, this church and the palace in front of it are the earliest examples of neo-Gothic in Russia.

ECLECTIC DÉCOR
Behind the classical exterior of St Isaac's is a lavish interior: here painted frescos have been supplanted by mosaics (right) and marble wall-surfaces. The columns of the iconostasis are covered with lapis lazuli and malachite.

A HOMAGE TO TRADITIONAL RUSSIAN ART
Built between 1883 and 1907 by Alfred Parland on the site of Alexander II's assassination, this church was intended as a celebration of Russian art's enduring values. The aim was not so much to imitate traditional construction methods as to draw on the decorative repertoire of medieval Russia and 12th-century mosaic techniques.

THE PEDIMENTS
The décor of the exterior pediments was executed from cartoons by the greatest Russian painters of the time, among them V.M. Vaznetsov.

CHURCH OF THE RESURRECTION ▲ *228*
The building was directly inspired by St Basil's Cathedral in Moscow (1555–60). Its main features include a variety of onion domes, central tower with a pyramidal roof, *kokoshniki* or halo-like decorated arches, and tall drums supported by columns. It is now open to the public and contains some magnificent restored mosaics.

THE PORCHES
With their stout balusters and hanging arches the porches at ground level are built to a pattern common in Russia until the late 17th century.

The brick exterior heightens the overall impression of lavishness.

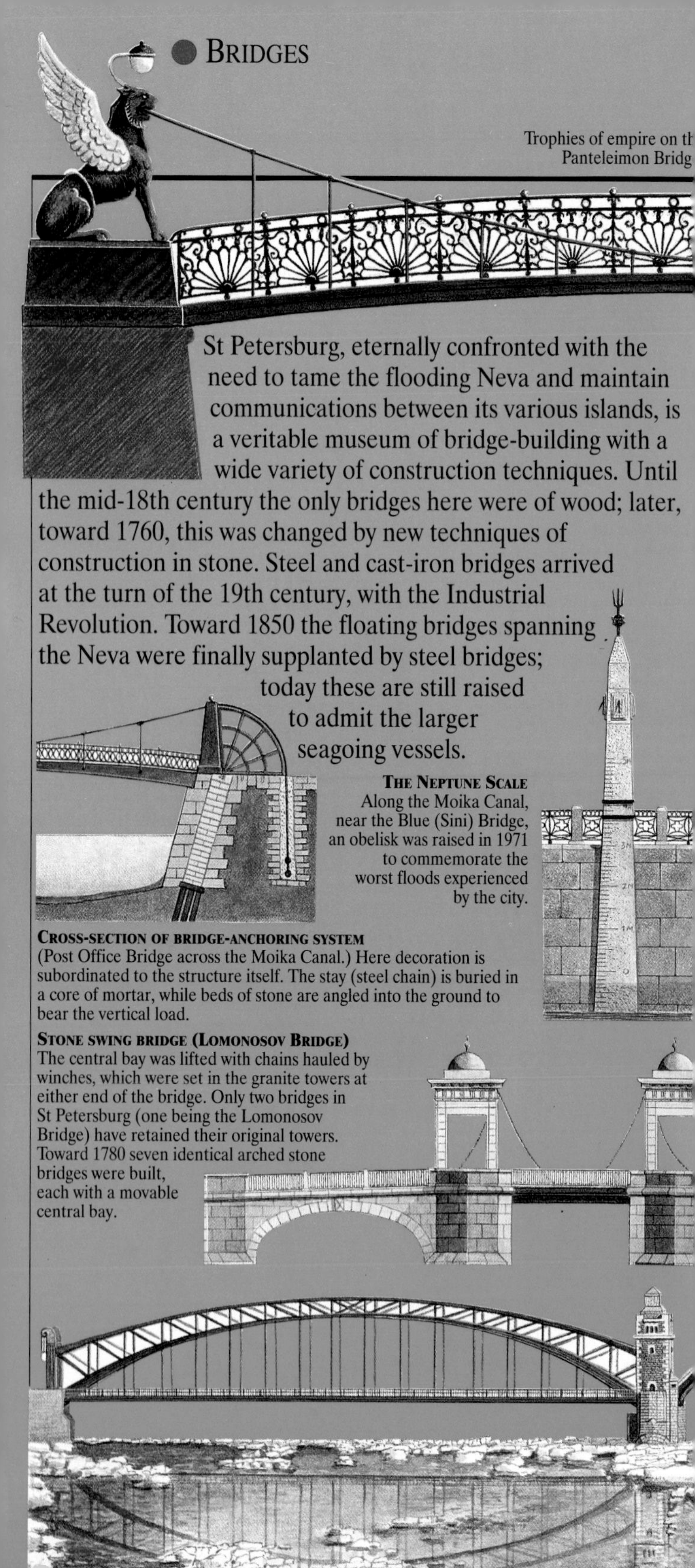

Trophies of empire on th
Panteleimon Bridg

St Petersburg, eternally confronted with the need to tame the flooding Neva and maintain communications between its various islands, is a veritable museum of bridge-building with a wide variety of construction techniques. Until the mid-18th century the only bridges here were of wood; later, toward 1760, this was changed by new techniques of construction in stone. Steel and cast-iron bridges arrived at the turn of the 19th century, with the Industrial Revolution. Toward 1850 the floating bridges spanning the Neva were finally supplanted by steel bridges; today these are still raised to admit the larger seagoing vessels.

The Neptune Scale
Along the Moika Canal, near the Blue (Sini) Bridge, an obelisk was raised in 1971 to commemorate the worst floods experienced by the city.

Cross-section of bridge-anchoring system
(Post Office Bridge across the Moika Canal.) Here decoration is subordinated to the structure itself. The stay (steel chain) is buried in a core of mortar, while beds of stone are angled into the ground to bear the vertical load.

Stone swing bridge (Lomonosov Bridge)
The central bay was lifted with chains hauled by winches, which were set in the granite towers at either end of the bridge. Only two bridges in St Petersburg (one being the Lomonosov Bridge) have retained their original towers. Toward 1780 seven identical arched stone bridges were built, each with a movable central bay.

SUSPENSION BRIDGE
The Bank Bridge (Bankovsky Most) was built by Georg Tretter in 1825–6, across the Griboedov Canal. The anchoring of the stays holding up the plank roadway is hidden inside the bronze griffons, sculpted by Pavel Sokolov. Of six similar bridges constructed between 1823 and 1826 only three have survived.

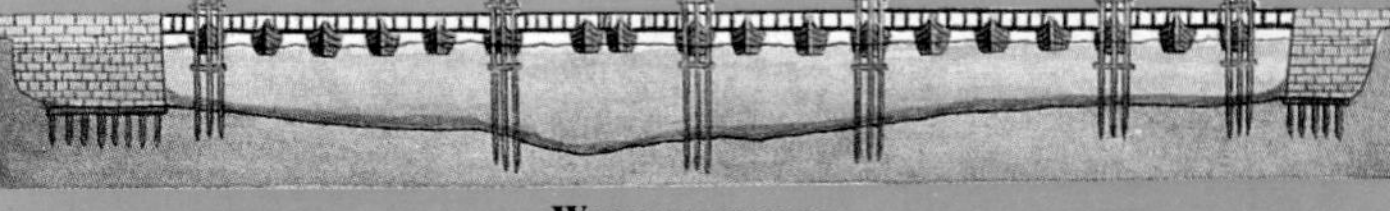

WOODEN PONTOON
The first bridges, built in about 1720, were of wood. The largest consisted of a succession of connected barges. For the small canals Dutch-style drawbridges were used.

STRUCTURE
The cross-section above shows the abutment pier of the steel arch and the way its thrust is absorbed by the masonry. The entire abutment pier rests on a substructure of wooden pilings.

THE PANTELEIMON BRIDGE
Built in 1907–8 by the engineer Andrei Pchenitsky, this bridge spans the Fontanka near the Summer Garden. For its decoration (parapets and lampposts) the architect Lev Ilin used Empire motifs.

METAL SWING BRIDGE
The Peter the Great bridge (Bolshoy Okhtinsky), built between 1908 and 1911 to a prize-winning design by V. Apychkov, allows ships to pass freely along the waterway. The lateral bays, each about 400 feet in length, are the longest in St Petersburg.

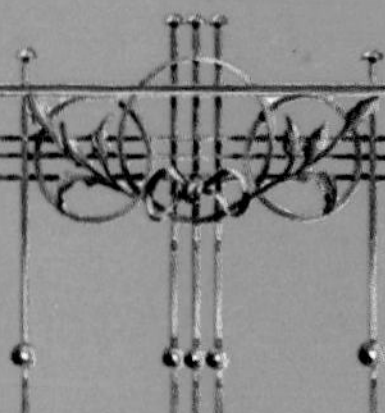

Wrought-iron "entrelac" design.

In the early 20th century St Petersburg, like other European capitals, was affected by modernist trends. The Art Nouveau style, popular almost everywhere, seems to have acquired certain typically regional characteristic when it reached the banks of the Neva. The majestic architecture of the classical age, the exuberance of Baroque and the innovations of Art Nouveau in Europe and Scandinavia were metamorphosed in a highly original manner in St Petersburg.

RESIDENTIAL BLOCKS
In the Petrograd district a number of Art Nouveau buildings were constructed, notably that of no. 28 Bolshaya Zelenina (19th century), which included both artists' studios and ordinary apartments. The façade is varied by two oriels, and crowned by an extensive mosaic.

THE PRIVATE TOWNHOUSE
The townhouse of the ballerina Mathilda Kshesinskaya, on Kronversky Avenue, is a typical example of a picturesque yet elegant European-style Art Nouveau structure. It was built (1904–6) by the architect A.I. Hogen.

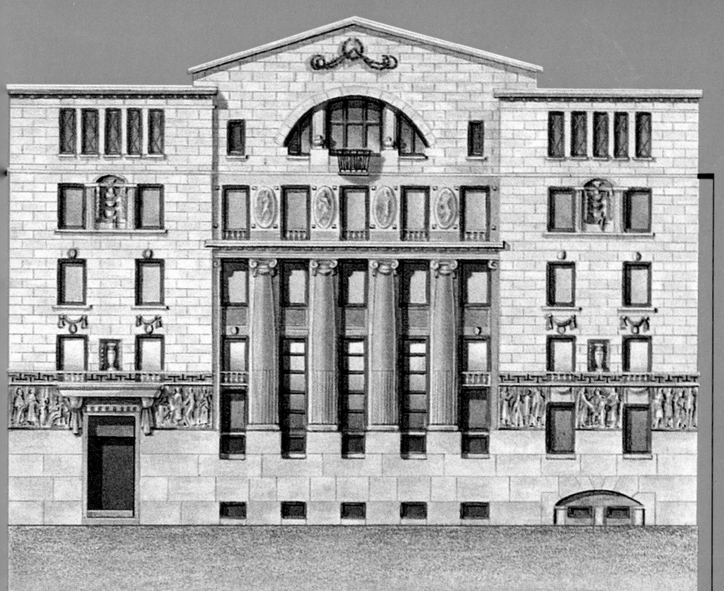

THE COMMERCIAL BUILDING
The Azovsko-Donskoy bank was built (1908–9) by the architect F.I. Lidval and the sculptor V.V. Kuznetsov. Designed in every way to reflect the grand scale of the capital, this building was inspired by the classicism of Catherine II's reign.

BAS-RELIEFS
Neoclassical Art Nouveau also had its place, in the bas-reliefs, decorative friezes and medallions of the bank's façade.

MATERIALS OF ART NOUVEAU
The door of the Zimmerman building, built in 1906 on Avenue Kamennoostrovsky, shows the diversity of the materials and construction techniques used in Art Nouveau. Rough-hewn projecting stones, bricks and mortar surfaces combine for a colorful yet formal effect.

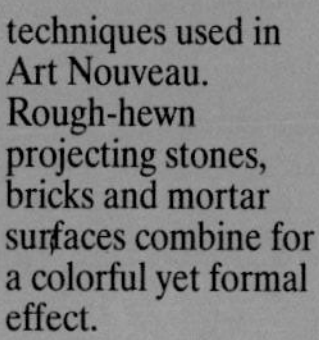

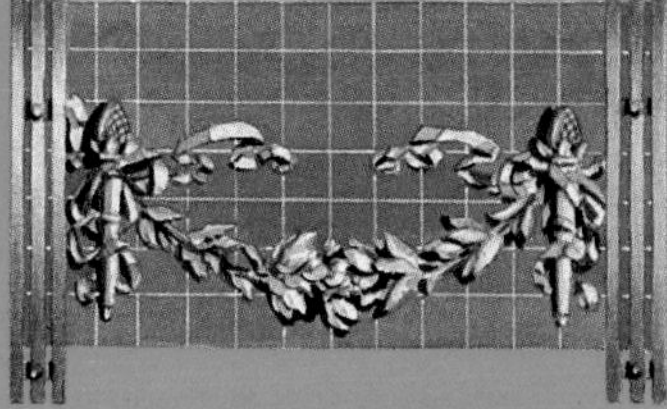

BLUE CERAMIC AND WROUGHT IRON
These supply the decorative motif for the cornice, which is handled in the classical manner. Note the foliated ribbon pattern on the flambeaux, with their pine-cone tops.

PROFILING
The profusion of glass, wrought iron, natural stone and vegetable ornamentation in the details of the surrounding balustrade and the projecting window show that the architect has fully mastered the new style without succumbing to eclecticism.

The Revolution of October 1917 marked a turning point in the development of Russian architecture. Thereafter the vogue was for the "Soviet style", or Constructivism, which could suitably represent the new ideology and exonerate architects from the charge of Formalism. Soon enough, Russian architects accomplished a stylistic transition, assimilating their classical heritage into a relatively human brand of Constructivism. This style, which developed in the 1940's and 1950's, was later baptized "Stalinist Empire".

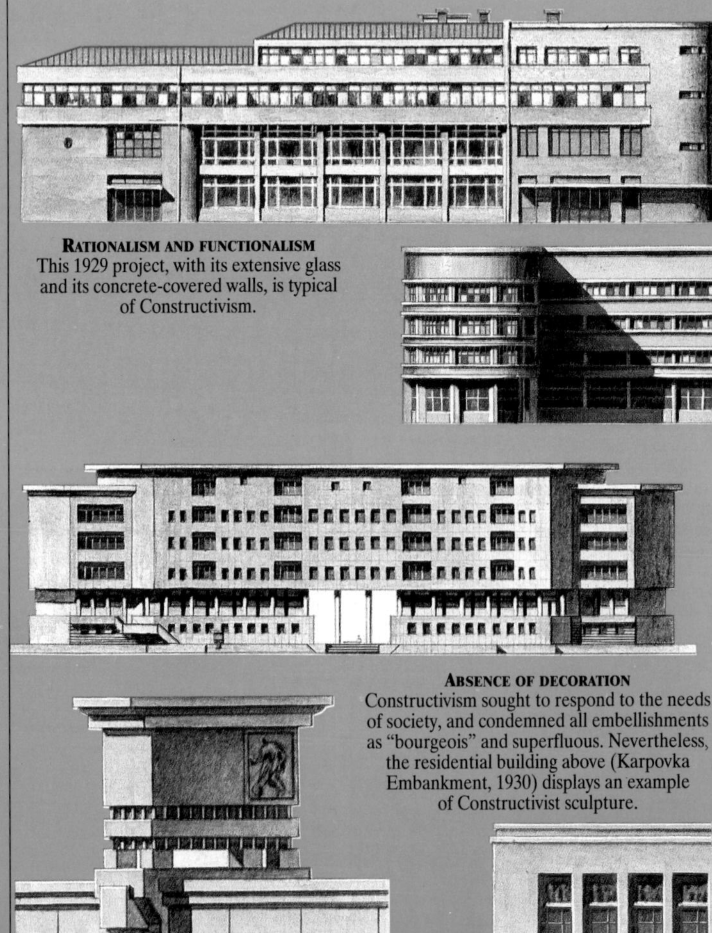

RATIONALISM AND FUNCTIONALISM
This 1929 project, with its extensive glass and its concrete-covered walls, is typical of Constructivism.

ABSENCE OF DECORATION
Constructivism sought to respond to the needs of society, and condemned all embellishments as "bourgeois" and superfluous. Nevertheless, the residential building above (Karpovka Embankment, 1930) displays an example of Constructivist sculpture.

HE REVIVAL OF ECORATION
ater attitudes changed nd decoration became ıseful" again. The frieze n the façade of the Ioscow cinema (top) ssimilated – and ıterpreted – the Russian assical heritage.

THE CLASSICAL MANNER
This building on Kamennoostrovsky Avenue was designed by the architect N. Lanser in 1936. The central part is flanked by slightly projecting wings, and the profiling is carefully worked, with faceted stonework, pilasters, arabesques and medallions.

MONUMENTALISM (THE KIROVSKY SOVIET)
This effect is achieved by emphasizing the horizontal lines in contrast to the vertical tower.

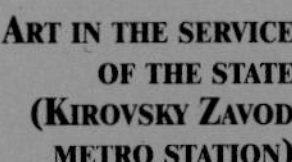

ART IN THE SERVICE OF THE STATE (KIROVSKY ZAVOD METRO STATION)
The building of the metro system, of the highest quality and very costly indeed, was meant to serve the Soviet ideal.

A MOVE TOWARD THE OUTSIDE WORLD
The Finland Station (Finlyandsky Vokzal), built in 1957, represented a timid gesture toward international modernism.

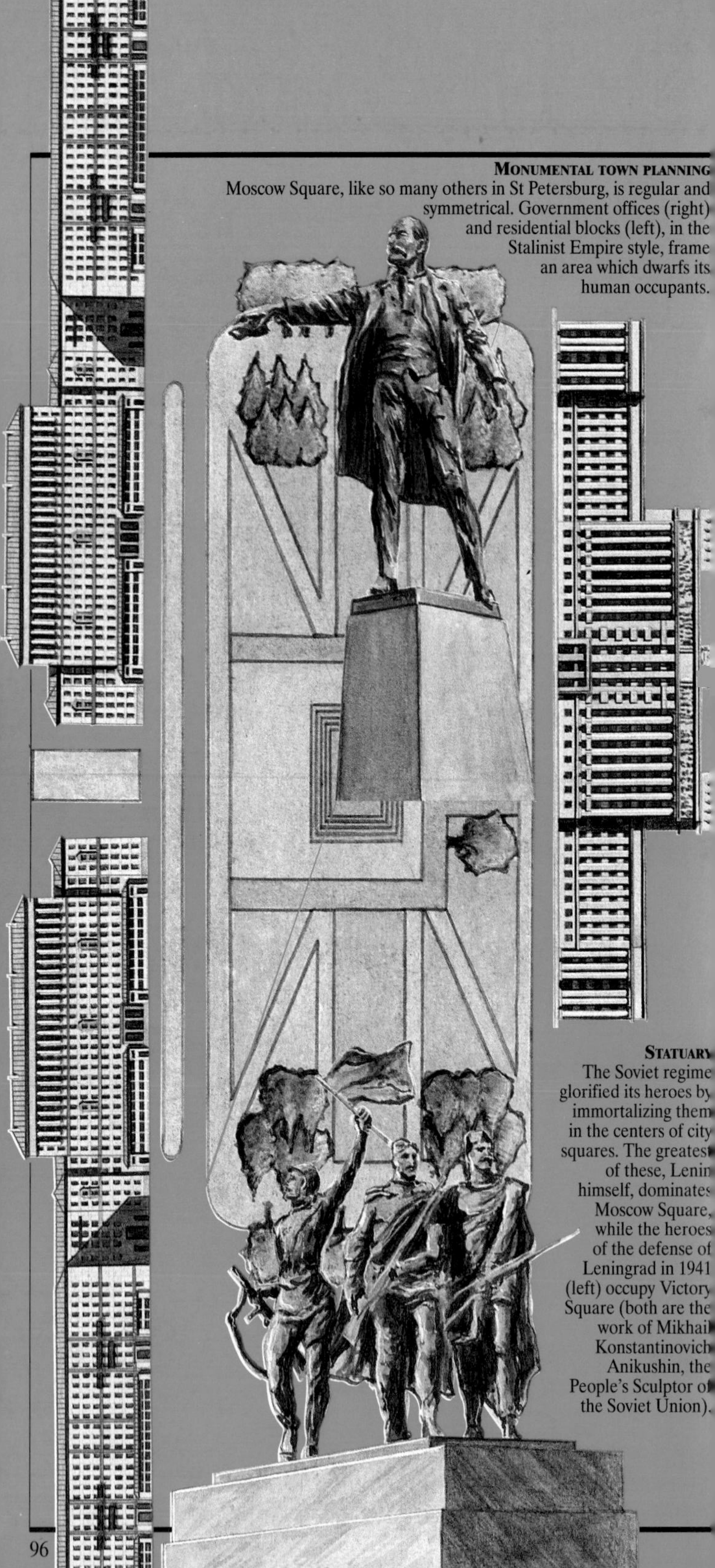

Monumental town planning
Moscow Square, like so many others in St Petersburg, is regular and symmetrical. Government offices (right) and residential blocks (left), in the Stalinist Empire style, frame an area which dwarfs its human occupants.

Statuary
The Soviet regime glorified its heroes by immortalizing them in the centers of city squares. The greatest of these, Lenin himself, dominates Moscow Square, while the heroes of the defense of Leningrad in 1941 (left) occupy Victory Square (both are the work of Mikhail Konstantinovich Anikushin, the People's Sculptor of the Soviet Union).

St Petersburg as seen by painters

Like many of his Swedish compatriots Benjamin Patterssen (1750–1815) came to seek his fortune in St Petersburg. His arrival coincided with an important moment in the history of the city. The avenues were under construction and the people were impatient to see how their town would look once they were completed; above all, they had become acutely planning-conscious and were fascinated by major architectural ensembles. Profiting from this vogue, Patterssen began painting detailed views of St Petersburg in 1793; these were very popular on account of their refined technique and architectural exactitude. Patterssen also excelled as an engraver and draftsman; but his paintings of the city's monuments belong in the realm of poetry. His *View of the Kutuzov and Palace Embankment* (opposite) is remarkable for its rendering of the atmosphere and luminosity of springtime.

Fyodor Alexeyev (1753–1824) was launched by the Fine Arts Academy as a painter of theater décors and a master of perspective. The result was that he was unable to give free rein to his own brand of classicism until 1790, at which time his views of St Petersburg had become so successful that Czar Paul I commissioned Alexeyev to paint several other cities in the empire, most notably Moscow. Below, his *View of the Palace Embankment from the Peter and Paul Fortress*.

St Petersburg as seen by painters
Chernetsov

Grigory Chernetsov (1801–65) shifted the artistic focus from topography to portraiture. As a former pupil at the Fine Arts Academy, he followed his master Maxim Vorobiov (1787–1855) on the path of Romanticism. His *Neva Embankment in Front of the Fine Arts Academy: Night* (**2**) (about 1830) is a subject also treated by Vorobiov. This picture is not so much a representation of the city but more a picture of the river itself, and of the dreamlike atmosphere investing it during the hours of darkness, while *Parade on the Marsovo Pole (Field of Mars)* (1831–7) (**3**), commissioned by Czar Nicholas I is a veritable portrait of St Petersburg society. The main interest of this huge painting lies in the figures that people it, which include, most notably, literary lions such as Krylov, Pushkin, Griboedov and Zhukovsky (**1**).

3

1

2

At the St Petersburg Fine Arts Academy the art of interior painting reached its apogee in the mid-19th century. The teaching of perspective was revived by the efforts of Maxim Vorobiov (1787–1855). One of his pupils, Constantin Ukhtomsky (1818–81), along with two St Petersburg-based foreign painters (Edward Hau, 1807–87, and Luigi Premazzi, 1814–91), were chosen to paint the Winter Palace and the rooms of the New Hermitage (Novy Ermitazh) designed for the imperial collections. The three artists faced an identical challenge: to paint as much space as possible with the maximum number of details, juggling angles of view from perspectives that were impossible in real life. The commission was brilliantly carried out, as attested by Ukhtomsky's *Cimmerian Bosphorus Antiquities Room* (**2**), Hau's *Italian School Gallery* (**3**) and *History of Painting Gallery* (**4**), and Premazzi's *Artist's Apartment, Winter Palace* (**1**). The three artists' talents as watercolorists and their mastery of trompe l'oeil were also much admired by contemporaries, who followed the Czar's example in having the interiors of their palaces and houses similarly recorded.

1	4
2	
3	

BENOIS

From the time of their arrival in Russia in the late 18th century until the October Revolution of 1917 the Benois family remained implacably French. Nevertheless the painter Alexander Benois (1870–1960) was able to make the connection between the culture of his origins and that of St Petersburg, which he always considered his home. An avid historian, he maintained that his feelings about the past were "... more tender and affectionate" than his feelings about the present. As leader of the World of Art movement Benois created a completely new genre, the historical landscape, which allowed him to bring the 18th century back to life. His city of St Petersburg, whose image he held so clearly in his mind that he tirelessly painted it from memory, is peopled by courtesans and more or less enlightened monarchs. In much of his work St Petersburg is the background for ballet and theater décors. Real landscapes, personal memories and Benois' own deep knowledge allowed him to fill these décors with childlike innocence and freshness, as in *Holy Week Fair on Admiralty Square, about 1830* (right).

St Petersburg as seen by painters Ostrumova-Lebedeva

1

2

Anna Ostrumova-Lebedeva (1871–1955) illustrated another aspect of the historical landscape, with St Petersburg as the central theme. For her the only significant epoch was that of classicism, whose architecture and ambiance she painted in preference to people, as seen in *Columns of Our Lady of Kazan* (1903) (**2**). Until her death, she continued to perfect her art, using watercolors and xylographs to depict the four elements and above all the waters of the Neva, which she viewed as the fountainhead of the city's poetry. *The Fontanka and the Summer Garden* (1922) (**1**).

The Russian Avant-Garde

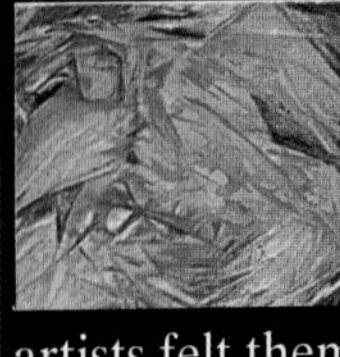

In the early 20th century the intellectual and artistic catalyst of St Petersburg (renamed Petrograd in 1914 and Leningrad in 1924) produced several avant-garde movements, led by creative talents of the first rank. Russian artists felt themselves on a par with their European counterparts notably the French Cubists and Italian Futurists. They also expressed themselves within the context of various trends dominated by the new painting.

The Young Movement (1910–14), which generated most of the avant-garde's initiatives, attracted artists as different as Matiushin, Rozanova, Malevich, Tatlin and Filonov. Their links with Parisian Cubists and the Expressionists of Munich (Kandinsky) eventually produced a conceptual stru (Rozanova, 19 which led to th blossoming of Cubo-Futurism the abstract ar associated with Malevich. The movement whi to reverberate through the rest of the 20th century came to th forefront in Decem 1915 with the "Last Futurist Exhibition: 0, 10", at which Tatlin's "counter-reliefs" firmly established the trend toward Constructivism. Thus the dialectic of the decades that followed was inaugurated in St Petersburg. The 1917 Revolution led many of the most prominent artists to migrate to Moscow, but after 1921 the fo modern ar subordinat Productivism, again shifted to Petrograd. Artists met at th Institute of Artis Culture (GINHUK), by whose agency their works were assembled in the Russian Museum ▲ *226* and the Zubov Art History Institute. The latter, which was opened in 1912, was intended to give St Petersburg's art an international dimension. Formalist (or Abstract) art, as championed by the Institute, fell into disfavor in the later 1920's, and eventually disappeared altogether.

MIKHAIL LARIONOV
Autumn (1912), a Primitivist work

Olga Rozanova, *Suprematist Composition* (1916–17)

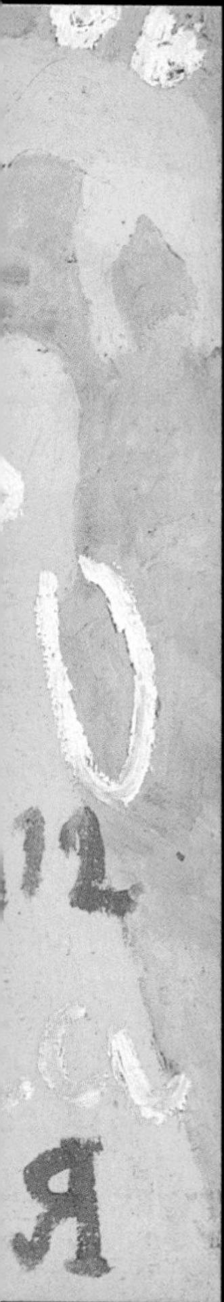

Kasimir Malevich
Portrait of Ivan Klium (1913)

Goncharova (1881–1962) and Larionov (1881–1964), the leaders of Futurism in Moscow, featured strongly in the exhibitions of 1910–14.

Natalia Goncharova
Peasants Carrying Fruit (1911–12)

Kasimir Malevich
Supremus no. 55 (1916)

The brilliant Cubo-Futurist theories of Matvejs (1877–1914) were championed by Olga Rozanova (1886–1918). This artist, whose notions of color emerged in the form of Futurist-Expressionist paintings between 1911 and 1913, went on to produce striking "trans-rational" compositions (1915) in which the figurative element was used as a metaphor rather than an object. The Cubist work of Pavel Filonov (1883–1941) was inspired by Russian folklore and mystical aspirations, while the Suprematism of Malevich (1879–1935) took its cue from European culture. With its intuitive, abstract construction, Malevich's work moved away from material reality to celebrate "pure sensibility" (Suprematism, or "pure non-objectivity" as he himself defined it). Malevich's approach, inspired by Cubism but refined by him, demonstrates a basic unity; and it was this above all which characterized his first Suprematist constructions.

Kasimir Malevich
The Carpenter (1930–1)

Pavel Filonov
Orient and Occident
(1912–13)

Mikhail Matiushin
Movement in Space
(1919–22)

This passage to the "third dimension" led to a theorization of his thought and an individual approach to spatial reality, to which the artist applied himself in the 1920's. Mikhail Matiushin (1861–1934), a friend of Malevich, was one of the most original artists in the Futurist group. A musician, painter, sculptor and theorist of the plastic arts, he developed an original view of the multi-dimensional space revealed by supra-sensorial experience. According to his theory of "enlarged vision" our perception of the world can go beyond the real to a different level of subjective and intuitive experience. His work as a teacher and publisher established the literary and theoretical validity of the Russian Avant-Garde.

Olga Rozanova
Office (1915)

VLADIMIR TATLIN
Project for the Monument to the Third Internationa (1920)

It is also in St Petersburg that the most famous work of Vladimir Tatlin (1885–1953), the model for his monument to the Third International, was created in 1919–20. This emblematic Constructivist piece, inspired by the Eiffel Tower, was supposed to ally the "logic of materials", which had fascinated Tatlin since 1914, with the Functionalist demands of the dawning technical age. The fame of the monument eclipsed the purely pictorial decline of this artist, who embraced the ideology of "renunciation of painting" in 1920–21. After the brief Formalist (Abstract) period epitomized by the work of Altman and Lebedev (now in the Russian Museum), the Avant-Garde period was supplanted by Socialist Realism, which faithfully reflected the new "restrictive" ideology.

Relief, 1914

● Alexander Pushkin

"An extraordinary phemonemon and a unique expression of the Russian spirit," said Nikolai Gogol ● *122* of Alexander Sergeivich Pushkin (1799–1837). One of Russia's greatest poets, he was born into ancient Russian gentry on his father's side and, on his mother's, was descended from the Ethiopian Ibrahim Hannibal. After a rebellious childhood and the restrictive life of a courtier in St Petersburg, he lived through censorship, exile, close surveillance . . . and complete isolation. Revered as a national genius and a liberator of the Russian language, he is still considered to be a major figure in world literature. At his funeral a distraught elderly man, asked if he was close to the poet, replied "No, but I am a Russian."

A classical education
At an early age Pushkin discovered the major classical writers in the extensive family library. His taste for French writers (Voltaire especially) earned him the nickname of "Frenchman" at the Tsarskoe Selo Lyceum ▲ *267* (1811) where he was a pupil. It was here, at this famous school for the sons of nobility, that Pushkin first began writing poetry at the age of fifteen.

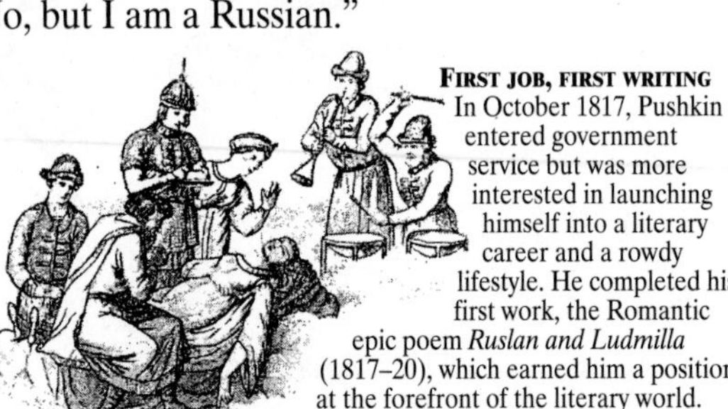

First job, first writing
In October 1817, Pushkin entered government service but was more interested in launching himself into a literary career and a rowdy lifestyle. He completed his first work, the Romantic epic poem *Ruslan and Ludmilla* (1817–20), which earned him a position at the forefront of the literary world.

"Dear friend have faith . . . Russia shall from her age-old sleep arise"
In 1819, Pushkin belonged to a circle known as "The Green Lamp"; the Tsar's discovery of his revolutionary writings led to his exile (1820–4) in the south, followed by a period under close surveillance in Mikhailovskoe. The Decembrists' rising ● *42* changed his life. In a letter to the Tsar, he swore he had had nothing to do with this plot and requested permission to leave Mikhailovskoe. In exchange, Nicolas I offered his protection . . . and his own personal censorship.

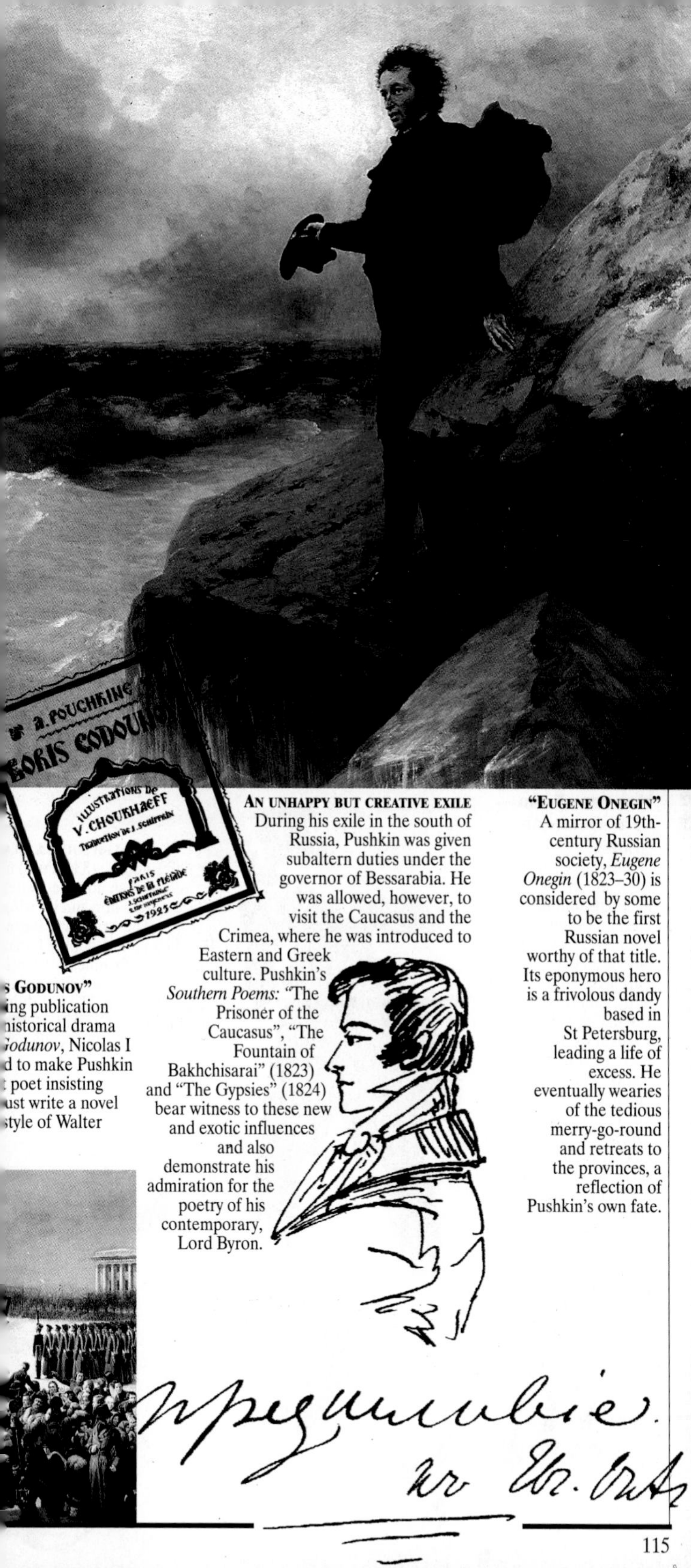

An unhappy but creative exile
During his exile in the south of Russia, Pushkin was given subaltern duties under the governor of Bessarabia. He was allowed, however, to visit the Caucasus and the Crimea, where he was introduced to Eastern and Greek culture. Pushkin's *Southern Poems:* "The Prisoner of the Caucasus", "The Fountain of Bakhchisarai" (1823) and "The Gypsies" (1824) bear witness to these new and exotic influences and also demonstrate his admiration for the poetry of his contemporary, Lord Byron.

"Eugene Onegin"
A mirror of 19th-century Russian society, *Eugene Onegin* (1823–30) is considered by some to be the first Russian novel worthy of that title. Its eponymous hero is a frivolous dandy based in St Petersburg, leading a life of excess. He eventually wearies of the tedious merry-go-round and retreats to the provinces, a reflection of Pushkin's own fate.

s Godunov"
ing publication
historical drama
Godunov, Nicolas I
d to make Pushkin
: poet insisting
ust write a novel
style of Walter

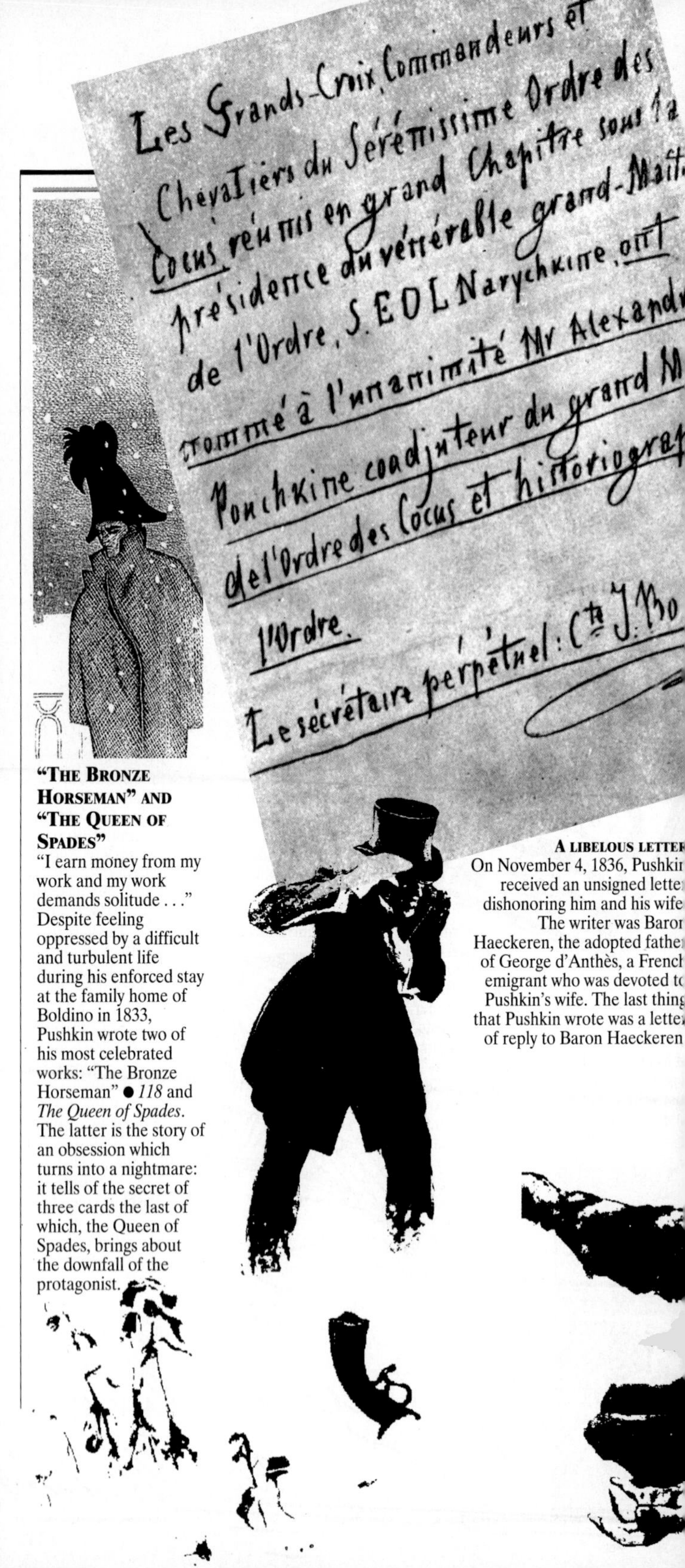

Les Grands-Croix, Commandeurs et
Chevaliers du Sérénissime Ordre des
Cocus réunis en grand Chapitre sous la
présidence du vénérable grand-Maît
de l'Ordre, S. E O L Narychkine, ont
nommé à l'unanimité Mr Alexand
Pouchkine coadjuteur du grand M
de l'Ordre des Cocus et historiograp
l'Ordre.

Le secrétaire perpétuel: Cte J. Bo

“THE BRONZE HORSEMAN” AND “THE QUEEN OF SPADES”

“I earn money from my work and my work demands solitude . . .” Despite feeling oppressed by a difficult and turbulent life during his enforced stay at the family home of Boldino in 1833, Pushkin wrote two of his most celebrated works: “The Bronze Horseman” ● *118* and *The Queen of Spades*. The latter is the story of an obsession which turns into a nightmare: it tells of the secret of three cards the last of which, the Queen of Spades, brings about the downfall of the protagonist.

A LIBELOUS LETTER

On November 4, 1836, Pushkin received an unsigned letter dishonoring him and his wife. The writer was Baron Haeckeren, the adopted father of George d'Anthès, a French emigrant who was devoted to Pushkin's wife. The last thing that Pushkin wrote was a letter of reply to Baron Haeckeren.

СРЕДА. **ТОМ. I. №. 8.** ФЕВРАЛЯ 5-.

ЛИТЕРАТУРНАЯ ГАЗЕТА.

1830 ГОДЪ.

Literary criticism
Pushkin was one of the first Russian writers to make a living almost entirely from writing. Following his return from exile, he became involved with his friend Delvig's *Literary Gazette*. In 1836, he obtained permission to start his own literary review, *Contemporary Life*, a collection of articles and critical studies on contemporary Russian and foreign literature. Only four editions were published during Pushkin's lifetime.

СОВРЕМЕННИКЪ,

ЛИТТЕРАТУРНЫЙ ЖУРНАЛЪ,

ИЗДАВАЕМЫЙ

АЛЕКСАНДРОМЪ ПУШКИНЫМЪ.

“Venus and the Vulcan”
On February 18, 1831, Pushkin and Natalia Goncharova were married in Moscow. The poet was then caught up in a whirl of celebrations (and growing debts). In 1831 at Tsarkoe Selo, Natalia was officially presented to the Empress . . . and was soon after courted by the Emperor.

The duel
On January 26, 1837, George d'Anthès challenged the poet to a duel. On January 27, on the banks of the Moika Canal, Pushkin was mortally wounded and carried back to his home at 12, Moika Quay ● *82*. He died on January 29. Several days later the young Lermontov hurled these vengeful lines: “All of your vile blood can never wash away/The fair blood of the poet!”

MAJESTY

PETER'S CREATION

"The Bronze Horseman" (1833) is an epic poem in which Etienne-Maurice Falconet statue of Peter the Great, erected by Catherine the Great, comes to life and chases clerk through the city during the 1824 flood. In this poem Alexander Pushki (1799–1837) ● 114 *uses the contrast between the menacing equestrian statue and th hero Eugene to symbolize the destructive effect of Peter the Great's imperialist Russi upon the ordinary man.*

"I love you, Peter's creation, I love your stern
Harmonious look, the Neva's majestic flow,
Her granite banks, the iron tracery
Of your railings, the transparent twilight and
The moonless glitter of your pensive nights,
When in my room I write or read without
A lamp, and slumbering masses of deserted
Streets shine clearly, and the Admiralty spire
Is luminous, and, without letting in
The dark of night to golden skies, one dawn
Hastens to relieve another, granting
a mere half-hour to night. I love
The motionless air and frost of your harsh winter,
The sledges coursing along the solid Neva,
Girls' faces brighter than roses, and the sparkle
And noise and sound of voices at the balls,
And, at the hour of the bachelor's feast, the hiss
Of foaming goblets and the pale-blue flame
Of punch. I love the warlike energy
Of Mars' Field, the uniform beauty of the troops
Of infantry and of the horses, tattered
Remnants of those victorious banners in array
Harmoniously swaying, the gleam of those
Bronze helmets, shot through in battle. O martial
Capital, I love the smoke and thunder
Of your fortress, when the empress of the north
Presents a son to the royal house, or when
Russia celebrates another victory
Over the foe, or when the Neva, breaking
Her blue ice, bears it to the seas, exulting,
Scenting spring days."

"THE BRONZE HORSEMAN",
SELECTED POEMS OF ALEXANDER PUSHKIN,
TRANS. D.M. THOMAS, PUB. SECKER & WARBURG, LONDON 1982

ST PETERSBURG MORNING

Vladimir Nabokov (1899–1977) and his family left Russia for Germany in 1919, and he lived thereafter in Berlin, Paris, the US and finally Switzerland. He wrote mainly in Russian until he moved to the US in 1940.

"How utterly foreign to the troubles of the night were those exciting St. Petersburg mornings when the fierce and tender, damp and dazzling arctic spring bundled away broken ice down the sea-bright Neva! It made the roofs shine. It painted the slush in the streets a rich purplish-blue shade which I have never seen anywhere since. On those glorious days *on aller se* ɔromener en équipage – the old-world expression current in our set. I can easily ·efeel the exhilarating change from the thickly padded, knee-length *polushubok*, vith the hot beaver collar, to the short navy-blue coat with its anchor-patterned ɔrass buttons. In the open landau I am joined by the valley of a lap rug to the ɔccupants of the more interesting back seat, majestic Mademoiselle, and riumphant, tear-bedabbled Sergey, with whom I have just had a row at home. I am kicking him slightly, now and then, under our common cover, until Mademoiselle sternly tells me to stop. We drift past the shop windows of Fabergé whose mineral nonstrosities, jeweled troykas poised on marble ostrich eggs, and the like, highly appreciated by the imperial family, were emblems of grotesque garishness to ours. Church bells are ringing, the first Brimstone flies up over the Palace Arch, in another month we shall return to the country; and as I look up I can see, strung on ropes rom housefront to housefront high above the street, great, tensely smooth, semitransparent banners billowing, their three wide bands – pale red, pale blue, and merely pale – deprived by the sun and he flying cloud-shadows of any too blunt connection with a national holiday, but undoubtedly celebrating now, in the city of nemory, the essence of that spring day, the swish of the mud, the beginning of mumps, the ruffled exotic bird with one blood-shot eye on Mademoiselle's hat.❞

❝When museums and movie houses failed us and the night was young, we were reduced o exploring the wilderness of the world's nost gaunt and enigmatic city. Solitary treet lamps were metamorphosed into sea creatures with prismatic spines by the icy noisture on our eyelashes. As we crossed he vast squares, various architectural phantoms arose with silent suddenness ight before us. We felt a cold thrill, generally associated not with height but with depth – with an abyss opening at one's feet – when great, monolithic pillars of polished granite (polished by slaves, repolished by the moon, and rotating smoothly in the

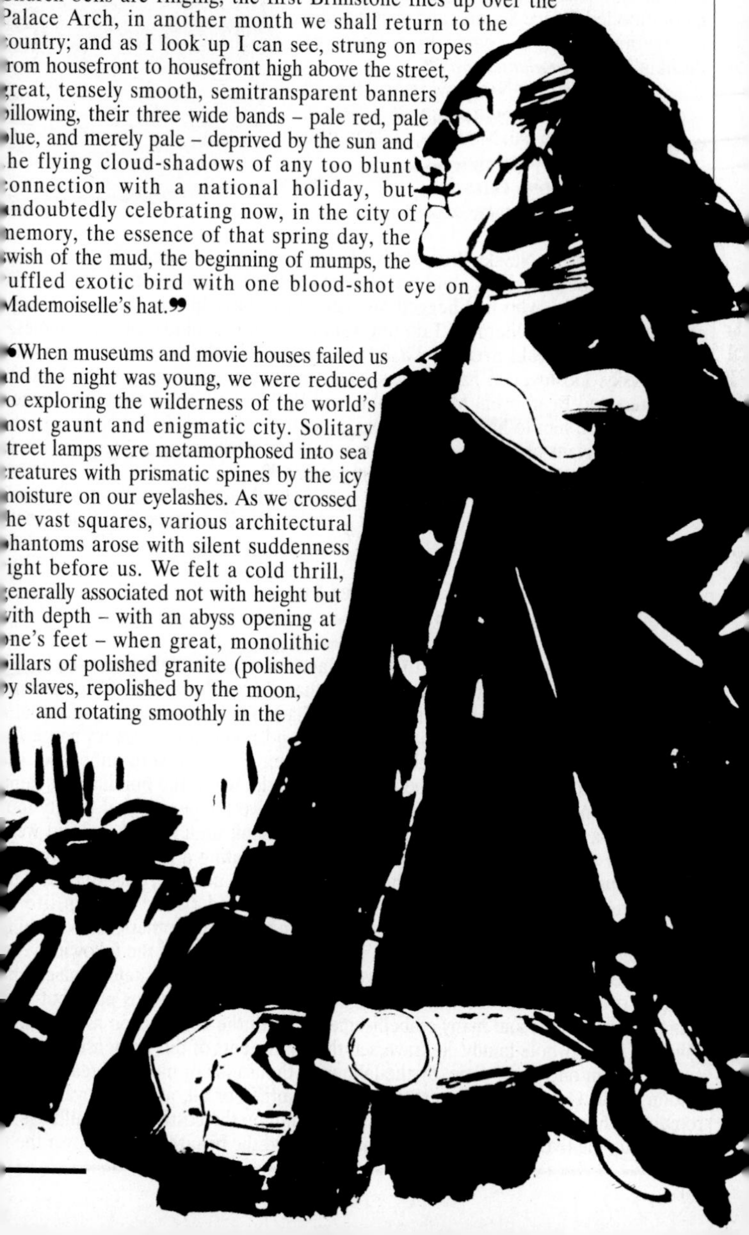

polished vacuum of the night) zoomed above us to support the mysterious rotundities of St. Isaac's cathedral. We stopped on the brink, as it were, of these perilous motifs of stone and metal, and with linked hands, in Lilliputian awe, craned our heads to watch new colossal visions rise in our way – the ten glossy-gray atlantes of a palace portico, or a giant vase of porphyry near the iron gate of a garden, or that enormous column with a black angel on its summit that obsessed, rather than adorned, the moon-flooded Palace Square, and went up and up, trying in vain to reach the subbase of Pushkin's *'Exegi monumentum'*.❞

VLADIMIR NABOKOV, *SPEAK, MEMORY: AN AUTOBIOGRAPHY REVISITED*, WEIDENFELD AND NICOLSON, LONDON 1960

AMONG FRIENDS?

In which Dostoyevsky makes arrangements. . . .

❝At the end of the Nevsky Prospekt is Alexander Nevsky Square . . . with the grea convent and the church . . . and two ancient cemeteries, in one of which, Tikhvin rests Dostoyevski, who had begged his wife not to bury him in the Volkovskoye cemetery among the literati. ('I do not want to lie in the middle of my enemies.' Around Dostoyevski are Glinka, Mussorgsky, Rimsky-Korsakov, Borodin Tchaikovsky. Dostoyevski had never shown a particular inclination toward music he appreciated Beethoven, Mendelssohn, and Rossini and could not bear Wagner Destiny wished him to have as neighbors in death, besides his friend Nekrasov, the greatest musicians of Russia. After our companions in school, in military service, in hospital or prison, these are our final companions.❞

ALDO BURGYS, "CHEKHOV IN SONDRIO" TRANS. ANN GOLDSTEIN, PUB. *NEW YORKER* SEPT. 14, 199

THE WINTER PALACE

After the great fire of 1837, the Winter Palace was rebuilt in a year.

❝Under the Empress Elizabeth the palace had taken eight years to build Kleinmichael completed it in one. True it is that almost the whole of the masonry resisted the fire, but the whole of the interior had to be reconstructed, and what a task that was! The work went on literally day and night; there was no pause for meals; the gangs of workmen relieved each other. Festivals were unheeded; the seasons themselves were overcome. To accelerate the work, the building was kept the winter through, artificially heated to the excessive temperature of twenty-four to twenty-six degrees Réaumur. Many workmen sank under the heat, and were carried out dead or dying; a painter, who was decorating a ceiling, fell from his ladder struck with apoplexy. Neither money, health, nor life, was spared. The Emperor, who, at the time of the conflagration, had risked his own life by penetrating into the innermost apartments to save the lives of others, knew nothing of the means employed to carry out his will. In the December of the following year and in proud consciousness of his power, he entered the resuscitated palace and rejoiced over his work. The whole was constructed on the previous plan, but with some improvements and many embellishments. With the Empress on his arm, and followed by his whole family, he traversed the apartments of this immense building completed, in one year's time, by the labour of thousands of men. He reached the saloon of St. George, the largest and most beautiful of all, and the royal family remained there longer than anywhere else, examining the costly gold mouldings of the ceiling, the five colossal bronze chandeliers, and the beautiful relievo over the

hrone, which represents St. George slaying the dragon. The Empress was tired, nd would have sat down; – the patron spirit of Russia prevented her: as yet there 'as no furniture in the hall so she leaned on the Emperor's arm and walked into he next room, followed by the entire retinue. The last of these had scarcely passed hrough the door when a thundering crash resounded through the palace, which rembled to its very foundations, and the air was darkened by clouds of dust. The mbers of the ceiling of the saloon of St. George had yielded to the weight of the handeliers; and the whole had fallen in, crushing everything beneath its enormous nass. The saloon, a moment before so brilliant, was a heap of ruins. The splendid alace was again partly destroyed, but the genius of Russia had watched over her lestiny – the imperial family were saved.”

EDWARD JERRMANN, *PICTURES OF ST PETERSBURG*,
TRANS. BY FREDERICK HARDMANN, LONDON 1852

COLORS

'he poet and novelist Andrey Biely (1880–1935) describes a walk along the loika Canal.

“Below, to one side of them, the Moika Canal appeared blue; on the other side tood the familiar three-story colonnaded building with the same familiar series of nodeled ornaments: ring after ring, and inside each ring a coat of arms – a Roman elmet between two crossed swords.

Before them, where the canal took a turn to the left of a stone projection, loomed he dazzling dome of St. Isaac's Cathedral against a background of exquisite urquoise.

'hey had reached the Embankment: the deep waters of the Neva looked green-lue. Far, far away, appearing ever so remote, the islands looked incredibly flat and ow; and their buildings seemed so flat too that the deep green-blue waters hreatened suddenly to wash over and submerge them. A pitiless sunset hovered bove this green blue surface, scattering its gleams here and there: the Troitsky 3ridge and the Winter Palace glowed purple.

uddenly, a clearly defined silhouette appeared above these green-blue waters and gainst the background of the red sky; the flaps of a coat cape beat in the breeze ke a pair of wings; carelessly, a waxen face with protruding lips came into view; he eyes seemed to search for something in the blue expanse of the Neva and, nable to find what they sought, took refuge under the visor of a modest cap; the yes saw neither Sofya Petrovna nor Varvara Evgrafovna: they saw only the green-lue depths; they rose and fell – beyond the Neva, where the buildings glowed urple on the sunken banks of the island. A bulldog, carrying in his mouth a whip with a silver handle, ran snorting ahead of the silhouette. As he passed them, the young man barely blinked his eyes, touched the band of his cap with his fingers, and walked on without a word. The buildings glowed purple.❞

ANDREY BIELY, *ST PETERSBURG*, TRANS. BY JOHN COURNOS,
PUB. GROVE PRESS INC., NEW YORK, 1959

PETERSBURG SOCIETY

WORKING PEOPLE

Dramatist and prose writer Nikolai Gogol (1809–52) was born in the Ukraine but moved to St Petersburg in 1828. He wrote a series of short stories set in the city in the mid 1830's, which are satirical and exaggerated in tone yet brilliantly descriptive.

❝Let us begin with earliest morning when all Petersburg smells of hot, freshly-baked bread and is filled with old women in ragged gowns and pelisses who are making their raids on the churches and on compassionate passers-by. Then the Nevsky Prospect is empty: the stout shopkeepers and their assistants are still asleep in their linen shirts or washing their genteel cheeks and drinking their coffee; beggars gather near the doors of the confectioners' shops where the drowsy Ganymede who the day before flew round like a fly with chocolate, crawls out with no cravat on, broom in hand, and thrusts stale pies and scraps upon them. Working people move to and fro about the streets: sometimes peasants cross it, hurrying to their work, in high boots caked with mortar which even the Ekaterinsky canal, famous for its cleanness, could not wash off. At this hour it is not proper for ladies to walk out, because Russian people like to explain their meaning in rude expressions such as they would not hear even in a theatre. Sometimes a drowsy government clerk trudges along with a portfolio under his arm, if the way to his department lies through the Nevsky Prospect. It may be confidently stated that at this period, that is, up to twelve o'clock, the Nevsky Prospect is for no man the goal, but simply the means of reaching it: it is filled with people who have their occupations their anxieties, and their annoyances, and are thinking nothing about it. Peasant talk about ten kopecks or seven coppers, old men and women wave their hands o talk to themselves, sometimes with very striking gesticulations, but no one listens t them or laughs at them with the exception perhaps of street boys in homespu smocks, darting like lightning along the Nevsky Prospect with empty bottles o pairs of boots from the cobblers in their arms. At that hour you may put on wha you like, and even if you wear a cap instead of a hat, or the ends of your collar stic out too far from your cravat, no one notices it.❞

NIKOLAI GOGOL, "THE NEVSKY PROSPECT"
FROM *THE OVERCOAT & OTHER STORIES*
TRANS. BY CONSTANCE GARNET
PUB. CHATTO & WINDUS, LONDON, 192

EXODUS

Born in Moscow, Fyodor Dostoevsky (1821–81) first moved to St Petersburg in 1838 t study at the St Petersburg Engineering Academy. During the 20th century, Dostoevsk has become the most widely read and influential of Russian writers in Britain and th US. He was a powerful thinker, influenced by Socialism and liberal ideas in the firs half of his life, and then by the Russian Orthodox Church. In this extract from his shor story "White Nights", written in 1848, is Dostoevsky's description of what he considere to be an alarming trend in St Petersburg society.

“It was only this morning that at last I discovered the real ause of my unhappiness. Oh, so they are all running away from me to the country, re they? I'm afraid I must apologise for the use of this rather homely word, but 'm not in the mood now for the more exquisite refinements of style, for everybody n Petersburg has either left or is about to leave for the country; for every worthy entleman of a solidly-prosperous and dignified position who hails a cab in the treet is at once transformed in my mind into a worthy parent of a family who, after is usual office duties, immediately leaves town and, unencumbered by luggage, astens to the bosom of his family – to the country; for every passer-by now wears uite a different look, a look which almost seems to say to every person he meets, As a matter of fact, sir, I'm here by sheer chance, just passing through, you nderstand, and in a few hours I shall be on the way to the country.' If a window is hrown open and a most ravishing young girl, who a moment ago had been rumming on it with her lovely white fingers, pokes out her pretty head and calls to he man selling pots of plants in the street, I immediately jump to the conclusion hat the flowers are bought not for the purpose of enjoying the spring and the lowers in a stuffy old flat in town, for very soon everybody will anyway be leaving or the country and will take even the flowers with them. Why, I've got so far in my ew discovery (quite a unique discovery, you must admit) that I can tell at once, ust by looking at a man, in what sort of a cottage he lives in the country. The esidents of the Stone and Apothecary Islands can be recognised by their studied xquisiteness of manners, their smart summer clothes, and their wonderful arriages in which they come to town. The inhabitants of Pargolov and places eyond 'inspire' your confidence at the first glance by their solidly prosperous osition and their general air of sobriety and common sense; while the householder f Krestovsky Island is distinguished by his imperturbably cheerful look. Whether I appen to come across a long procession of carters, each walking leisurely, reins in and, beside his cart, laden with whole mountains of furniture of every description - tables, chairs, Turkish and non-Turkish divans, and other household chattels – nd, moreover, often presided over by a frail-looking cook who, perched on the

very top of the cart, guards the property of her master as though it were the apple of her eye; or whether I look at the barges, heavily laden with all sorts of domestic unk, sailing on the Neva or the Fontanka, as far as the Black River or the Islands – oth carts and barges multiply tenfold, nay, a hundredfold in my eyes. It really eems as though everything had arisen and set off on a journey, as though everything were moving off in caravan after caravan into the country; it seems as hough the whole of Petersburg were about to turn into a desert, and it is hardly urprising that in the end I am overwhelmed with shame, humiliation, and adness.”

DOSTOEVSKY, "WHITE NIGHTS",
FROM *THE BEST SHORT STORIES OF DOSTOEVSKY*,
TRANS. BY DAVID MAGARSHACK,
PUB. THE MODERN LIBRARY, NEW YORK, 1955

Entrance to a Ball

It took Count Lev Nikolaevich Tolstoy (1828–1910) almost seven years to write "War and Peace", an epic novel following the fortunes of three aristo cratic families through the Napoleonic invasion.

❝Natasha had not had a moment free since early morning and had not once ha time to think of what lay before her.

In the damp chill air and crowded closeness of the swaying carriage, she for th first time vividly imagined what was in store for her there at the ball, in thos brightly lighted rooms – with music, flowers, dances, the Emperor, and all th brilliant young people of Petersburg. The prospect was so splendid that she hardl believed it would come true, so out of keeping was it with the chill darkness an closeness of the carriage. She understood all that awaited her only when, afte stepping over the red baize at the entrance, she entered the hall, took off her fu cloak and, beside Sonya and in front of her mother, mounted the brightl illuminated stairs between the flowers. Only then did she remember how she mus behave at a ball, and tried to assume the majestic air she considered indispensabl for a girl on such an occasion. But, fortunately for her, she felt her eyes growin misty, she saw nothing clearly, her pulse beat a hundred to the minute and th blood throbbed at her heart. She could not assume that pose, which would hav made her ridiculous, and she moved on almost fainting from excitement and tryin with all her might to conceal it. And this was the very attitude that became her best Before and behind them other visitors were entering, also talking in low tones an wearing ball-dresses. The mirrors on the landing reflected ladies in white, pale blue, and pink dresses, with diamonds and pearls on their bare necks and arms.

Natasha looked in the mirrors and could not distinguish her reflection from th others. All was blent into one brilliant procession. On entering the ball-room th regular hum of voices, footsteps, and greetings deafened Natasha, and the light an glitter dazzled her still more. The host and hostess, who had already been standin at the door for half an hour repeating the same words to the various arrivals *'Charmé de vous voir,'* greeted the Rostovs and Peronskaya in the same manner.

The two girls in their white dresses, each with a rose in her black hair, both curtsie in the same way, but the hostess's eye involuntarily rested longer on the slin Natasha. She looked at her and gave her alone a special smile, in addition to he usual smile as hostess. Looking at her she may have recalled the golden irrevocable days of her own girlhood and her own first ball. The host also followe Natasha with his eyes and asked the count which was his daughter.

'Charming!' said he, kissing the tips of his fingers.

In the ball-room guests stood crowding at the entrance doors awaiting th Emperor. The countess took up a position in one of the front rows of that crowd Natasha heard and felt that several people were asking about her and looking a her. She realized that those noticing her liked her, and this observation helped t calm her.

'There are some like ourselves and some worse,' she thought.❞

Leo Tolstoy, *War and Peace*,
trans. by Louise and Aylmer Maude,
pub. Everyman's Library, London,
and Alfred A. Knopf, New York, 1992

Backstabbing

Anton Chekhov (1860–1904) deplored theatrical society in St Petersburg. The premiere of "The Sea Gull" at the State Theatre in 1896 was disastrous yet it was later a great success when staged at the Moscow Arts Theatre, and he took all his subsequent plays to the latter:

❝I am tired out, like a ballerina after five acts and eight tableaux. Banquets, letters which one is too lazy to answer, conversations and all sorts of bosh. Right now I've got to take a cab to Vasilievsky Island, to dine there, yet I am bored and I have to work. I will stay here for three days more and see: if this ballet continues I'll either go home or to Ivan in Sudoroga.

I am enveloped by a dense atmosphere of ill will, extremely vague, and to me inexplicable. They are tendering me dinners and chanting banal dithyrambs to me and at the same time are all set to devour me. Why? The devil knows. If I had shot myself I would have afforded great pleasure to nine-tenths of my friends and admirers. And in what petty ways people express their pettiness! Burenin berates me in a *feuilleton*, even though it is not customary for newpapers to berate their own contributors; Maslov (Bezhetsky) no longer goes to dine with the Suvorins; Shcheglov tells all the gossip current about me, and so on. All this is dreadfully foolish and boring. They're not people, but some sort of mold.❞

LETTER TO M.P. CHEKHOVA, ST PETERSBURG, JANUARY 14, 1891,
IN *LETTERS OF ANTON CHEKHOV*, TRANS. BERNARD GUILBERT GUERNEY,
PUB. VIKING PRESS, NEW YORK, 1968

❝There is in Petersburg a species of men whose speciality it is to jeer at every aspect of life; they cannot even pass by a starving man or a suicide without saying something vulgar. But Orlov and his friends did not jeer or make jokes, they talked ironically. They used to say that there was no God, and personality was completely lost at death; the immortals only existed in the French Academy. Real good did not and could not possibly exist, as its existence was conditional upon human perfection, which was a logical absurdity. Russia was a country as poor and dull as Persia. The intellectual class was hopeless; in Pekarsky's opinion the overwhelming majority in it were incompetent persons, good for nothing. The people were drunken, lazy, thievish, and degenerate. We had no science, our literature was uncouth, our commerce rested on swindling – 'No selling without cheating.' And everything was in that style, and everything was a subject for laughter.❞

ANTON CHEKHOV, "AN ANONYMOUS STORY",
FROM *THE LADY WITH THE DOG*, TRANS. CONSTANCE GARNETT,
PUB. CHATTO & WINDUS, LONDON, 1919

LERMONTOV

The writings of Ivan Turgenev (1818–83) were the first by a major Russian author to find success in Europe. Here he describes a meeting with the Romantic poet and novelist Mikhail Lermontov (1814–41), just over a year before the latter was killed in a duel.

❝Lermontov, too, I saw only twice: at the house of Princess Sh[akhovskoy], a Petersburg high society woman, and a few days later at a New Year's fancy dress ball at the Noblemen's Club on the eve of 1840. At Princess Sh[akhovskoy]'s I, a very rare and unaccustomed visitor at high society parties, saw him only from a distance, observing the poet, who had become famous in so short a time, from a corner where I had secreted myself. Lermontov sat down on a low stool in front of a sofa on which, wearing a black gown, was sitting one of the society beauties of those days, the fair-haired Countess [Emilia] Mussin-Pushkin, who died young and who really was a strikingly beautiful girl. Lermontov wore the uniform of the Life Guards Hussar Regiment. He had removed neither his sword nor his gloves and, frowning and hunching his shoulders, gazed sullenly at the Countess. She only exchanged a few words with him, talking mostly to Count Sh[akhovskoy], also a Hussar officer, who was sitting beside him. There was something ominous and tragic in Lermontov's appearance: his swarthy face and large, motionless dark eyes exuded a sort of sombre and evil strength, a sort of pensive scornfulness and passion. His hard gaze was strangely out of keeping with the expression of his almost childishly tender, protruding lips. His whole figure, thick-set, bow-legged, with a large head on broad, stooping shoulders, aroused an unpleasant feeling; but everyone had at once to acknowledge its immense inherent strength. It is, of course, a well-known fact that he had to some extent portrayed himself in Pechorin. The words: 'His eyes did not laugh when he laughed,' from *A Hero of Our Time*, etc., could really have been applied to himself. I remember that Count Sh[akhovskoy] and the young Countess suddenly burst out laughing at something and went on laughing for some time; Lermontov, too, laughed, but at the same time he kept looking at them with a sort of offensive astonishment. For all that I could not help feeling that he was fond of Count Sh[akhovskoy] as a fellow-officer and that he was also well-disposed towards the Countess. There could be no doubt that, following the fashion of those days, he was trying to assume a Byronic air together with a number of other even worse eccentricities and whimsicalities. And he paid dearly for them! At heart Lermontov was probably terribly bored; he felt stifled in the airless atmosphere where fate had forced him to live.❞

Ivan Turgenev, *Literary Reminiscences and Autobiographical Fragments*,
trans. by David Magarshack, pub. Faber & Faber, London, 1959

Fashion

Russian revolutionary Alexander Herzen (1812–70) combined his personal life and his opinions with political views in his autobiography published in 1885.

❝The Petersburghers laugh at the costumes seen in Moscow; they are outraged by the caps and Hungarian jackets, the long hair and civilian moustaches. Moscow certainly is a non-military city, rather careless and unaccustomed to discipline, but whether that is a good quality or a defect is a matter of opinion. The harmony of uniformity, the absence of variety, of what is personal and whimsical, a traditional obligatory dress and external discipline are all found on the largest scale in the most inhuman condition in which men live – in barracks. The uniform and a complete absence of variety are passionately loved by despotism. Nowhere are fashions followed so respectfully as in Petersburg, and that shows the immaturity of our culture; our clothes are alien. In Europe people dress, but we dress up, and so are terrified if a sleeve is too full, or a collar too narrow. In Paris all that people are afraid of is being dressed without taste; in London all that they are afraid of is catching cold; in Italy every one dresses as he likes best. If one were to show an Englishman the battalions of fops on the Nevsky Prospect, all wearing exactly similar, tightly buttoned coats, he would take them for a squad of 'policemen'.❞

Alexander Herzen, *My Past and Thoughts*,
trans. by Constance Garnett,
pub. Chatto & Windus, London, 192-

Festivities

English tutor William Coxe (1747–1828) witnessed an enormous and ultimately rather dangerous party in St Petersburg.

❝On the 6th of December we were witness to a very singular entertainment given to the public by a Russian, who had acquired a large fortune by farming, during four years only, the right of vending spirituous liquors. On surrendering his contract, he gave, as proof of his gratitude to the lower class of people, by whom he had enriched himself, a feast near the garden of the summer-palace . . . announced by hand-bills distributed throughout the city . . . which commenced at two o'clock in the afternoon. A large semicircular table was covered with all kinds of provision, piled in different shapes, and in the greatest profusion. Large slices of bread and caviare, dried sturgeon, carp, and other fish, were ranged to a great height, in the form of pent-houses and pyramids, and garnished with craw-fish, onions, and pickles. In different parts of the grounds were rows of casks full of spirituous liquors, and still larger vessels of wine, beer, and quass. Among the decorations, I observed the representation of an immense whale in pasteboard, covered with cloth and gold or silver brocade, and filled in the inside with bread, dried fish, and other provisions.

All sorts of games and diversions were exhibited for the amusement of the populace. At the extremity of the grounds was a large square of ice well swept for the scaters; near which were two machines like the swinging vehicles at Bartholomew Fair. One of these machines consisted of two cross-beams fixed horizontally to a pole in the center by means of a pivot; from the ends of the beams hung four sledges, in which people seated themselves, and were turned round with great velocity; the other had four wooden horses suspended from the beams, and the riders were whirled round in like manner. . . . Beyond these were two ice-hills. . . . Two poles, above twenty feet in height, were also erected, with colours flying; and at the top of each was placed a piece of money, as a prize for those who could swarm up and seize it. The poles, being rubbed with oil, soon froze in this severe climate; many and tedious were the attempts of the various competitors in this slippery ascent to fame. The scene was lively and gay; for about 40,000 persons of both sexes were assembled on the occasion. . . .

It was preconcerted, that, on firing a rocket, the people were to drink a glass of spirituous liquor, and, on the discharge of a second, to begin the repast. But the impatience of the populace anticipated the necessity of a second signal; and the whole multitude was soon and at once in motion. The whale was the chief object of contention; within the space of a few minutes he was entirely divested of his gaudy trappings, which became the spoils of his successful invaders. . . . They rend him into a thousand pieces, to seize the provision with which his inside was stored. The remaining people . . . were employed in uncovering the pent-houses, and pulling down the pyramids. . . . Others crowded around the casks and hogsheads; and with great wooden ladles lapped incessantly wine, beer, and spirits. The confusion and riot, which soon succeeded, is better conceived than described; and we thought it expedient to retire. . . .

But the consequences of this feast were indeed dreadful. The cold had suddenly increased with such violence, that Fahrenheit's thermometer, which at mid-day

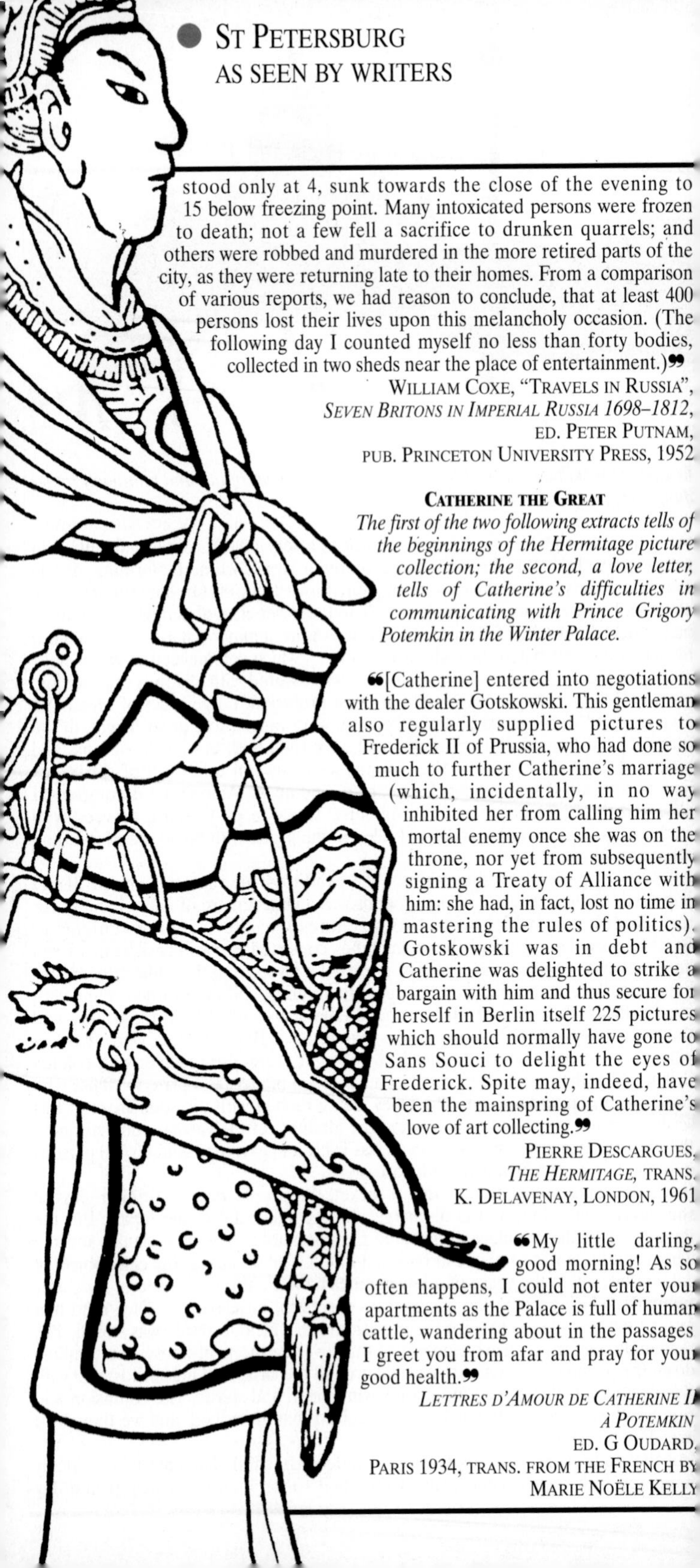

stood only at 4, sunk towards the close of the evening to 15 below freezing point. Many intoxicated persons were frozen to death; not a few fell a sacrifice to drunken quarrels; and others were robbed and murdered in the more retired parts of the city, as they were returning late to their homes. From a comparison of various reports, we had reason to conclude, that at least 400 persons lost their lives upon this melancholy occasion. (The following day I counted myself no less than forty bodies, collected in two sheds near the place of entertainment.)”

WILLIAM COXE, "TRAVELS IN RUSSIA", *SEVEN BRITONS IN IMPERIAL RUSSIA 1698–1812*, ED. PETER PUTNAM, PUB. PRINCETON UNIVERSITY PRESS, 1952

CATHERINE THE GREAT

The first of the two following extracts tells of the beginnings of the Hermitage picture collection; the second, a love letter, tells of Catherine's difficulties in communicating with Prince Grigory Potemkin in the Winter Palace.

“[Catherine] entered into negotiations with the dealer Gotskowski. This gentleman also regularly supplied pictures to Frederick II of Prussia, who had done so much to further Catherine's marriage (which, incidentally, in no way inhibited her from calling him her mortal enemy once she was on the throne, nor yet from subsequently signing a Treaty of Alliance with him: she had, in fact, lost no time in mastering the rules of politics). Gotskowski was in debt and Catherine was delighted to strike a bargain with him and thus secure for herself in Berlin itself 225 pictures which should normally have gone to Sans Souci to delight the eyes of Frederick. Spite may, indeed, have been the mainspring of Catherine's love of art collecting.”

PIERRE DESCARGUES, *THE HERMITAGE*, TRANS. K. DELAVENAY, LONDON, 1961

“My little darling, good morning! As so often happens, I could not enter your apartments as the Palace is full of human cattle, wandering about in the passages. I greet you from afar and pray for your good health.”

LETTRES D'AMOUR DE CATHERINE II À POTEMKIN ED. G OUDARD, PARIS 1934, TRANS. FROM THE FRENCH BY MARIE NOËLE KELLY

A COMIC WEDDING

ı 1740 Empress Anne, displaying an extraordinary sense of humour, organized Prince ·alitzine's bizarre wedding to Avdotaya Ivanovna.

"The winter of 1739–40 was unusually cold, and the scientists of the Academy mbarked on a programme of experiments to test the properties of ice that was vailable in such abundance. Knowing this, a court Chamberlain called Alexander atishchev thought of combining it with a new entertainment for the court – uilding a palace of ice on which artists and artisans as well as scientists could xercise their skills. In the end it turned out to be a setting for another of the mpress's macabre jokes for which poor Golitsyn was again the butt. . . . One iorning a huge and astonishing procession formed up in the streets. Goats, pigs, ows, camels, dogs and reindeer were seen harnessed to various vehicles each of hich contained a representative pair from each of the 'Barbarous Races' in the mpire. There were Lapps and Kirghiz, Tunguses and Tatars, Bashkirs and Finns – ach couple in 'national dress'. But the centrepiece was an elephant with an iron age on its back. The cage contained Golitsyn and his unlovely bride. To the ccompaniment of cymbals, bells and the occasional roaring of an angry beast, the rocession passed the Palace and eventually arrived at Ernest Biron's covered iding school, where a banquet had been prepared for the captive bridal pair and ıeir guests. By the Empress's express command each couple was served with its wn traditional dishes – including such culinary delights as reindeer meat, horse-esh and fermented mare's milk. There was entertainment too. A poet named

redyakovski declaimed an ode composed specially for the occasion entitled: Greetings to the Bridal Pair of Fools', and each pair of guests was made to dance s own 'national dance' for the amusement of onlookers. Then the procession ormed up again to accompany the bride and groom to their home for the night – he palace made of ice. No other material had been used in its construction – walls nd steps, baroque bald columns, even the decorative figurines and window-panes vere made of ice. So was the furniture – a huge four-poster bridal bed, chairs, ables, chandleliers, a clock, a commode, a set of playing cards, with the markings oloured in, and a statue of a Cupid. Outside there were other marvels of ngineering and the sculptor's art – flowers and trees complete with perching birds, ce cannon which fired real charges, a pair of dolphins which breathed out flames f fire (thanks to a device inside which pumped out naptha), and a life-sized model f an elephant equipped with a machine to squirt out water to a height of two undred and fifty feet. Everything had been done to excite the eye and astonish the magination – and all at a cost of only thirty thousand roubles.The Empress ccompanied the bridal pair inside, saw them undressed and laid upon their bed of ce. Then she withdrew. From her bedroom she had an excellent view of the Ice 'alace, and next morning she saw Golitsyn and his wife emerge apparently none he worse for their experience. The stove installed inside their chilly bedroom, as he scientists of the Academy took careful note, had proved effective."

PHILIP LONGWORTH, *THE THREE EMPRESSES*, LONDON, 1972

HISTORY

ASSASSINATIONS

"Under Western Eyes" by Joseph Conrad (1857–1924) describes the fate of a studen who is caught up in the Russian Revolution.

“Mr. de P– was being driven towards the railway station in a two-horse uncovere sleigh with footman and coachman on the box. Snow had been falling all nigh making the roadway, uncleared as yet at this early hour, very heavy for the horse It was still falling thickly. But the sleigh must have been observed and marke down. As it drew over to the left before taking a turn, the footman noticed peasant walking slowly on the edge of the pavement with his hands in the pocke of his sheepskin coat and his shoulders hunched up to his ears under the fallin snow. On being overtaken this peasant suddenly faced about and swung his arm. I an instant there was a terrible shock, a detonation muffled in the multitude c snowflakes; both horses lay dead and mangled on the ground and the coachma with a shrill cry, had fallen off the box mortally wounded. The footman (wh survived) had no time to see the face of the man in the sheepskin coat. Afte throwing the bomb this last got away, but it is supposed that, seeing a lot of peopl surging up on all sides of him in the falling snow, and all running towards the scen of the explosion, he thought it safer to turn back with them. In an incredibly sho time an excited crowd assembled round the sledge. The Minister-President, gettin out unhurt into the deep snow, stood near the groaning coachman and addresse the people repeatedly in his weak, colourless voice. ‘I beg of you to keep off. Fc the love of God, I beg of you good people to keep off.’ It was then that a tall youn man who had remained standing perfectly still within a carriage gateway, tw houses lower down, stepped out into the street and walking up rapidly flun another bomb over the heads of the crowd. It actually struck the Minister-Presider on the shoulder as he stooped over his dying servant, then falling between his fee exploded with a terrific concentrated violence, striking him dead to the grounc finishing the wounded man and practically annihilating the empty sledge in th twinkling of an eye. With a yell of horror the crowd broke up and fled in a directions, except for those who fell dead or dying where they stood nearest to th Minister-President, and one or two others who did not fall till they had run a littl way. The first explosion had brought together a crowd as if by enchantment, th second made as swiftly a solitude in the street for hundreds of yards in eac direction. Through the falling snow people looked from afar at the small heap of dead bodies lying upon each other near the carcases of the two horses. Nobody dared to approach till some Cossacks of a street-patrol galloped up and, dismounting, began to turn over the dead. Amongst the innocent victims of the second explosion laid out on the pavement there was a body dressed in peasant’s sheepskin coat; but the face was unrecognizable, there was absolutely othing found in the pockets of its poor clothing, and it /as the only one whose identity was never stablished.❞

JOSEPH CONRAD, *UNDER WESTERN EYES*, EVERYMAN'S LIBRARY, LONDON, AND ALFRED A. KNOPF, NEW YORK, 1992

REVOLUTION

:nglish writer William Gerhardie 1895–1977 was born in St Petersburg and later served in the British Embassy there.

❝One morning, as I was about to cross the Troitski Bridge to meet the Admiral, I /as stopped by the police and was compelled to go home and change into uniform. Vhen I returned the revolution had already broken out. The Admiral had just /itnessed the sacking of the Arsenal by a disorderly crowd. Regiment after egiment was going over to the revolution. Solitary shots, and now and then nachine-gun fire, were heared from varius quarters of the city. The Admiral and I tood at the window and watched. Lorry after lorry packed with armed soldiery and /orkmen, some lying in a 'ready' attidtude along the mudguards, went past us in a .ind of wild and dazzling joy ride, waving red flags and revolutionary banners to houts of 'Hurrah!' from the crowds in the street. The Admiral stood with his hands olded on the window-sill, unable to withhold his enthusiasm. It was a clear, bright lay, I think and very cold.

'hat evening following the outbreak of the revolution was vividly impressed upon ny memory. During the day I had listened to innumerable speeches, some of a .iberal loftiness; others of a menacingly proletarian character, threatening death to apital and revolution to the world at large. There was a tendency to flamboyant :xtravagance and exaggeration. 'Down with Armies and Navies!' shouted one peaker hysterically. 'Down with militarism! Through red terror to peace, freedom .nd brotherhood!' Therewere placards and banners and processions. 'Land and .iberty!' was a popular watchword. Red was the dominant colour, and the opening ars of the Marseillaise were a kind of recurring *Leitmotiv* in the tumult. Crossing a ridge I passed a company of soldiers newly revolted. They marched alert and oyous to the sound of some old familiar marching song till they came to the words for the Czar.' Having sung these words they stopped somewhat abruptly and erplexed. '*How* for the Czar?' one of them asked. '*How* for the Czar?' they epeated, looking at each other sheepishly. Then they marched on without singing. 'here were peasants who did not know the 'revolution' and thought it was a /oman who would supersede the Czar. Others wanted a republic with a czar. And here were others still who interpreted the word republic as 'rezshpublicoo,' thinking that it meant 'cut up the public'.

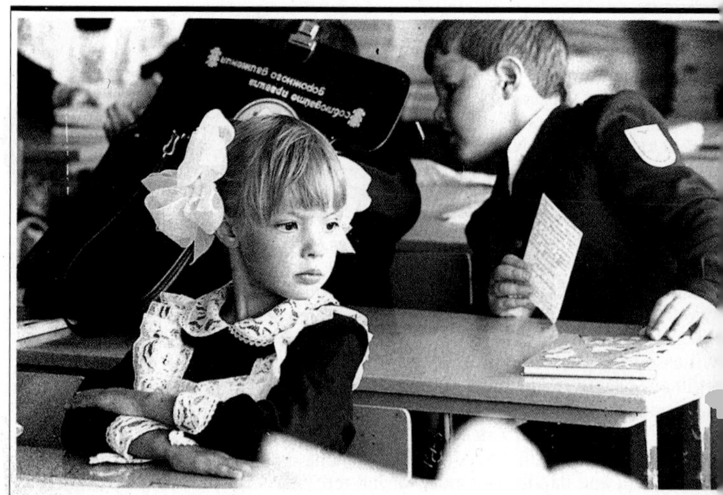

In the Troitski Square I was stopped by a young enthusiastic Russian officer, wh attracted by my British uniform, spoke to me in English, his eyes glittering wit excitement. 'Sir,' he said, 'you now will have more vigorous Allies.' And then in th Nevski I passed a procession of Anarchists who are regarded by the Bolsheviks wit about the same degree of unmitigated horror as the Bolsheviks are regarded by th *Morning Post*. They marched with a gruesome look about their faces, bearing the horrible colours of black, crested with a human skull and cross-bones.❞

WILLIAM GERHARDIE, *FUTILIT*
PUB. DUCKWORTH, LONDON, 192

AN ARISTOCRATIC REVOLUTIONARY

Prince Peter Kropotkin (1842–1921) was born into the Russian aristocracy but hi political beliefs were left-wing extremist. He left the army in 1872 to work for th International Working Man's Association. Arrested and imprisoned in 1874, h escaped to England in 1876, and spent the next forty years in exile, not returning t Russia until the 1917 Revolution.

❝One day I received a quite unexpected visit. The Grand Duke Nicholas, brothe of Alexander II, who was inspecting the fortress, entered my cell, followed only b his aide-de-camp. The door was shut behind him. He rapidly approached me saying 'Good-day, Kropótkin.' He knew me personally, and spoke in a familiar good-natured tone, as to an old acquaintance. 'How is it possible, Kropótkin, tha you, a page de chambre, a sergeant of the corps of pages, should be mixed up i this business, and now be here in this horrible casemate?'
'Every one has his own opinions,' was my reply.
'Opinions! So your opinions were that you must stir up a revolution?'
What was I to reply? Yes? Then the construction which would be put upon m answer would be that I, who had refused to give any answers to the gendarmes 'avowed everything' before the brother of the Tsar. His tone was that of commander of a military school when trying to obtain 'avowals' from a cadet. Yet could not say No: it would have been a lie. I did not know what to say, and stoo without saying anything.
'You see! You feel ashamed of it now' –
This remark angered me, and I at once said in a rather sharp way, 'I have given m replies to the examining magistrate, and have nothing to add.'
'But understand, Kropótkin, please,' he said then, in the most familiar tone, 'that don't speak to you as an examining magistrate. I speak quite as a private person, quite as a private man,' he repeated, lowering his voice.
Thoughts went whirling in my head. To play the part of Marquis Posa? To tell th

Emperor through the grand duke of the desolation of Russia, the ruin of the peasantry, the arbitrariness of the officials, the terrible famines in prospect? To say that we wanted to help the peasants out of their desperate condition, to make them raise their heads, and by all this try to influence Alexander II? These thoughts followed one another in rapid succession, till at last I said to myself: 'Never! Nonsense! They know all that. They are enemies of the nation, and such talk would not change them.'

I replied that he always remained an official person, and that I could not look upon him as a private man.

He then began to ask me indifferent questions. 'Was it not in Siberia, with the Decembrists, that you began to entertain such ideas?'

'No; I knew only one Decembrist, and with him I had no talks worth speaking of.'

'Was it then at St. Petersburg that you got them?'

'I was always the same.'

'Why! Were you such in the corps of pages?' he asked me with terror.

'In the corps I was a boy, and what is indefinite in boyhood grows definite in manhood.'

He asked me some other similar questions, and as he spoke I distinctly saw what he was driving at. He was trying to obtain avowals, and my imagination vividly pictured him saying to his brother: 'All these examining magistrates are imbeciles. He gave them no replies, but I talked to him ten minutes, and he told me everything.' That began to annoy me; and when he said to me something to this effect, 'How could you have anything to do with all these people – peasants and people with no names?' – I sharply turned upon him and said, 'I have told you already that I have given my replies to the examining magistrate.' Then he abruptly left the cell.

Later, the soldiers of the guard made quite a legend of that visit. The person who came in a carriage to carry me away at the time of my escape wore a military cap, and, having sandy whiskers, bore a faint resemblance to the Grand Duke Nicholas. So a tradition grew up amongst the soldiers of the St. Petersburg garrison that it was the grand duke himself who came to rescue me and kidnapped me. Thus are legends created even in times of newspapers and biographical dictionaries.❞

PETER KROPOTKIN, *MEMOIRS OF A REVOLUTIONIST*,
PUB. DOVER PUBLICATIONS, INC., NEW YORK, 1971

CAFÉ LIFE

American novelist John Dos Passos (1896–1970) visited St Petersburg in 1928.

❝In the evening the café under the Europskaya Hotel seems a great relief. Here's something a guy doesn't have to cudgel his wits to understand. It's like Europe, it's like the East Side of New York. Beer, jingly music, white tablecloths, shoddy whores. You can give your order to the waiter and he politely brings you a breaded cutlet. There are businessmen at the tables, tricky-looking articles who will assist you to buy a genuine antique ikon or a young lady's recumbent halfhour. There are speculators who will change your dollars for rubles in the black market. It's the kingdom of money again, the blessed land of valuta. After a while the nightlife begins to get a stale look, the beer begins to taste sour; best thing to do's to go to bed. It's too drearily obvious that the café's a grimy microcosm of the capitalist world across the Frontier, too obvious to be funny even. I'm no Y.M.C.A. secretary,

but Red Putilov has somehow taken the edge off it. When I ask my Russian friends about it they laugh and say, 'That's the underworld. The police let that place stay open so that they can always know where the criminals are when they want to put their hands on them.'❞

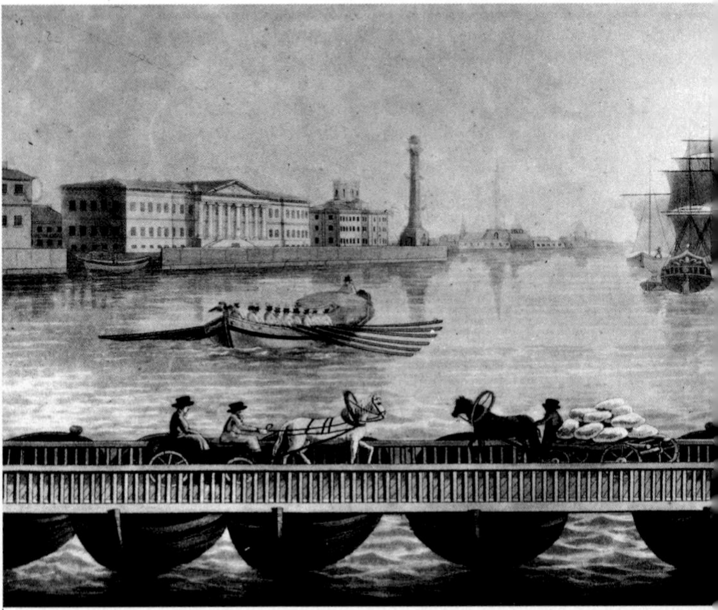

JOHN DOS PASSOS, *JOURNEYS BETWEEN WARS*, PUB. HARCOURT BRACE & COMPANY, NEW YORK, 1938

SEASONS

SNOW

English traveler E.D. Clarke (1769–1822) found Russian snow extraordinary.

❝The season began to change before we left Petersburg. The cold became daily less intense; and the inhabitants were busied in moving from the Neva large blocks of ice into their cellars. A most interesting and remarkable phænomenon took place the day before our departure, – the thermometer of *Fahrenheit* indicating only nine degrees of temperature below the freezing point; and there was no wind. At this time, snow, in the most regular and beautiful crystals, fell gently upon our clothes, and upon the sledge, as we were driving through the streets. All of these crystals possessed exactly the

same figure, and the same dimensions. Every one of them consisted of a wheel or star, with six equal rays, bounded by circumferences of equal diameters; having all the same number of rays branching from a common centre. The size of each of those little stars was equal to the circle presented by the section of a pea, into two equal parts. This appearance continued during three hours, in which time no other snow fell.❞

E.D. CLARKE, *TRAVELS IN VARIOUS COUNTRIES OF EUROPE, ASIA AND AFRICA*, PUB. T. CADELL & W. DAVIES, LONDON, 1816

NEVA

Now regarded as one of the major poets of the 20th century, Osip Mandelstam (1891–1938?) fell out of favor with the Soviet regime and died of a heart attack after his second arrest in 1938.

❝I'm feeling cold. Transparent springtime is
clothing Petropolis in a green down.
But still the Neva's wave, like a medusa,
inspires in me a slight sense of aversion.
On the embankment of the northern river
the fireflies of the automobiles whirl,
steel dragon-flies and beetles rush along,
the gold pins of the stars are flickering,
but no stars, no stars whatever, will kill
the weightly emerald of the sea's waves.❞

OSIP MANDELSTAM, "TRISTIA", FROM *POEMS FROM MANDELSTAM*, TRANS. BY R.H. MORRISON, PUB. ASSOCIATED UNIVERSITY PRESSES, LONDON, 1990

EARLY MORNING

Russian poet and essayist Joseph Brodsky was born in St Petersburg in 1940.

❝Once upon a time there was a little boy. He lived in the most unjust country in the world. Which was ruled by creatures who by all human accounts should be considered degenerates. Which never happened.

ALEXANDRE DUMAS
ILLUSTRÉ

IMPRESSIONS DE VOYAGE

En Russie

ILLUSTRATIONS
DE
DE LA CHARLERIE, GUSTAVE DORÉ, GERLIER, PHILIPPOTEAUX,
RAFFET, ETC.

And there was a city. The most beautiful city on the face of the earth. With an immense gray river that hung over its distant bottom like the immense gray sky over that river. Along that river there stood magnificent palaces with such beautifully elaborated façades that if the little boy was standing on the right bank, the left bank looked like the imprint of a giant mollusk called civilization. Which ceased to exist.

Early in the morning when the sky was still full of stars the little boy would rise and, after having a cup of tea and an egg accompanied by a radio announcement of a new record in smelted steel, followed by the army choir singing a hymn to the Leader, whose picture was pinned to the wall over the little boy's still warm bed, he would run along the snow-covered granite embankment to school.

The wide river lay white and frozen like a continent's tongue lapsed into silence and the big bridge arched against the dark blue sky like an iron palate. If the little boy had two extra minutes, he would slide down on the ice and take twenty or thirty steps to the middle. All this time he would be thinking about what the fish were doing under such heavy ice. Then he would stop, turn 180 degrees, and run back, nonstop, right up to the entrance of the school. He would burst into the hall, throw his hat and coat off onto a hook, and fly up the staircase and into his classroom.

It is a big room with three rows of desks, a portrait of the Leader on the wall behind the teacher's chair, a map with two hemispheres, of which only one is legal. The little boy takes his seat, opens his briefcase, puts his pen and notebook on the desk, lifts his face, and prepares himself to hear drivel.❞

JOSEPH BRODSKY, *LESS THAN ONE*
PUB. FARRAR, STRAUS, GIROUX, NEW YORK, 1986

THE TSAR'S MANIFESTO

The ambassador Maurice Paléogue was the only foreigner present at the ceremony, in St George's Gallery in the Winter Palace, when the Tsar proclamed Russia's entry into the 1914 War.

❝After the final prayer the court chaplain read the Tsar's manifesto to his people – a simple recital of the events which have made war inevitable, an eloquent appeal to all the national energies, an invocation to the Most High, and so forth. Then the Tsar went up to the altar and raised his right hand toward the gospel held out to him. He was even more grave and composed, as if he were about to receive the sacrament. In a slow, low voice, which dwelt on every word he made the following declaration.

'Officers of my guard, here present, I greet in you my whole army and give it my blessing. I solemnly swear that I will never make peace so long as one of the enemy is on the soil of the fatherland.'

A wild outburst of cheering was the answer to this declaration which was copied from the oath taken by the Emperor Alexander I in 1812. For nearly ten minutes there was a frantic tumult in the gallery and it was soon intensified by the cheers of the crowd massed along the Neva.❞

MAURICE PALÉOGUE, "AN AMBASSADOR'S MEMOIRS 1914–1917"
FROM *ST PETERSBURG, A TRAVELLERS' COMPANION*
SELECTED AND INTRODUCED BY LAURENCE KELLY
PUB. CONSTABLE, LONDON, 198[illegible]

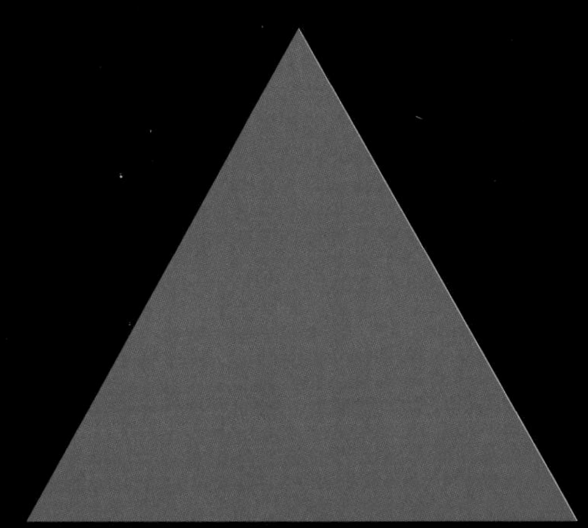

Itineraries in St Petersburg

Palace of Pavlovsk ▲

Palace of Tsarskoe Selo and detail of Atlas figure (right) ▼

Winter Palace, Hermitage Museum ▼

By the Fortress in winter ▲

The Moika Canal ▲

The Sphinx landing stage, University Embankment ▼

asilyevsky Island, from the Admiralty Embankment ▲ Palace Embankment and the Hermitage ▼

The frozen Neva and the Peter and Paul Fortress ▼

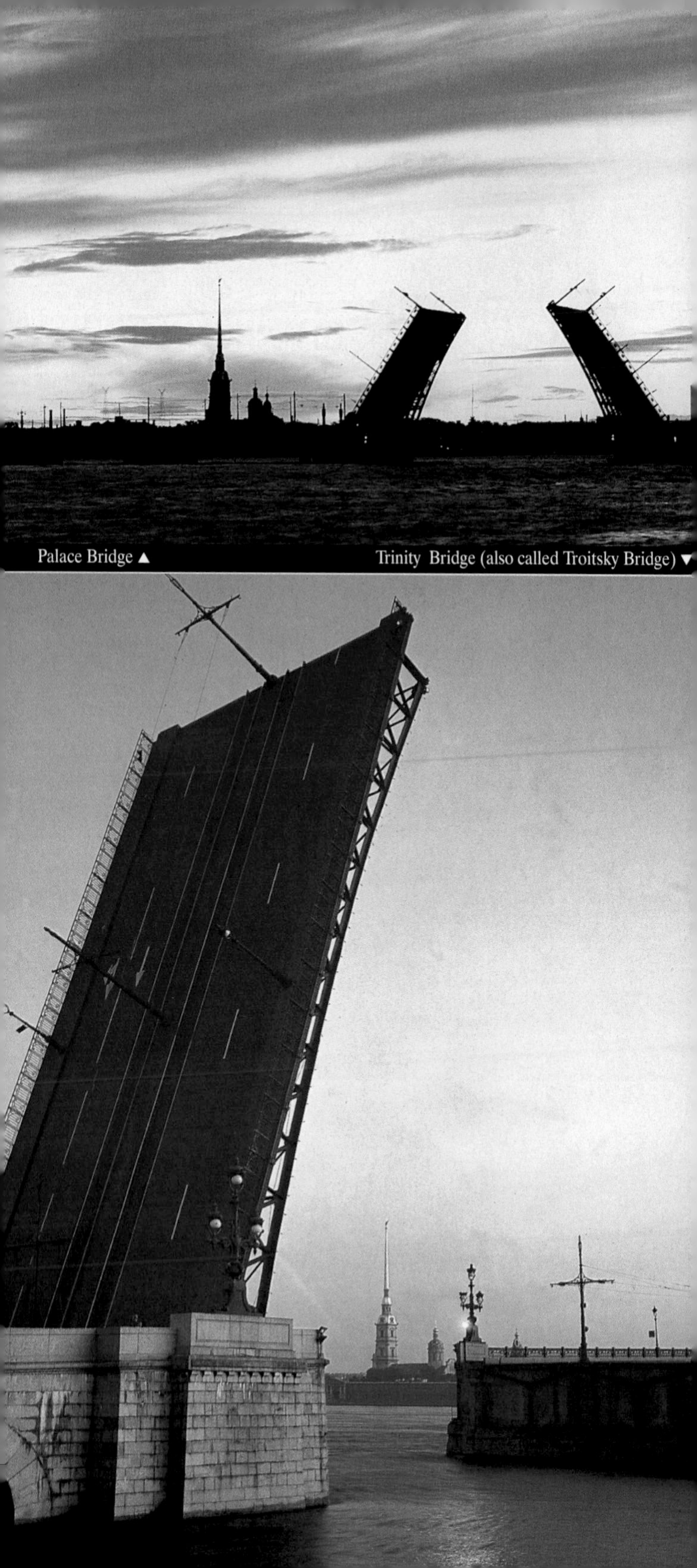

Palace Bridge ▲

Trinity Bridge (also called Troitsky Bridge) ▼

From the Peter and Paul Fortress to the islands of the delta

1. PETER AND PAUL FORTRESS
2. PETER AND PAUL CATHEDRAL
3. TRINITY BRIDGE

⏲ **Half a day**

◆ **A-B-C**

FROM THE BASTION TO THE MAUSOLEUM CHAPEL
The Peter and Paul Fortress has never been a residential area. Its only inhabitants were the garrison and the clergy attached to the Cathedral. It was, however, the symbolic center of the Russian Empire because successive sovereigns from Peter the Great onward (including the executed Czarevich Alexei ● *36*) are buried there.

FORTIFICATIONS

With the coming of the age of artillery a Vauban-style fortress with bastions was planned for the defense of the island. It is likely that Peter the Great was inspired in this by what he had seen in the West (1696–8). After the first earthworks had been raised the walls were continued in stone under the supervision of the architect Trezzini. The bastions bore the name of the princes who were given responsibility for each military sector. Thus, from Peter's (Petrovsky) Gate these are known as the CZAR, NARYSHKIN, TRUBETSKOY, ZOTOV, GULUKIN AND MENSHIKOV BASTIONS. In about 1740 the initial fortifications were doubled around each gate leading to the mainland by a curtain wall with moats; the latter were filled in during the 19th century. As a result it is necessary to pass through St John's Gate in order to reach Peter's Gate. When she built up the Neva embankment Catherine II added a granite dressing to the fortifications in 1779. Although it stands on the Petrograd Side the Arsenal, or Kronverk, complements the ramparts of the fortress and is an integral part of them. In the event, the Peter and Paul Fortress never had to play the defensive role for which it was designed.

THE GATES

PETER'S GATE. The decoration of this gate, with its imperial eagle and wooden bas-relief, refers to the victories of Peter the Great. On either side statues of the goddesses Bellona and Minerva serve as reminders of Peter's military prowess and political sagacity.

NEVA GATE. Built by Lvov between 1784 and 1787, this gate leads to the Fortress' only deep-water landing stage. It is crowned by a triangular pediment and framed by two groups of twin columns, joined by two blocks of facetted stone. The image of SAINT NICHOLAS guards this gate, which serves as the fortress exit toward Vasilyevsky Island, while SAINT BASIL stands sentry over the gate between the Trubetskoy and Zotov bastions.

"The fortress of St Petersburg was built, like all fortresses, to be a visible symbol of the antagonism between the people and its sovereign. No doubt it defends the city, but it threatens it to a far greater extent; no doubt it was built to repel the Swedes, but in practice it has been a prison for Russians."

Alexandre Dumas, *Voyage en Russie*

After the annexation by Russia of the mouth of the Neva during the Northern War the first fortress was built, in May 1703. This structure was close to the sea and naturally defended by the Neva itself. The island of Petersburg on which it stood was small enough to be entirely enclosed, leaving no room for enemy forces to gain a foothold. It was the last upstream island of the delta, and no ship could enter the waterway without passing it.

PETER'S GATE
The wooden relief shows the fall of Simon Magus, a reference to the Russian victory over Sweden.

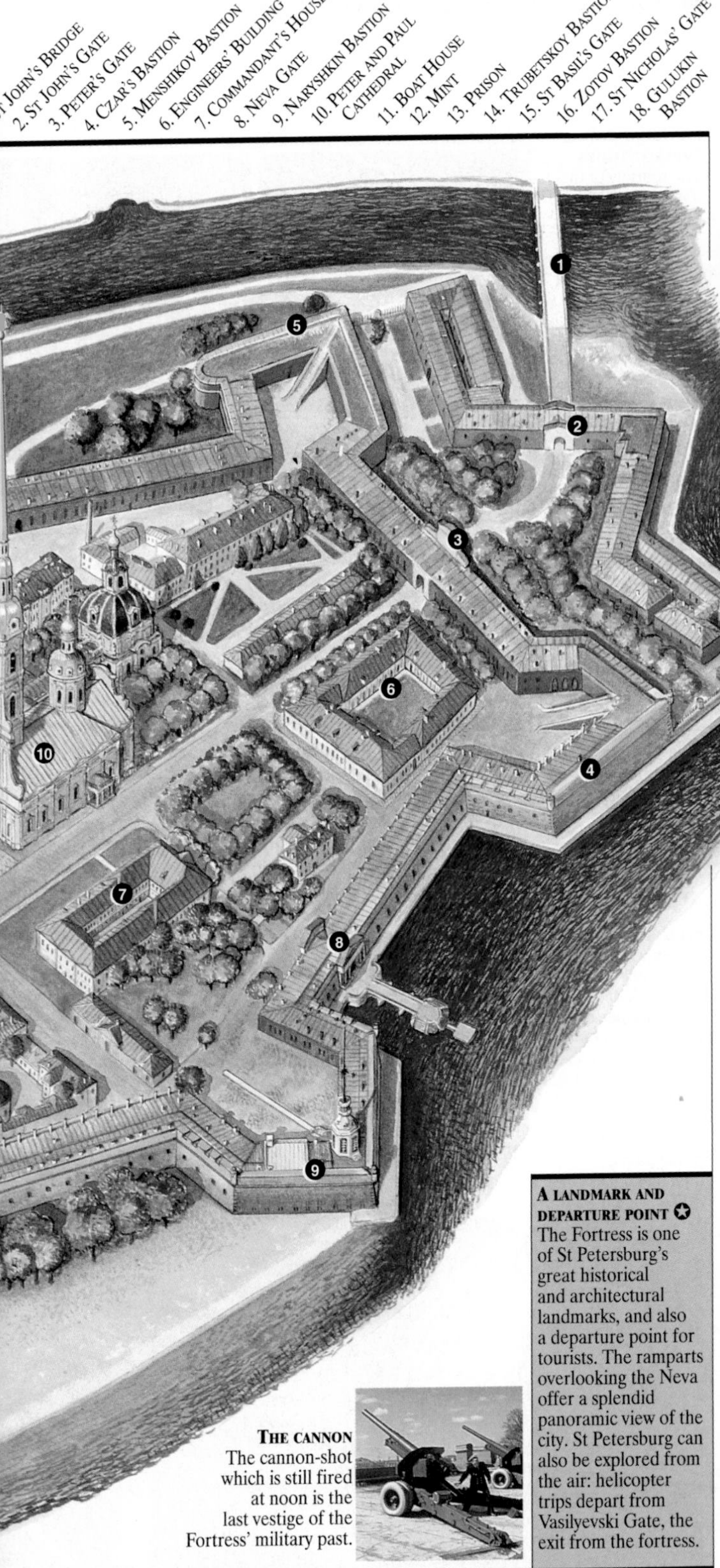

THE CANNON
The cannon-shot which is still fired at noon is the last vestige of the Fortress' military past.

A LANDMARK AND DEPARTURE POINT ✪
The Fortress is one of St Petersburg's great historical and architectural landmarks, and also a departure point for tourists. The ramparts overlooking the Neva offer a splendid panoramic view of the city. St Petersburg can also be explored from the air: helicopter trips depart from Vasilyevski Gate, the exit from the fortress.

IMPERIAL TOMBS
The sobriety of the tombs contrasts with the wealth of the trophies hanging from the walls, as if man's humility were being deliberately juxtaposed with the glory of his acts. The tradition of the mausoleum is once again alive; the last of the Romanovs, who died in France in 1992, is buried here. In 1998 the ashes of the last imperial family, executed by the Bolsheviks at Ekaterinburg in 1918, were transfered and interred here.

THE MINT
Peter I decided to move his state mint from Moscow to St Petersburg in 1719. From 1724 onward coins of

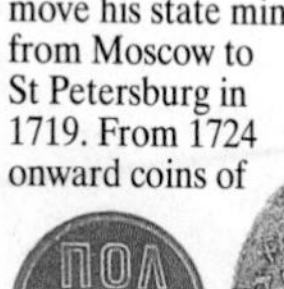

gold, silver and copper were struck here, along with medals. Although it served as the center of the national money supply under both the imperial and Communist regimes the Mint is now confined to the production of military medals.

PETER AND PAUL CATHEDRAL ★

The first church inside the fortress was built of wood. Its construction began on June 29, 1703, the feast day of Saint Peter and Saint Paul. The construction of the present cathedral (PETROPAVLOVSKY SOBOR; Петропавловский собор) was undertaken in 1712 under the direction of the architect Trezzini, who opted for the Western style of the period. The tower has been struck by lightning and rebuilt several times, and the cathedral was reconstructed following a fire in 1753. Its nave is conventional European Baroque, both in its floor plan and its elevation. There is also a pulpit, which is unusual for a Russian Orthodox cathedral.

ICONOSTASIS ● *56*. The architectural framework, which is ill-adapted to the Russian ritual, imposed an original solution for the iconostasis; in effect it occupies the entire breadth of the cathedral, and its royal doorway runs the width of the central nave.

CHIMING CLOCK. After 1724 the cathedral was equipped with a Dutch clock, presented by Peter the Great. Its bells originally sounded a carillon in honor of the Czar. Later, with the change of political regime, it sounded the Soviet anthem. Today every six hours it chimes *God Save the Czar*, a tune by the 18th-century composer Bortniansky and every hour the Orthodox *Alleluya*.

Artillery Museum
The Artillery Museum has a rich collection of swords, military souvenirs, uniforms and battle paintings. It is devoted to the military engineer corps. Don't miss the collection of cannons in the forecourt.

The Governor's mausoleum. Against the east wall of the cathedral is the mausoleum reserved for governors of the Fortress who died during their tenure. Among other duties the governors had to alert the sovereign to the fact that the Neva was once again navigable at winter's end, by bringing him a goblet of water from the river.

The Boat House

The pavilion. The Boat House (Botny Dom/Ботный дом), built by the architect Alexander Wist (1761–5) in the Baroque style, is crowned by an allegory of navigation sculpted by David Jensen (1891). Today it is occupied by a luxury souvenir shop.

St Petersburg History Museum

Engineers' Building. The whole Fortress precinct houses the St Petersburg History Museum; the collections in the Engineers' Building demonstrate certain aspects of daily life, in particular through a series of highly colored shop signs painted in a naive style. On the way through to the Commandant's House stands Mikhail Shemyakin's statue of Peter I (1990).
The Commandant's House. This building, which dates from the 1740's, contains an exhibition documenting the history of the Fortress, from the first human occupation of the site to the fall of the monarchy. The naval aspect of its history is especially well represented.

The Old Arsenal

Between 1705 and 1708 the Fortress was protected on the Petrograd Side by the construction of the original Kronverk. Of this auxiliary earthwork nothing remains today except ruins, with a stream running at their foot.
Monument to the Decembrists. The execution of the Decembrists ● *42* took place at the Arsenal. The obelisk commemorating the five victims bears a medallion showing their profiles.
Artillery Museum. The Arsenal building is a brick-built construction with a façade regulated by pilasters; each segment includes a carriage gateway and twinned bays on the second floor. In 1856 the military collections assembled since 1776 were installed in the arsenals of the Kronverk, where they may still be seen today.

The prison
Outside is the sauna bath which the prisoners were allowed to visit once a week. The cells were furnished with an iron bed and a table, both sealed to the wall, and a stool: they were heated one by one by a stove kept in the corridor. In the old days, one corner of the prison was known as the Dance Floor, in reference to a punishment inflicted on malingering soldiers, who were lashed to a stake with their bare feet resting on pointed sticks. The pain forced them to constantly shift their weight from one foot to the other, so that they looked as though they were dancing.

The ancestor of the Russian Fleet
For Peter I a powerful war fleet was the guarantor of Russia's opening up to the rest of the world. He personally sailed a large Dutch sloop from Moscow, his admirals plying the oars while he himself held the tiller. This vessel, known to this day as the "Grandfather of the Russian Fleet", was placed in the Boat House in 1761; since 1940 it has been in the Naval Museum (Stock Exchange) ▲ *157*.

THE FIRST MARKET BUILDING
In the early 18th century the island of Petersburg was the site of the city's food market, the first Gostiny Dvor (right), a restaurant, and the port with its customs house where foreign ships (mostly Dutch) unloaded their cargos. Later the customs officers were moved to Vasilyevsky Island ▲ *156*.

MATHILDA KSHESINSKAYA (1872–1971)
A pupil of the choreographer Petipa, Kshesinskaya (right) was one of the ballet stars who trained a new generation of dancers in the Paris schools.

MONUMENT TO THE "STEREGUSHCHY"
Built on a stone plinth, this monument on the corner of Kamennoostrovsky Avenue and the Gorky Prospekt commemorates a destroyer captured by the Japanese in 1907 and scuttled by her two surviving crewmen. The sculptor Karl Isenberg chose to represent his theme on a stele of sheet-metal. On the reverse side is an inscription describing the event and listing the names of the dead.

THE PETROGRAD SIDE

PETERSBURG ISLAND. In the early days of the city this island (known today as the Petrograd Side) was important because it was close to the Fortress. All commercial and social life was concentrated around the old Revolution Square, now renamed TROITSKAYA. It suffered decline with the development of the left bank; by the second half of the 19th century wooden houses without gas or running water were in evidence, just as they were on the right bank.

RAPID MODERNIZATION. At the turn of the 20th century land was cheap and the influx of money into St Petersburg gave a powerful incentive to construction. The Petrograd Side was quickly built up, almost uniformly in the Art Nouveau style ● *92*. The construction of the TRINITY BRIDGE (1897–1903) (Troitsky Most) gave the district further cachet by linking it to the grander quarters of the far bank. This bridge replaced a floating one ● *91*, which had to be dismantled each year when the Neva swept away all the ice from Lake Ladoga.
MUSEUM OF POLITICAL HISTORY. In 1904, the architect A.I. Hogen built a townhouse ● *92* for Mathilda Kshesinskaya, favorite ballerina of Nicholas II. It was commandeered by the Bolsheviks in March 1917, and later became the Museum of the Great October Socialist Revolution. Now the Museum of Political History, it also incorporates a display devoted to the life of Mathilda Kshesinskaya and is the venue for musical evenings.

ALEXANDER PARK

The Gorkovskaya metro station (Горьковская) is surrounded by an immense park, until recently named after Lenin but now with its old title of Alexander Park restored. It occupies the old military training grounds around the Kronverk ▲ *149* and is a favorite place for St Petersburgers.

The Zoological Gardens. West of the Kronverk is the zoo, converted from a 19th-century private menagerie. It has seen better days; nevertheless, although giraffes and elephants are currently absent, the zoo does have a comprehensive collection of northern animal species, some of them virtually unknown to the Western public. Children visiting this zoo will discover that minks, sables and martens exist in other forms than coats and stoles; they will also be interested by rare animals from Siberia, such as the long-eared hedgehog and the Przewalsky horse. In addition, there is a large aviary of birds of prey, and a number of bears, the emblem of Russia.

Cabin of Peter the Great ★

A wooden lodge ● *83.* Facing the Neva is the small cabin occupied by Peter the Great (Domik Petra; домик Петра) in the summer of 1703. The roof is made of wooden slats in the shape of tiles, while the brick imitation of the exterior is reminiscent of a Dutch cottage. One of the two rooms was made into a chapel under Nicholas I; dismantled in 1930, this was replaced by an 18th-century style interior. The stone house built around the cabin also encloses a boat built by Peter the Great himself, along with an exhibition of engravings.

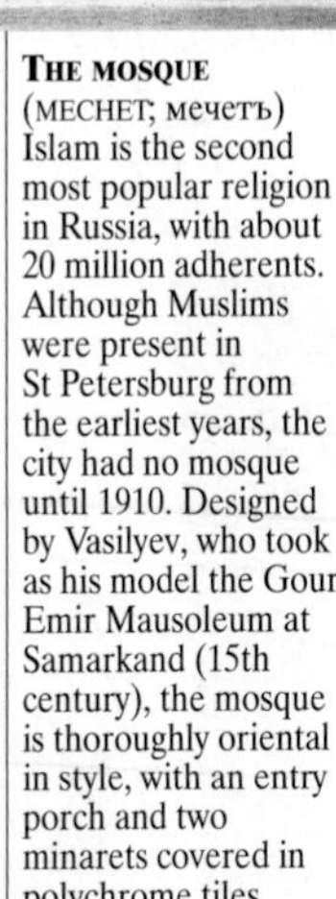

The mosque (Mechet; мечеть) Islam is the second most popular religion in Russia, with about 20 million adherents. Although Muslims were present in St Petersburg from the earliest years, the city had no mosque until 1910. Designed by Vasilyev, who took as his model the Gour Emir Mausoleum at Samarkand (15th century), the mosque is thoroughly oriental in style, with an entry porch and two minarets covered in polychrome tiles.

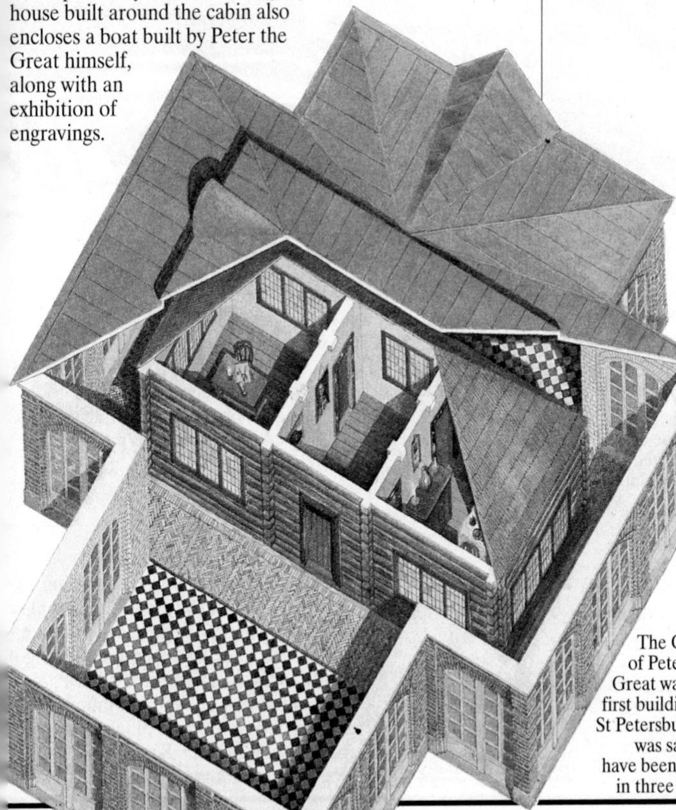

The Cabin of Peter the Great was the first building in St Petersburg; it was said to have been built in three days.

THE "AURORA"
Built in the city's shipyards, this cruiser inherited the name of a famous fighting frigate of the Crimean War. Moored in front of the Nakhimov Naval Academy since 1948, it is one of the most celebrated symbols of the Revolution.

THE CRUISER "AURORA" ★

The cruiser *Aurora* (KREISER AVRORA; крейсер Аврора) of the Baltic Fleet was launched in 1903; it became a cadet training vessel after the war with Japan in 1904. The crew, many of whom had progressive ideas, played a key role at the start of the Revolution ● *46*; at a signal given from the Fortress, one of the *Aurora*'s guns opened the people's attack on the Winter Palace. It is open to the public as part of the Naval Museum (Stock Exchange).

LENIN SQUARE

In the middle of Lenin Square (PLOSHCHAD LENINA; пл.Ленина) stands a bronze effigy of the great revolutionary sculpted by Sergei Yevseyev. The statue, unveiled in 1926, shows Lenin standing on the turret of an armored vehicle, his right arm thrust out and left thumb grasping his waistcoat. An inscription reads "Long Live the Socialist Revolution throughout the World".

FINLAND STATION. This station, rebuilt in the 1960's, is the boarding point for trains to Finland, Vyborg and the Isthmus of Carelia between Lake Ladoga and the Baltic Sea, and to resorts such as Zelenogorsk, Sosnovo, Repino and Komarovo (the burial place of the poet Anna Akhmatova). At weekends the station is packed with city families heading out of town to their garden plots, returning later with flowers, vegetables, mushrooms and blueberries. A sculpted frieze on the station front depicts the Revolution; Lenin ▲ *248* arrived here on his journey from Finland on April 3, 1917. Locomotive no. 293, which brought him secretly to Finland, was presented to the Soviet Union by the Finnish Railway Company in 1957; it still stands by the platform here, behind glass.

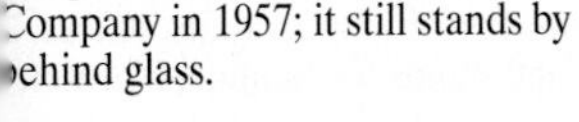

APOTHECARIES' ISLAND

BOTANICAL GARDENS (BOTANICHESKY SAD; Ботанический сад). Apothecaries' Island (APTEKARSKI OSTROV; Аптекарский остров), separated from the island of Petrograd by the river Karpovka, is named after the Botanical Gardens at no. 2 Professor Popov Street. As the successor of the medicinal garden founded by Peter I in 1714, this institution became the Imperial Botanical Garden in 1823. Its collections were enriched over the years by contributions from explorers in Asia, Siberia and Central and South America. At the close of the last century it became a center for agricultural research. The species from temperate climates are distributed around an English-style park (top right) while the greenhouses are reserved for tropical and subtropical plants. This garden is closely associated with the Botanical Museum built up around the vegetable samples collected by Peter the Great for his *cabinet de curiosités* in the Kunstkammer ▲ *160*.

SHALYAPIN HOUSE. The Apartment-Museum of Fyodor Shalyapin (Chaliapin) is at no. 2B Heinrich Graftio Street, in what used to be his private residence. Here the great singer received the artistic elite of St Petersburg. The building houses an exhibition that describes his work and includes recordings of his incomparable voice.

FYODOR SHALYAPIN (1873–1938)
Shalyapin was one of the great figures of Russian opera. He had a remarkable bass-baritone voice, and became especially famous for his interpretation of the role of Boris Godunov in Mussorgsky's eponymous opera.

THE ISLANDS OF THE DELTA

KAMMENY ISLAND (KAMENNY OSTROV; Каменный остров). This island has retained its old name, translated from a Finnish word meaning "stone". Several princely palaces were built here in the late 18th century, among them the Stone Island Palace (Kamennoostrovsky Dvorets), built (1776–81) by Yuri Felten, with the exception of its façade, attributed to Quarenghi. The Stone Island Palace was commissioned by Catherine II for her son Paul I. It was built on the point of the island, where the Neva divides into two. Its central part has a pediment supported by columns, with roof eaves enhanced by

Polovtsev's dacha.

CHURCH OF ST JOHN THE BAPTIST
This church was built on Kamenny Island in 1778 by Velten, to celebrate Catherine II's victory over the Turks.

ELAGIN PARK
The entire island is laid out in the English style, complete with pavilions, stables, landing stage, bandstands and orangeries. Today Elagin Island is St Petersburg's best-loved park.

"THE ISLANDS" ✪
Collectively known as "the islands" by St Petersburgers, Kammeny Island, Elagin Island and Krevstovsky Island were the favorite holiday spots for the gilded youth of the 19th century. Wealthy young people would come here to be entertained by gypsies and cabaret dancers, and to watch the sun go down over the Gulf of Finland. Although the islands are now part of St Petersburg, they are an oasis of greenery. Opposite Elagin Island (91 Primorski Prospekt) the largest Buddhist temple in Europe, built in 1915 and reestablished as a centre of worship in 1990, is worth a visit.

a long balustrade. Today the palace is surrounded by barracks, and is used as a military sanitarium; efforts are being made to restore it to its original splendor. In the early 20th century a number of dachas were built on Kammeny Island; many of these are now abandoned, but others have been restored for the use of Russian dignitaries and distinguished guests from abroad. POLOVTSEV'S DACHA is an old neoclassical palace with a façade of Ionic columns; it was built (1911–16) by Fomin, who modeled it on Russian gentlemen's residences of the 18th century. After the October Revolution Polovtsev's dacha was used as a rest home for workers. It now contains offices. By the road out to Elagin Island stands the Summer Theater,

which was built in 1827 by Shustov and altered later by Cavos, in 1844. This theater is entirely constructed of wood, including its frontal colonnade, which gives it the air of a Greek temple. The Ballroom Dancing Company puts on performances here.

ELAGIN ISLAND (OSTROV YELAGIN; остров Елагин). This island was a present to Ivan Elagin by Catherine the Great in 1770. In 1794 it passed to Count Orlov and in 1817 was purchased by Alexander I ● *36*, for his mother Maria Fyodorovna, the widow of Paul I. The transformation of ELAGIN PALACE was Carlo Rossi's ▲ *181* first project in St Petersburg (1818–22). The central feature of the façade overlooking the river is a colonnaded half-rotunda topped by a flat dome, whose upper floor gives access to a roof terrace more appropriate to the climate of Italy than to that of St Petersburg. The interior décor reflects the taste of the time, with a large amount of white and pastel-toned painted stucco as well as much sculpture. This palace was seriously damaged during World War Two, since when it has been carefully restored. It now contains a museum of decorative arts of the 19th and early 20th centuries.

KRESTOVSKY ISLAND (KRESTOVSKY OSTROV; Крестовский остров). As they always have done, St Petersburgers still go to the island of Krestovsky to bathe in the waters of the Neva and breathe the sea air, all for the price of a tram ticket. The island is also the location for a number of important sporting facilities, among them an Olympic Training Institute, and the KIROV STADIUM, which is the largest sporting complex in St Petersburg, having a capacity of 73,000 people.

Vasilyevsky Island

1. MINING INSTITUTE
2. LIEUTENANT SCHMIDT BRIDGE
3. STATUE OF ADMIRAL KRUSENSTERN
4. SPHINX PIER
5. PASSENGER PORT
6. ACADEMY OF ARTS
7. MENSHIKOV PALACE
8. PALACE BRID[illegible]

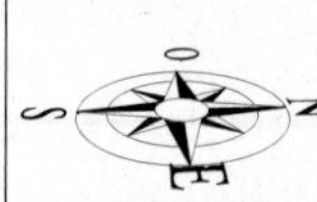

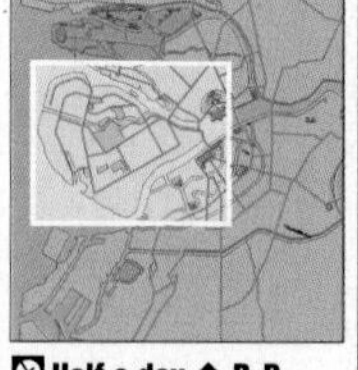

Half a day ◆ B-D

Vasilyevsky Island (VASILYEVSKY OSTROV; Васильевский остров) is the largest of the various islands in the Neva Delta. Its street plan was laid out by the architect Jean-Baptiste Leblond ● *82*, whose project was approved by Peter I on January 1, 1716. Leblond's idea was to divide the island into a network of streets and canals meeting at right angles. He also envisaged the excavation of a broad navigable canal, which would follow the line of the present Bolshoy Prospekt. Each side of the streets running at right angles to the canal was called a "line" and bore a number; this system still operates today. Shortly after Peter I's death the island was relegated to a secondary role in the development of St Petersburg, being too frequently subject to flooding, and the project for a canal network was shelved indefinitely.

ʼHE POINT (STRELKA)

)ne of the finest vantage points on Vasilyevsky Island is the ʼtrelka, meaning Arrow or Point. Peter I intended this site ɔ be the prestigious center of his capital, with a broad square ınd magnificent government buildings.

ɪAVAL MUSEUM (TSENTRALNY VOENNO-MORSKOY MUZEY; ʼентральный Военно-морской музей). The heart of this ɪrchitectural ensemble is the old Stock Exchange building *87*, rebuilt between 1804 and 1810 by Thomas de Thomon. ʼhe Exchange, with its massive granite base, was the place of ʼusiness to which merchants came on their arrival at the port ʼf St Petersburg ▲ *192*. Since 1940 the building has been ɪllocated to the Naval Museum.

HISTORY OF THE RUSSIAN FLEET
The collections of the Naval Museum include over 1,700 model ships, from the oldest (Peter I's small vessel) to the most modern, along with designs and maquettes.

ЦЕНТРАЛЬНЫЙ
ВОЕННО-МОРСКОЙ
ОРДЕНА
КРАСНОЙ ЗВЕЗДЫ
МУЗЕЙ

RARE SPECIES
The St Petersburg Zoological Museum is one of the largest of its kind in the world. It has examples of over forty thousand different animal species, with about fifteen million specimens in reserve.

ROSTRAL COLUMNS ★
● *87*. On the square in front of the Exchange are the two rostral columns (the term is derived from the Latin *rostrum*, the bows of a vessel), to which are attached metal ships' prows. These are flanked by colossal statues, allegories of the four great rivers of Russia – the Volga, the Dnieper, the Volkhov and the Neva – sculpted in stone from studies by I. Chamberlain and J. Thibaut. For some time beacons, fueled by hemp oil, burned on the top of the columns, and these functioned as lighthouses at the entrance to the port.

OLD PORT WAREHOUSES. On either side of the Exchange are port warehouses, built between 1826 and 1832 by the architect Giovanni Luchini. The south building is now the ZOOLOGICAL MUSEUM (ZOOLOGICHESKY MUZEY; Зоологический музей), founded in 1896. This was the former site of the palace of Czarina Prascovia Fyodorovna (1664–1723), the wife of Peter I's half-brother, Czar Ivan Alexeyvich (1666–96) and mother of the future Empress Anna Yoannovna ● *36*. The north warehouse is now the DOKUCHAYEV MUSEUM OF SOIL SCIENCE (TSENTRALNY MUZEY POCHVOVEDENIYA IM. V. DOKUCHAYEV; центральный музей Почвоведения им. В. Докучаева),

MUSEUM OF LITERATURE
(LITERATURNY MUZEY; Литературный музей). The old Customs House was built between 1829 and 1832 under the supervision of Luchini. Since 1927 this building has served as the Institute of Russian Literature (or Pushkin House) and the Museum of Literature. Both establishments were founded after the 1899 exhibition in honor of Pushkin's centenary ● *114*. Their archives include over two thousand manuscripts from the 13th to the 18th centuries, along with a number of texts by Tolstoy and Dostoevsky ▲ *207*. The museum houses an extraordinary collection of original oil paintings and watercolors.

AN UNUSUAL STUDENT
Lenin was a student of law at the University of St Petersburg, obtaining his diploma in 1891.

opened in 1904. This museum is devoted to the study and protection of Russia's soils and to increasing their productivity.

MAKAROV EMBANKMENT

The embankment is named for Stepan Makarov (1849–1904), the famous Russian Navy Admiral. The granite facing of the embankment was built between 1806 and 1809, as were the buildings by the Customs House pier (note the broad stairway with its sculpted lions).

LIBRARY OF THE ACADEMY OF SCIENCES (BIBLIOTEKA AKADEMII NAUK; библиотека Академии наук). The main façade completes the view from the main Neva waterway along the Mendeleev "line", named for the chemist Mendeleev (1834–1907). Founded in 1714, the Library of the Academy of Sciences (1912–25, architect R. Marfeld) is one of the oldest scientific establishments in the city. It contains over twenty million volumes, as well engravings, drawings, watercolors, manuscripts, maps and charts.

THE TWELVE COLLEGES (DVENADTSAT KOLLEGI; Двенадцать Коллегий). Constructed between 1722 and 1742 by Domenico Trezzini ● *83* and Theodore Schwertfeger and now attached to the University of St Petersburg, this complex is made up of twelve identical buildings in an unbroken line, intended for the various government bodies: the Senate, the Synod and the ten "colleges" or ministries. The glazed second floor is now the corridor of the University and is famed for its length. In 1835 all these buildings were handed over to the University authorities, by whom they were partially reconstructed. Visitors are admitted to the museum named after the chemist Mendeleev, who devised the periodic table of chemical elements, and lived and worked here from 1866 to 1890.

THE POINT (STRELKA), CENTER OF SCIENTIFIC RESEARCH ON VASILYEVSKY ISLAND ✪
Although Vasilyevsky Island did not in fact become the hub of the city, as Peter I had intended, it is however the nerve center of research and of the human sciences. Students, researchers and museum curators account for much of its population, hence its nickname "Island of Light". It is also pleasant to browse in the bookstores clustered around the university, and to stop at one of the many cafés were students can be seen putting the world to rights. The monument to Mikhail Lomosonov ● *53*, built in 1986 on University Embankment, is a fitting symbol of the spirit of the island.

A CONCENTRATION OF BUILDINGS
The Twelve Colleges constitute the west side of an immense architectural ensemble built in the early 1830's. Apart from the warehouses, it includes the Merchants' Courtyard of the New Exchange (now part of the University) along with an annex of the Museum of the Academy of Sciences, currently used by the St Petersburg department of the Nauka science publishing organization.

UNIVERSITY EMBANKMENT

At the beginning of the University Embankment (UNIVERSITETSKAYA NAB.; Университетская наб.) are a number of buildings which are linked to the history of the Academy of Sciences.

THE KUNSTKAMMER ★ ▲ *250*. The Kunstkammer, Peter the Great's gallery of curiosities, is an interesting example of earl Russian Baroque. Built between 1718 and 1734 by the architects G. Mattarnovy, N. Herbel, G. Ciaveri and M. Zemtsov, the Kunstkammer has wings of two stories with a tower between. The Kunstkammer was the first Natura Science Museum in Russia, and it included a library and an observatory. From 1783 to 1796 the Academy was directed by E. Dashkova, a friend of Catherine II and one of the most cultivated women of her time. In 1878 i became the Museum of Anthropology and Ethnology (MUZEY ANTROPOLOGII I ETNOGRAFII IM. PETRA VELIKOVO; музей Антропологии и Этнографии им. Петра Великого). The museum's displays include items which illustrate the daily lives and cultures of many different countries, along with their weapons, clothes and religious objects.

M. LOMONOSOV MUSEUM (MUZEY M. LOMONOSOVA; музей М. Ломоносова). In 1949 the M. Lomonosov Museum ● *53* was installed inside the Kunstkammer, ir memory of the great scientist. Among its attractions ar Lomonosov's scientific instruments and his writings, in addition to a reconstitution of the Academy of Sciences' conference hall.

ACADEMY OF SCIENCES (AKADEMIYA NAUK; Академия наук). Beside the Kunstkammer, also on the embankment at no. 5 is the main Academy of Sciences building, which was constructed between 1783 and 1789 by Giacomo Quarenghi ● *86*. In 1925 the main staircase in the vestible was embellished with a mosaic panel by Lomonosov, which was entitled *The Battle of Poltava*. In the same year the Academy became known as the Academy of Sciences of the Soviet Union, before its headquarters were transferred to Moscow nine years later, in 1934.

THE GLOBE
At the Lomonosov Museum is a reconstruction of the huge terrestrial globe of the Academy of Sciences. Made in the 1600's for the Duke of Holstein-Gottorp, it was presented as a gift to Peter the Great in 1713.

CABINET OF CURIOSITIES
The collections of monstrosities and curiosities in the Kikin Palace ▲ *250* were amassed by Peter I and transferred to the Kunstkammer in 1727.

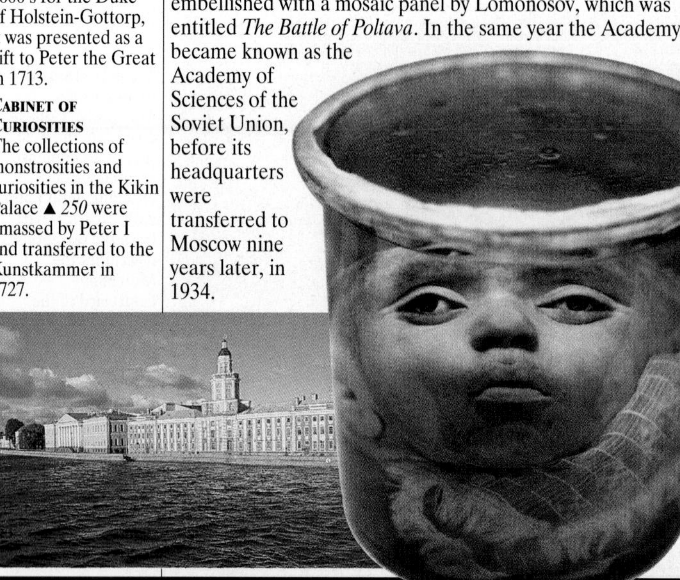

ALEXANDER MENSHIKOV (1672–1729)
The son of a baker, Menshikov was a childhood friend of Peter the Great. He wielded immense influence on affairs of state, and distinguished himself in a number of military campaigns (he was promoted to general in 1705). He later directed part of the construction of St Petersburg. Following the death of Peter the Great, Menshikov, who had become a member of the Secret Supreme Council and had married off his daughter to the future Peter II, was sole master of Russia for over two years. But he aroused the hostility of the nobility and his grip on power ended with his arrest in 1727. All his property was confiscated and he was deported with his family to Siberia, where he died two years later.

IENSHIKOV PALACE (DVORETS MENSHIKOVA; дворец Аеншикова) ★ ● *82*. At no. 15 on the embankment stands the rchitectural ensemble of the Menshikov Palace. In the early ears of the 18th century Prince Menshikov, who was a close riend of Peter the Great, had his private mansion here. The uilding has two floors and a mansard roof; it was designed y the architects Giovanni Maria Fontana and Gottfried chädell. It was here that Peter I held lavish assemblies nd celebrations of Russian victories, and received foreign mbassies. In 1781, two years after Menshikov's death, the alace was the barracks of an elite regiment, the Foot Guards, efore it was passed on to the Army's First Cadet Corps. The eft wing of the palace was enlarged by the addition of a new uilding, which was itself enlarged during the 1770's. Works nitiated in 1956 restored the palace's original aspect, which vas remarkable for its famously splendid interiors. A spacious estibule leads to the formal oak staircase, with wrought-iron anisters struck with the monograms of both Peter the Great nd Menshikov himself. The stairs go up to the apartments f Prince Menshikov and his sister-in-law Varvara Arseneva who had the responsibility of educating his children); the two reas are separated, however, by formal drawing rooms. The ASSEMBLY ROOM, which is over a thousand square feet in size, s the largest room in the palace. The WALNUT ROOM, with s painted ceiling and boiseries of Persian walnut wood, was Aenshikov's favorite room; his BEDROOM (below) is covered vith no fewer than 27,811 Delft tiles ● *64*. The restoring of he architectural decoration of the palace was completed in 002, with the installation of the princely crowns and vases. he palace is now an annex of the Hermitage and contains n exhibition on "Russian Culture 1700–30".

MENSHIKOV'S OFFICE
On the walls are portraits of Menshikov's four daughters.

PAINTING, SCULPTURE, ARCHITECTURE
The Academy of the "three noble arts" was founded in 1757, at the instigation of Lomonosov.

ACADEMY OF ARTS (AKADEMIYA KHUDOSHESTV; Академия художеств). Further along the embankment, at no. 17, the building of the Academy of Arts may be found, which was constructed between 1764 and 1768 by the architects Alexander Kokorinov and Jean-Baptiste Vallin de la Mothe ● *86*. The traditions of this academy are maintained today by the Repin Institute of Painting, Sculpture and Architecture. Also housed within the building is the Arts Academy of Research, and on the first floor a department exhibiting plaster casts of original artworks from all over the world. The department of architecture displays a variety of designs and projects, together with scale models of Smolny ● *84*, St Isaac's Cathedral ● *88*, the Engineers' Castle, and the Stock Exchange ● *87*.

LIEUTENANT SCHMIDT EMBANKMENT

SPHINX QUAY ★
(SPUSK SO SPHINXAMI; Спуск со Сфинксами) This quay was built (1832–4) to a plan by Konstantin Thon. The two sculpted sphinxes on either side of the steps leading down to the river were found at Thebes, the capital of ancient Egypt. Their features are those of the Pharaoh Amenophis III.

LIEUTENANT SCHMIDT BRIDGE. Both the bridge and the embankment are named for Nikolai Schmidt (center), who distinguished himself during the 1905 Revolution ● *44*. The Lieutenant Schmidt Bridge (originally named the Nicholas Bridge) was the first permanent bridge across the Neva; it was built between 1847 and 1850 by the engineer S. Kerbedz and the decoration (sea shells and sea horses) is by Bryulov.

THE ACADEMICIANS' HOUSE (DOM AKADEMIKOV; дом Академиков). At no. 1 Lieutenant Schmidt Embankment (NAB. LEYTENANTA SCHMIDT; наб. Лейтенанта-Шмидта) stands the Academicians' House, which was constructed in the 1750's by Savva Chevakinsky. The building was completely reshaped in the early 19th century by the architects A. Bezhanov and Andrei Zakharov ● *87*. The classical structure of the house is typical of the period; it has twenty-six plaques affixed to its walls, which commemorate the intellectuals who occupied it.

HE FRUNZE NAVAL STAFF COLLEGE (VYSSHEE VOENNO-/IORSKOYE UCHILISHCHE IM. M. FRUNZE; Высшее военно-юрское училище им. М. Фрунзе). This imposing building 'ith its Ionic colonnade is the Russian Navy's principal ducational institution. It was built between 1796 and 1798 by he architect F. Volkov, and succeeded the Navigation School, /hich had been founded in 1701 by an edict of Peter the ;reat. The Navigation School was converted into the Naval :adet Corps School in 1752.

TATUE OF ADMIRAL KRUSENSTERN (PAMYATNIK ADMIRALU ⟨RUSENSHTERNU; памятник адмиралу Крузенштерну). In ront of the Naval Staff College stands the statue of Admiral ⟨rusenstern (1770–1846), which was erected in 1873. Admiral ⟨rusenstern is famous as the commander of the first flotilla of ⟨ussian ships to circumnavigate the globe in the early 19th entury.

HURCH OF THE DORMITION (USPENSKAYA TSERKOV; 'спенская церковь). The pure lines of the monumental :hurch of the Dormition stand out clearly on the Neva's kyline. Built between 1893 and 1900 by B. Kosyakov, it tands on the former site of the Pskov Monastery's guest uarters, purchased in the 1880's by the Kiev Monastery ▲ *253*.

IINING INSTITUTE (GORNY INSTITUT; Горный институт). ieutenant Schmidt Embankment ends with the enormous Iining Institute, one of the oldest establishments of its kind n the world. When it was founded in 1773 it was known as the Mining School, later becoming the Mining Corps. The building, with its portico of twelve Doric columns, was built between 1806 and 1811 by Andrei Voronikhin. It houses a museum which contains one of the world's richest collections of minerals, stones and fossils. There are scale models of mines, and the museum also exhibits examples of the tools used in the mining industry.

THE "CHEKUCHI". Beyond the Mining Institute is the industrial and manufacturing quarter, which has always been known as the "Chekuchi" (The Crushers), on account of the mallets which were used to crush the lumps of damp flour piled in the warehouses here. Nowadays the area is a huge naval dockyard which, with its counterpart on the other bank of the Neva, frames the point where the river meets the Gulf of Finland.

PAVLOV (1849–1936)
Since 1949 there has been a museum at the Academicians' House dedicated to the work of the physiologist Pavlov, who lived at apartment no. 18 there from 1918 onward.

MIKHAIL FRUNZE (1885–1925)
This military commander distinguished himself during the Civil War (1918) and in 1924 was named Chief of Staff and Commandant of the Moscow Military Academy.

SMOLENSK CEMETERY ■ *26*
This is made up of three cemetries: a Russian orthodox cemetery, a Lutheran cemetery and an Armenian cemetery.

ST CATHERINE'S CHURCH
The Bolshoy Prospekt begins with St Catherine's Church, built (1768–71) by Yury Velten ● *86* for the Evangelical Lutheran community of Vasilyevksy Island.

BOLSHOY PROSPEKT

The buildings along the BOLSHOY PROSPEKT (Большой проспект) are less interesting for their architecture than for the memories that cling to them – above all, for the everyday life of the quarter.

ST ANDREW'S MARKET (ANDREEVSKY RYNOK; Андреевский рынок). The area between "lines" five and six is occupied by St Andrew's Market. The old part of the building dates from 1780–90, and its modern section from 1959.

ST ANDREW'S CHURCH (ANDREEVSKY SOBOR; Андреевский собор). The principal Orthodox church on the island, this building is a monument of mid-18th century Baroque architecture (1764–80, architect A. Vist). The carved iconostasis is a masterpiece in the genre.

PEL AND SON'S PHARMACY (APTEKA A. PELYA SYNOVEY; аптека А. Пеля и сыновей). On the first floor of a four-story house nearby was the original pharmacy of A. Pel (1900's). Pel, a doctor in chemistry, philosophy and pharmacology, was the first in Russia to make preparations based on organic constituents; he invented a number of medical compounds that are still in use today. Since 1983, a museum of Russian pharmacology has occupied Pel's old premises, with objects from the period filling the old shelves.

PASSENGER PORT
On Naval Glory Square, fronting the Gulf of Finland, the main building is the Passenger Port (1977–82), whose giant 240-foot spire is topped by a caravel, similar to the one at the Admiralty ▲ *190*.

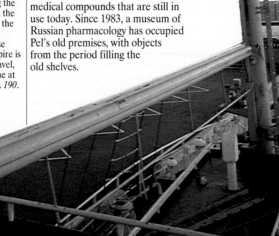

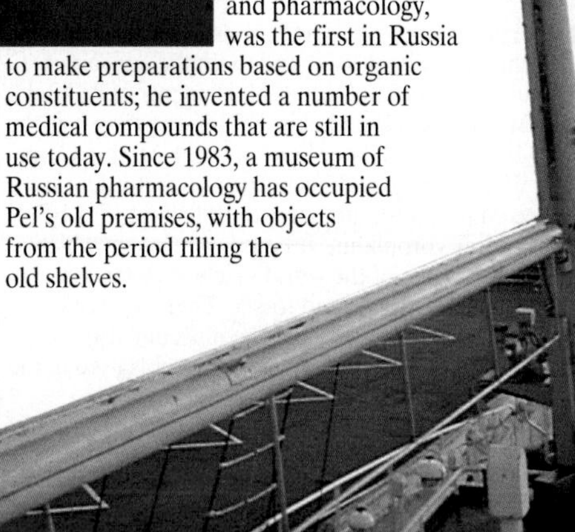

From the Hermitage to the Summer Palace

1. THE HERMITAGE
2. PALACE SQUARE
3. ALEXANDER COLUMN
4. ARCH OF THE GENERAL STA

⏱ One day

◆ A-E

THE HERMITAGE

THE FIRST WINTER PALACES. The Winter Palace, now known as the Hermitage Museum, is the fourth building to have bee constructed on this site. After the first "small Dutch-style house" built by Peter I it was probably the Italian architect Domenico Trezzini who built the nuptial palace which we consider to have been the first Winter Palace (1711–12). This building was destroyed in 1726. Meantime, the architec Mattarnovy had built a "winter house" next door (1716–19) for Peter I. In 1732 the Empress Anna Ivanovna from the Rastrellis another palace. It was razed in 1754 to make way for the current palace, built for Elizabeth Petrovna.
PALACE OF ELIZABETH. Built from 1754 to 1762 by Bartolome Rastrelli, this palace is renowned for its profusion of Baroqu decoration: two stories of columns cover the facades.

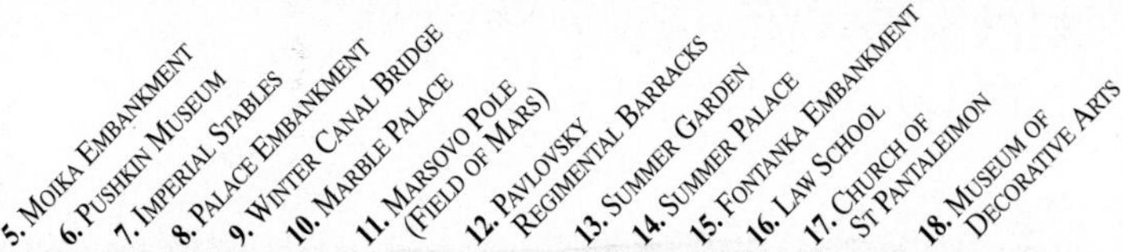

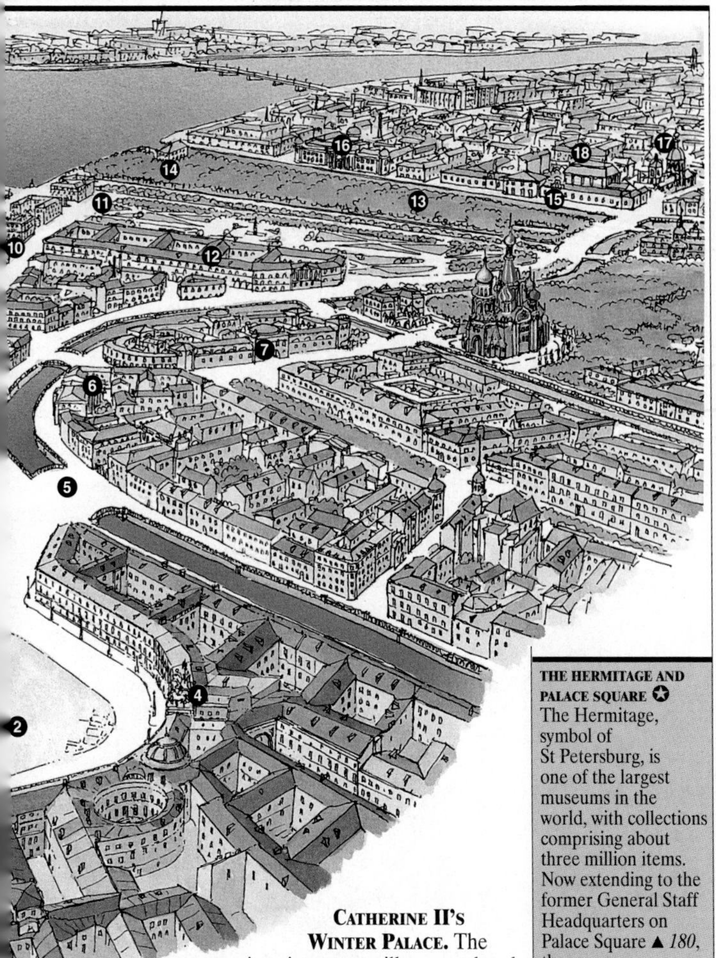

The Hermitage and Palace Square ✪
The Hermitage, symbol of St Petersburg, is one of the largest museums in the world, with collections comprising about three million items. Now extending to the former General Staff Headquarters on Palace Square ▲ *180*, the museum constitutes a major cultural center. "Under the Aegis of the Eagle", one of the displays there, is an exhibition of Empire artefacts.

Catherine II's Winter Palace. The interiors were still uncompleted when Rastrelli was dismissed by Catherine in August 1762. The director of the Buildings :hancellery, I. Betsky, called in several foreign architects to eplace him: Jean-Baptiste Vallin de la Mothe, Antonio :inaldi and the German Yury Velten. De la Mothe decorated :atherine II's private apartments (later destroyed in the 1837 .re), the Throne Room, the church, the partments of the ladies of honor on the nird floor, and the apartments of Count :rigory Orlov on the mezzanine floor. 'elten reorganized the Portrait and the Mirror galleries, and Rinaldi changed ne Throne Room into an oval salon. :atherine II had ten grandchildren, and ne imperial apartments (including the neater) were altered to meet their needs y Giacomo Quarenghi and Ivan Starov. :ut the really major changes were to ome with new construction work.

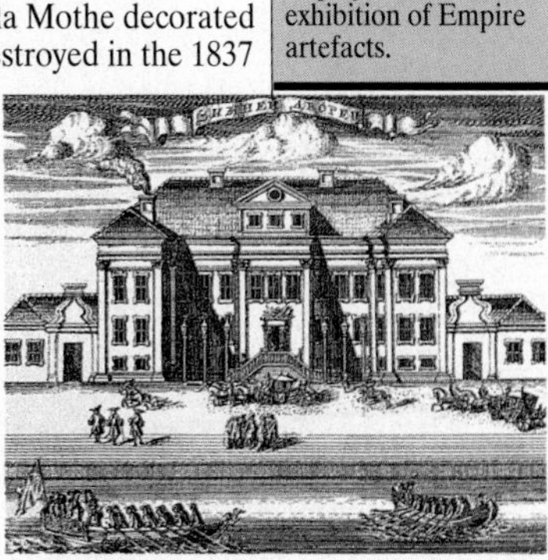

Built by Bartolomeo Rastrelli (1754–62), Elizabeth I's Winter Palace is laid out around an immense closed courtyard with four projecting pavilions at the corners. The main portions of the building facing the Neva and Palace Square are linked by closed lateral galleries with apartments, service areas and staircases giving on to them. The center of the façade giving onto the Neva is barely evident by comparison with the projecting pavilions on either side of it. Although the Palace Square was built much later, the entrance to the courtyard was always by way of the triple arch on the city side.

The entrance to the New Hermitage was from Khalturin (Millionaires') Street, through a monumental gateway. It was built by the German architect Leo von Klenze between 1839 and 1851 and is supported by ten sculpted figures of Atlas.

During the Revolution Guards occupying the Winter Palace, October 24, 1917.

The Theater (e)
Built in the antique style, it has a semicircular auditorium and décor inspired by the Olympic Theater at Vicenza (Italy).

The Winter Palace (a)
Major alterations were made to the Winter Palace's corner pavilions in the 19th century. The Ambassadors' Staircase (or Jourdain Staircase) was built in the northeast corner; the sovereign used this staircase on January 6 (Epiphany) each year on his way to bless the waters of the Neva in memory of Christ's Baptism.

The Small Hermitage (B)
Beginning in 1736, Vallin de la Mothe built a hanging garden here, with a pavilion at each end. The north pavilion, which was called the Hermitage, was finished in 1770. But Catherine II's growing art collection eventually required another building, the Large Hermitage, to be built.

The Large Hermitage (C)
Built in two stages, the Large Hermitage was the work of Yury Velten (1771–87). It occupies a site between the palace and the Winter Canal dug by Peter the Great between the Neva and the Moika. Its name was changed in the 19th century to the Old Hermitage.

The New Hermitage (d)
The imperial collections were saved from the fire which devastated the Winter Palace in December 1837. To house and display them to the public, it was decided in 1839 that a New Hermitage should be built. The museum was opened by Nicholas I in 1852.

"Composition VI"
The work of Vasily Kandinsky is displayed on the third floor of the south wing of the Winter Palace, after the Fauvist section. This painting, *Composition VI*, is an example of a work from the artist's Abstract period.

After the 1837 fire Stasov rebuilt the Ambassadors' Staircase. He also restored the curve of the stairs, recreated the fanciful golden moldings against their white background, and reinstated the trompe-l'œil windows with their mirrors.

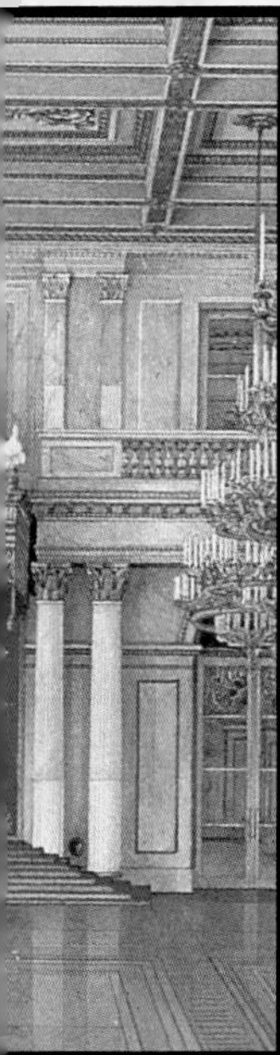

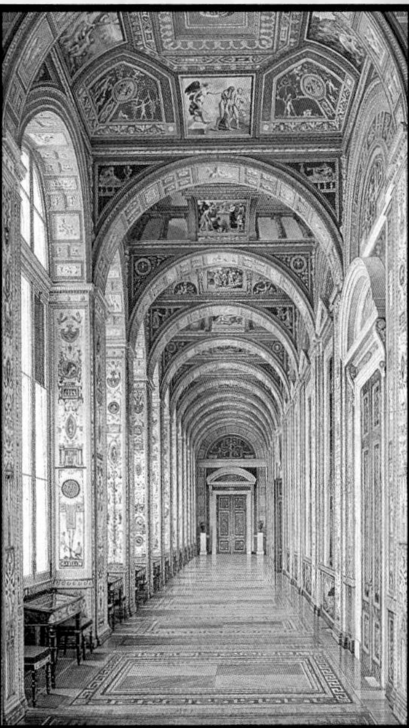

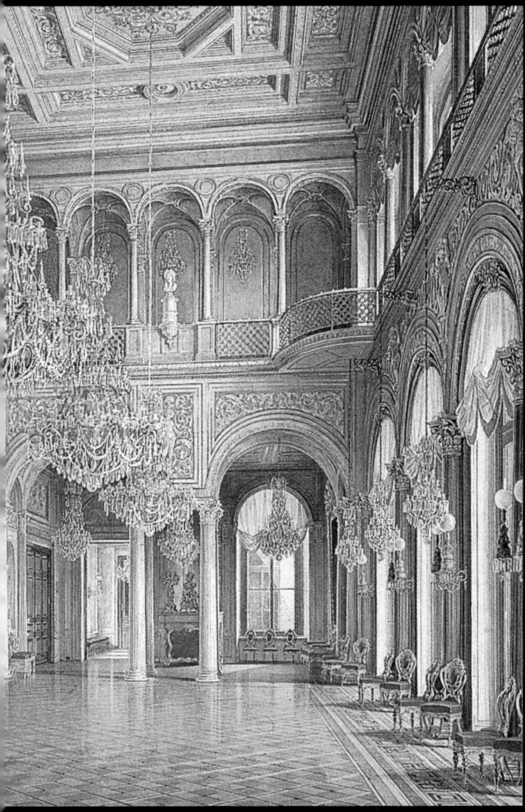

Th[illegible] 1812 Ga[illegible] still bears the [illegible] of Rossi, its decorator. Here are displayed the portraits of the Russian generals who took part in the war against Napoleon. The Alexander Hall (**1**) contains a medallion with the profile of Alexander I, and moldings of warlike themes symbolizing t[illegible]zar's victory in t[illegible]ar of 1812–14. Bry[illegible]decorated this [illegible] clusters of Goth[illegible]olumns, two-headed eagles and classical medallions. The Hall of St George (**3**) is decorated with Carrara marble columns with gilded bronze capitals. The Throne, now installed in the Hall of Peter I, formerly stood below the bas-relief of Saint George and the Dragon. In the Pavilion Hall (**4**) copies of mosaics from Roman spas are set in the floor. This hall also contains reproductions of the Fountain of Tears from the Bakhtchisarai Palace in the Crimea. On the orders of Catherine II Quarenghi painted a reproduction of Raphael's *Loggia* (**5**) at the Vatican along the Winter Canal side of this room (1783–92).

[illegible]	3	5
2	4	

The history of the Hermitage as a museum began with Peter the Great, who himself bought a number of works of art – among them *David and Goliath* by Rembrandt and the *Tauride Venus*. In the reign of Catherine II the imperial collections occupied rooms in the Hermitage of the Winter Palace, which gave its name to the museum. The museum is considered to have been officially born in 1764, when the Berlin dealer Gotzkowski sent the Empress of Russia 225 paintings intended for Frederick II of Prussia, in payment of a debt. Later, on the advice of Diderot among others, Catherine bought many more works of art (and above all complete collections) in Paris, Dresden and London.

VENETIAN PAINTERS
The series of galleries at the Old Hermitage includes works such as *Judith* (left) and *Madonna and Child* by Giorgione (1477–1510). One room is devoted to paintings by Titian (c. 1490–1576), among which are several masterpieces, including *Danaë*, *Mary Magdalen*, *Portrait of a Woman*, *Christ Carrying the Cross* and *Saint Sebastian*.

17TH–18TH CENTURY SPANISH PAINTINGS
The collection includes works by El Greco (*Saint Peter and Saint Paul*), Velasquez (*The Meal*, also known as *The Drinkers*), Zurbaran (*Saint Laurence*), Murillo (*Child with Dog*) and (right) Goya's *Portrait of Antonia Sarate*.

THE GOLDEN COMB OF SOLOKHA (above)
The collections of antique, oriental and Scythian jewelry, as well as gold and silverwork from Western Europe, are displayed in a special area. This golden comb is from the collection of Scythian jewelry, of which the Hermitage has some outstanding examples.

ITALIAN ART, 13TH–18TH CENTURIES
Among the many masterpieces in the section, don't miss the following: *The Virgin of the Annunciation* (Simone Martini); *The Vision of Saint Augustine* (a fresco by Filippo Lippi); *Virgin and Child with Saint Thomas and Saint Dominic* (Fra Angelico); *Saint Dominic and Saint Jerome* (Botticelli). The Italian majolica room has two paintings by Raphael: *Madonna Conestabile* (above) and *The Holy Family*. In the first glazed gallery are Veronese's *Conversion of Saint Paul* and Tintoretto's *Birth of John the Baptist*. In the large glazed gallery are 17th- and 18th-century paintings, including works by Tiepolo and Canaletto.

THE "BENOIS MADONNA"
The great gallery of the Old Hermitage exhibits two famous piantings by Leonardo da Vinci : *Benois Madonna*(1478, above) and the *Litta Madonna* (early 1490-1). This painting, previously known as the *Madonna of the Flower*, is named after one of its former owners.

Crouching Youth (right), the only work by Michelangelo in Russia, was created for the Medici Tombs in Florence.

Dutch painting in the 15th and 17th centuries

The most remarkable works in this collection are Campin's diptych, *The Trinity* and the *Virgin at the Hearth*, *Saint Luke Painting the Virgin* by Van der Weyden, *The Healing of the Blind Man at Jericho* by Van Leyden, and *The Adoration of the Magi* by Van der Goes. All 17th-century genres and great masters are represented, except for Vermeer. There are two portraits by Hals, landscapes by Van Goyen and Van Ruisdael, and pictures by Van Ostade, Steen, De Hooch and Ter Borch. In the Rembrandt Room are twenty-five pictures spanning the painter's entire career, from *The Sacrifice of Abraham* (1635) (right) and *The Descent from the Cross* (1634) to *David and Uriah* and *The Return of the Prodigal Son* (mid-1660's).

17th–19th century English painting

This section of the museum comes after the room devoted to works by Fragonard and Greuze. Note in particular *Love Untying Venus's Girdle* and *The Infant Hercules Killing the Serpents* (below, by Reynolds); and *The Duchess of Beaufort* (by Gainsborough). Also here is the work of landscape painters contemporary with Constable, including *Boats near the Shore* by Richard Parkes Bonington (1801–28

Detail of Rembrandt's *The Return of the Prodigal Son* (left)

"Saskia as Flora"
This painting by Rembrandt dates from the first years of his marriage to Saskia van Uylenborch, shown here as a goddess of Roman mythology.

15th–19th century German painting

n this section eligious painting is isplayed alongside Renaissance portraits nd 17th-century till lifes. The great nasterpieces here nclude Cranach the Elder's *Venus and Cupid* (below), *Virgin nd Child Under n Apple Tree* and *Portrait of a Woman*; s well as *Portrait f a Young Man* by Ambrosius Holbein nd *Erasmus of Rotterdam* by Hans Holbein the Younger 1497–1543). There are also ome fine still ifes by Christoph Paudiss (1618–66) nd Hendrik an der Borcht he Elder 1583–1660).

Nineteenth-century German paintings are shown on the third floor, in a series of rooms parallel to those housing the Matisse collection. The group of paintings by the Romantic artist Caspar David Friedrich (1774–1840) are not to be missed.

17th-century Flemish paintings

Many of the paintings exhibited in this section are works by the major Flemish portraitists of the period. The section includes twenty-six pictures by Van Dyck, including his fine *Portrait of Charles I*, *Self-Portrait* and *St Peter the Apostle*. Of the forty works by Rubens the most notable are *Christ with Crown of Thorns* (above), *The Alliance of Earth and Water*, *Perseus and Andromeda*, *Landscape with Rainbow* and *Portrait of Isabella of Spain's Lady-in-Waiting*. The fame of the collection of Flemish paintings in the Hermitage rests on the museum's holdings of works by these two masters.

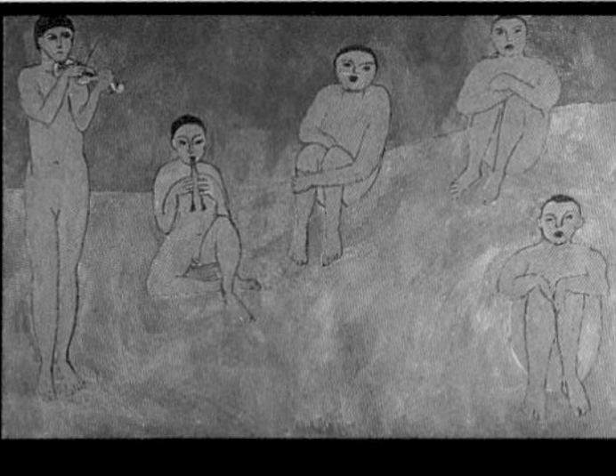

"La Musique" The collection of paintings by Matisse (1869–1954) in the Hermitage is one of the largest and most representative in Europe. The thirty-seven paintings exhibited include *La Danse* and *La Musique*.

15th–18th century French painting This collection of French painting rivals that of the Louvre itself. The major works here are Le Nain's *The Milkmaid's Family*, Poussin's *Tancredi and Hermine* and *Landscape with Polyphenus*, Watteau's *The Little Savoyard* and *The Awkward Proposal*, and Fragonard's elegantly suggestive *Stolen Kiss* (left).

19th century French art This collection is the pride of the Hermitage, particularly because it includes some paintings of international importance. Among the works dating from the first half of the 19th century are *Bonaparte at the Bridge of Arcole* (Gros); *Morpheus and Iris* (Guérin, left *Portrait of Count Guriev* (Ingres); *Lion Hunt in Morocco* and *Arabs Saddling a Horse* (Delacroix).

FRENCH PAINTING, LATE 19TH TO EARLY 20TH CENTURY
Mainly assembled by the Muscovite collectors Morozov and Shchukin at the beginning of this century, this collection is one of the finest in the world. It includes six paintings by Renoir (among them *Portrait of Jeanne Savary* and *Young Woman with a Fan*), five pastels by Degas, including *Young Woman at her Toilet* (below, left); eight landscapes by Monet, eleven Cézannes, four van Goghs (including *The Bush*, above left), fifteen Gauguins from the artist's Tahiti period (left), eight paintings and thirteen panels by Denis, eight canvases and triptychs by Bonnard, two Vuillards and six Vallotons. The Fauvists are represented by nine Marquets, five Vlamincks, fourteen Derains and five Van Dongens. To cap it off, there are thirty-one paintings by Picasso and thirty-seven by Matisse. Below, *Absinthe Drinker*, 1901, by Picasso.

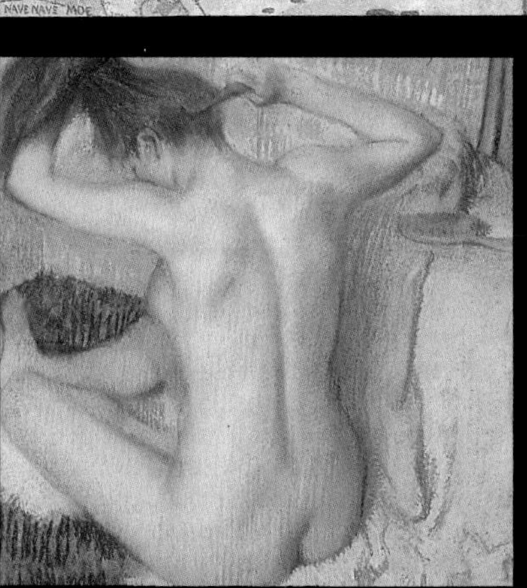

Bloody Sunday
Gathered on Palace Square on January 22, 1905, the demonstrators asked to be allowed to present a petition to the Czar Nicholas II (who was not in the palace).

The police fired on the crowd; the resultant carnage created an unbridgeable gulf between the Czar and his people and provided the impetus for revolution.

Palace Square

An imperial esplanade. Even though the entrance to the courtyard of the Winter Palace ▲ *168* was originally planned not for the Neva side but for the city side of the building, Palace Square (Dvortsovaya Ploshchad; Дворцовая площадь) was laid out at a relatively late date. The architect Bartolomeo Rastrelli ● *84* had proposed a semicircular colonnade to transform the area into a gigantic courtyard and provide a counterpoint to the Baroque façade of the Winter Palace. But Empress Elizabeth died before the completion of the project and Catherine II dismissed Rastrelli when she ascended the throne. All this time the square was no more than a huge field; but in 1772 the architect Starov resurrected the idea of a colonnade, which Catherine had rejected, although the semicircular plan appealed to her. Finally, in 1779 the Arts Academy launched a competition, which was won by Yury Velten ▲ *162*. Opposite the palace he built a half-circle of houses with identical façades. Still, the ensemble lacked real grandeur, and Carlo Rossi ● *86* was commissioned in 1819 to lay out a more regular square.

The General Staff Headquarters. The main function of the buildings fronting the square was to provide a general headquarters for the Army's main staff. In 1819 it was decided that Russia's administrative center should also be moved here, concentrating the Ministry of Finance and the Foreign Ministry in the same place. Carlo Rossi went back to the old semicircular layout as defined by the existing buildings, and put all of them behind a single façade, the center of which was pierced by a huge triumphal arch, the Arch of the General Staff. The skill with which this was accomplished is famous in the annals of architecture. The arch, sited directly on the axis of the main palace entrance, had to link the square with the curved street coming from the

Palace Square
The Winter Palace, Admiralty Gardens, former headquarters of the General Staff, and the Guards' former headquarters bound this huge area.

Nevksy Prospekt. Rossi therefore devised a "turning" arch – that is, one doubled with a part forming an arc of a circle which made it possible to pass from the fixed plane to the curve of the street while preserving the illusion of depth. The Arch is decorated Roman-style with military trophies and laurel-crowned worthies. On its top is a team of six bronze horses harnessed to the chariot of Glory. In 1840 the square was rounded off on its east side by the Headquarters of the Guard, designed by Alexander Bryulov.

THE ALEXANDER COLUMN (ALEKSANDROVSKAYA KOLONNA; Александровская колонна). This gigantic column was raised in the middle of the square (1830–4) in honor of Alexander I ● *36*, who prevailed against the armies of Napoleon. The idea came from Rossi, but the design was completed by Auguste Ricard de Montferrand. The 90-foot monolith of pink Finnish granite is crowned by an angel: the total height of the monument is nearly 150 feet. The pedestal is decorated with allegorical bas-reliefs of the rivers Nieman and Vistula (crossed by the Army in pursuit of Napoleon) on one side, and Wisdom and Abundance, Peace and Justice, Victory and Peace on the other.

CARLO ROSSI (1775–1849)
Rossi was born in St Petersburg, the son of an Italian ballerina. Beginning his career as the assistant of Brenna, he studied in Italy before returning to Russia to complete his architectural masterpieces, among them the Palace Square.

THE ALEXANDER COLUMN
The 600-ton column, brought from Finland in 1832, was raised onto its base using a system of winches similar to that later used for St Isaac's Church ▲ *195*. Myth has it that the column is perfectly balanced and whoever can lift it will find gold and treasure hidden underneath.

PUSHKIN'S HOUSE
The poet's study and his 4,000-book library (above) have been carefully preserved as they were when the Pushkin family lived here. Pushkin died in this house on January 29, 1837 ● *117*.

THE MOIKA EMBANKMENT

CAPELLA ● **72.** The original Capella (no. 20), known as the Glinka Singing Academy in this century, was founded by Peter the Great; the present school was built in 1880 by the architect Leonty Benois at the end of a courtyard. The auditorium is separated from the street by high cast-iron railings which link two identical buildings. The Capella ensemble is a fine example of eclectic late 19th-century décor.

DLT STORE (Dom Leningradskoi Torgovli). This store backs on to the Moika Embankment (NAB. REKI MOIKI; наб. реки Мойки), although its main entrance is at no. 21 Bolshaya Konnushenaya. Built by the architect E.V. Virrich (1908–10), it is important in the history of St Petersburg architecture as one of the first metal-and-glass structures in the city. The huge salerooms were patterned on the Parisian *grands magasins* built at the turn of the century.

PUSHKIN MUSEUM (MUZEY-KVARTIRA PUSHKINA; музей-квартира Пушкина). An earlier house on this site (no. 12, built in the 1730's) belonged to the Volkonsky family. This mansion was replaced in 1770 by another in the classical Russian style, and subsequently altered extensively. Six fluted Corinthian pilasters distinguish the projecting central section, of the height of two floors, with a curved façade reflecting the bend in the river. On the courtyard side are broad arches (now glassed in) which still incorporate elements of the original building. The Pushkin family rented the second floor here in 1836.

Arms of the Volkonsky Family.

IMPERIAL STABLES. The first imperial stables were built in 1720 for Peter the Great, by the architect N.F. Gerbel. The buildings were laid out around a polygonal courtyard. Although entirely reconstructed on the same site by Vasily Stasov between 1816 and 1823, they have retained their original form, specifically the curve imposed by the Moika. The CHURCH is contained in the square central portion of the façade giving on to the square. This somewhat complex ensemble included not only the stables and the riding ring, but also several warehouses, the administrative offices (the master of the stables was an

"The Neva, with its bridges and piers, is the true glory of St Petersburg. The prospect of it is so immense that everything else is tiny by comparison. The Neva is a basin filled to the brim; its banks merge with the water, which seems about to overflow on every side. Venice and Amsterdam seem to me much better defended against the sea than is St Petersburg."
Astolphe de Custine, *La Russie en 1839*

mportant figure in the imperial service), the lodgings of the taff and the church.

ALACE EMBANKMENT

HE WINTER CANAL BRIDGE. The Winter Canal meets the Neva by the Old Hermitage. The bridge that spans it is haracteristic of those built by Yury Velten in the 1770's as art of the works carried out on the banks of the Neva, its ributaries and the various canals.

HE FORMER / NEW MIKHAIL PALACE. Built by htakenshneider (1857–61) for Mikhail Nicolayevich, son of Nicholas I ● *36*, this palace (no. 18) occupies a site bordered n one side by the Palace Embankment (DVORTSOVAYA NAB.; Дворцовая наб.) and on the other by Millionaires' Street. It ollows the alignment of the other houses, blending well with he other private mansions of the quarter, although its lower evel is notable for its French Renaissance-style panels and ilasters. The rear façade, however, is much more modest, nd was reserved for the Grand Duke's domestic servants and taff. The dimensions of the palace are impressive, and it is aid that one of the Grand Duke's sons would borrow a icycle to visit his sister-in-law, whose quarters were located n another part of the palace.

Left to right: The galleried bridge across the Winter Canal, built by Yury Velten to link the Winter Palace with the theater ▲ *168*; the façade of the Hermitage ▲ *168* on the Neva side; and a detail of the façade of the Academicians' House. This former palace at no. 26 Palace Embankment, built by Alexander Rezanov (1867–71), includes many Italian Renaissance and Baroque elements. The red sandstone façade is itself strongly reminiscent of Florentine palaces.

BESIDE THE NEVA
The Palace Embankment owes its name to the residence of the Czars, today's Hermitage Museum ▲ *168*. The consolidation of the river banks with granite was undertaken over fifteen years, beginning in 1763, with the architect Yury Velten playing an important role.

THE MARBLE PALACE

FLOOR PLAN OF THE MARBLE PALACE
This follows the traditional U-design of urban palaces, with a courtyard fronting the main entrance.

A GIFT OF THE EMPRESS. For nearly twelve years Catherine II was the mistress of Count Grigory Orlov (1734–83). During this time she presented him with the Marble Palace (MRAMORNY DVORETS; Мраморный дворец). Orlov, with his brothers Alexei and Fyodor, led the conspiracy against Peter III that placed Catherine II on the Russian throne. The palace was built (1768–85) by the architect Antonio Rinaldi on a site between the Palace Embankment and Millionaires' Street. The main façade has four Corinthian columns at its center. The original entrance was via the Red Canal, which ran along the west side of Marsovo Pole. This canal was filled in during the 19th century, when a service wing was added and a new main entrance was built in the courtyard at the side of the palace.

GRANITE AND MARBLE. The contrast between the rough granite of the first floor and the refined marble of the upper levels, from which its name derives, gives the Marble Palace an original if somewhat severe aspect. Its roof was formerly covered in copper sheeting, while the window frames of the *piano nobile* were of gilded bronze, with polished glass panes. Marble was as much in evidence inside the building as outside. The main FORMAL STAIRCASE and the MARBLE ROOM (left) are still in their original state. From 1937 to 1991 the Marble Palace housed the Lenin Museum. Serving since 1992 as an annex of the Russian Museum ▲ *225*, it now contains an exhibition of works by foreign artists living in Russia, and the Lüdwig Donation.

A RECENT ARRIVAL
In the courtyard of the Marble Palace stands an equestrian statue of Alexander III, which replaced Lenin's armored car in November 1994. The statue, originally erected on Insurrection Square (Pl. Vostaniya) ▲ *244*, was brought from the Russian Museum, its home since 1937.

THE FIELD OF MARS

MARSOVO POLE (MARSOVO POLE; Марсово поле). With the Summer Garden to eastward, the Moika to the south, the Red Canal to the west and the Neva to the north, this broad area was not given its final form until 1817–19, when the architect Vasily Stasov (1769–1848) built the Pavlovsky barracks at the same time as Carlo Rossi was completing the Mikhail Palace. Their joint efforts led to a definitive project for the quarter, and the layout of the various green spaces was dictated by the architecture they designed.

BARRACKS OF THE PAVLOVSKY GUARDS REGIMENT (KAZARMY PAVLOVSKOVO POLKA; казармы Павловского полка). The west side of the square is entirely occupied by this gigantic building. At the center of its long yellow façade are twelve Doric columns, crowned by a monumental pediment

decorated with the usual trophies, weapons and winged victories. There are pavilions on either side in front of the building topped by a triangular pediment, which is echoed by a similar arrangement fronting Millionaires' Street. In the middle of Marsovo Pole, now laid out as a park, stands the Liberty Monument (right), formerly known as the Monument to Revolutionary Fighters. On the Neva side the quadrilateral ends at Suvorov Square; and in the center is a statue of Field Marshal Suvorov ▲ *252*.

Marsovo Pole
Like its Paris equivalent, Marsovo Pole (Field of Mars) was used for military events, which played an important part in the daily lives of the Czars, notably that of Paul I.

Adamini House. On the southwest side of Marsovo Pole, the corner house (no. 7) with a semicircular colonnade was built by the architect D. Adamini (1823–7) in the later classical style ● *86*. The basement of this building was a meeting-place during World War One and the Revolution for Russian artists like Vsevolod Meyerhold, Alexander Blok, Anna Akhmatova, Mikhail Kuzmin, Vladimir Mayakovsky and Anatoly Lunacharsky.

"Montagnes russes"
In the old days Marsovo Pole was a favorite venue for the thoroughly Russian sport of sliding down an artificial slope on a small sledge or vehicle. In the rest of Europe this was known as *montagnes russes*; it was practiced as much by the Czars in their palaces as by peasants in the countryside. *Montagnes russes* could be extremely sophisticated, as at Oranienbaum ▲ *262*.

Saltykov and Betsky houses. On the north side, fronting the waters of the Neva, Giacomo Quarenghi built the Saltykov House (1784–8); in 1820 it became the Austrian Embassy. It was celebrated for the salon over which presided the ambassador's wife, the grand-daughter of Marshal Kutuzov.

The *Tauride Venus*.

SUMMER GARDEN (LETNY SAD; Летний сад)

A GARDEN IN THE FRENCH STYLE. In 1704 Peter the Great made a rough sketch of a Western-style garden, with rare plant species brought from Siberia, the Urals, Holland and Kiev. The French model won the Czar's favor after his visit to Versailles in 1717, and as a result the gardens, which extend between the Neva to the north, the Fontanka to the east and the Moika to the south, are regular and symmetrical. The gardens were divided into quadrilaterals which were planted with trees and (in the old days) shrubs and flowers. There were also cunningly devised fountains and sculptures.

STATUES FROM ITALY. Most of the statuary in the Summer Garden was bought in Italy, according to the vogue of the early 18th century. Subjects from Greek mythology include

GATES OF THE SUMMER GARDEN After consolidating the Neva's banks, Velten worked on the Embankment fronting the gardens and on the Summer Palace. The wrought-iron garden gates that he competed in 1784 were considered to be one of the finest examples of metalwork of the period.

SUMMER GARDEN ✪ Praised by poets, the Summer Garden is particularly attractive in summer. From November to April its famous statues, masterpieces of European sculpture, are clothed in wooden cases to protect them from frost.

"The Summer Garden is the Jardins du Luxembourg of the St Petersburgers; they are designed to form a square, with the Fontanka on one side and a ditch on the other. Everything, both inside and outside, is precisely measured."

Alexandre Dumas

upid and Psyche, and the *Tauride Venus*, excavated at Rome; while real-life history is represented by the busts of Agrippina, hristina of Sweden and Jean Sobiesky. The *Venus*, ransported with the utmost care from Italy, was Peter the Great's favorite piece. He placed it in the gallery at the ntrance to the garden, but moved it later to the grotto, where he had it guarded by a sentinel for fear that it would e damaged. Today the *Venus* is in the Hermitage Museum *168*.

LEASURE GARDENS. Pavilions, a grotto, an aviary, a nenagerie and an orangery were installed in the Summer Garden, as Peter directed. Thirty-six granite monoliths, with lternating urns and vases as amortizements, frame the lements of the wrought-iron railing with its gilded points. In 777 serious flooding destroyed the machinery, the channels nd all the fountains, which were never repaired. Finally, arlo Rossi built a COFFEE HOUSE (1826) and Louis harlemagne a TEA HOUSE (1827) in the park. In 1855 a nonument by Piotr Klodt was raised to Ivan Krylov, the Russian Aesop".

"As I was smiling at this extraordinary collection, I saw the Czarina, preceded by Count Gregorius Orloff, and followed by two ladies, approaching . . . I stood by the hedge to let her pass, but as soon as she came up to me she asked, smilingly, if I had been interested in the statues. I replied . . . that I presumed they had been placed there to impose on fools, or excite the laughter of those acquainted with history."

Jacques Casanova

UMMER PALACE

ETER I'S PROPERTY. In 1711 Peter the Great built his Summer Palace ● *83* LETNY DVORETS; Летний дворец) at he juncture of the Fontanka and the Neva beside his Summer Garden. The onstruction was based on the "model ouse" commissioned from the rchitect Domenico Trezzini ● *83*. n 1713 the German Andreas Schlüter oubled the size of the Summer Palace nd completed the building's decoration, making bay windows in the pale yellow brick-and-staff walls. Between the windows he placed terracotta bas-reliefs; these were inspired by various mythological themes which could be seen to reflect Russia's military victories.

THE ROOMS. The interior of the Summer Palace is arranged in the Dutch style, with tall faience stoves and furniture which is simple in style. The walls of the vestibule are lined with beautifully carved panels, and also feature a relief depicting Minerva, who was the goddess of wisdom and of war.

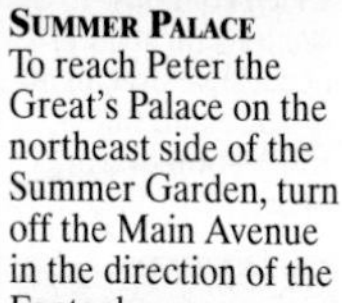

SUMMER PALACE
To reach Peter the Great's Palace on the northeast side of the Summer Garden, turn off the Main Avenue in the direction of the Fontanka.

A WALK IN THE SUMMER GARDEN
In the 19th century the trees in the gardens were allowed to grow unpruned, in the English manner, and its shady avenues became famous. Pushkin, who lived nearby, often came here to read in the mornings, wearing his dressing gown.

FONTANKA EMBANKMENT

LAW SCHOOL. The houses which ran along the Fontanka Embankment (NAB. REKI FONTANKI; наб. реки Фонтанки) in the 18th century were mostly rebuilt in 1835 by Melnikov, who adapted them for a new purpose. The Law School (no. 6) has two floors above a tall stylobate. A colonnade occupies the center and domes stand at the corners; the interior was completed by Vasily Stasov.

BRIDGES ACROSS THE FONTANKA
The Prachechny Bridge (Laundry Bridge) was so named because of the laundries on the left bank of the Neva. Built at the junction of the Fontanka and the Neva (1766–9), it was one of the elements in the project to consolidate the banks of the Neva and was the city's first three-arched stone bridge. Between the Prachechny Bridge and the Panteleimon Bridge (right) runs the "green wall" of the Summer Garden.

THE CHURCH OF ST PANTELEIMON (TSERKOV SV. PANTELEIMONA; церковь св. Пантелеймона). This church is the last remaining vestige of the old merchant shipyards, which occupied this quarter after 1739, and to which the salt warehouses were added at the end of the 18th century. It was dedicated to Saint Panteleimon, to commemorate the Russian fleet's victory over the Swedes in 1714 in Hangö Bay on St Panteleimon's Day. The church, which has a dome on an octagonal drum, is completed by a Baroque bell tower.

MUSEUM OF DECORATIVE AND APPLIED ARTS (MUZEY DEKORATIVNO- PRIKLADNOVO ISKUSSTVA; музей декоративно-прикладого Искусства). The glass cupola visible from the Fontanka Embankment is that of an art school (no. 12, Solyanoi Street) founded by Baron Stieglietz and built (1879–81) at his expense by the architects Krakau and Hedich. Within the complex is the museum, built (1885–96) by the architect Mesmacher for the students.

MUSEUM OF DECORATIVE AND APPLIED ARTS
A huge dome spans the main exhibition room, covering a surface of nearly 4,000 square feet. The buildings belong to an art school, which contains sections on styling, decorative arts, haute couture and the restoration of works of art.

From the Admiralty to the Haymarket

▲ From the Admiralty to the Haymarket

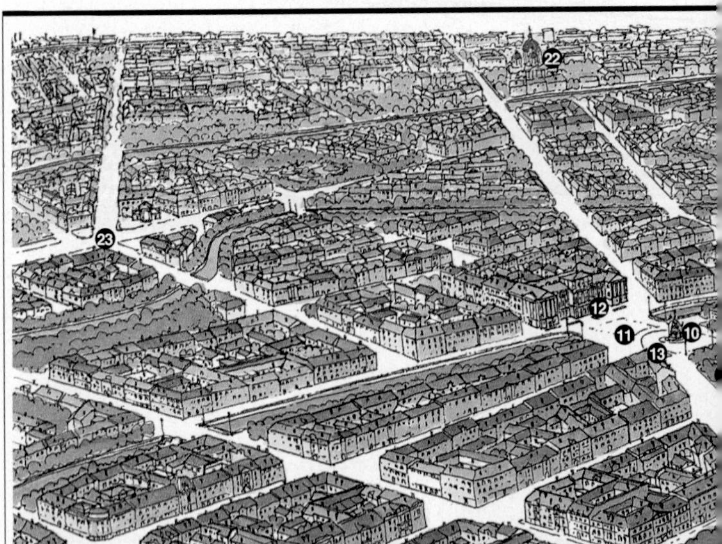

1. Admiralty
2. Admiralty Embankment
3. Decembrists Square
4. Monument to Peter I
5. Riding School
6. Senate and Synod
7. Alexander Gar
8. St Isaac's Cathed

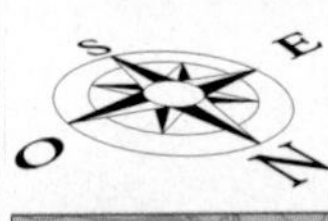

One day

◆ A-D

In the early years of St Petersburg the smartest residential quarters extended over what is now the Petrograd Side ▲ *148* and Vasilyevsky Island ▲ *156*. By contrast, those of the Admiralty were purely utilitarian, occupied by craftsmen and soldiers in their barracks. With the closure of the Admiralty's naval dockyards an altogether grander kind of house began appearing on the far side of the Neva.

The Admiralty

The naval dockyards. The Admiralty (Admiralteistvo; Адмиралтейство) is a focal point of the city: three major thoroughfares converge on it, and its spire is one of the great landmarks of St Petersburg. The first Admiralty building marked the edge of the dockyards and gave onto the Neva. It was protected by a line of fortifications, with moats and bastions. After it was rebuilt in brick in 1738 the Admiralty was made up of two major constructions separated by an

9. St Isaac Square
10. Monument to Nicolas I
11. Blue Bridge
12. Mary's Palace
13. Astoria Hotel
14. Bolchaya Morskaya
15. Central post Office
16. New Holland
17. Yusupov Palace
18. Mariinsky Theater
19. Conservatoire
20. Synagogue
21. St Nicolas's Cathedral
22. Trinity Church
23. Haymarket

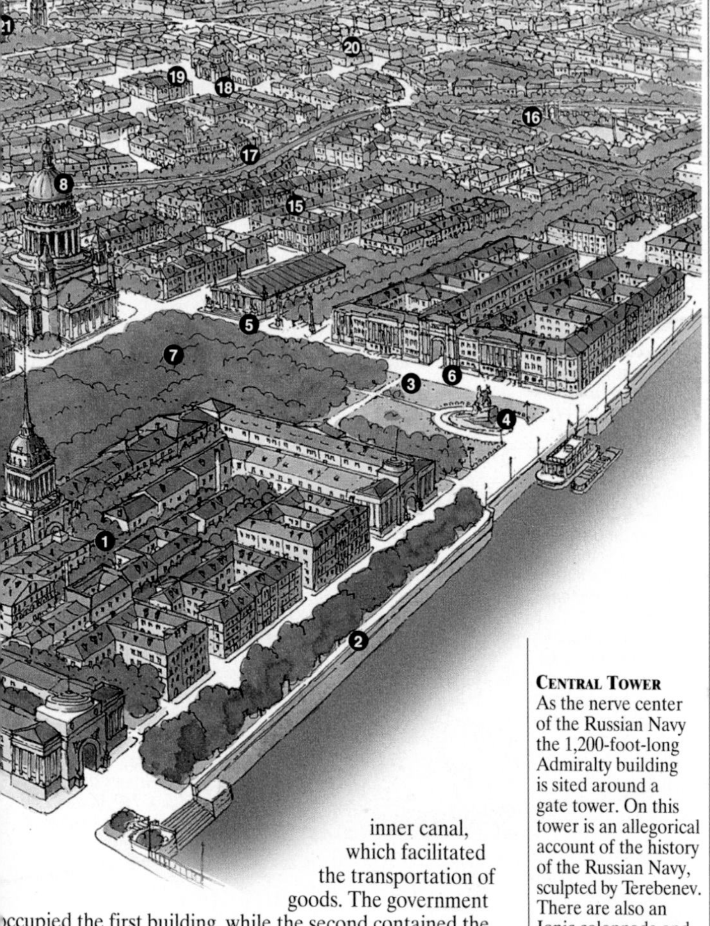

Central Tower
As the nerve center of the Russian Navy the 1,200-foot-long Admiralty building is sited around a gate tower. On this tower is an allegorical account of the history of the Russian Navy, sculpted by Terebenev. There are also an Ionic colonnade and various statues.

inner canal, which facilitated the transportation of goods. The government ›ccupied the first building, while the second contained the :arpentry shops, the forges, the cordwainers' shops, the ;eneral workshops and the reserve supplies ıeeded for each body of craftsmen.

Headquarters of the General Staff. In 1718 :he Admiralty became the Headquarters of Peter I's General Staff. For a while after this :he porches of the pavilions at its ends were ronted by a canal on its way to the Neva, which vas not filled in until the mid-19th century. In :he old days red flags would be hoisted on the :oofs of these pavilions to warn the people of ımpending floods. Later a complex of buildings vas erected on the site of the old dockyards ›etween the Neva and the two wings, effectively :oncealing the Admiralty from passers-by on the :mbankment. It is now a military zone, closed to the public with the exception of the central tower.

THE "POLTAVA"
The keel of the first Russian ship of the line, the *Poltava*, was laid in December 1709.

Confronted by the naval power of Sweden Peter the Great, the "Father of the Russian Navy", decided to build a fleet worthy of the name. Originally the port of St Petersburg was set on Birch Island, where the city center evolved later in the 18th century. In 1733 i was transferred to the point of Vasilyevsky Island, and a stock exchange, a customs house, a merchant's court and other port installations were built. The Admiralty served both as the Navy Ministry and as a naval dockyard until 1844. At the close of the 19th century its precinct was densely built up and became known as the Admiralty Embankment.

KRONSTADT
From the 18th century onward Kronstadt was Russia's principal naval base; but after the appearance of steamships in the 1850's merchant cargoes began to be unloaded there, for transportation to St Petersburg on lighters. According to a popular saying of the period, "The voyage from London to Kronstadt is much shorter than the voyage from Kronstadt to the point of Vasilyevsky Island." In 1885 the port was moved to Gutuyevsky Island.

THE "GRANDFATHER OF THE RUSSIAN FLEET"
This was the name given to Peter the Great's first ship ▲ *149*, in which he learned to navigate.

THE ADMIRALTY
Toward 1738 the Admiralty was rebuilt. Its initial floor plan remained the same, but stone now replaced the original wood and clay materials. The Tower was raised to a height of over 200 feet. In 1823, after reconstruction works undertaken by the architect Andrei Zakharov, the building assumed its present appearance. Even before the completion of the works in 1829 the Navy Ministry was transferred here from Moscow, and a bureau was set up for the use of Czar Alexander I.

THE GALLEYS
In Russia the word "galley" was applied to any warship with oars. The crews of these vessels were made up of soldiers and sailors in the pay of the Army. The construction and repair of the galleys was carried out at the dockyards of Galley Island, west of the Admiralty.

THE FIRST DOCKYARDS
The construction of the first factory in St Petersburg, the Admiralty's naval dockyard, began on November 5, 1704. Peter I noted in his diary: "This day we laid the foundations of the Admiralty amid great joy and celebration. The building is to be 200 sagens in length and 100 sagens broad [1 sagen = 6½ feet]."

THE EMBLEM OF THE CITY
A spire was added to the Admiralty Tower in 1719, with a golden apple and a weathercock in the form of a caravel.

MONUMENT

ÉLEVÉ A LA GLOIRE

DE PIERRE-LE-GRAND.

PETER THE GREAT
Peter I surveys the city he founded from horseback, in the pose imagined for him by the French sculptor Etienne Falconet, who won a competition arranged by Catherine II in 1765. The sculpture was not completed until 1778; it represents the Czar ascending a rock and trampling a serpent (symbolizing the Swedes) underfoot. This statue was the inspiration for one of Pushkin's most celebrated poems, "The Bronze Horseman" ● *118*.

DECEMBRISTS SQUARE

DECEMBRISTS SQUARE (PL. DEKABRISTOV; пл. Декабристов) owes its name to the protagonists of one of the more painful episodes in the history of St Petersburg and Russia ● *42*.

EQUESTRIAN STATUE OF PETER I. Contrary to the fashion of the day, the Czar is represented neither as a Roman emperor nor as a prince of his own time. Instead he wears a long robe, a mantle, soft leather boots and a simple sword at his side – the garb of an ordinary Russian prince. Only the crown of laurels on his head, sculpted by a pupil of Falconet's, Anne-Marie Collot, reminds us of his rank. On either side of the plinth are four words, which translate: "To Peter I, Catherine II".

THE RIDING SCHOOL (THE MANÈGE). Designed by Quarenghi (1804–7), with sculpted décor by Paolo Triscorni, the Riding School is a low quadrangular building not unlike a Greek temple, with a double colonnade and pediment.

VICTORY COLUMNS. Following the disappearance of the Admiralty dockyards the canal connecting the site with the New Holland district was covered by a brick arch which became the Horseguards Boulevard. On a granite pedestal here are winged Victory figures in bronze, modeled by Christian Rauch (1845–6) and presented to the Czar by the King of Prussia in commemoration of their joint victory over Napoleon.

SENATE AND SYNOD. By creating new institutions for Russia Peter the Great managed to disarm those of his opponents who were obstructing his reforms. He suppressed the Patriarchate which had hitherto wielded absolute power over the Church, and replaced it by a Synod, with authority to settle all religious questions. Likewise in 1711 he outmaneuvered the Duma of the Boyars by setting up a nine-member Senate to manage affairs of state in his absence. The architects Rossi and Stasov designed twin buildings for these institutions

A VISTA OF BRIDGES ✪
On summer evenings, when the bridges ● *90* spanning the Great Neva are bathed in the mysterious light created by diffused sun beams ● *28* (known in Russia as 'white nights'), enthusiasts for the nightly opening of the bridges gather around the statue of the Bronze Horseman. As orchestras assemble on the English Embankment and Admiralty Embankment, bankside cafés and restaurants begin to fill with customers. It is worth being there when the bridges are opened: Palace Bridge opens at 1.35am and Lieutenant-Schmidt Bridge at 1.40am.

(1829–34), which were connected by an arch spanning Galernaya Street. The columns are set forward, with a heavy entablature decorated with statues of angels. A frieze in bas-relief emphasizes the attic, in the center of which is a sculpted group featuring allegories of Probity and Justice. In the direction of the Neva, the Senate building is distinguished by a colonnade which curves round to meet the embankment. Today the Senate and Synod buildings contain historical archives; they also incorporate the Palace of Count Laval, whose daughter followed her husband, the Decembrist Trubetskoy, into exile in Siberia.

ALEXANDER GARDEN. The Alexander Garden (ALEKSANDROVSKY SAD; Александровский сад) was planted for the two-hundredth anniversary of the birth of Peter the Great, and covers the fortifications and moats which formerly defended the Admiralty. The statues here are mostly copies of antique originals made in the 18th century, along with busts of famous Russians like Gogol, Lermontov, Glinka and Zhukovsky.

ST ISAAC'S CATHEDRAL

St Isaac's Cathedral had difficult beginnings. Between the first church, built of wood on the present site of the Senate, and the project of Rinaldi, inherited by Renna and rejected by Montferrand, nearly a dozen architects seem to have tried to build this cathedral on its sodden, unstable site.

MONUMENT TO PRZEVALSKY
This statue in the Alexander Garden, sculpted by Schroeder in 1882, celebrates the explorer Przevalsky (1839–88), who went out to discover Asia on behalf of the Imperial Geographical Society. In his account of his travels Przevalsky described the wild camel whose image now graces his statue's plinth, along with the rare Siberian horse species which was named after him ▲ *151*.

THE FIRST ST ISAAC'S CHURCH
Wishing to honor the saint on whose feast day he was born, Peter I dedicated what was later to become St Petersburg's largest place of worship to an obscure Dalmatian monk.

Montferrand left an album of watercolors showing the different stages of the cathedral's construction, from the transportation of the columns to their erection.

A technical exploit. The architect Auguste Ricard de Montferrand, who designed the cathedral as we know it (1818–58), gave it a Byzantine floor plan, somewhat lengthened. He solved the problem of unstable foundations by setting the 300,000-ton building on 11,000 pilings, reconciled the dictates of the disposition of the square and the orientation of the Christian sanctuaries, and added deep porches with double rows of columns to the north and south façades. These monolithic columns, made of Vyborg granite brought by sea from Finland, are over 50 feet high and weigh 114 tons each. Before constructing the main dome Montferrand made a study of similar European buildings; his greatest innovation was his use of cast iron for the rafters.

Realistic décor. To give his monstrous brainchild at least a veneer of lightness, the architect used materials of contrasting colors: for example, the gray granite of the walls offsets the pink columns, while the bronze of the pediments, statues, monumental doors and capitals echoes the gold of the domes. The décor of the interior ● *88* is extremely lavish; the two columns supporting the central door of the iconostasis ● *56* are paneled wit lapis lazuli, while all the inside columns are coverec in malachite.

St Isaac's Cathedral
The upper parts of the building are classical in style, with a huge dome, four smaller bell towers, and abundant statuary on the roof.

St Isaac's Square ★

Conceived as a whole and remodeled by Montferrand as part of the work on the cathedral, St Isaac's Square (Isaakievskaya Pl.; Исаакиевская пл.) was no more than a huge building site at the time when Rossi was busy with the Senate and the Synod.

Monument to Nicholas I. This equestrian statue (1859), the work of the sculptor Piotr Klodt, represents the Czar in the uniform of the Horse Guards. The pedestal is decorated with four bronze bas-reliefs of the principal episodes of his reign.

The pedestal is decorated with four bronze bas-reliefs of the principal episodes of his reign. Between the motifs are allegorical statues of Justice, Strength, Faith and Wisdom, which have the features of the Empress and the daughters of the Czar, who together commissioned the monument.

Mariinsky Palace (Mariinsky Dvorets; Мариинский дворец). This palace, built (1839–44) by Shtakenshneider, is the final element of the square. Intended for the Grand Duchess Maria, daughter of Nicholas I, it replaced an older construction of Vallin de la Mothe. It was purchased by the State in 1884 and was used thereafter by the Council of the Czar's Ministers. After the Revolution it became the seat of the Provisional Government of the Russian Republic; today it is the headquarters of the St Petersburg Municipal Council.

The Blue Bridge
Despite its diminutive span the Blue Bridge (Siny Most; Синий мост) across the Moika is the broadest in St Petersburg (nearly 300 feet). It was once made of wood and painted blue – hence the name – while its neighbors were red and green.

Bolshaya Morskaya

This main thoroughfare (once Herzen Street) begins at the Arch of the General Staff ▲ *180* and intersects Nevsky Prospekt ▲ *214* and St Isaac's Square.

Astoria Hotel. The Astoria (neoclassical and Art Nouveau) was designed by the architect Lidwal in 1911. The first and second floors are faced with granite decorated with medallions, garlands and mascarons, while the façades are punctuated with pilasters. In 1917 the Astoria was a focus of resistance to the Revolution, which was invested on November 7 by Red Guards and sailors. In the first years of the Soviet regime it was the headquarters of the Petrosoviet. In 1990 it was merged with the neighboring Angleterre Hotel (where the poet Sergei Esenin committed suicide in 1925) and entirely renovated.

Lobonov-Rostovsky mansion
This majestic private mansion on the corner of Decembrists Square and the Voznesensky Prospekt occupies a three-cornered site. It was built by the architect of St Isaac's Cathedral, Auguste Ricard de Montferrand (1817–20).

DEMIDOV MANSION
The gateway here is flanked by Atlas figures and caryatids supporting a richly sculpted balcony. At the turn of the century Demidov Mansion was the Italian Embassy; today it is a machine-tool training institute.

GAGARIN HOUSE
The pavilion at no. 45, next door to Demidov Mansion, was built in the 1840's. It is now the Composers' House.

DEMIDOV MANSION. This building (no. 43) bears the name of an industrialist whose family made a fortune from mines in the Urals. Constructed between 1836 and 1840, the Demidov Mansion was inspired by Italian Renaissance architecture and is laid out around an inner courtyard. Formerly it had a hall that was entirely covered in malachite taken from its owner's mines, and this served as the model for the one in the Winter Palace ▲ *172*.

NABOKOV'S HOUSE. Vladimir Nabokov (below, with his mother) was born in St Petersburg in 1899 and grew up in no. 47. The scion of a liberal aristocratic family, Nabokov was a privileged child and idolized by his mother; he recalls his happy youth in his memoir, *Other Shores*. Following the October Revolution the Nabokovs left Russia for Europe; the writer then emigrated to the United States in 1940, adopting U.S. citizenship. The house contains the Nabokov Museum.

POLOVTSEV MANSION. This lavish townhouse (no. 52), also called the Architects' House, was built (1835–6) by Pel. The Senator A. Polovtsev, who acquired it in 1860, was also the president of the Russian Historical Society. The interior is notable for its neo-Gothic library, a gilded hall and a salon decorated with malachite and bronze. The restaurant at Polovisev Mansion, which was once used exclusively by architects, is now open to all.

CENTRAL POST OFFICE

The first post office, or Postamt, founded by Peter I in 1714, was on Suvorov Square ▲ *186*. It was later transferred to larger premises on the present Millionaires' Street; and in 1782 Catherine II moved it to the present site. This was the departure point for the post coaches which criss-crossed the Russian Empire; all the milestones in the nation indicated their exact distance

rom the Postamt. In 1859, when the Post Office was in need
f more space, it expanded to the other side of Postamt Street
nd a covered gallery in the form of an archway was built to
onnect the two buildings. Clocks were hung here, showing
he time in the major foreign capitals. Today the Postamt still
ulfills its original function.

NOVAYA GOLLANDIYA (NEW HOLLAND DISTRICT)

HE FORMER TIMBER STORES. The Novaya Gollandiya
istrict covers an area that was once a Navy storage depot
onstructed on an artificial island skirted by the Admiralty,
ryukov and Moika canals. Before the depot was built,
imber used for shipbuilding was kept at the Admiralty
▲ *190*, in close proximity to the yards, where it was seasoned
n the Dutch fashion; for this reason the wood store was
nown as "New Holland". The immense building with
s rounded corners is characteristic of the work of the
rchitect Vallin de la Mothe, who was commissioned
o construct the market galleries. The bare brick
difice that ultimately resulted is virtually blind
n its exterior, with nothing but small-paned bay
vindows on the corners.

HE ARCH ● *88*. A large pool stands at the center of
he store area, which can be reached by boat through
n archway high enough to admit fairly substantial
uperstructures. This arch is classical in design,
ramed by two columns bearing a Doric frieze.
he arch itself rests on smaller columns. The
usterity of the architectural design is relieved
o some extent by the colors of the brick walls and
he metopes, which contrast with the gray granite
olumns and triglyphs. The district of Novaya
Gollandiya has been associated with the Russian
Navy for as long as it has been in existence; today it
emains a military zone, and is not open to the public.
n the 19th century it was used as a prison. In more recent
imes it has been suggested that the Novaya Gollandiya
istrict should be converted into a cultural center, or a
ourist area which would incorporate hotels and boutiques.
A third project has been proposed that would move the
Naval Museum into the precinct, as this institution is at the
noment somewhat cramped in its present building at the
Stock Exchange ▲ *157*.

"My mother's boudoir had an overhanging window, which was convenient for looking outside, since it had a view across Morskaya Street toward Mariya Square . . . from this window, a few years later, at the start of the Revolution, I observed more than one skirmish, and for the first time in my life I saw a dead man."

Vladimir Nabokov

APARTMENT OF ALEXANDER BLOK
The apartment in which the writer spent a few months (no. 57, Decembrists Square) is now a museum displaying mementos of his life, amid the sober surroundings he favored.

From the 18th century onward the Mariinsky was the imperial ballet theater. Among the five theaters maintained by the court (two in Moscow and three in St Petersburg) it was especially favored from the time of Nicholas I. Nothing was too lavish for the ballets of the Imperial Theater, which was endowed with sumptuous décors created by court artists such as Roller and (later) Golovin and Benois. Known as the Kirov under the Sovie regime, the Mariinsky reverted to its original name in 1992.

Marius Petipa (1818–1910)
A world-renowned choreographic genius, Petipa was ballet master at the Mariinsky from 1869 to 1903. He put on more than sixty performances and was one of the architects of academic ballet.

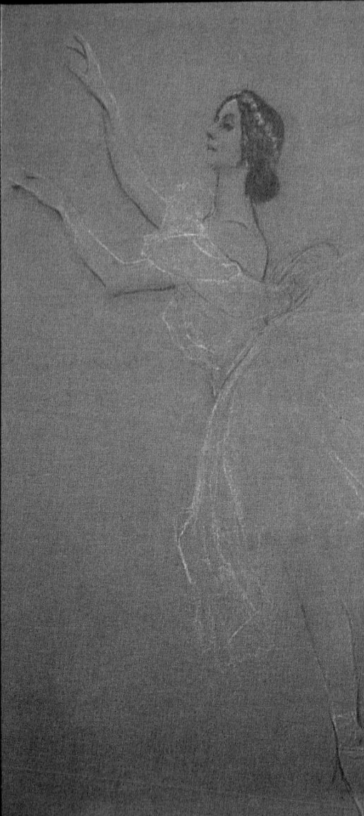

The Kirov Ballet
From 1935 the Mariinsky Ballet was known as the Kirov Ballet, in honor of Sergei Kirov ● *49*. The repertoire of the Soviet period included Tchaikovsky's *Queen of Spades*, among other productions.

Mikhail Baryshnikov
In the 1950's and 1960's a new generation of dancers emerged. The most gifted of these, like Mikhail Baryshnikov, crossed the Iron Curtain, preferring to try their luck in the West.

Pavlova (1881–1931)
No choreographer before Petipa had celebrated the ballerina with so much brio. His ballets brought a whole constellation of dancers to the fore, including Mathilda Kshesinskaya, O. Presbrazhenskaya and Anna Pavlova.

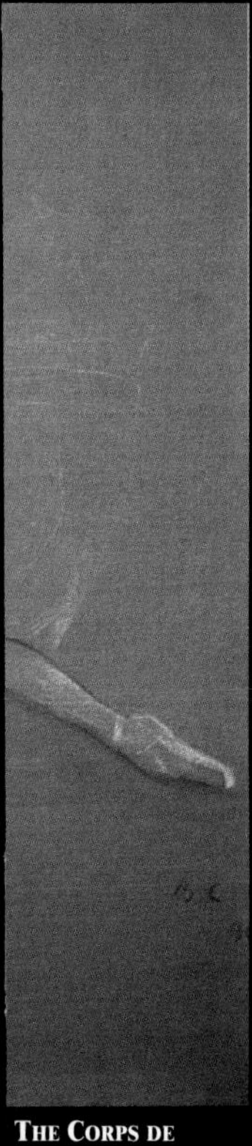

The Corps de Ballet
The genius of Petipa reached its climax in his collaboration with the composers Tchaikovsky and Glazunov. With *The Sleeping Beauty* (1890), *Swan Lake* (1895) and *Raymonda* (1898) Petipa created a style in which the *corps de ballet* became an essential component of the choreographic language.

Yusupov Palace

Built by Vallin de la Mothe in the 1760's, the Yusupov Palace (Yusupovsky Dvorets; Юсуповский дворец) was converted at the end of the 19th century for Princess Zinaida Yusupov. Seriously damaged during World War Two, it has since been heavily restored and its magnificent art collection moved to the Hermitage. The interior decoration of the palace testifies to its former brilliance; the formal salon, the Moorish Salon, and the Buffet Room (where the acoustics are extraordinary) in particular. So as not to overload the slender vaulting of the Ballroom, which was not strong enough to support crystal or gilded bronze, the chandeliers were fashioned of gilt papier-maché so that they resembled metal. An Italianate theater (above) is situated in the North Wing of the building.

The death of Rasputin. On the first floor of the Moika side of the building a concealed entrance leads to a salon in which exclusive parties were given; it was in this salon that Rasputin ● *37*, the hypnotic monk who oscillated between spirituality and debauchery, met his horrible end. In the uneasy atmosphere of the period, Rasputin's mesmeric gift had given him enormous power over the Empress and her entourage. To rid the court of this inconvenient character Prince Felix Yusupov plotted his murder, in which the Grand Duke Dmitry also had a hand. Felix Yusupov died in Paris in 1967.

The poisoning of Rasputin
In the basement of the Yusupov Palace there is a waxwork which recreates the décor and atmosphere of Rasputin's gruesome murder.

Theater Square ✪

Theater Square (Teatralnaya Pl.; Театральная пл.) contains, in close proximity, two of the main institutions of the musical life of St Petersburg.

The Mariinsky Theater. Between 1847 and 1848, A. Kavos, St Petersburg's chief theatrical architect, built a theater that also doubled as a circus. Circus acts with performing horses, acrobatic shows and trapeze acts took place in its central arena. Badly damaged by fire in 1859, the building was replaced the following year by a conventional theater. Named the Mariinsky Theater in honor of the Empress Maria Alexandrovna, consort of the Emperor Alexander II, the theater began its first season with *A Life for the Czar*, a work by Glinka that signaled the birth of classical Russian opera. It was nationalized in 1917, and from 1935 to 1993 was known as the Kirov Ballet. It has now

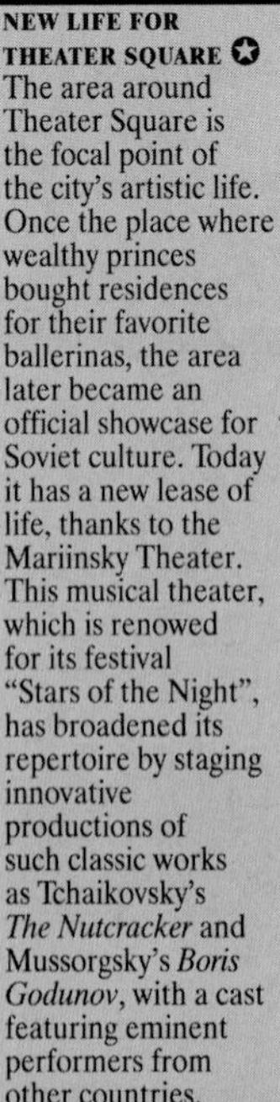

New life for Theater Square ✪
The area around Theater Square is the focal point of the city's artistic life. Once the place where wealthy princes bought residences for their favorite ballerinas, the area later became an official showcase for Soviet culture. Today it has a new lease of life, thanks to the Mariinsky Theater. This musical theater, which is renowned for its festival "Stars of the Night", has broadened its repertoire by staging innovative productions of such classic works as Tchaikovsky's *The Nutcracker* and Mussorgsky's *Boris Godunov*, with a cast featuring eminent performers from other countries.

reverted to its original name. During the Soviet era the theater continued to mount operas and ballets by native Russian composers such as Prokofiev and Shostakovich. The theater's current director is Valery Gergiev, whose primary objective is to revive the great masterpieces of Russian opera. The ballet company, which still enjoys international renown, continues to tour the major capitals of the world.

The Conservatoire. The site on which the Conservatoire now stands was originally occupied by the Great Theater. Built in the late 1770's, during the reign of Catherine the Great, it was at the time the only permanent theater in St Petersburg. Between 1891 and 1896 it was completely rebuilt: the new building, designed by the architect V. Nicol, was to house the Conservatoire that the pianist Anton Rubinstein had founded in 1862. It was the first advanced music school in Russia, teaching seven disciplines; these were musical theory and composition; choir and orchestra conducting; singing; orchestral instruments; piano and organ; ballet and opera direction; and traditional instruments. The Conservatoire has two auditoriums: in the larger of the two, pupils give public performances; the smaller one, which has magnificent acoustics, a painted ceiling and a gallery of portraits of musicians, is used for Russian and international festivals and competitions.

Statue of Nikolai Rimsky-Korsakov ▲ *239* in front of the Conservatoire.

Synagogue
The Jewish community of St Petersburg was heavily repressed prior to the reforms of Alexander II ● *36*. In 1893 the construction of a synagogue and cultural center confirmed these reforms; the synagogue, at no. 2 Lermontov Street, is built in the Moorish style.

In an area once overwhelmingly inhabited by sailors, this cathedral was understandably dedicated to their patron, Saint Nicholas. With its blue, white and gold exterior, St Nicholas' Cathedral is similar in many ways to Smolny, which was built by Rastrelli; indeed Chevakinsky, the architect of St Nicholas, was a pupil of the Italian. A remarkable illustration of religious Baroque, this church remained open throughout the Soviet era.

BESIDE THE KRYUKOV CANAL

The cathedral is built to the classic Greek cross plan, with a central cupola and four turrets at each corner, topped by onion domes ● *57*. On the exterior the composition is punctuated by columns backed against the walls. The lower church (there is no crypt, because of likely flooding) supports a richly embellished upper one. Services are held on the upper level, where the décor is especially lavish because of the largesse of Catherine II, who presented ten gold-covered icons to commemorate ten naval victories. The equally gold-laden iconostasis ● *57*, of carved wood, was executed between 1755 and 1760. The bell tower is separate from the church proper ● *85*, standing at the entrance to the cathedral precinct, where it is reflected in the Kryukov Canal ▲ *210*.

2

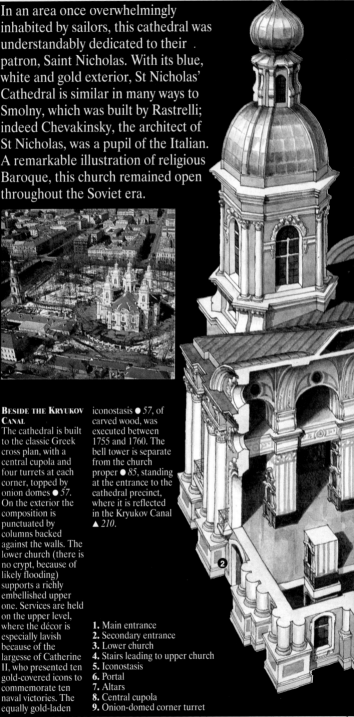

1. Main entrance
2. Secondary entrance
3. Lower church
4. Stairs leading to upper church
5. Iconostasis
6. Portal
7. Altars
8. Central cupola
9. Onion-domed corner turret

8
9
5
6
7
3
1

SENNAYA PLOSHCHAD
In Dostoevsky's time the crowded and filthy Haymarket was known for its low dives, taverns, cabarets, brothels and prostitutes' hotels. The district exercised a deep fascination on Raskolnikov, the hero of *Crime and Punishment*: at the close of the novel, visiting the Haymarket for the last time, "... he let himself fall to the ground ... on his knees in the center of the square, he bent and kissed the muddy stones with ecstasy and delight ... then he straightened, and prostrated himself a second time."

HAYMARKET SQUARE

From St Nicholas' Cathedral, Sadovaya Street (SADOVAYA UL.; Садовая ул), typical of 19th-century St Petersburg, leads through to Haymarket Square (SENNAYA PL.; Сенная пл.). At the end of the 18th century there was a huge market here where hay, oats and straw were sold, hence the name. The Haymarket area was once one of the worst slums of St Petersburg, but today the old buildings have been replaced by buildings constructed after World War Two. The only original edifice still standing is the Police Station, with its four-columned classical portico.

THE CHURCH OF THE ASSUMPTION IN HAYMARKET SQUARE, now demolished, was built in the mid-18th century to a project by A. Kvasov, in which Rastrelli had a hand. It was the architectural focus of the square. Closed in 1938, the church was knocked down in 1961 to make way for the Sennaya metro station.

DOSTOEVSKY DISTRICT ★

A HERMETIC SPACE. Dostoevsky never had a house of his own in St Petersburg; instead he was constantly on the move,

"Few places exercise on the human spirit so somber, violent, and strange an influence . . ."

Fyodor Dostoevsky

hanging his domicile a score of times in ıe eight years he lived in the city center. ıs a rule he chose buildings that faced hurches. Whether large and spacious or arrow and closed off, a room for ostoevsky had a profound underlying ıeaning. Time and again the image of ıe oppressive, constricting bedroom ppears in his books. This hermetic pace, bounded by a corner, a wall, a alisade or an alleyway, is a frequent haracteristic of his work; it has the value f a symbol, expressing the inner life of ıe hero and his state of mind.

UT OFF FROM THE WORLD. Dreamers, men of the underworld" with ravaged onsciences, the heroes of Dostoevsky lways live in "corners"; they flee the eality that surrounds them. The writer imself nearly always lived on street-corner houses, hich made him feel even more isolated from the rest f the world than he actually was. He had a clear reference for Vladimir Square ▲ *238* and the Haymarket. It was here that he set his characters, who alked the same streets as he did and saw the same uildings and scenes from their windows as he saw. he lives of both Dostoevsky and his heroes are eamlessly blended with the life of St Petersburg self. Indeed, this may be one reason why ostoevsky moved with such regularity: once he ad completed a novel, he became impatient to leave the places which his art and his imagination had transformed into fiction.

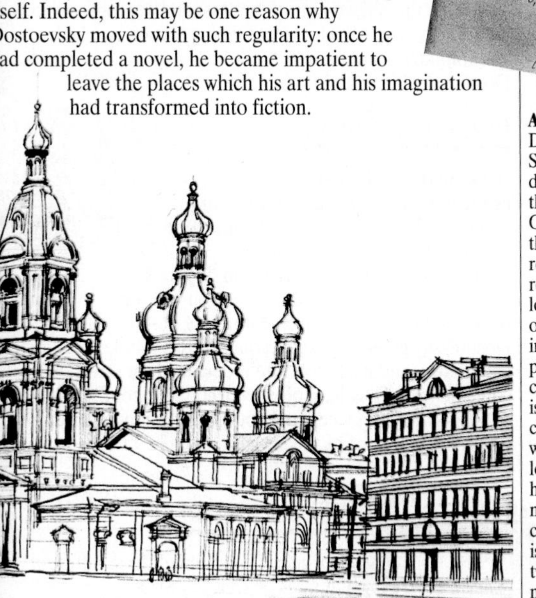

A CITY REINVENTED Dostoevsky's St Petersburg has two dimensions, one real, the other imaginary. On the one hand, there is the city which really existed, with real people and locations; and on the other, there is the imagined metropolis, peopled by invented characters, which is such a strong characteristic of his work. Dostoevsky loved his city, where he had grown up and made his literary career. St Petersburg is present in about twenty of his thirty novels, sometimes as a background but more often as a character in its own right.

DOSTOEVSKY DISTRICT

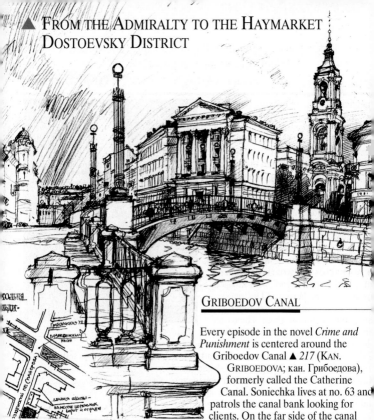

GRIBOEDOV CANAL

Every episode in the novel *Crime and Punishment* is centered around the Griboedov Canal ▲ *217* (KAN. GRIBOEDOVA; кан. Грибоедова), formerly called the Catherine Canal. Soniechka lives at no. 63 and patrols the canal bank looking for clients. On the far side of the canal stands the building occupied by the moneylender Alena Ivanovna, the old woman whom Raskolnikov robs and kills with an axe. No. 65 was the old Police Station to which Raskolnikov is summoned, and which Dostoevsky himself visited.

ASCENSION BRIDGE
❝Raskolnikov went straight to X Bridge, stopped in the middle of it, leaned his elbows on the parapet, and looked down . . . with his head craned over the water, he began mechanically to contemplate the last pink rays of the setting sun … Eventually red circles emerged before his eyes, and the houses, passers-by, quays, coaches and everything else began spinning and dancing around him.❞
Crime and Punishment

PRZEVALSKY STREET

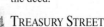

RASKOLNIKOV'S HOUSE. The corner house here, no. 5, is thought to be the model for Raskolnikov's. In the mid-19th century this three-story building belonged to a man called Joachim. If you turn right after entering the porch you will see in the corner the door which gives onto the staircase described in the novel. Dostoevsky gives an exact account of Raskolnikov's comings and goings, and his hero's fate is decided by a series of coincidences. Thus Raskolnikov, who has carefully thought out everything he needs to do before he commits his crime, finally forgets to bring an axe with which he intends to do the deed.

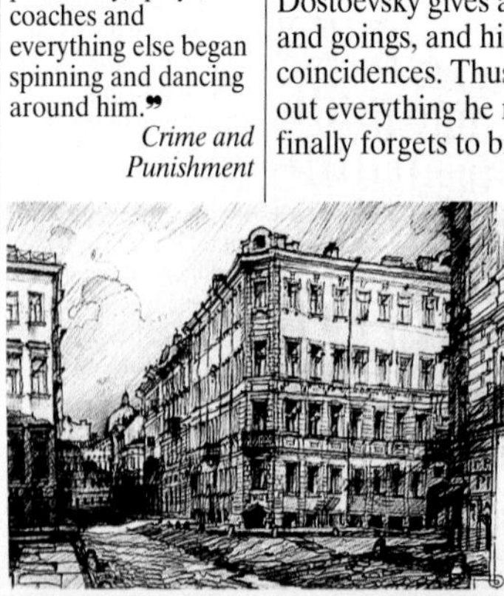

TREASURY STREET

Dostoevsky occupied three different houses in Treasury Street (KAZNACHEYSKAYA UL.; Казначеская ул.), close by the Haymarket, known as Petit Bourgeois Street until the turn of the century. The writer, who was already famous, lodged in one of the most wretched slums in St Petersburg; not

"He hadn't the least desire to go into the street like that. And as for going home, that would be even worse. 'A beautiful opportunity, lost forever!' he muttered, standing with dangling arms under the porch just in front of the concierge's tiny lodge, which was also open. Suddenly he gave a start. Within the lodge two steps away, something was shining on the bench, just to the right."
Crime and Punishment

because he liked the romantic, meandering Catherine Canal, or because he wanted to study the sordid existence of the tenants of the surrounding buildings, but because he simply did not have the means to live elsewhere. Considering that "the mind is narrowed by small lodgings", he preferred to have two spacious rooms, a luxury which was very expensive in the grander districts of the city.

OLONKIN HOUSE. This house (no. 7), on the corner of Treasury and Przevalsky streets (the latter used to be called Carpenters' Lane), was Dostoevsky's home from August 1864 to January 1867. It was here that he wrote *Crime and Punishment* and received his second wife, Anna Grigorievna Snitkina, for the first time. The two also worked together for the first time at this house, when Anna (whom he had engaged to help him finish a novel, *The Gambler*, in double-quick time) took down his dictated text in twenty-six days. The building contained a wine-shop and tavern kept by a tradesman, Efimov; and although the district was noisy at all hours Dostoevsky mostly worked at night.

THE "TIMES". Dostoevsky's elder brother also lived on Petit Bourgeois Street; together they edited and published the *Times* and *Epoch* reviews.

ASCENSION PROSPEKT

Ascension Prospekt (VOZNESENSKY PR.; Вознесенский пр.) features in nearly every one of Dostoevsky's novels set in St Petersburg. He lived there himself between 1847 and 1849, and again in 1867. In the 1860's one of his friends, Apollo Grigoriev, also lived in the street, which appears often on the itineraries of Raskolnikov, of Arkady Dolgoruky in *Raw Youth*, and of the characters in *Insulted and Injured* and *The Eternal Husband*.

THE CHIL HOUSE. Dostoevsky lived here, at nos. 8–23, from spring 1847 to April 23, 1849 while he was writing *White Nights*, *The Landlady* and *Netoshka Nezvanova*. And it was here, also, that he was arrested, in the night of April 22–3, 1849.

"With his heart failing him, trembling with nerves, he approached an enormous house, one side of which backed on to the canal, with the other overlooking X Street. This building was divided into a crowd of small apartments, whose tenants were artisans of every kind: tailors, locksmiths, cooks, Germans, prostitutes, petty functionaries, etcetera. People went in and out through the two carriage entrances."
Crime and Punishment

THE KOLOMNA DISTRICT 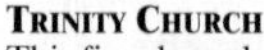
Between Kryukov Canal and the Great Neva to the west lies the Kolomna district. This quiet quarter of the city seems still to be slumbering in the 19th century, and this is how Pushkin described it in his poem "The Little House in Kolomna". Consisting of four islands and having nine embankments and twenty bridges, the appealing Kolomna district can be explored by boat, revealing yet another aspect of St Petersburg, "the Venice of the North".

TRINITY CHURCH
This five-domed building, constructed by Stasov between 1828 and 1830, supplanted an 18th-century wooden church.

KRYUKOV CANAL

Beside the Kryukov Canal stands the clock tower of St Nicholas' Cathedral ▲ *204*, a fine three-story building of harmonious proportions. This is one of the most romantic corners of St Petersburg, and it was not for nothing that Dostoevsky set what is perhaps his most poetic novel, *White Nights*, around the Kryukov and Catherine canals.

2ND ISMAILOV BATTALION STREET

From this street, where Dostoevsky lived in 1872 and 1873, the writer could see the Trinity Church, which was where he was married to Anna Grigorievna Snitkina in 1867.

PIONEERS' SQUARE

"We, the Petrashevtsy, heard out our sentence of death standing on the scaffold without a trace of remorse. I cannot speak for all of us, but I do not think I am mistaken when I affirm that at that instant, in that minute, the majority among us were very close to dishonoring themselves by forsaking their convictions."
Journal of an Author

It was on Pioneers' Square (PIONERSKAYA PL.; Пионерская пл.), formerly known as Semenovsky Square, that the members of the Semenovsky circle were led to believe they

had been condemned to death (December 22, 1848). Those who had been present at the meetings of this literary and political group, at which Vissarion Bielinsky's letter was read out ▲ *237*, appeared before a military tribunal, who condemned them to death after eight months' imprisonment in the Peter and Paul Fortress ▲ *146*. At the last moment the sentence was commuted to deportation to a labor camp. Afterward Dostoevsky recorded in *The Idiot* Prince Myshkin's description of the minutes they spent in the full expectation of death.

Around Nevsky Prospekt

▲ Nevsky Prospekt

The buildings along Nevsky Prospekt recount the history of this main thoroughfare, laid down through the forest in the decade following 1710. The road was originally laid with tree-trunks; gradually houses and palaces began to be built along its length, the most beautiful structures concentrated between Palace Square and the Fontanka (the original limit of the city). In the mid-18th century it was baptized Nevsky Prospekt, after the monastery to which it led. This avenue, over 2½ miles long, is “at once the most elegant street and the chief shopping area of St Petersburg . . . being an original blend of shops, palaces and churches; on the signs gleam the beautiful characters of the Russian alphabet.” (Théophile Gautier)

AT THE HEART OF THE CITY ✪
In St Petersburg, every street leads to Nevksy Prospekt, which, according to Nikolai Gogol, was “the hub of all communication”. Shops selling all sorts of goods attract a cosmopolitan crowd. At the corner of no. 56 Malaya Sadovaya Street, a pedestrianized thoroughfare lined with cafés, benches and old-fashioned street lights, is a fountain with a granite globe that is turned by the flow of water. Visitors will also admire the attractive interior courtyards that line the street.

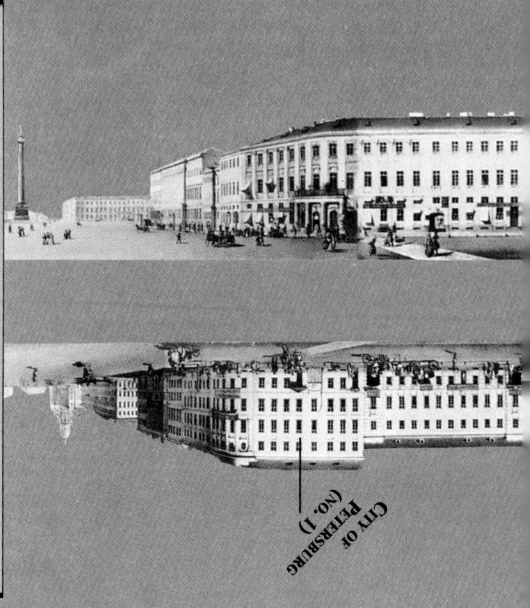

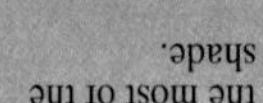

Shady Side (uneven numbers) Here the buildings were provided with galleries, loggias and colonnades to make the most of the shade.

City of Petersburg (No. 1) This late 18th-century building was altered between 1910 and 1912 by Ziedler, on behalf of the Commercial Bank of Petersburg.

Sunny Side (even numbers)
Despite their diversity the façades of the buildings along the sunny side of the Prospekt give an overall sense of elegance and unity.

Karl Bryulov (no. 6)
The painter Karl Bryulov stayed at this address in 1836, where Nikolai Gogol visited him several times to pose for his portrait.

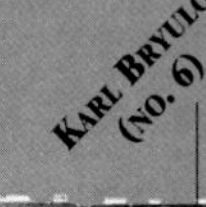

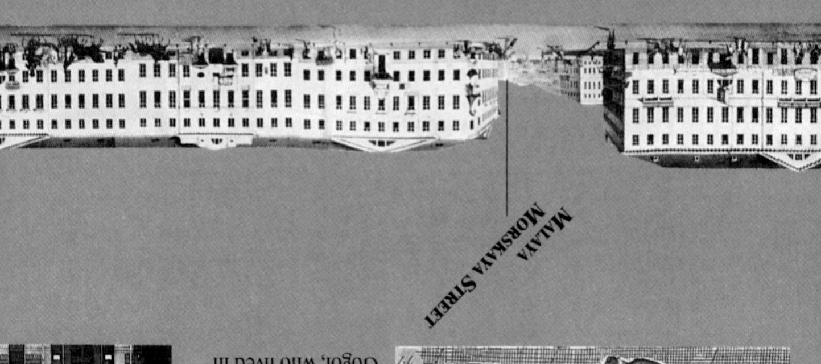

Malaya Morskaya Street

Malaya Morskaya Street
From 1902 to 1992 this street bore the name of one of its most famous residents, Nikolai Gogol, who lived in an apartment at no. 17 between 1833 and 1836. He wrote *Taras Bulba* here.

During the siege
No. 14 has a poignant reminder of the siege of Leningrad: a plaque reads, "Comrades! In the event of artillery fire, this side of the street is the most dangerous."

Bolshaya Morskaya Street
Before reverting to its original name Bolshaya Morskaya Street was rebaptized Herzen Street, after the writer (right) who lived at no. 14. Bolshaya Morskaya Street cuts directly across Nevsky Prospekt. The even street numbers end at the Arch of the General Staff. At nos. 3–5 the former Azovsko-Donskoy bank (1908–9) provides another example of the luxurious tastes of the old financiers. This building has now been converted into a telephone exchange.

"Wolff and Béranger" (no. 18)
Pushkin met his second, Danzas, at this pastry-shop on January 27, 1837, before his final duel ● *116*. The literary café here opened in 1985.

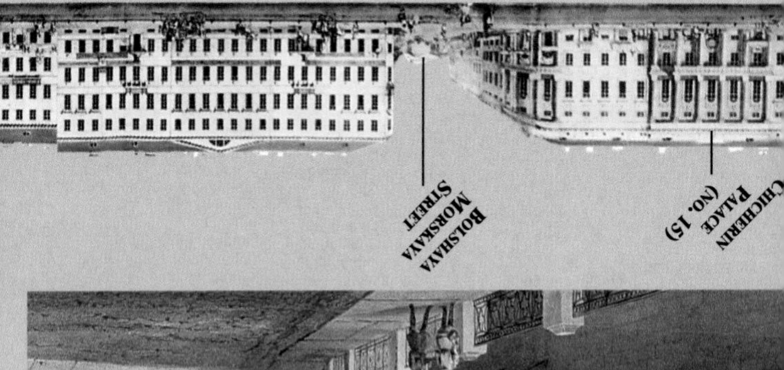

Police Bridge
The rearrangement of the banks of the Moika took place earlier than that of the other canals. Nevertheless it was only in the years 1798–1810 that these were completely reconstructed in granite. The Police Bridge, which spans the Moika, owes its name to its proximity to the Chicherin Palace (no. 15) and the central police building.

DUTCH CHURCH (NO. 20)
The central part of this long building (1830–3, designed by Paul Jacot) had a massive portico behind which the church was situated; the wings contained the residences of the pastor and the members of the Dutch mission. In the 19th century the offices of the Society for the Encouragement of Painters occupied the first floor.

STROGANOV PALACE (NO. 17)
This palace was built between 1752 and 1754 by Rastrelli for his friend Baron Sergei Stroganov. The latter's son Alexander, an art lover and patron, commissioned Andrei Voronikhin to redecorate the interior. A good part of the restoration work on the Palace, an annex of the Russian Museum ▲ 225, was completed in 2003 for the tricentenary of the foundation of St Petersburg.

CHICHERIN PALACE (NO. 15)
Built in the 1760's fo[r] the Chief of Police, this palace was a gift of Catherine II to he[r] servant. Today it is the Barrikada Cinema.

SMYRDIN PUBLISHING HOUSE (NO. 22)
Formerly the bookseller A. Smyrdin, the publisher of Pushkin and Gogol, occupied the right wing of the Lutheran church building.

"DOMINIQUE" (NO. 24)
Before the Revolution no. 24 was the famous restaurant *Dominique* where the young Dostoevsky habitua dined in the 184 Later the interior w sketched by t painter Rep

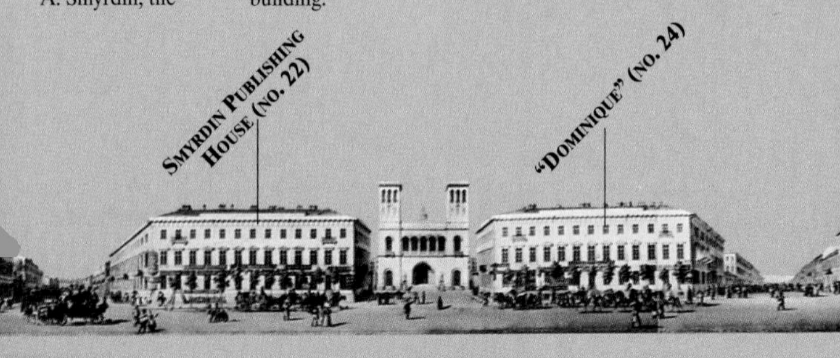

MERTEN'S STORE (NO. 21)

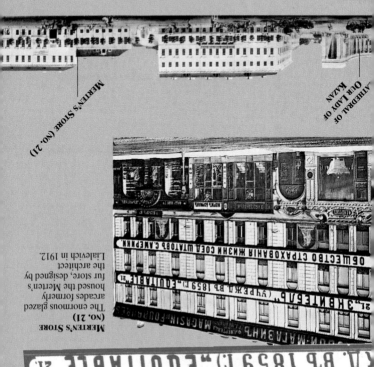

ATHEDRAL OF OUR LADY OF KAZAN

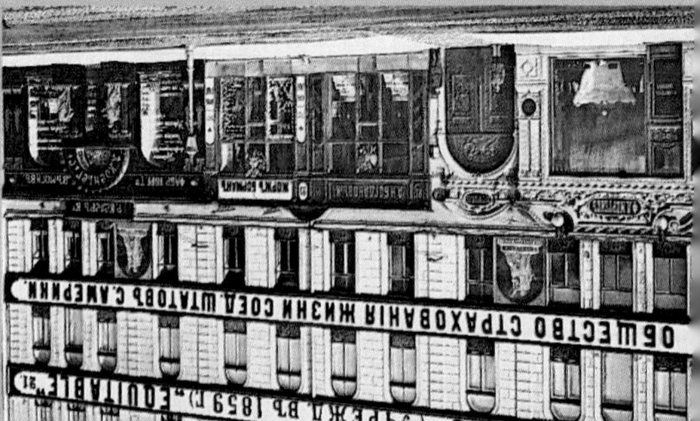

MERTEN'S STORE (NO. 21)
The enormous glazed arcades formerly housed the Merten's fur store, designed by the architect Lialevich in 1912.

Griboedov Canal
This waterway was cut between 1764 and 1790 to avoid flooding. Hilarion Kutuzov, the father of Marshal Kutuzov, originally proposed this idea to Elizabeth I.

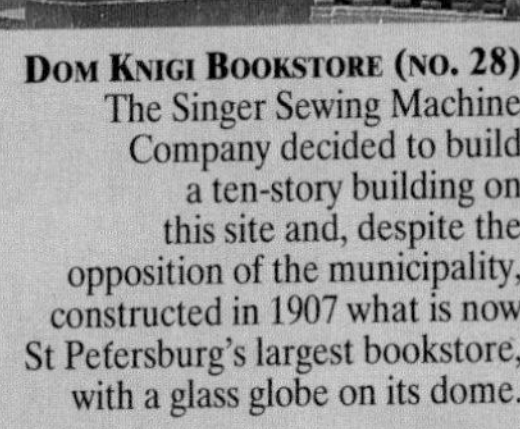

Dom Knigi Bookstore (no. 28)
The Singer Sewing Machine Company decided to build a ten-story building on this site and, despite the opposition of the municipality, constructed in 1907 what is now St Petersburg's largest bookstore, with a glass globe on its dome.

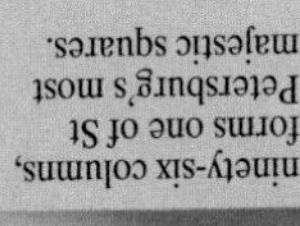

Church of Our Lady of Kazan
Designed by Voronikhin and built between 1801 and 1811, this church reflects both Russian and Western styles. While it respects the Orthodox canon of an altar facing east, its lateral colonnade (like that of St Peter's in Rome) is very striking. It was reinstated as a functioning church in 1999.

Kazan Square
The church of Kazan, with its semicircular colonnade of ninety-six columns, forms one of St Petersburg's most majestic squares.

The tomb of Marshal Kutuzov (1745–1813) is preserved in the cathedral.

ST CATHERINE'S CHURCH (NOS. 32–4)
The refined Baroque elegance of St Catherine's (1763–83, Vallin de la Mothe) contrasts strongly with the massive buildings around it.

TOWER OF THE DUMA (NOS. 31–3)
It was decided that the Municipal Duma (town hall) would occupy a part of Quarenghi's building. The tower, built between 1799 and 1804 by the architect Giacomo Ferrari, is the tallest construction on the Prospekt. It served as a semaphore for the optical telegraph and as a beacon for fires (the signals informed the fire brigade of the location of conflagrations).

Grand Hotel Europe (no. 36)
Beyond the Grand Hotel Europe, now restored by European investors to its pre-Revolutionary glory, cross Mikhailovskaya Street, to reach the Arts Square.

Armenian Church
This wonderful little church was built by Yury Velten in 1780 and restored between 1835 and 1837 by the architect A. Melnikov.

САНКТ-ПЕТЕРБУРГ
ST. PETERSBURG
НЕВСКИЙ ПРОСПЕКТ
NEVSKY PROSPECT
30 ← 36

Meeting place of the Decembrists (no. 42)
The Decembrist Gavril Batenkov (1793–1863) lived at no. 42, where he entertained other conspirators such as Kondraty, Ryleyev, Trubetskoy and Bestuzhev (left).

The "Portik
This neoclassica portico, the work the architect Rusc (1802–6), wa restored in 197 Today it is a sale office for theater an exhibition ticket

Gostiny Dvor (no. 35)
After a series of fires and lootings, the tradespeople of Nevsky Prospekt decided to finance the construction of a stone galleried market by Vallin de la Mothe. Behind these façades, which have a total length of more than half a mile, is the largest store in the city. Maintenance work on the gallery in 1965 brought to light over 300 lbs of gold hidden by merchants.

THE "PASSAGE" (NO. 48)
This 180-yard gallery, built in 1846, was commissioned by Count Essen-Stenbock from the architect R. Zheliazevich as a site for shops, a concert hall and a *salon de thé*. The façade, which the tradesmen thought t[oo] modest, was altered [in] 1902 by the enginee[r] Kozlov.

THE "PASSAGE" (NO. 48)

SADOVAYA STREET

SCHROEDER PIANO WORKS (NO. 5[…])

SALTYKOV-SHCHEDRIN LIBRARY (NO.37)

A MAJOR RESERVE
In addition to a large stock of French books (among them the 7,000 books of Voltaire's library) are a number of other treasures, notably rare 11th- and 12th-century manuscripts such as the *Ostromir Gospels* (1056), documents and autographs of Peter the Great and Mozart

▲ 231.

chroeder Pianos (no. 52)
lo. 52 belonged to Karl Schroeder, he piano manufacturer. Today it a bookshop.

Malaya Sadovaya treet
he "Street of the Gardens" (left) leads hrough to the Michael Garden, the ummer Garden and he Engineers' Castle.

Eliseev Store (no. 56)
This foodshop was built in 1907 by G. Baranovsky for the Eliseev brothers. Don't miss its magnificent Art Nouveau interior.

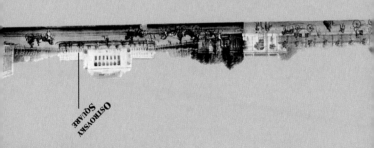

Saltykov-Shchedrin Library (no. 37)
The curving façade giving onto Nevsky Prospekt is the work of the architect Sokolov, built between 1796 and 1801; the rectilinear colonnade was added by Rossi thirty years later, when the Library (inaugurated 1814) needed to be enlarged. It is named for the Russian writer Saltykov-Shchedrin (1826–89).

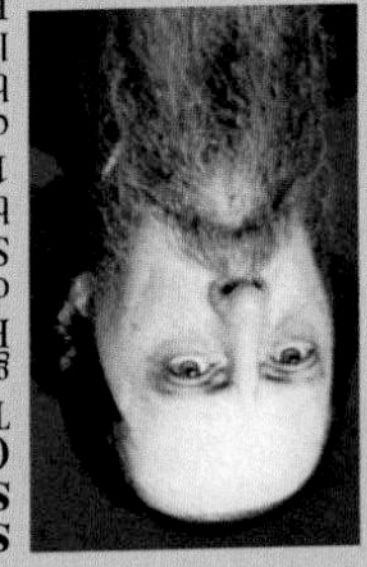

Many well known figures, including Tolstoy, Gorky, Mendeleev, Pavlov, Plekhanov and Lenin all frequented the Saltykov-Shchedrin Library.

Anichkov Palace (no. 39)
This palace, completed by Rastrelli in 1751 after a project by Zemtsov, was frequently altered prior to the 19th century. First of all it was given by Elizabeth I to her morganatic husband Alexei Razumovsky. Later Catherine II gave it to Prince Potemkin, on two occasions: the first time in 1776, then a second time after he had sold it to pay his debts. Potemkin gave lavish balls here.

Apartment blocks (nos. 64–6)
Nos. 64–6 are typical of late 19th-century St Petersburg apartment buildings.

Anichkov Bridg
The four horses an their tamers (a different) on th Anichkov Bridg were sculpted b Klodt in 1849 an 185

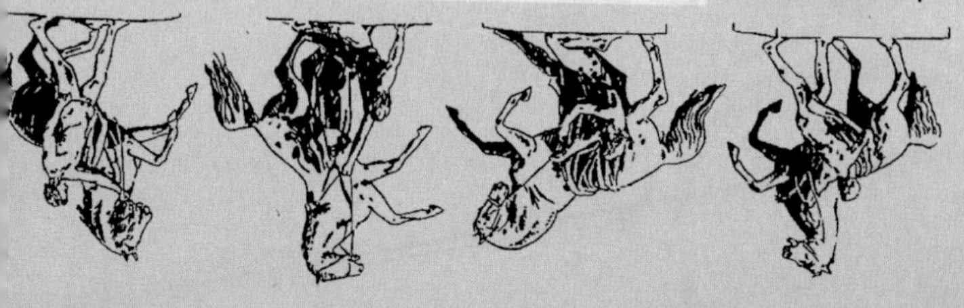

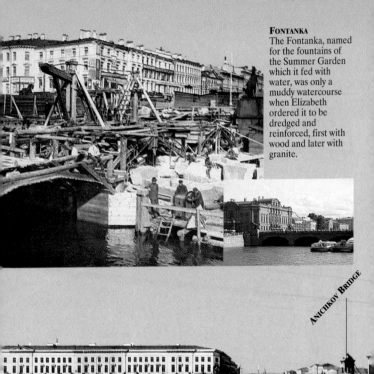

Fontanka
The Fontanka, named for the fountains of the Summer Garden which it fed with water, was only a muddy watercourse when Elizabeth ordered it to be dredged and reinforced, first with wood and later with granite.

Anichkov Bridge

Anichkov Palace (No. 39)

"A perpetual stream of carriages goes by at full speed, and crossing the Prospekt is no less perilous an undertaking than cutting over the boulevard from Rue Drouot and Rue de Richelieu in Paris."
Théophile Gautier

The heirs of the pioneers
After 1817 the Anichkov Palace became the residence of the heirs to the Russian throne. Alexander III liked it so much that he remained there after his coronation, filling the house with his art collections, which were later to be exhibited at the Russian Museum ▲ 225. In 1935 the Anichkov buildings became the Palace of the Pioneers, where the red-scarfed pioneers came to spend their free time.

1. ARTS SQUARE 2. STATUE OF PUSHKIN 3. BRODSKY MUSEUM 4. MUSSORGSKY THEATER 5. BENOIS PAVILION 6. MIKHAIL PALACE 7. ETHNOGRAPHIC MUSEUM 8. SHOSTAKOVICH PHILHARMONIA 9. CHURCH OF THE RESURRECTION 10. MIKHAILOVSKY GARDEN 11. ENGINEERS' CASTLE 12. STATUE OF PETER THE GREAT 13. RUSSIAN MUSEUM (ENTRANCE)

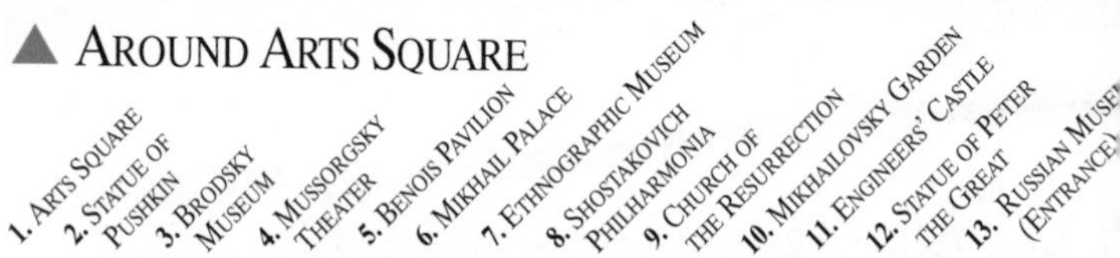

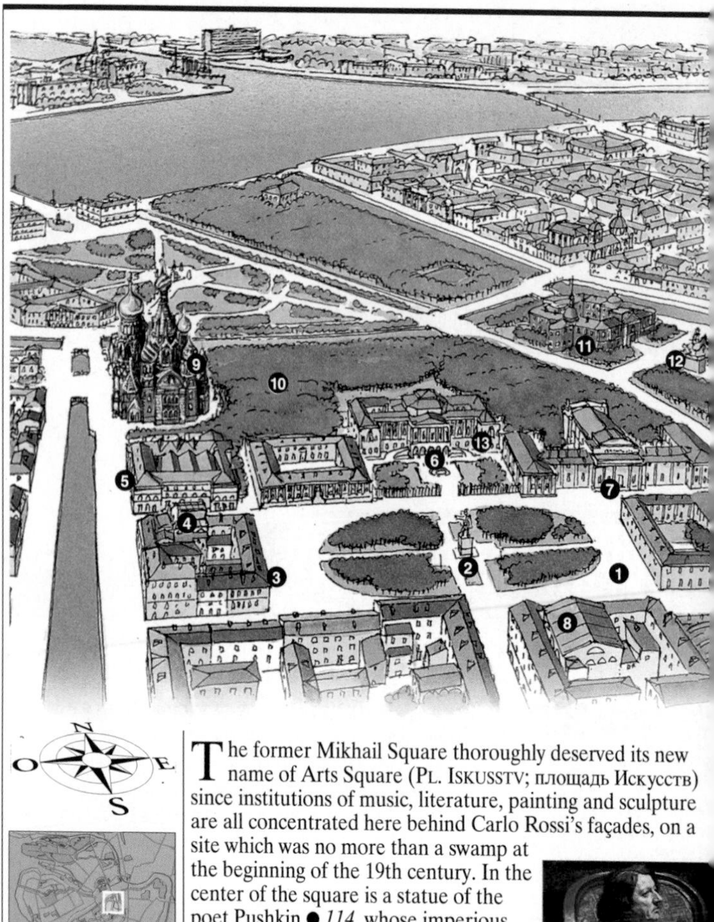

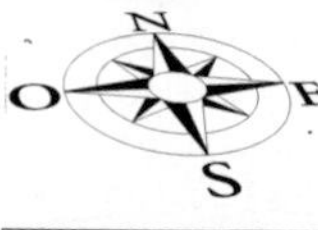

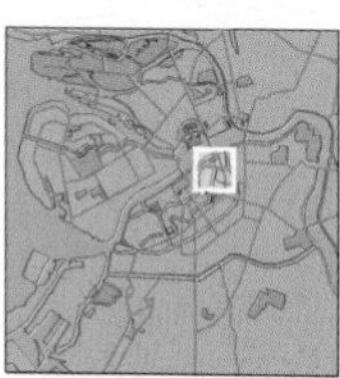

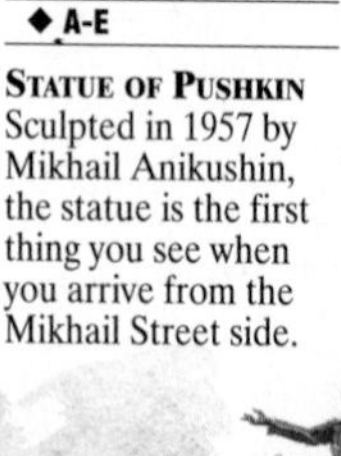

⏱ Half a day

◆ A-E

STATUE OF PUSHKIN
Sculpted in 1957 by Mikhail Anikushin, the statue is the first thing you see when you arrive from the Mikhail Street side.

The former Mikhail Square thoroughly deserved its new name of Arts Square (PL. ISKUSSTV; площадь Искусств) since institutions of music, literature, painting and sculpture are all concentrated here behind Carlo Rossi's façades, on a site which was no more than a swamp at the beginning of the 19th century. In the center of the square is a statue of the poet Pushkin ● *114*, whose imperious gesture seems to invite you to begin your visit on the left hand side of the square.

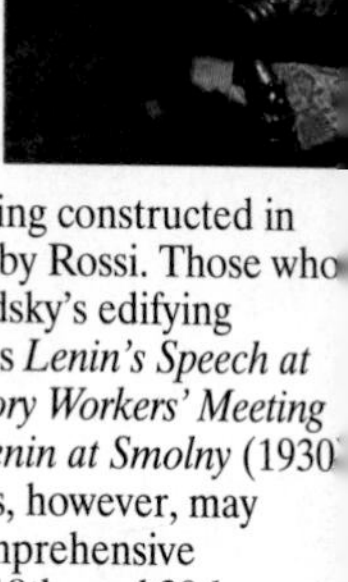

BRODSKY MUSEUM

The painter Isaac Brodsky (1883–1939), after whom Mikhail Street was named during the Soviet era, lived between 1924 and 1939 at no. 3, which was a building constructed in the early 19th century according to plans by Rossi. Those who admire socialist realism will look for Brodsky's edifying canvases, such as *Lenin's Speech at the Putilov Factory Workers' Meeting* (1929) and *Lenin at Smolny* (1930) ▲ *248*. Others, however, may prefer his comprehensive collection of 19th- and 20th-century paintings, which includes works by Repin, Surikov and Serov.

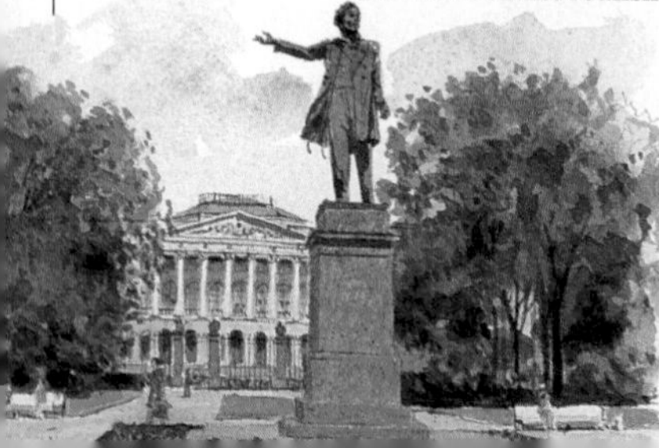

E GUITRYS IN ST PETERSBURG
ie French actor Lucien Guitry was a leading man at the Iikhailovsky Theater. He lived close by, at no. 12 Nevsky Prospekt, where his son Sacha as born on February 21, 1885.

ITTLE THEATER OF)PERA AND BALLET

THE FORMER MIKHAILOVSKY THEATER
68. At no. 1 Arts Square is the old Aikhailovsky Theater (now called the .ittle Theater of Opera and Ballet, Aaly Theater or Mussorgsky Theater), ɔuilt by the architect Alexander Bryulov, ɔartly to plans by Rossi, between 1831 ınd 1833. "Certain productions have heir premieres in St Petersburg almost at he same time as in Paris. We may be orgiven a certain pride at seeing, some ix or seven hundred leagues from Paris, ıt a latitude of sixty degrees, that our anguage is sufficiently widely spoken o maintain full houses in an exclusively French theater." Thus Théophile Gautier lescribed the "French Theater of St Petersburg", as it was ometimes known at that time; it is now a mecca for ballets ınd musical productions.

ARTS SQUARE ✪
With three museums, two theaters and the Shostakovich Philharmonia building, Arts Square is an artistic hub. A café on the square, the Stray Dog (Brodiarchaya Sobaka), was popular in the 1910's with artists and writers like Vladimir Mayakovsky and Anna Akhamatova. Nearby, beside the Mikhailovsky Garden, is the art market, a picturesque place between four bridges.

RUSSIAN MUSEUM ★

MIKHAIL PALACE (RUSSKY MUZEY/MIKHAILOVSKY DVORETS; Михайловский дворец). The central building of the Russian Museum, with its Corinthian façade, was built between 1819 ınd 1825 for the Grand Duke Mikhail, brother of Alexander I, ɔy Carlo Rossi. This architect, who laid out Mikhail Square in ts entirety, also arranged the interior details of the palace. All that survives of this today is the vestibule and main staircase, along with the White Room (where visitors can see sculptures by Mikhail Kozlovsky, bas-reliefs by Stepan Pimenov and murals by Vighi).

FIRST RUSSIAN MUSEUM. In 1898 Nicholas II transformed he Palace into the Russian Museum of Alexander III, ɔringing in some of the paintings and art objects earlier ıssembled by his father at the Anichkov Palace ▲ *223*. Works from private collections, from the Hermitage ▲ *168* ınd from the Fine Arts Academy ▲ *162* were added to hese, leading to the construction of a west wing in the lirection of the Griboedov Canal, by Leonty Benois, ɔetween 1914 and 1916. The ıationalization of private ɔroperty in 1917 also greatly enriched he museum.

Created by an *ukaze* of the Emperor Alexander III, the Russian Museum opened its doors on March 7, 1898 in Carlo Rossi's Mikhail Palace. Today it is one of the largest museums in the world, with reserves of over 380,000 paintings and *objets d'art*. The purpose of the museum is to exhibit Russian works of art that range in date from the 10th century to our own time; among them is an extraordinary collection of some six thousand icons.

"THE SWAN PRINCESS" (1900)
Superb and disquieting, *The Swan Princess* by Mikhail Vrubel (1856–1911) illustrates Pushkin's story *The Czar Saltan*

"EVGRAV DAVYDOV" (1809)
Since the creation of the Academy of Arts of St Petersburg the teaching reflected mainly French art. The Russia of the early 19th century did not escape the vogue for Romanticism, fueled by the patriotic war of 1812, as this portrait of Evgrav Davydov by Orest Kiprensky (1782–1836) shows.

"THE DINNER" (1902)
The collections of the museum reflect the artistic and cultural blossoming of Russia on the eve of the Revolution. One of the movements of the period, the World of Art, adopted an esthetic that was simultaneously predominant in Berlin, Vienna and Paris. Leon Bakst (1868–1924) went to the French capital; a lover of 18th-century painting and the poetry of the French Symbolists, he knew how to pay homage to them without compromising any of the essentially Russian character of his art.

"The Zaporozhian Cossacks Write a Letter to the Turkish Sultan", Ilya Repin (1891)
National traditions, historical episodes, legends and tales supplied many favorite themes of the 19th century.

"The Promenade" (1917)
Marc Chagall, who was initially influenced by the World of Art movement, later looked for a means of escape into the world of fantasy.

"Anna Yoannovna" (1741)
Artists whose destinies were closely linked to that of Russia were also represented: left, the Empress Anna Yoannovna and her servant, by Rastrelli.

Details of the faça
of the Church of t
Resurrectic
representing the ar
of all the regions
Russ

ETHNOGRAPHIC MUSEUM

The Mikhail Palace is flanked, on its left, by a wing built (1900–11) by Vasily Svinin to house the ethnographic section of the Ethnographic Museum (MUZEY ETNOGRAFII; Государственный музей Этнографии). Founded in 1901, it was not opened to the public until 1923; it became a separate museum in its own right in 1934. The richness of its collection makes it far and away Russia's most important ethnographic museum. All the peoples of the former Soviet Union are represented: for example, Moldavians and Bielorussians, Azeris and Turkmens, Evenks and Nenets.

MARBLE HALL. The great entry hall of the museum is sumptuous: Svinin had its walls covered with delicate pink Carelian marble, while the sculptor Kharlamov executed a 300-foot frieze representing all the peoples of the former Russian Empire.

SHOSTAKOVICH PHILHARMONIA

The building constructed by Paul Jacot in 1839 for the Assembly of the Nobility was the scene of major concerts organized by the St Petersburg Philharmonic Society; here, in the Great Hall, Tchaikovsky, Berlioz and Wagner came to conduct their own works, and Isadora Duncan danced. After the Revolution the Great Hall and auditorium became the property of the Philharmonic Society (founded in 1921); a year after the death of Shostakovich (left) in 1976 it was renamed after him. The Philharmonia building projects into the ITALIANSKAYA with two further theaters, the MUSICAL COMEDY THEATER (no. 13) and the KOMISSARZHEVSKAYA THEATER (no. 19). The latter opened in October 1942, hence its nickname the "Blockade Theater".

THE "LENINGRADSKAYA". On the evening of August 9, 1942, the date that had been fixed by Hitler for the fall of Leningrad, the Philharmonia gave the city's first performance of Shostakovich's *Leningrad Symphony*, or *7th Symphony*, which was broadcast from the Great Hall by all the nation's radio stations. Some of the members of the orchestra were still in uniform, having been recalled from the front for the occasion. Others wore the traditional white tie and tails.

CHURCH OF THE RESURRECTION

THE NEO-RUSSIAN STYLE ● *89*. The twisted onion domes, proliferating mosaics and asymmetry of the Church of the Resurrection (KHRAM VOSKRESENIYA KHRISTOVA; храм Воскресения Христова) come as a surprise in this city known for its Baroque curves and classical rigor. The mosaics have just been restored and are magnificent.

THE ASSASSINATION OF ALEXANDER II
On March 1, 1881 the carriage of Czar Alexander II was bowling along the Griboedov when a bomb, hurled by the Narodnaya Volia ("People's Will"), missed its target; but a second bomb mortally wounded the Czar. The members of the commando were tried and executed on April 3.

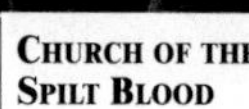

CHURCH OF THE SPILT BLOOD
Alexander III built the Church of the Resurrection on the very spot where his father Alexander II was assassinated. This explains why the church projects so far out into the street, and why it is also called the Church of the Spilt Blood.

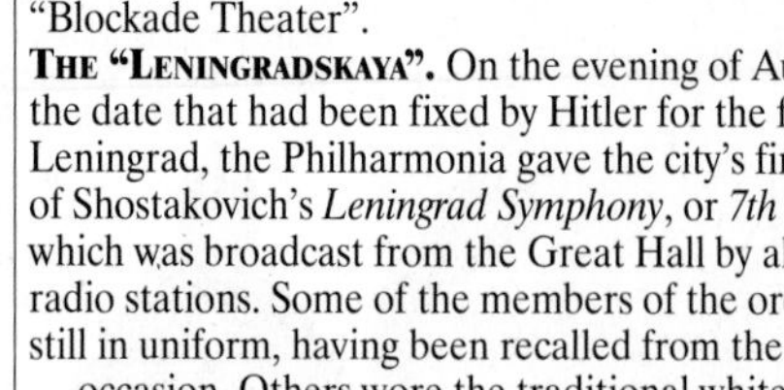

Alfred Parland, who built the church (1883– 1907), won the competition set up by Alexander III, which stipulated that it had to be in the "purely Russian style of the 17th century".

ENGINEERS' CASTLE ★

A walk through the MIKHAILOVSKY GARDEN will take you past the rear façade of the Mikhail Palace to the Engineers' Castle (INZHENERNY ZAMOK; Инженерный замок), which since 1991 has served as an annex of the Russian Museum ▲ *225*.

STATUE OF PETER THE GREAT. Bartolomeo Carlo Rastrelli, the father of the architect, began this equestrian statue of Peter I while the Czar was still alive, and ultimately used his death-mask as a model. In 1800 Paul I placed the statue in front of the Castle's main entrance, with the inscription: "To the great-grandfather, the great-grandson."

MIKHAILOVSKY CASTLE. Paul I decided to build a secure fortress on the site of Empress Elizabeth's Summer Palace. The castle was inaugurated on November 8, 1800, St Mikhail's Day in the Orthodox calendar. The name Mikhailovsky, contrary to that of Arts Square or the Russian Museum, has nothing to do with the Grand Duke Mikhail; instead it refers to the Archangel Mikhail, who, according to Paul I, appeared and commanded him to build a chapel bearing his name on this site. This inspiration, which obliged the architect Brennan to design each of his four façades completely differently, did not mitigate the castle's frowning, military aspect.

SCHOOL OF ENGINEERING. Alexander I abandoned the castle, with its sinister associations. It later became the barracks of a squadron of the Imperial Guard, the headquarters of an institute for the blind, and the Chancellery of the Ministry of Instruction and Religious Affairs. In 1822 the Military Engineering School moved here, and it assumed the name of Engineers' Castle. Fyodor Dostoevsky ▲ *207* was a student at the school in 1838, occupying a corner room on the third floor overlooking the Fontanka, where he liked to read and work.

MIKHAILOVSKY CASTLE
Designed by Bazhenov, this massive building was built by Brenna to a medieval plan. The castle was surrounded by water (the Fontanka, the Moika and two other canals, now running underground), and was linked to the city by drawbridges, which were raised every evening.

ASSASSINATION OF PAUL I
In the night of March 11, 1801, supporters of Alexander murdered Paul I in Mikhailovsky Castle, where he had resided for only forty days. The secret rooms and passages Paul I (justifiably paranoid) had devised stopped many of the plotters from reaching the murder scene.

▲ AROUND OSTROVSKY SQUARE

1. CATHERINE II SQUARE
2. STATUE OF CATHERINE II
3. SALTYKOV-SHCHEDRIN LIBRARY
4. ALEXANDRINSKY THEATER
5. THEATER MUSEUM
6. ROSSI STREET
7. VAGANOVA ACADEMY
8. LOMONOSOV SQUARE
9. LOMONOSOV BRIDGE
10. FONTANKA EMBANKMENT
11. TOVSTONOGOV THEATER

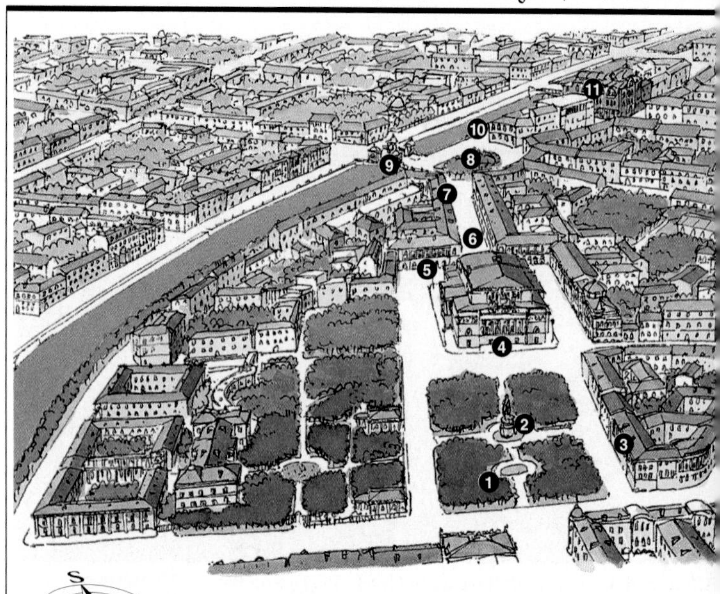

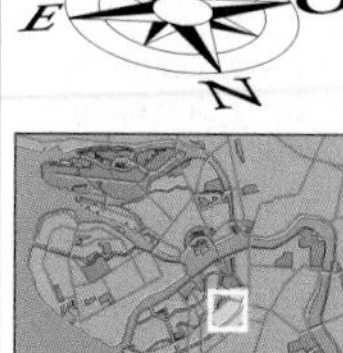

⏲ Three hours

◆ A-E

OSTROVSKY SQUARE (PL. OSTROVSKOVO; площадь Островского) is bordered on one side by Rossi's Saltykov-Shchedrin Library ▲ *221*, and on the other by the pavilions of the Anichkov Palace ▲ *223* and its gardens. This square, even more than Arts Square, is an example of the architectural ensemble of balanced proportions and restrained ornamentation for which Carlo Rossi was famous ▲ *181*. It formerly bore the name of the wife of Nicholas I, Alexandra; in 1923 this was changed in honor of the celebrated Russian dramatist Alexander Ostrovsky, whose most famous works were *Poverty No Vice* (1854), *The Storm* (1860) and *Snegurochka* (1873), which had been performed at the Alexandrinsky Theater.

"If God did not exist, it would be necessary to invent him." One of the famous Voltaire manuscripts in the Public Library.

CATHERINE II SQUARE

STATUE OF THE EMPRESS. This massive monument (over 40 feet tall) standing in the center of the square was sculpted in 1873 by Matvei Chizhov and Alexander Opekuchin, after a project by Mikhail Mikechin. Catherine the Great is shown in her state robes, while around the plinth cluster sundry personalities of the period: the officers Suvorov ▲ *252*, Rumantsev, Orlov ▲ *184* and Chichagov, the statesmen Potemkin ▲ *251*, Bezborodko and Betskoy, the poet Derzhavin and Princess Dashkova, President of the Academy of Sciences.

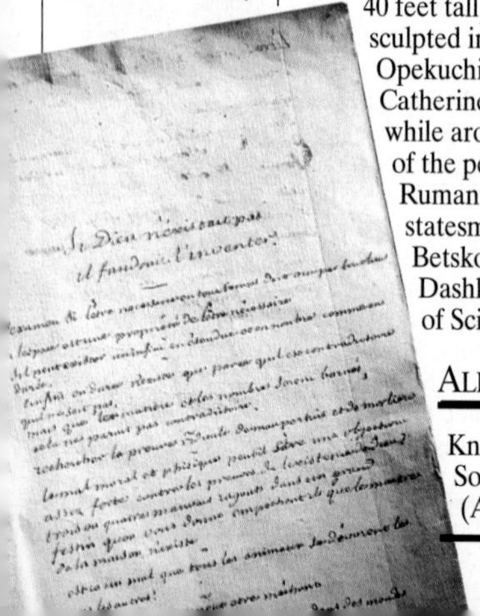

ALEXANDRINSKY THEATER ★

Known as the Pushkin Theater during the Soviet era, the Alexandrinsky Theater (ALEXANDRINSKY THEATR; Александринский театр) was built in 1832, to a project by Carlo Rossi in the Russian classical style ● 86. It was named in honor of the Empress Alexandra Fyodorovna. The troupe at this theater, one of the oldest in Russia, was founded in 1756 during the reign of Elizabeth I ● 36. In 1836 it staged the first production of Nikolai Gogol's *The Government Inspector*.

RUSSIAN DRAMA. The history and development of theatrical genres in Russia (classicism, Romanticism, Realism) are linked to the evolution of this theater, which became the *de facto* national dramatic academy. The repertoire during the second half of the 18th century included the works of Russian authors such as Alexander Sumarokov, Iakov

Kniazhnin, Vasily Kapnist and Ivan Krylov, as well as Western European masters, such as the French playwrights Corneille, Racine, Molière and Beaumarchais. At the dawn of the 20th century the Imperial Alexandrinsky Theater turned to the new drama of Anton Chekhov, whose *Seagull* flopped badly in 1896. After the 1917 Revolution the theater actively promoted new Soviet-style plays, and today it remains one of the most popular with the St Petersburg public. Its repertoire is a blend of Russian and Western classics, along with contemporary plays. The leading actors of the decades between 1950 and 1980 used the title of "Artists of the People of the USSR".

ORIENTAL MANUSCRIPTS The Saltykov-Shchedrin Library has, among its oriental treasures, this manuscript of the Hindu poem, the *Bhagavad-Gita*.

THEATER MUSEUM ★

This museum, founded in 1918, was established on the premises of the former Management of the Imperial Theaters of Russia. Its collections were assembled from the imperial archives and from the private collections of people connected with the theater; today the Theater Museum includes many items, all of which are on display, which document 250 years of Russian music and theater.

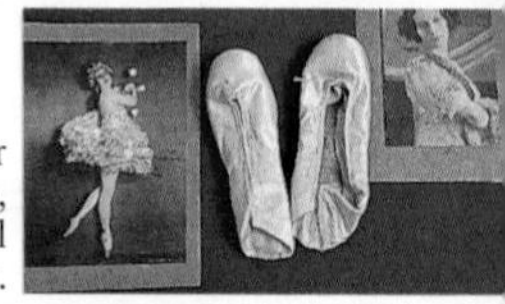

Another special jewel of the Theater Museum is its collection of ballet shoes, which gives an idea of the technical evolution of the ballerina's art.

Agrippina Vaganova (1879–1951)
From 1921 until her death Agrippina Vaganova reigned supreme over the dance school which was named after her in 1957. A former pupil of O. Preobrazhenskaya, E. Vazem and P. Gerdt, she became the star dancer of the Mariinsky Theater ▲ *200*. Nicknamed the "Czarina of Variations", she described her teaching system in her book *The Foundations of Classical Dance* (1934). According to Vaganova all the expressive power of dance derives from the assimilation of technique combined with a rigorous mastery of the body and of the positioning of the feet and hands.

Collections. The museum also displays the personal archives of Marius Petipa, Maria Savina and Fyodor Shalyapin (including the jeweled robe that he wore as Boris Godunov), along with the autographed musical scores of Nikolai Rimsky-Korsakov, letters of Piotr Tchaikovsky and projects for costumes and décors of many different periods throughout the history of Russian theatrical production. The museum's collection of costumes is one of the world's largest, and includes, among others, those of Sleeping Beauty (1890).

For music lovers. In the evenings people crowd into the museum's small concert hall. The piano on which Tchaikovsky once played bursts into sound; recordings of former stars are played; contemporary artists perform, and videos of the greatest ballets and operas are screened.

ROSSI STREET

VAGANOVA CHOREOGRAPHIC SCHOOL. In 1737 the dance teacher of St Petersburg's Polish aristocracy, the Frenchman Jean-Baptiste Landet, who had danced professionally in Paris and Dresden and had been master of ballet in Stockholm, suggested to the Empress Anna Yoannovnathat a dance school should be founded to train the leading dancers of the imperial court's ballet troupe. In 1738 Her Majesty's Dance School was inaugurated, exclusively for children of Russian families of modest means. The first class was made up of twelve girls and twelve boys. The best pupils of this first generation (1742) soon demonstrated a mastery of their art that astonished everyone. In the 19th century the director Charles Didelot ● *71* was replaced by Marius Petipa ▲ *200*, who formed a strong pedagogical team. Since that time the school has regularly sent its pupils on to glittering careers on the Russian stage. The School of St Petersburg has exercised a very powerful influence on the development of European and American ballet; indeed ballet of the 20th century would have been considerably the poorer had it not been for such figures as George Balanchine, Rudolph Nureyev, Natalia Makarova, Anna Pavlova, Tamara Karsavina and Mikhail Baryshnikov, brilliant choreographers and dancers who were all trained at the Vaganova Choreographic School.

ROSSI STREET
The height of the buildings and the width of Rossi Street are exactly equal (66 feet), while its length is exactly ten times this (660 feet). The street was laid out by Carlo Rossi between 1828 and 1834, and was originally known as Theater Street.

LOMONOSOV SQUARE

Rossi Street leads on to another of that architect's projects, Lomonosov Square (PL. LOMONOSOV; Ломоносова). The austerity of the buildings here accorded well with the use that was made of them, prior to the Revolution, by the Ministry of Public Instruction and the Interior Ministry. At that time the square was named after Peter the Great's companion-in-arms, Chernyshev. In the middle of the square stands a bust of Mikhail Lomonosov ● *53* by Sabello (1892).

LOMONOSOV BRIDGE ● *90*. The turrets of this bridge formerly concealed the chains used to raise and lower its ramp. Today the turrets are purely ornamental. The Lomonosov Bridge was identical to another bridge further along the Fontanka, opposite the Anichkov Palace, before the latter was reconstructed and provided with its celebrated horses ▲ *222*.

FONTANKA EMBANKMENT

To the right, on the way down the Fontanka Embankment (NAB. REKI FONTANKI; наб. реки фонтанки), is the Press Building, the offices of several newspapers and at one time the *Leningrad Pravda*'s nerve center. Beside it stands the Tovstonogov Theater ● *69*.

TOVSTONOGOV THEATER
The Tovstonogov was one of the first post-Revolutionary theaters in the city. Its inaugural play, performed in 1919, was Schiller's *Don Carlos*; later repertoires included contemporary pieces such as Mayakovsky's *The Bedbug* and *The Bath-House* (both 1929). The theater originally bore the name of one of its founders, Maxim Gorky, before adopting that of Tovstonogov, the director who ran it from 1956 onward.

Details of the various bridges spanning St Petersburg's canals.

From the Fontanka to Insurrection Square

1. Insurrection Square
2. Moscow Station
3. Ligovsky Pr

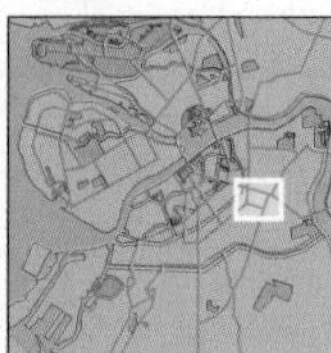

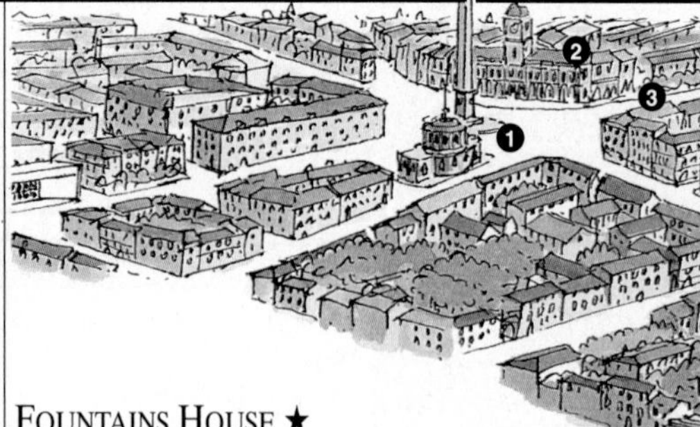

Half a day

◆ E

Fountains House ★

On the Fontanka Embankment the regularity of the 19th-century façades is broken by a green park, at the end of which is Fountains House (no. 34) (Fontanny Dom; Фонтанный дом).

Sheremetev Palace. In 1712 Marshal Sheremetev was allotted a large building site beside the river, where he erected a wooden country house. This was replaced in the 1730's by a stone house. In 1750–5 the architect Argunov, who came from a family of serfs famous for their artistic talents, added a floor to the palace and transformed its façades, giving it its present aspect. The central façade of the main building was heightened by the addition of a mezzanine and a semicircular pediment.

Music and culture. Many famous writers, artists and intellectuals have lived and worked in Fountains House, beginning with the actress Prascovia Kovaleva (Zhemchugova), who married Nikolai Sheremetev in 1801. From the mid-18th century to the 1870's the house was the venue for the concerts of the Sheremetevs' Capella, which was one of the best private choirs in Russia and greatly admired by such figures as Glinka, Liszt and Berlioz. After the Revolution the house was used by a series of different organizations and its interior was much altered. A few years ago it was reallocated to the State Museum of Theater and Music, which is currently restoring the prestige of this former center of musical and cultural life. The building's reception rooms and the Museum of Music that has been laid out there are now open to the public.

"Over that noble abode
I have no rights nor pretensions,
But it happens that I have spent
Almost all my life beneath the roof
Of the Palace of Fountains:
I was poor when I entered it,
And I leave it poor"
Anna Akhmatova

. Nevsky Prospekt
5. Actors' House
6. "Nevsky Palace"
7. Samoilov Museum
8. Museum of the Arctic and Antarctic
9. Marata Street
10. Dostoevsky Museum
11. Vladimir Church
12. Vladimir Square
13. Fountains House
14. House of Letters
15. Fontanka
16. Beloselsky-Belozersky Palace

\<AKHMATOVA MUSEUM. (MUZEY ANNY AKHMATOVOI; музей \<Анны Ахматовой). The poet Anna Akhmatova lived from 1924 to 1952 in the apartment on the third floor of the south wing, overlooking the courtyard. During the 1920's this place was frequented by poets, painters and writers, among them Mayakovsky, Tatlin, Lebeder and Tyrssa. Akhmatova's rooms were made into a museum in 1989; one of them has been redecorated to look as it would have appeared between 1938 and 1941. Here Akhmatova's husband and later her son were arrested. In the other room a display of her poetry explains how she won so important a place in the history of Russian society, culture and literature between 1910 and 1960. There is also a portrait of the poet by Modigliani, executed during a visit to Paris in 1911.

HOUSE OF LETTERS

The house that was situated at the intersection of Nevsky Prospekt and the Fontanka Embankment (nos. 40–68) was entirely destroyed during the siege of World War Two ● 50 but subsequently rebuilt. The critic Vissarion Bielinsky lived here from 1842, in what was known during the 19th century as the "House of Letters". Bielinsky was an influential journalist, and had a powerful effect on the younger generation of writers. He gathered around him a circle of Russia's intellectual avant-garde which included the writers Nekrasov, Turgenev, Grigorovich and Dostoevsky. Today the house is used by the regional tax office.

VISSARION BIELINSKY (1811–48)
Bielinsky's ideas about the condition of the people and the role of Russian writers are expressed in his letter to Gogol, which was clandestinely circulated among the intelligentsia. Dostoevsky spent four years in a labor camp and six years in exile in Siberia, partly because he had read this letter.

BELOSELSKY-BELOZERSKY PALACE

The house of Prince Shakhovskoy was bought in the mid-18th century by Myatlev, the head of the Assignat bank. It was subsequently altered by the classical architect Thomas de Thomon and became the palace of Prince Beloselsky-Belozersky. The new owners were wealthy and famous, members of a family that dated back to Vladimir Monomachus, the Kievan Grand Duke. Their double-barreled name originated in 1798, when Paul I gave Beloselsky the right to use the name of Belozersky, in recognition of his ancestors' services to Russia. The palace was rebuilt between 1846 and 1848 by the architect Shtakenshneider. From 1898 to 1917 it belonged to the imperial family; one of its last owners was the son of Alexander II, Prince Sergei Alexandrovich.

MUNICIPAL CULTURE CENTER AND WAXWORKS MUSEUM
After the Revolution the Beloselsky Palace was occupied by the Communist Party's regional committee. Today it is the Municipal Culture Center. The Hall of Mirrors and the Oak Room are used for plays and concerts, while other rooms provide exhibition areas for classical and contemporary art. The palace also contains a Waxworks Museum featuring the likenesses of the great figures of Russian history.

VLADIMIR SQUARE
Vladimir Prospekt leads to the square of the same name, whose buildings form a circle around the Vladimir Church (dedicated to the Virgin and Saint John of Damascus).

VLADIMIR PROSPEKT

LITTLE (MALY) DRAMATIC THEATER ● *69*. At no. 18, on the corner of Rubinstein and Count streets, is the Little Dramatic Theater (MALY DRAMATICHESKY TEATR; Малый драматичесий театр). Since its creation in 1944, it has gained worldwide fame under the direction of Lev Dodin.
LENSOVIET THEATER (LENSOVETA TEATR; Леисовета театр). This single-story building (no. 12) has a striking façade with an eight-column portico, Ionic pilasters and masks. It was built in the 1820's by the architect Mikhailov as a wealthy mansion for the Korsakov family. After the Revolution it was occupied by a number of different theatrical institutions. Today it is once again known by its original name, the Lensoviet Theater, and is under the direction of Vladimir Paze.

LADIMIR SQUARE (VLADIMIRSKAYA PL.; Владимирская пл). 'he first church in the center of this square was built in 1747 nd replaced in 1761 by a stone building. Its anonymous rchitect may have been Trezzini, who worked under Rastrelli. In 1783 a two-story bell tower was erected alongside ne church by Quarenghi; in 1848 the architect Ruska added wo further stories. Closed since 1932, the Vladimir Church as been reopened by the Russian Orthodox authorities.

"LOUSE EXCHANGE"
The intersection of Nevsky Prospekt, Vladimir Prospekt and Liteiny Prospekt used to be known as the "Louse Exchange"; porters and craftsmen looking for work used to gather here, along with itinerant barbers who sat their clients on stools to cut their hair.

RIMSKY-KORSAKOV MUSEUM

'he famous composer Rimsky-Korsakov lived for the last fteen years of his life at no. 28 Zagorodny Prospekt. In 1971 is apartment was transformed into a museum MUZEY-KVARTIRA RIMSKOVO-KORSAKOVA; музей-вартира Римского-Корсакова). The vestibule, tudy, salon and dining room here recreate the tmosphere of what was one of the centers f St Petersburg culture, where Rimsky-Korsakov held his musical venings, the "Korsakov Wednesdays". Glazunov, Lyadov, Rachmaninov, 'aneyev and Shalyapin all attended these vents. Today an entire room is devoted to nusical life in St Petersburg in the late 19th nd early 20th centuries, and every Wednesday meetings of singers and musicians are once more held in the concert room. In this apartment Rimsky-Korsakov wrote over forty romances, as well as his *Principles of Orchestration*, *Chronicle of My Musical Life* and the operas *Sadko*, *Czar Saltan*, *The Czar's Bethrothed* and *Kashchey the Immortal*.

RIMSKY-KORSAKOV (1844–1908) ● 72
The composer's name is closely linked with the Conservatoire, where he taught the composition class.

DOSTOEVSKY MUSEUM ★

This museum (MUZEY-KVARTIRA F.M. DOSTOYEVSKOVO; музей-квартира Ф. М. Достоевского) was opened in 1971, ninety years after the death of Dostoevsky ▲ *206*. The apartment had to be reconstituted, but its atmosphere remains faithful to the personality of the master and to the spirit of his time.

A WRITER'S PRIVACY. Dostoevsky lived in this apartment on two occasions (for a few months in 1846, and during the last years of his life) with his wife Anna Grigorievna and their two children, Lyuba and Fedya. Here he wrote his celebrated *Discourse on Pushkin*, as well as *The Brothers Karamazov*. Dostoevsky liked his study (above) because it was spacious and isolated from the rest of the apartment. The place was austere and ascetic. Above the sofa on which he slept is a reproduction of Raphael's *Virgin of Saint Sixtus*, a painting he especially loved. Beyond the windows are the domes of the Vladimir Church, of which he was a parishioner. The streets and the passers-by in this district still compose the same "... inexhaustible, magnificent almanac, which one can leaf through in one's spare moments, when one is bored, after a meal ...".

RADISHCHEV (1749–1802)
This celebrated writer, the first thoroughgoing Russian dissident, lived at no. 14 Marata Street from 1775 to 1790. He was arrested, imprisoned at the Peter and Paul Fortress, and sent to Siberia on the orders of Catherine II for his revolutionary *Journey from Petersburg to Moscow*. Freed in 1796 by Paul I, he was amnestied in 1801 by Alexander I, but killed himself in 1802.

MARATA STREET

MUSEUM OF THE ARCTIC AND ANTARCTIC (MUZEY ARKTIKI I ANTARKTIKI; музей Арктики и Антарктики). The former St Nicholas Church is the only building of the United Schismatics (a branch of the Old Believers ● *56*) which remains intact at St Petersburg; it was closed in 1932 to make way, in 1937, for the Museum of the Arctic and Antarctic, which houses, among other exhibits, stuffed polar wildlife and items from expeditions. Today there is a project to return the church to the Old Believers and move the museum elsewhere.

NEVSKY PROSPEKT

On the section of Nevsky Prospekt between Liteiny and Vladimir prospekts and Marata Street is a series of apartment blocks dating from the second half of the 19th century and early 20th century. At no. 60 lived the satirical writer Mikhail Saltykov-Shchedrin ▲ *221*; in 1815 Vladimir Zhukovsky, the translator of English, French and German poetry, lived at no. 82.

ACTORS' HOUSE. This building (no. 86), with its white-columned portico, is known in St Petersburg as the Actors' House. It unites several theatrical associations, such as the Union of Theater Workers, the Russian Theater Society and the Stanislavsky Palace of the Arts. Built in the 18th century as a private mansion, then reconstructed between 1820 and 1830 by the architects Ovsianikov and Fossati, it belonged in the 19th century to the Yusupov family, who organized concerts and exhibitions there. Today the Actors' House still mounts soirées, seminars, conferences, and exhibitions of theater décor as well as international festivals and competitions.

"NEVSKY PALACE". No. 57, opposite the Actors' House, was built in 1861 by the architect Langé and belonged to the craft school of Czarevich Nicholas ● *36*. It was formerly the Renommée Hotel, which rented furnished rooms, before it became the Hermès and finally the Baltic Hotel at the end of World War Two. It was restored in 1993, and is today a luxury establishment.

SAMOILOV MUSEUM. In the same block as the Nevsky Palace, on the Groom Street side, is the Samoilov family museum which was opened 1994. From 1869 onward a number of famous actors, composers, painters and writers frequented this house.

PUSHKIN STREET

On a square halfway down Pushkin Street (PUSHKINSKAYA UL.; Пушкинская ул.) is a statue of the writer, which was the first to be erected to him in St Petersburg. It is the work of the sculptor Opekushin, who was also responsible for the Moscow statue of Pushkin (1880), this monument was unveiled in 1884.

NO. 10 PUSHKIN STREET. Today a number of artists inhabit this derelict house. As representatives of alternative culture in St Petersburg they organize exhibitions, entertainments and concerts in the courtyards of the building and in the street outside. The creative drive behind this unusual center is currently a popular phenomenon in St Petersburg.

VASILY SAMOILOV MUSEUM
This establishment pays homage to Vasily Samoilov, an actor at the Alexandrinsky Theater, where he played more than fifty different roles. His personal effects are displayed in the main rooms, along with 19th- and 20th-century theatrical mementos and the interior of one of the imperial boxes. Costumes made in the workshops of the imperial theaters are also exhibited, on Yves Saint-Laurent dummies from the *200 Years of the Ballets Russes* exhibition at the Paris Opera.

MUSEUM OF THE ARCTIC AND ANTARCTIC
This museum contains several sections (The Nature of the Arctic, History of Polar Scientific Expeditions, Economy and Art of the Nordic Peoples). One of its major curiosities is a 1930 three-seater amphibious plane, which hangs above the entrance.

ST PETERSBURG IN THE MOVIES

The first Russian production company was founded in 1907. St Petersburg at that time appears (with the help of Czarist censors) as a 19th-century city, a sumptuous décor perfect for adaptations such as *The Queen of Spades* (1916) by Iakov Protazanov, the greatest director of the early Russian cinema.

Max Linder, immensely popular in Russia, came to St Petersburg in 1913. The public flocked to see his movie, which ended with a ballooning scene. Then the theater lights came on, and Linder himself appeared on the end of a rope, as if he had come in through the roof.

St Petersburg's first movie theater was established on the Nevsky Prospekt, on the initiative of the Lumière brother. Although Moscow was the cinematic capital for Russia under the Czars, St Petersburg was an inspiration to a number of directors and developed a distinct cinema tradition of its own. Today directors no longer seem threatened by censors, but the new economic situation of the Russian cinema is making movie production extraordinarily difficult.

КВАРІУМЪ

го Мая 1896 года

Вниманіе! Отк

Съ 4 Мая и ежед. первый разъ въ Ро

Живая фотографія Синемотографъ-

міэръ послѣднія чудеса науки.

Завтра, въ Воскресенье, 5 Мая, выходъ

ВАЯ ФОТОГРАФІЯ послѣднія чудеса на

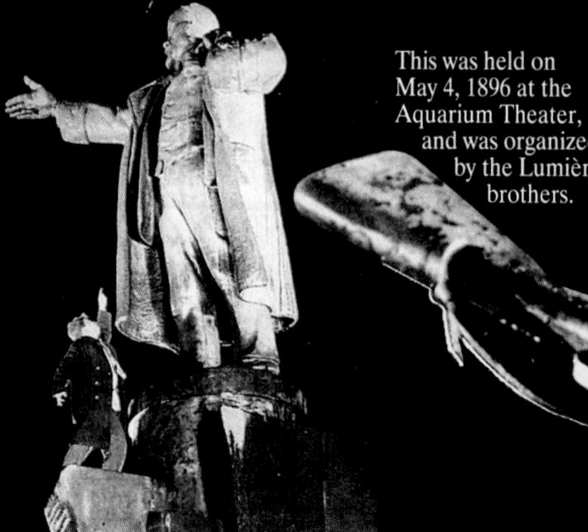

Certain Soviet directors rapidly established their "Leningrad" credentials, notably Kozintsev and Trauberg. Ermler (with Johanson) was mainly concerned to film a city transformed by socialism (*Ruins of Empire*, 1929).

This was held on May 4, 1896 at the Aquarium Theater, and was organized by the Lumière brothers.

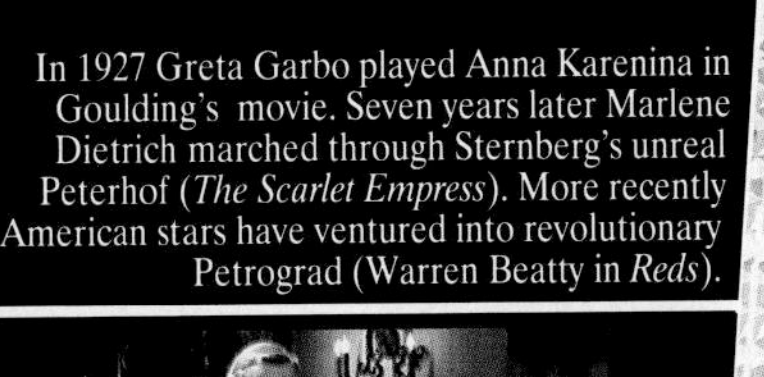

In 1927 Greta Garbo played Anna Karenina in Goulding's movie. Seven years later Marlene Dietrich marched through Sternberg's unreal Peterhof (*The Scarlet Empress*). More recently American stars have ventured into revolutionary Petrograd (Warren Beatty in *Reds*).

With the Russian vogue of the 1930's pasteboard Petersburgs sprang up like ushrooms. Harry Borg played a disquieting Rasputin in the French movie *La Tragédie Impériale* (1938).

The recasting of the Leningrad studios under the name of Lenfilm in 1936 (the name has survived to this day) sounded the death-knell of their creative insolence. Experimentation was definitely out of favor when Heifitz and Zarkhy filmed *The Baltic Deputy* (1936).

For its epics the oviet cinema often used the streets of eningrad. Crowds of xtras, directed by isenstein, flooded ast in his theoretical and disturbing *October* (1927).

INSURRECTION SQUARE
In 1909 a statue of Alexander III by Trubetskoy was erected in the center of the square; at the time this monumental sculpture ▲ *184* was nicknamed "The Scarecrow".

BREAD MUSEUM
At no. 73 Ligovsky Prospekt is an industrial bakery; on the fourth floor is the Bread Museum. The exhibition here traces the history of breadmaking from the foundation of St Petersburg, and describes the various uses to which bread has been put over the centuries.

LIGOVSKY PROSPEKT

Nevsky Prospekt intersects Ligovsky Prospekt (LIGOVSKI PR Лиговский пр.), laid out in the late 19th century on a part o the canal of that name, now filled in, which fed the fountain in the Summer Garden ▲ *186*. In the 18th and 19th centurie this street was famous for its queues of carriages, its supply drinks, its tearooms, taverns and cheap hotels.

OCTOBER CONCERT HALL. At the head of the Prospekt there used to be a remarkable Greek Orthodox church. This was built between 1861 and 1866 in a Byzantine style that was highly unusual for St Petersburg. It was demolished in 1961 and replaced by the October Concert Hall (1967).

"WRITERS' WALKWAYS". In the Volkovskoe Cemetery at the end of Ligovsky Prospekt is a mausoleum where some great Russian intellectuals, including the writer Turgenev and the chemist Mendeleev, are buried.

INSURRECTION SQUARE

INSURRECTION SQUARE (PL. VOSTANIYA; пл. Восстания) was the original terminal point of Nevsky Prospekt before it was extended to the Alexander Nevsky Monastery ▲ *253*. It was the scene of some of the most violent encounters between police and demonstrators during the February Revolution.

FROM THE CHURCH TO THE METRO. Until 1918 this square was called Our Lady of the Sign, after the church built her by Elizabeth I in 1767. At the end of the 18th century plans were made for the original wooden church to be replaced by stone one. Work began in 1794 and continued for ten years. The result was a five-domed church dominating the square. remained in use until 1938 but was demolished in 1940. The Ploshchad Vostaniya metro station now stands on the site.

MOSCOW STATION (MOSKOVSKY VOKZAL; Московский вокзал). The inauguration on November 1, 1851 of the railway linking St Petersburg with Moscow was a momentou event in the life of the capital. The original Nicholas Station was designed by Thon. The central part of its grand green a white façade was decorated on two levels, with Corinthian columns, and now this is all that remains of the old building, as it has now been completely modernized inside. In 1967 a bust of Lenin was placed in the main hall on a monument pedestal, and on its walls were inscribed the decree of t second Party Congress of 1924 which changed Petrogra to Leningrad ● *33*. Now that the city has reassumed its original name the bust of Lenin has been replaced by that of Peter the Great. For St Petersburg's statues "musical chairs" has always been the norm.

From Smolny to the Alexander Nevsky Monastery

▲ From Smolny to the Alexander Nevsky Monastery

Smolny

Smolny Monastery and Cathedral
Visitors can attend concerts and view an exhibition on the site's history. From the top of the bell tower (accessible on request) are fine panoramic views.

Suvorov Avenue leads to the remarkable Smolny architectural complex. Behind the Dictatorship of the Proletariat Gardens rises the austere yellow and white façade of the Smolny Institute, while to the left, behind the trees, rise the Baroque domes of the Cathedral and Monastery. The origin of the name Smolny goes back to the time of Peter the Great. Until 1723 this site was occupied by the Smolny Dvor (tar depot), where tar was prepared and stored for caulking ships' timbers.

Dictatorship of the Proletariat Square
(Pl. Proletarskoy; пл. Пролетарской Диктатуры Diktatury). The access to the Smolny Institute, which played so prominent a role in the Revolution, had to be on a par with its symbolic importance; this, at any rate, is what the architects Vladimir Shchuko and Vladimir Guelfreikh must have thought when they erected their massive neoclassical propylaea (1923–4) on either side of the main thoroughfare, and complemented them ten years later with a rectilinear garden. In the garden the architects installed busts of Karl Marx and Friedrich Engels, sculpted by Sergei Yevseyev.

…KIN PALACE
2. TAURIDE PALACE
3. TAURIDE GARDENS
4. SMOLNY MONASTERY
5. DICTATORSHIP OF THE PROLETARIAT SQUARE
6. SMOLNY INSTITUTE
7. SUVOROV MUSEUM
8. SUVOROV AVENUE
9. BOLSHEOKHTINSKY MOST

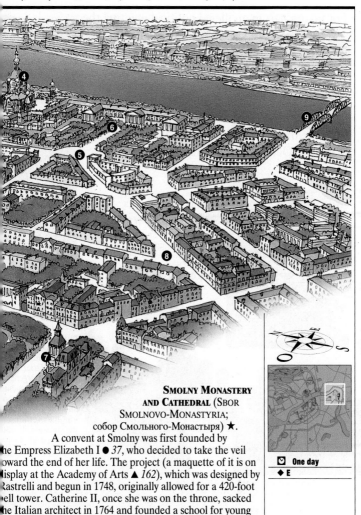

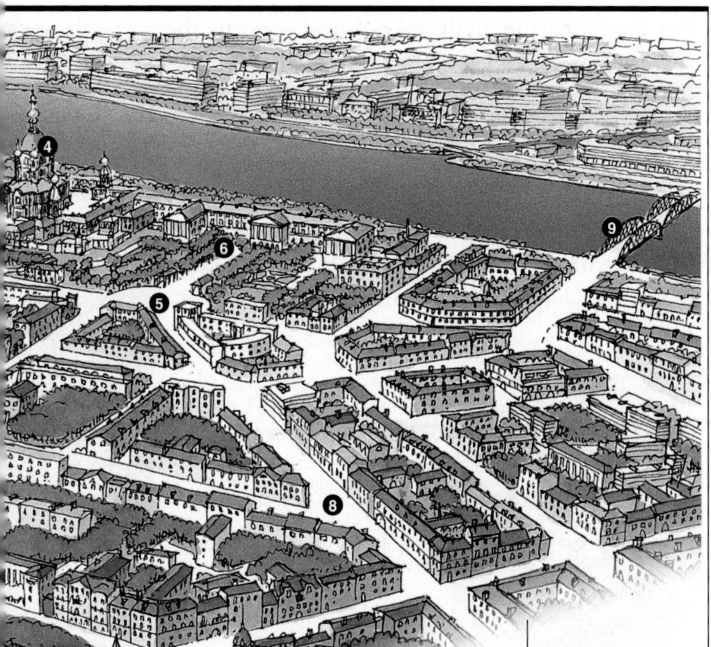

SMOLNY MONASTERY AND CATHEDRAL (SBOR SMOLNOVO-MONASTYRIA; собор Смольного-Монастыря) ★.
A convent at Smolny was first founded by he Empress Elizabeth I ● *37*, who decided to take the veil oward the end of her life. The project (a maquette of it is on lisplay at the Academy of Arts ▲ *162*), which was designed by Rastrelli and begun in 1748, originally allowed for a 420-foot ell tower. Catherine II, once she was on the throne, sacked he Italian architect in 1764 and founded a school for young adies in the convent.

One day
◆ E

A LAVISH CATHEDRAL
● *85*
The cathedral as completed by Vasily Stasov in 1835 preserves the style of Rastrelli, in which the ornamental exuberance of Baroque includes purely Russian elements such as the five onion domes.

For taking part in an illegal political meeting the seventeen-year-old student Vladimir Ilyich Ulyanov was arrested, banned from the University and exiled to a distant village in Kazan. Thus began Lenin's life as a dedicated revolutionary. By 1916 he was living in Zurich and had despaired of any revolution in his lifetime; the spontaneous rising of the Russian masses in October 1917 came as a total surprise to him.

A CLANDESTINE EXISTENCE
Lenin lived clandestinely in St Petersburg during the 1905–7 Revolution ● *44* and in the same city (by then named Petrograd) under the Kerensky regime from July 5 to October 25, 1917. Left, Lenin disguised as a worker, under the name of K. Ivanov.

APRIL 1917
Lenin outlined his program at the Tauri Palace in April 1917. declared the "Tasks of the Proletariat" to be the utmost urgency; to the astonishment of his listeners he propo an immediate end to war, the overthrow of the government, and handing over of all political power to the soviets.

LENIN AT THE SMOLNY INSTITUTE
Lenin arrived at the headquarters of the Petrograd Soviet, the Smolny Institute, on the evening of October 24, 1917 to direct the coup d'état. He stayed there until the government left for Moscow on March 11, 1918. He ran the Council of People's Commissars within the Palace, wrote, and received delegations and journalists; among the latter was J. Reed, author of a celebrated account of the October Revolution, *Ten Days that Shook the World*.

Power to the Bolsheviks
On October 25, 1917, at 10.40pm, even as the attack on the Winter Palace ● *44* was under way, the Second Pan-Russian Congress of Soviets opened at Smolny. The Mensheviks and right-wing Socialist Revolutionaries disapproved of Lenin's coup d'état. They proposed to open talks with the Provisional Government, with a view to setting up a democracy. After a short, violent debate they walked out in a body, abandoning the field to the Bolsheviks.

Back in Petrograd
In July 1920 Lenin took part in the Second Congress of the Komintern at the Tauride Palace. The same month he sent a message to Stalin, then fighting at Kharkov: "The situation in the Komintern is excellent. Zinoviev, Bukharin and I believe that we should immediately encourage the Revolution in Italy. In my view, we should first Sovietize Hungary and perhaps the Czech state and Romania. This requires mature consideration. Let us know your conclusion."

Lenin's tragedy
On May 25, 1922 Lenin fell ill, with a paralyzed right arm and leg and acute aphasia. He returned to work in October, but by December was once more confined to his bed. His health declined progressively thereafter, and he was cut off from the levers of power within the Kremlin.

The deification of Lenin
Krupskaya, Lenin's wife, entreated the Politburo in vain not to embalm his body but to bury it as he had wished.

Nikolai Karamzin (1766–1826)
The great historian and writer Nikolai Karamzin spent the final years of his life at the Tauride Palace.

Smolny Institute (Smolny Institut; Смольный институт) ★. This long neoclassical building, built by Quarenghi in 1806–8, was a school for young ladies until August 1917, at which time the Soviet of Workers' and Soldiers' Deputies of Petrograd ● *46* was installed there. On October 24, 1917, in the evening, Lenin arrived to seize control of the insurrection. The long corridors of the Institute swarmed with Red Guards, soldiers, sailors and factory delegates seeking weapons, tracts or newspapers. On October 25, while the fighting was still going on, the Second Pan-Russian Congress of Soviets opened, at 10.40pm in the Lecture Hall. At 3.10am the delegates greeted the news of the fall of the Winter Palace with wild cheering. That evening they ratified the decrees proposed by Lenin on peace and land ownership, as well as on the formation of the Council of People's Commissars. The Council, headed by Lenin, operated from Smolny until it was moved to Moscow in March 1918. Since 1991 the Institute has housed the offices of the Mayor of St Petersburg, but the historic Lecture Hall, Lenin's study and the bedroom he occupied with his wife, Nadezhda Krupskaya, now form part of the Smolny Memorial Museum. There is also a permanent exhibition about the Institute as it was at the time of Catherine II.

The first Kunstkammer
After Kikin's death his palace was used for the Kunstkammer, Peter the Great's assemblage of curiosities. Here was displayed a collection bought from the Dutch anatomist Frederik Ruysch (1717), a specialist in embalming. In 1727 the Kunstkammer was transferred to Vasilyevsky Island ▲ *160*.

Kikin Palace

At the Stavropol intersection stands one of the oldest buildings in St Petersburg, the palace of the Boyar Alexander Kikin. Kikin was an opponent of Peter the Great's policies who supported the Czarevich Alexei in his doomed attempt to overthrow the Emperor ● *39*. After fleeing to Austria on the advice of Kikin the Czarevich returned to Russia in January 1718 and was condemned to death a few months later. Most of the people he denounced as his accomplices, among them Kikin, were executed. Nowadays the Kikin Palace building houses a music school.

NCING CLASSES
:and up straight and speak French!" was the monishment given to the six- to eighteen-ar-old pupils at the Smolny Institute. Here young ladies were taught such subjects as igion, languages, arithmetic, drawing, ncing, sewing and good manners.

AURIDE PALACE

earby, on the left-hand side of Shpalernaya reet, runs the 760-foot yellow façade of the Tauride alace (TAVRICHESKY DVORETS; Таврический дворец), hich has a stark Doric pediment crowned by a green ome. Constructed between 1783 and 1789, this was one f the first classical buildings in Russia ● *86*.

OTEMKIN'S REWARD. Catherine II was much given to owering palaces on her favorite, Prince Potemkin. After resenting him with the Anichkov Palace ▲ *222* she had the auride Palace built for him, modeled on the Pantheon in ome. Scarcely was it finished than she offered to buy it ack for 460,000 roubles; Potemkin, a notorious spendthrift, as always heavily in debt and needed the money. In ebruary 1791, on his return from Iasi, the former capital of Ioldavia, where he had negotiated an advantageous peace ith the Turks, Catherine gave the palace to Potemkin a econd time. He used it to throw parties of legendary xtravagance.

THER OCCUPANTS. After Prince Potemkin's death the auride in 1792 was decreed an imperial palace. When the mpress died Paul I revenged himself on his mother and her vorite by stripping the place bare and converting it into a

barracks. The Column Room was converted into a stable, and its furnishings and works of art were moved to the Mikhail Castle ▲ *229*. Alexander I had the palace restored by Luigi Rusca (1802–4).

FROM THE DUMA TO THE SOVIETS. After the February Revolution ● *46* the left wing of the palace was occupied by ie Soviet of the Workers and Soldiers of Petrograd, while ie right wing was used by the Committee of the Duma which ormed the Provisional Government. The Tauride Palace was iter used as the Leningrad Higher Party School before ecoming the seat of the Assembly of the CIS.

AURIDE GARDENS. (TAURICHESKI SAD; Таврический сад). Although probably not as luxuriant today as in Potemkin's me these gardens are still a pleasant place to walk. In winter s avenues are used by cross-country skiers.

POTEMKIN, PRINCE OF THE TAURIDE
The Greeks called the Crimea the Tauride; they believed that its barbarian inhabitants were in the habit of burning foreigners on sight (Euripides states this categorically in his *Iphigenia*). When the Crimea was annexed to Russia in 1783 it reverted to its original name; and Potemkin, who led the campaign against the Ottomans, was named Prince of the Tauride by Catherine II. His palace, built at this time, was given the same name.

THE ASSEMBLY
Between 1906 and 1917 the Palace became the seat of the Duma ● *46*.

A MAJESTIC FAÇADE
The stylistic restraint shown by the architect Starov in his design for the palace provoked the enthusiasm of the poet Gavril Derzhavin: "Its exterior is distinguished neither for its sculptures, nor its gilding . . . old-fashioned, elegant good taste is the true source of its dignity and majesty."

ALEXANDER SUVOROV (1729–1800)
Alexander Suvorov was born in Moscow. His father was a general who had fought with Peter the Great. During the Russo-Turkish War (1787–91) Catherine II conferred on him the rank of Field Marshal after he crushed the Polish uprising (1794).

SUVOROV MUSEUM

The popularity of Field Marshal Alexander Suvorov made possible a nationwide subscription toward the Suvorov Military History Museum (Voenna-Istorichesky Muzey Suvorova/военно-исторический музей А. В. Суворова). In 1904 the architects Guerman Grimm and Alexander Gogen completed this building, with its enormous panels of mosaic illustrating the principal events in Suvorov's life. Inside, a selection of the general's possessions is on display, together with maps, weapons and various other items that have survived from his campaigns.

TOWARD THE MONASTERY

SUVOROV AVENUE (SUVOROVSKY PROSPEKT; Суворовский проспект). This broad thoroughfare, which leads to the Smolny District, used to be known as Elephant Avenue. In the early 18th century the Persian shahs were in the habit of sending elephants as gifts to the Russian emperors (indeed, i 1741 Nadir Shah gave a total of fourteen elephants). One of the special stables constructed for these somewhat cumbersome offerings stood by the side of today's Suvorov Avenue; it was by this route that the elephants would travel on their way to drink from the waters of th river Neva.

NEVSKY PROSPEKT. The section of the Nevsky Prospekt ▲ *212* which leads to the Alexander Nevsky Monastery was built shortly after the foundation of the monastery; the idea behind its constructior was to give the monks access to the road to Novgorod, where the metropolitan resided Close by what has now become Insurrectio Square ▲ *244* the monks' route joined with the road linking the dockyards of the Admiralty to this same Novgorod road. It was during the reign of Anna Ivanovna – in fact on April 20, 1738 – that it was finally decreed that "the great thoroughfare from the Admiralty to the Nevsky Monastery should be called the Nevsky Prospekt".

ALEXANDER NEVSKY
Prince Alexander Novgorod was given this sobriquet after he won the 1240 battle by the Neva.

1. Lazarus Cemetery
2. Church of the Annunciation
3. Trinity Cathedral
4. Alexander Nevsky Square
5. Tikhvin Cemetery

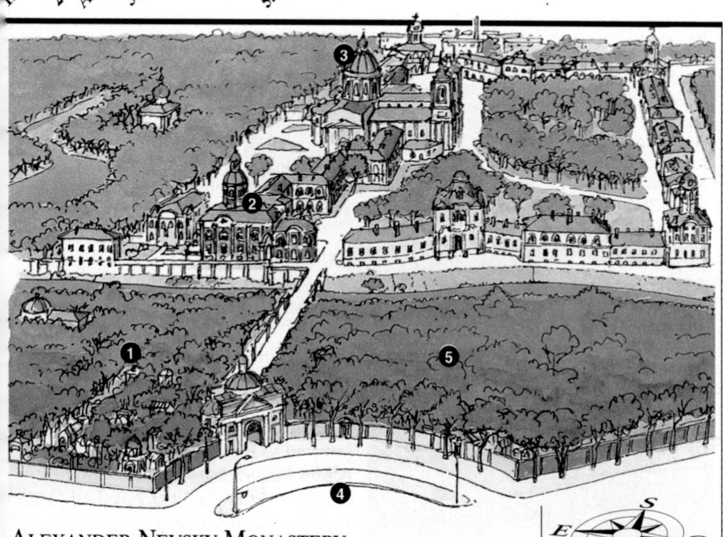

Alexander Nevsky Monastery

By Peter's will. In 1710 Peter the Great built the Alexander Nevsky Monastery (Aleksandro-Nevsky Lavra; Александро-Невская Лавра) in honor of Prince Alexander Novgorod, on the site of his victory over the Swedes in 1240. The construction work began in 1712, and by the following year a wooden church had been consecrated and monks had moved in. After the death of Peter the Great the works continued, but the building was not completed until the last years of the 18th century, during the reign of Catherine II. In 1797 the Alexander Nevsky Monastery took the title of *lavra*, reserved for the most important monasteries. In addition to the St Petersburg *lavra*, there are others at Pechersky (Kiev, Ukraine), Trinity-St-Sergei (Sergiyev Posad) and Pochaevsky-Uspensk (Volhynia, Ukraine).

Touring the monastery. In the recess of the curving monastery wall rises the dome of the main entrance, built between 1783 and 1785 by the architect Ivan Starov. Once through the gateway arch you will see beyond the walls surrounding them the Lazarus cemetery (on the left) and the Tikhvin cemetery (on the right). Some of the tombstones here are the work of famous sculptors, such as Ivan Martos, Mikhail Kozlovsky, Auguste Montferrand and Vasily Demut-Malinovsky.

Lazarus Cemetery (Lazarevskaye Kladbishche; Лазаревское кладбище). The Lazarus Cemetery, also known as the 18th-century Necropolis, is the oldest cemetery in St Petersburg. It was inaugurated in 1716 with the burial of Natalia Alexeyevna, who was the much-loved sister of Peter the Great. Later it was mainly used for the deceased of the great aristocratic families, but it also harbors the remains of such luminaries as the encyclopedist Mikhail Lomonosov (1711–65) ● *53*, the architects Adrian Zakharov (1761–1811), Carlo Rossi ▲ *181*, Giacomo Quarenghi (1744–1817), Andrei Voronikhin (1759–1814), as well as Thomas de Thomon ● *87*, who had been appointed court architect in 1802.

S E O N

Two hours

◆ E

Russia's national mausoleum ✪

The Alexander Nevsky Monastery is one of the rare architectural complexes to have survived intact from the early 18th century. The Museum of Sculpture keeps more than 2,000 funerary monuments of great historical or artistic value here. Don't miss the Artists' Necropolis (in the Tikhvin cemetery), where are laid to rest the great figures of Russian culture, such as Dostoevsky and Tchaikovsky.

RELICS OF ALEXANDER NEVSKY
In 1742 Peter the Great decided to move the relics of Alexander Nevsky (then in the town of Vladimir) to St Petersburg. To begin with they were displayed at the Church of the Annunciation, and then transferred to Trinity Cathedral in 1790, where they were placed in a silver sarcophagus (now at the Hermitage).

CHURCH OF THE ANNUNCIATION (BLAGOVESHCHENSKAYA TSERKOV; Благовещенская церковь). The avenue between the two cemeteries crosses a small canal (which joins the Obvodny "lateral" canal, built between 1805 and 1834, to the southward) and leads on to the Monastery entrance. The Church of the Annunciation, which lies immediately to the left, is the oldest in the Monastery. Built between 1717 and 1725 by Domenico Trezzini, it was from the start used as a burial place for major figures such as Vasily Dolgoruky, who traveled to Europe with Peter the Great; Alexei Razumovsky, the morganatic husband of the Empress Elizabeth; Ivan Shuvalov (who was another celebrated favorite of the Czarina's); and the great strategist Field Marshal Alexander Suvorov ▲ *252*. At Suvorov's funeral on December 6, 1800, his coffin appeared to be too wide to be able to pass through the door, but one of the soldiers carrying the bier gave the order: "Forward! Nothing ever stopped Suvarov!" and somehow they managed to force it through. Today the church contains a part of the collection belonging to the Sculpture Museum. Among the items on display are maquettes of a variety of different monuments and statues of St Petersburg (including the Alexander Column ▲ *181* and the Monument to Peter I ▲ *194*).

LAVISH DECORATION
The interior décor of Trinity Cathedral contains an altar of marble and agate, and walls covered in copies of works by Guercino, Van Dyck, Rubens and such Russian painters and other masters as Grigory Ugriumov, Marcin Bielsky and Nikolai Utkin.

TRINITY CATHEDRAL (TROITSKY SOBOV; Троицкий собор). A church built by Schwertfeger originally stood on this site, but its walls were so fissured that in 1753 the Empress Elizabeth I ● *37* ordered its demolition. The stones were reused to pave Nevsky Prospekt; and the subsequent cathedral was built by Ivan Starov between 1778 and 1790, with a restrained pediment, colonnade and single dome, in the classical style that was then in fashion. It is the only place of worship in the Monastery precinct that is still open for services. Behind it stretches the St Nicholas Cemetery (NIKOLSKOYE), where many prominent personalities from the Soviet era are buried.

FEDOROVSKAYA CHURCH (FEDOROVSKAYA TSERKOV; Федоровская церковь). This church (right), built between 1742 and 1750 by Trezzini, to the south of Trinity Cathedral, was also used as a mausoleum for the last kings and princes of Georgia.

Palaces on the outskirts of St Petersburg

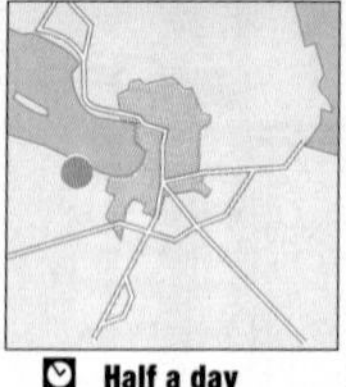

Half a day

STRELNA
On the way to Peterhof note (on the right) Strelna Palace (dating from the first half of the 18th century), along with the grand-ducal residences of Mikhailovka and Znamenka, which were built for the sons of Nicholas I. Strelna Palace, which is currently undergoing restoration, is to be the new coastal residence of the president of Russia.

Peterhof (Петергоф) is one of the oldest summer palaces in the region of St Petersburg, and it is perhaps the most exotic of all because of its unusual seaside situation. In the 19th century Peterhof was one of the world's most extraordinary palace and garden complexes, covering a total area of nearly 2,500 acres. Like the city 20 miles away it is named for the first Emperor of Russia (Peterhof means "Peter's Court"). Peter the Great built a preliminary residence here in 1710, on the edge of a plateau of land commanding fine views of the Gulf of Finland. Then, in place of this small wooden building, in which he would habitually stay on his way to Kronstadt ▲ *192*, he proceeded to construct a far bigger palace (1714), broadly sketched out by himself as a basic plan from which his architect Johann Braunstein worked.

UPPER PARK

The Upper Park (VERKHNY SAD; Верхний сад) ". . . is no less beautiful than that of the King of France" according to the archives. This area served as an ostentatious front courtyard to the Great Palace, the main residence of Peterhof. It was to the Great Palace that Peter the Great summoned the entire corps of foreign diplomats to celebrate the official inauguration of the building that became known a the "Russian Versailles".

GREAT PALACE ★

As we see it now the Great Palace (BOLSHOY DVORETS; Большой дворец) still has the exterior planned by the Empress Elizabeth I ● *37*. After 1745 she had the initial building altered by the architect Bartolomeo Rastrelli ● *84*, who, after enlarging Peter I's original palace, added to it a couple of single-floor galleries, each ending with a pavilion (a church on the east side and an armorial pavilion of the west side). He also surrounded the Upper Park with a long railing punctuated by broad pillars, later designing a formal enfilade in the purest Baroque style.

BAROQUE STAIRCASE
The grand staircase was entirely restored in 1985.

FORMAL STAIRCASE. The stairway to the second floor is typical of the Russian Baroque period. Its décor, designed by Rastrelli in about 1750, combines richly carved and gilded elements in wood (mostly limewood) with numerous trompe-l'oeil features.

CHESME HALL. Contiguous with the ballroom is a large space dedicated to the naval victory of Chesme (1770); this was altered by Yury Velten ● *86* to house major commemorative paintings by Hackert (1737–1807).

THRONE ROOM. In the Throne Room, alongside portraits of Russian sovereigns, is a canvas by the Danish painter Vigilius Erichsen of Catherine II on her horse Brilliant. There are also four pictures of the Battle of Chesme by Joseph Wright of Derby. The Audience Chamber, with its décor by Rastrelli, offers an interesting collection of Russian marquetry gaming tables which date from the latter part of the 18th century.

WHITE DINING ROOM ★. The table set in the White Dining Room, whose neoclassical décor was redesigned by Velten toward 1775, displays a complete set of Wedgwood china delivered from England in 1768.

CHINESE ROOMS. On either side of the Portrait Hall are extravagant Chinese Rooms decorated by Vallin de la Mothe with walls set with lacquer screens and exotic marquetry floors.

LAVISH STUCCO
The walls of the White Dining Room are decorated with white stucco bas-reliefs.

▲ FOUNTAINS AT PETERHOF

The wide variety of fountains at Peterhof is the principal feature of the park. Elsewhere (notably at Versailles) all the surviving fountains are classical in design; not so at Peterhof, where their extravagance and sheer playfulness give us a vivid idea of the atmosphere that must have reigned in a park of this kind during the early 18th century. The Great Cascade, with its Samson Fountain, is the most impressive of all.

FESTIVALS AT PETERHOF ✪
The Baroque masterpiece of Peterhof is now a site for several festivals, the most popular of which are those marking the opening and closing of the fountains (in May and October respectively). Cultural events held between these two festivals include the music festival (June) and the festival of the city of Peterhof (July).

GREAT CASCADE
On the slope between the upper and lower terraces, the Great Cascade is a major feature of Peterhof. The statue of *Samson and the Lion* symbolizes the Russian victory over the Swedes at Poltava (1709).

MARLY CASCADE
▲ *260*. Also called the "Golden Mountain", the Marly Cascade is made of white marble and plaques of gilded copper, which cover its successive levels.

Checkerboard Cascade
The water spouts from the jaws of fierce dragons above giant sloping checkerboards.

The Sun
The perpetually spinning sun and its silvery rays.

Roman fountains
Erected in 1739 at the foot of the Checkerboard Cascade, these statues are reminiscent of those by the fountains of St Peter's in Rome. They were reconstituted in 1792; gilded bronze masks spout water from their plinths.

Portrait Hall. In 1764 the Portrait Hall in the central part of the Palace was decorated by the architect Vallin de la Mothe ● *86* with a rare ensemble of 368 portraits of women painted by Count Pietro Rotari.

Oak Study
This room, with its carved oak boiseries after drawings by Nicolas Pineau (1684–1754), contains assorted personal possessions of Peter I.

Partridge Room. The adjoining Partridge Room takes its name from its partridge-design hangings. These hangings were woven in Lyons, France, afte cartoons by Philippe de la Salle.

Divan Room. This room has walls covered with Chinese silk, and contains an enormous sofa framed by a balustrade in the Turkish manner.

Crown Room. The Crown Room is also covered in 17th-century Chinese silk. During the 18th century the imperial crown was kept in this room when the Court was residing at Peterhof.

Lower Park

Lower Park (Nizhny Park; Нижний парк) was originally planted with lime trees, oaks, elms and maples from Holland Germany, Estonia and the regions of Moscow and Novgorod The geometrical parterres are crowded with the sculptures and fountains that were at that time deemed to be the essential features of any princely park. At the ends of the domain's various prospects there are pavilions designed for the pleasures of the Russian sovereigns and their courtiers.

A sea view
Monplaisir, on the seafront, was a favorite with Peter the Great, who liked to spend several months a year there. William Coxe, visiting the palace in 1784, wrote: "We can form an idea of the austere simplicity in which this sovereign was accustomed to live . . .".

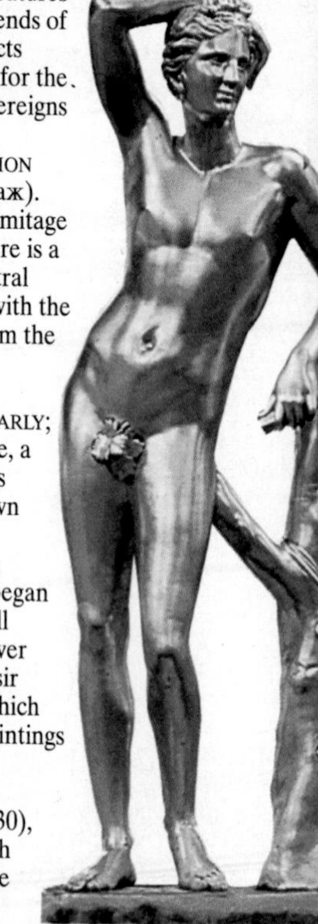

Hermitage Pavilion (Pavilion Ermitazh; павильон Эрмитаж). In the main room of the Hermitage Pavilion, used for dining, there is a mechanism that lifts the central section of the table, loaded with the dishes ordered by guests, from the first floor straight to the second floor.

Marly Palace (Dvorets Marly; дворец Марли). Marly Palace, a favorite of Peter the Great, is furnished according to his own simple taste.

Monplaisir ★ (Monplezir; Монплезир). In 1714, work began on the construction of a small palace the far end of the Lower Park. It was named Monplaisir after the French palace on which it was based. Monplaisir's paintings gallery, which has a ceiling decorated to a design by Philippe Pillement (1684–1730), contains a collection of Dutch and Flemish pictures of battle scenes. In 2001, some of the

Benois Museum
East of the Palace are former court buildings which now contain a museum dedicated to the Benois family ● *104*.

Monplaisir
In 1723 the Marquis de Campredon gave this report to Louis XV: "One enters the house by way of a remarkably well-kept garden. It is square in shape, with double banks of greenery on either side, contiguous to the rooms, in which one can walk unseen . . . lulled by the sound of the great fountain in the garden."

palace's attractive buildings, including the imperial baths and the Chinese garden around them, were opened to the public.
Catherine Wing (Ekaterininsky Korpus; Екатерининский корпус). In the Catherine Wing, added to Monplaisir in the 1740's, a remarkable china service , made at the imperial St Petersburg works between 1809 and 1817, is on display. It is known as the Guriev Service, after the director of the factory. The gilded chandeliers in the Yellow Salon, of pasteboard and carved wood, are remarkable for their quality.

Nicholas I's study.

Alexandria Park

Imperial Stables (Tsarskie Koniushni; Царские конюшни). Beyond the Benois Museum stand the extensive imperial stables (which are now a rest home and closed to the public). They are the work of the architect Nikolai Benois (1856–1928) and their extraordinary neo-Gothic style bears witness to the Czar Nicholas I's pronounced taste for this style.
Gothic chapel (Kapella; капелла). By continuing toward the east through the gates of the Alexandria Park you will reach the imperial family's private oratory, a Gothic chapel built (1831–3) to a design by the Berlin architect Karl Schinkel (1781–1841).
Cottage (Kottedzh; Коттедж)★. You can reach this small pavilion (right) either by walking through Alexandria Park or by car. The cottage was constructed by the architect Adam Menelaws between 1826 and 1829, and it has now been carefully restored to display collections of objects and furniture, along with Russian porcelain and crystal in the dining room. The original stairway leads to the study of Nicholas I, from which he communicated with his fleet by semaphore. The Czarina's study has a stained-glass screen and a remarkable frieze around the bay window. Another interesting feature is the intricate star-burst ceiling of the Grand Drawing Room next door to the Czarina's study.
Neo-Gothic station. To the north of Alexandria Park stands the picturesque neo-Gothic railway station, which was built by Nikolai Benois.

"[The Cottage] is a small house built in the new Gothic style currently fashionable in England."
Astolphe de Custine

COURTYARD/GARDEN
Like Peterhof, the Great Palace is fronted by a huge courtyard/garden surrounded by open land. Two levels of terraces and steps link it to a lower garden area.

About 25 miles from St Petersburg, not far from Peterhof ▲ *256*, is the Oranienbaum estate, which occupies a comparable sloping site and dates from exactly the same period. It was originally given in 1710 by Peter the Great to his companion-in-arms and political advisor Prince Alexander Menshikov ▲ *161* as a summer residence, but it soon reverted to the Crown and was regularly embellished in the 18th century. Until recently, foreign tourists were excluded from Oranienbaum, which stands directly opposite the Kronstadt Naval Base ▲ *192*. Nevertheless, it is one of the very few residences around St Petersburg that did not suffer heavily during World War Two, and has more or less remained in its original state.

CHINESE STUDY
The fine marquetry floors and boiseries of the Chinese Study illustrate large exotic scenes. All are by Russian master cabinet-makers.

GREAT PALACE

Giovanni Maria Fontana began the building works in 1710. The Great Palace (BOLSHOY DVORETS; Большой дворец) takes full advantage of its elevated position, with a central section and two single-story galleries curving round on either side to domed pavilions (a chapel to the west and a Japanese pavilion to the east). Long occupied by government bodies, the Great Palace is currently under restoration and is not open to the public.

CHINESE PALACE ★

Detail of the Glass Study in the Chinese Palace.

The stucco walls and ceilings of the Chinese Palace (KITAISKY DVORETS; Китайский дворец), built by Rinaldi ● *86* in 1762, provide the background for frescos and oil paintings by Italian artists. The interior style is Rococo, while outside it is a less flamboyant Baroque.

GLASS STUDY. On the floor, once of glass, are two extraordinary "smalt" marquetry tables.

CHINESE KITCHEN. In the Chinese Kitchen and the Cavalry House, both nearby, are objects from the Far East and 17th- and 18th-century paintings.

ᑭETER III'S PALACE

ᑎear the Great Palace is the Palace of Peter III (DVORETS ᑭETRA III; дворец Петра III), to which Oranienbaum devolved ɪn 1743. Peter III, nephew of Empress Elizabeth I ● *36* and a ɪnonarch of rabid military bent, built a fortress here called ᑭeterstadt, where he had Russian troops parade about in ʒerman uniforms. Nothing remains of it but this small, two-tory palace, constructed by Antonio Rinaldi ● *86* and ɪecorated in Chinese style with silk hangings, lacquer ɪaintings and dress cabinets. The Picture Hall houses Italian ɪnd Flemish paintings.

PEARL GLASS
The Glass Study in the Chinese Palace, a masterpiece of extravagance, has eleven panels and two door lintels in pearl glass made in the workshops of the great Russian scientist and writer Mikhail Lomonosov, after whom Oranienbaum was renamed in 1948.

'SLIDING HILL" ★

Ɪeading toward the sea, you come to "Sliding Hill" PAVILION KATALNOY GORKY; павильон Катальной горки), ɪlso designed by Rinaldi (1762–74). Built on a helical plan, ɪntil the early 19th century it had an extension in the form ɪf a 1,500-foot wooden colonnade, in the middle of which ɪvas a *montagne russe* ▲ *185* for the diversion of the court a model of this is displayed on the first floor). From the econd-floor windows you can see the island of Kronstadt, ɪnd notably the dome of its huge Byzantine-style cathedral 1902–13).

ᖇOUND ROOM. The central salon, or Round Room, still has its ɪriginal *scagliola* floor, made of powdered marble mixed to ɪmitate colored marble marquetry.

MEISSEN PORÇELAIN
In the Porcelain Room is a rare series of Meissen figurines, which symbolize the prestige of the Russian Empire.

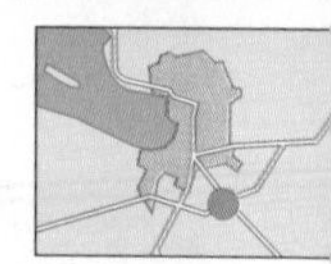

Half a day

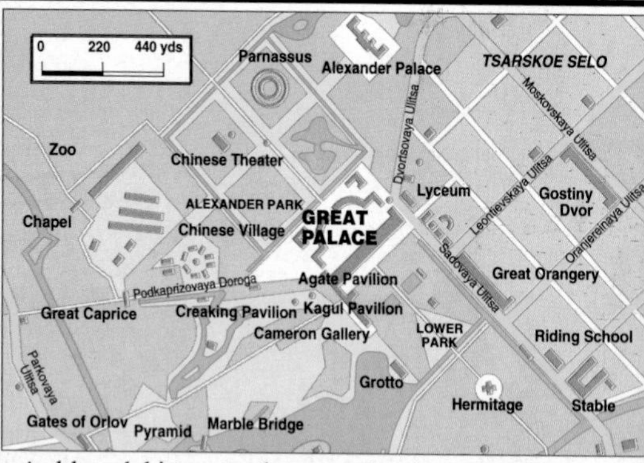

Although history tends to associate its name with Catherine the Great the palace of Tsarskoe Selo (TSARSKOÏE SELO; Царское Село) was built at the beginning of the 18th century. In 1710 Peter the Great gave his second wife, Catherine, a small property 15 miles south of St Petersburg. When Elizabeth, Catherine's daughter, came to the throne in 1741 she found the house too small; and in 1743 she commissioned Mikhail Zemtsov to enlarge it. This he did by adding two wings, linked to the main building by single-story galleries leading to pavilions. The finished

ensemble, however, lacked unity, and in 1752 Bartolomeo Rastrelli ● *84* was asked to entirely redesign it. The building we see today is the result of his work, is a surprising 900 feet in breadth.

CATHERINE PALACE ★

FAÇADE. The columns, with composite capitals, are themselves supported by massive Atlas figures; they punctuate most of the bays in the façade of the Catherine Palace (BOLSHOY EKATERININSKY DVORETS; Большой Екатерининский дворец), which incorporates no fewer than five projecting and pedimented buildings. The series of diverse rooms within, restored in the 1960's, gives an idea of the development of the Russian interior through three very different epochs.

State Staircase. This was installed between 1860 and 1864 by Hippolyte Monighetti (1819–78) in the center of the palace. On the upper landing are folding chairs with the monogram of Elizabeth I, made in the workshops of Tula ● *60*.

Catherine Palace.

Great Hall. Decorated in a generous Baroque style, with a painted ceiling representing "The Triumph of Russia", this immense room is the focal point of the palace as it was redesigned by Rastrelli in the late 18th century.

State Staircase.

Knights' Banqueting Hall. In this hall the table is set with china that was made to order for Catherine II by the Gardner works in Moscow. The banqueting hall was formerly heated by a pair of enormous Dutch faience stoves.

Great Hall (detail below).

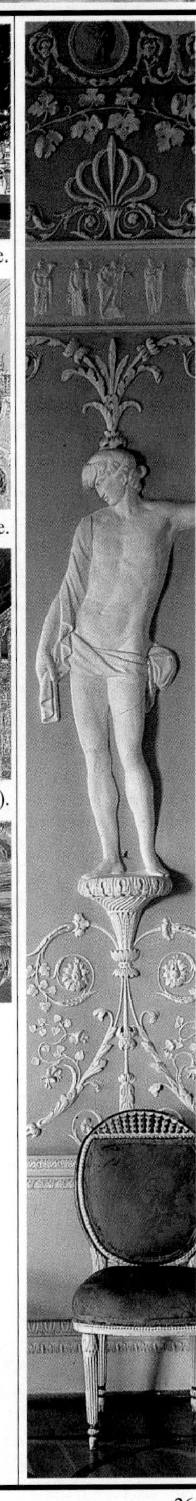

Picture gallery. There are 117 works altogether, by painters such as Luca Giordano, David Teniers and Jean-Marc Nattier, which hang here side by side in the decorative spirit of the 18th century.

Amber Room. The Amber Room, whose tall panels were presented to Peter the Great by the King of Prussia in 1716, is currently under restoration and is not open to the public.

First apartment. The rooms of the first apartment, converted by the Scottish architect Charles Cameron ● *86* for the heir to the throne Czarevich Paul Petrovich ● *37*, are decorated in the neoclassical style, Catherine II's favorite. In the Green dining room ★ (details on the left and right of these pages) the accent is deliberately innovative; on the ceiling, which is bare of ornamentation, are ample white stucco figures in relief, alternating with tall matching antique tripods. The Bedroom is even more surprising, with its multiple colonnettes delineating the alcove and punctuating the walls.

The Creaking Pavilion
The badly oiled weathercocks on the roof of the Chinese Pavilion (Kitaisky Pavilion; Китайский павильон) earned it the name of Creaking Pavilion.

Old Garden

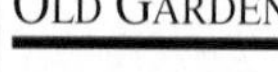

All too often the visit to Tsarskoe Selo is confined to the Catherine Palace, but the park and its many pavilions hold much of interest. Below the eastern façade of the Palace extends the Old Garden (Stary sad; Старый сад); here are the Upper and Lower Baths, built by the architect Ilya Neelov in the late 1770's.

Hermitage

Down from the Old Garden stands the Hermitage (Ermitazh; павильон Эрмитаж), built by Rastrelli, where receptions were held in the summer; nearby is the Hermitage Kitchen, in a remarkably composite style.

Cameron Gallery
Catherine II wrote to Baron Grimm in Paris: "If you could only see what a magnificent gallery and what marvelous hanging gardens I shall soon have . . ."

Agate Pavilion ★

In the vicinity of the Palace the Old Garden is delineated by two of the most interesting buildings of Tsarskoe Selo: the Agate Pavilion (Agatovy Pavilion; Агатовый павильон) and the Cameron Gallery, both built after 1780.

Cold baths. The first floor of the Agate Pavilion was occupied by the Tsarina's cold baths. On the second floor the Agate bedrooms open on to a hanging garden, which in turn gives access to the elegant Cameron Gallery. There are also a large salon and two studies with walls richly covered in semi-precious agate from the Urals, after which the pavilion is named. (These rooms are currently closed to visitors.)

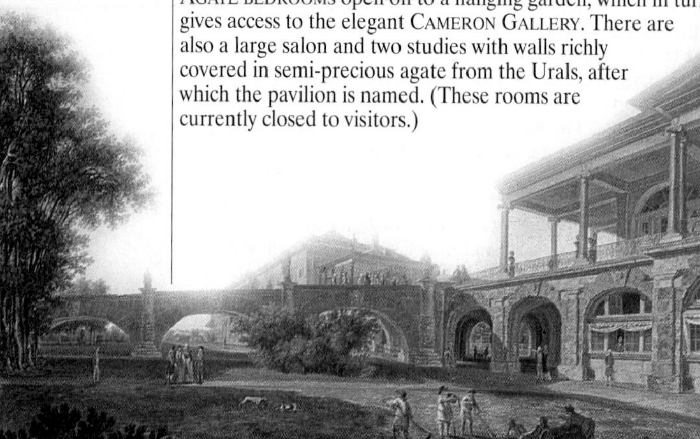

Catherine Park

The lower reaches of Catherine Park (Ekaterininsky Park; Екатерининский парк) are taken up by a lake; nearby is a series of follies.

Grotto, or Morning Salon. Originally decorated with thousands of seashells, the grotto was built in the reign of Elizabeth I by Rastrelli. Catherine II liked to come here from time to time, early in the morning, after her marathon work sessions.

Around the lake. The Turkish-inspired "Admiralty" and the Chesme Column (Chesmenskaya Kolona; Чесменская колонна) in the middle of the lake are succeeded by the Turkish baths built by Monighetti toward 1850. The Pyramid, where Catherine II's dogs are buried, is close to the Palladian bridge. Other monumental features include the Orlov Gate and the impressive ruined tower designed by Yury Velten ● *86*.

Upper garden. North of Catherine Park are the Evening Hall, the Concert Hall and the Creaking Pavilion. The Great Caprice, an elaborate arch standing at the end of the avenue that separates Catherine Park from Alexander Park, has a pagoda-like roof supported on Ruskeala marble columns.

Kagul obelisk
This monument stands opposite the side wing of Catherine Palace.

The arch
On the way to Catherine Palace you pass beneath an arch; this communicates with the Lyceum, a building converted into a school in the 19th century. The poet Pushkin was educated here.

Alexander Park

Alexander Park (Alekandrovsky Park; Александровский парк) is named for the Grand Duke Alexander Pavlovich, the future Alexander I and favorite grandson of Catherine II.

Chinese Village. This echoes the pavilions described, with its painted roofs, its theater and its various quaint bridges, such as the cross-shaped one with four lamps.

Alexander Palace (Aleksandrovsky Dvorets; Александровский дворец). This classical building, built by Quarenghi in 1792 for the future Emperor, was also the favorite residence of the last members of the imperial family.

▲ PALACES ON THE OUTSKIRTS PAVLOVSK

Pavlovsk is the most elegant of the summer palaces around St Petersburg, in its decoration and the quality and quantity of the objects it contains. Although PAVLOVSK (Павловск) is no more than four miles from Tsarskoe Selo, visitors from abroad seldom take the trouble to go there. None the less, there is a striking contrast between the majestic aspect of the latter and the more homely character of the former. The histories of the two palaces would have been very similar had it not been for an adventure unique in the annals of the 18th century. In order to get away from the court, and above all to visit the capitals of Western Europe and acquire works of art for their residence, Paul Petrovich and the Grand Duchess Maria Fyodorovna set out on a tour lasting over a year. They left St Petersburg on September 19, 1781 and embarked on a 428-day journey that would take them the length and breadth of Europe, with the objective of embellishing the palace of Pavlovsk.

Paul Petrovich and Maria Fyodorovna.

PAVLOVSK
The original wooden houses on the site, known as Krik and Krak, were succeeded by two small palaces, also in wood, called Marienthal ("Maria's Valley") and Paulslust ("Paul's Joy"). No doubt these were still considered inadequate, so the decision was made to build yet again. The result was what we know as Pavlovsk Palace (Pavlovsky Dvorets; Павловский дворец), much larger and in brick; it was designed by Charles Cameron ● *86*, one of Catherine II's favorite architects.

GREAT PALACE ★

STATE APARTMENTS. The central block of the building is classical in structure. On the second floor are the apartments of Paul and Maria Fyodorovna, set around a central salon known as the Greek Hall. On the Grand Duke's side this leads on to a room called the Hall of War and on the Grand Duchess's side the Hall of Peace. The décor, begun by Charles Cameron ● *86*, was mostly completed by Vincenzo Brenna (1740–1819), an Italian artist whom Paul and Maria Fyodorovna met in Poland on their travels.

GALLERIES. After Paul I's accession in 1796 Brenna was commissioned to enlarge the palace, now an imperial residence. He heightened the two single-story side galleries

A lavish gift
Originally a hunting estate, the domain of Pavlovsk was given by Catherine II to her son Paul, when the Grand Duchess produced a male heir for the dynasty, Alexander, on December 12, 1777.

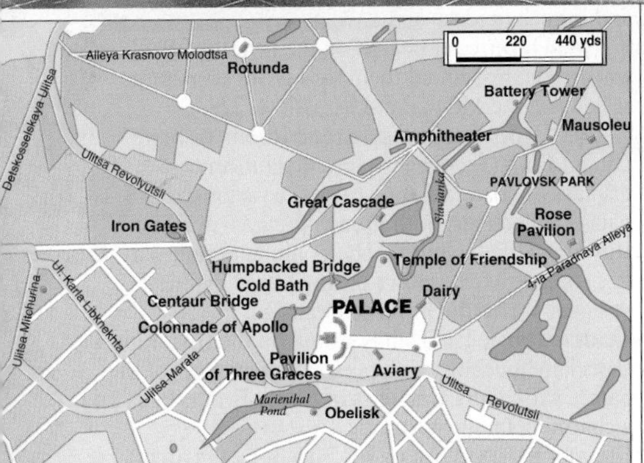

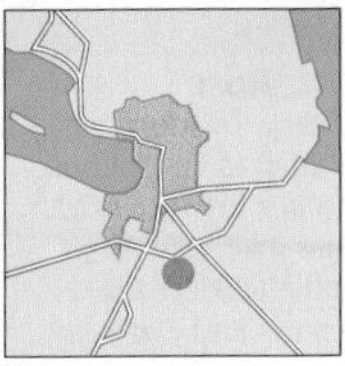

Half a day

Vestibule
The Vestibule (where the tour begins) was decorated by Voronikhin with twelve allegorical sculptures in the Egyptian style, very fashionable at the time. On the upper landing can still be seen the elaborate stucco décor designed by Brenna.

built by Cameron. He then added two ample pavilions to house the new Throne Room and chapel; and finally he included two other service wings, on the same quarter-circle plan.

Hall of War. The carved and gilded wooden *torchères* of the Hall of War (opposite page, top left) are additional tangible proof of the special talent of Russian artisans for woodwork, such as the chairs in the Greek Hall and the marquetry floors of the Grand Duchess's apartment.

Boudoir. The Boudoir is decorated with porphyry columns and painted pilasters brought from Italy by the royal couple (left page, center).

Vase from the toilet service of Maria Fyodorovna.

GRAND DUCHESS'S STATE APARTMENTS. In the apartments of Maria Fyodorovna (center) is a magnificent series of Gobelins and Savonnerie tapestries, along with a sixty-four piece toilet service in Sèvres porcelain kept in a glass cabinet opposite the bed, which was given to Paul I and the Grand Duchess by Louis XVI and Marie-Antoinette during their visit to France.

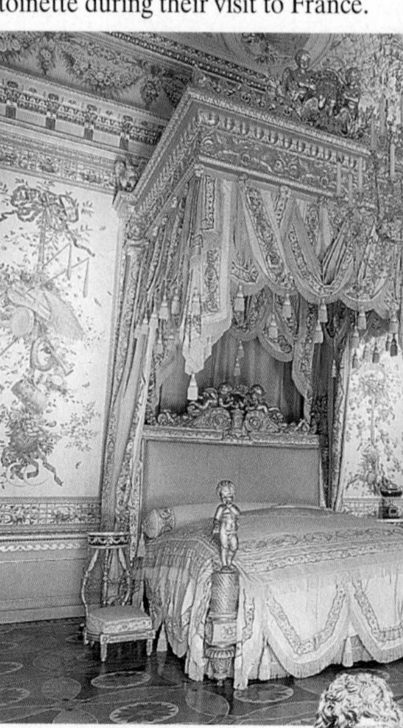

THE ROSE
Maria Fyodorovna dedicated a pavilion to her favorite flower, the rose, a motif which covers the chairs and everyday objects.

"... 1,500,000 roubles are invested in perpetuity for the upkeep of Pavlovsk .. I give to my son the Grand Duke Mikhail the castle of Pavlovsk ... the Grand Duke Mikhail will gain possession of Pavlovsk on condition that the castle, the gardens, parks, orangeries, hospital and invalids' home ... that, in a word, all the dependencies of that beautiful place, are maintained ..."
Maria Fyodorovna

PICTURE GALLERY. In the picture gallery Russian furniture and vases relate harmoniously with European paintings and French objects in gilded bronze purchased on the orders of Paul I, who originally wanted them for his St Petersburg residence, the Mikhailovsky Castle ▲ *229*.

THRONE ROOM ★. In the Throne Room, or State Dining Room (above left), are magnificent displays of porcelain ● *64* from the various palace collections, both French (Sèvres) and Russian (St Petersburg). The dominant feature of this room is its enormous ceiling fresco by the set designer Pietro di Gottardo Gonzaga.

FAMILY ROOM. The Family Room on the first floor is especially touching, with personal mementos of the palace's founders, drawings of Maria Fyodorovna and a charming family portrait.

CORNER SALON. With its 1815 décor by the architect Carlo Rossi ● *86*, the Corner Salon shows the evolution of taste during the reign of Alexander I.

BALLROOM. In the gay pink and blue ballroom are four major canvases by the French artist Hubert Robert, of which Paul I was particularly fond.

MUSEUM OF INTERIORS. On the third floor the Museum of Interiors exhibits a collection of Russian furniture and objects from the late 18th and 19th centuries.

"A home, a colonnade, a temple at Pavlovsk give me greater joy than all the beauties of Italy."
Maria Fyodorovna

Park at Pavlovsk

Aviary. Near the palace stands an aviary, designed by Cameron, in which the Grand Duchess bred her songbirds.
Temple of Friendship. Further on is the Temple of Friendship, also built by Cameron, which symbolized the reconciliation between Paul Petrovich and Catherine II. The walls bear depictions of platonic and romantic love.

The Slavyanka
On the banks of the Slavyanka, and overlooking it, are the foundation obelisk and the Marienthal staircase, formerly a landing stage.

Pil Tower. Beyond the cast-iron bridge designed by Rossi and the amphitheater is the thatched Pil Tower.
New Woods. In the New Woods overlooking the Slavyanka are the monument to Maria Fyodorovna's parents, the Duke and Duchess of Württemberg (their profiles appear on a marble pyramid inside) and the mausoleum of Paul I.
Vanished pavilions. Other favorite retreats of the owners of Pavlovsk (the Old Chalet, the Elizabeth Pavilion by the Slavyanka Valley, the New Chalet and the farm in the Great Star area) have disappeared since World War Two. The Great Star is formed by twelve paths which converge on a statue of Apollo at the center. A statue of a mythological figure stands at the entrance to each path.
Rose Pavilion. This place, much loved by Maria Fyodorovna (especially after she became a widow), stands on an expanse of parkland known as the White Birch. It was here that the Dowager Empress met her son Alexander I ● *36* after his victory over Napoleon. In seventeen days the decorator Pietro Gonzaga managed to add a ballroom, dedicated to the liberator of Europe. The current restoration of this building, so dear to the creator of Pavlovsk, at a time when Russia is going through times of special difficulty, is a striking symbol of the nation's deep attachment to its history and culture.

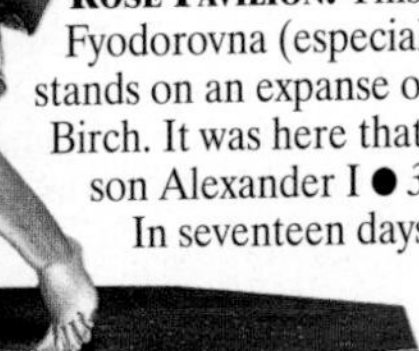

Pavlovsk Park
(Pavlovsky Park; Павловский парк). The grounds of Pavlovsk, covering nearly 2,000 acres, were a major interest of Paul Petrovich and Maria Fyodorovna from the start. They beautified the estate with artificial lakes and follies. The meandering river Slavyanka served as the basis for Cameron's first landscape project.

APARTMENTS
The State Staircase leads directly to the Great Antechamber, which is followed by the Marble Dining Room and Paul I's Throne Room (the tapestries here were a gift from Louis XVI). In the White Room (below) the walls are covered in stucco by Rinaldi.

In 1766 Catherine II gave Gatchina (Гатчина) to Count Orlov. On this estate, 28 miles from St Petersburg, the architect Antonio Rinaldi ● *86* built a country residence. After 1783 Gatchina belonged to Paul Petrovich, who had it altered to some extent by the architect Vincenzo Brenna ▲ *268*. Following Paul I's assassination, the palace was left empty until Nicholas I ordered its restoration in 1844.

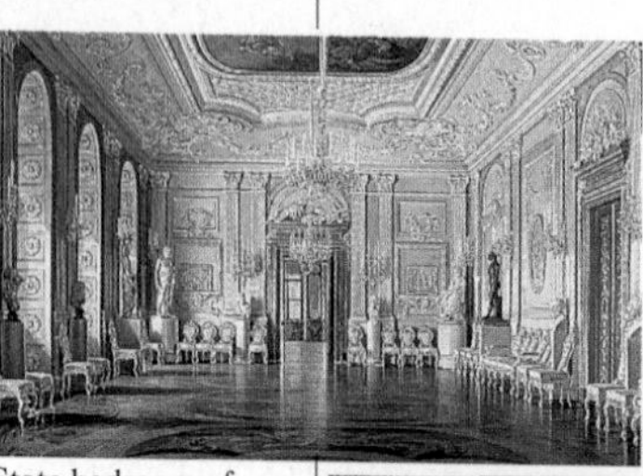

State bedroom of Maria Fyodorovna (right).

GATCHINA PALACE

FAÇADE. Gatchina Palace (GATCHINSKY DVORETS; Гатчинский дворец), faced entirely in limestone, is made up of a central block with galleries on either side leading to service wings. The plan is quadrilateral, with an inner courtyard.

"SQUARE" WINGS OF THE ARSENAL AND KITCHENS. Under Nicholas I the main central building was converted into a memorial of filial devotion, and comfortable apartments were set up in the lateral wings.

INTERIOR DÉCOR. The décor of the central building nearly all dates from Rinaldi's time (elaborate marquetry floors and fine stuccos).

ENGLISH GARDEN
An English garden was fashioned from the original hunting estate, described by Orlov in a letter to Rousseau: "Sixty versts from St Petersburg I have a property where the knolls surrounding the lakes are an inspiration . . . to reverie." The park is filled with picturesque monuments, notably the Chesme Obelisk.

GATCHINA PARK

After the death of Orlov the park at Gatchina (GATCHINSKY PARK; Гатчинский парк) was embellished with several new buildings. By the White and Silver lakes are two pavilions: the Venus Pavilion, a copy of the Prince de Condé's original at Chantilly, in France, and the Birch Pavilion, whose rustic exterior belies an interior of great refinement.

Practical information

USEFUL ADDRESSES

→ CONSULATES OF THE RUSSIAN FEDERATION

■ **Canada**
3655 Avenue du Musée
Montreal
Quebec H3G 2EI
Tel. (514) 843 5901

■ **United Kingdom**
5 Kensington Palace Gardens
London W8 4QP
Tel. 020 7229 8027
Visa Information:
Tel. 09065 508 960 (£1/min.)
Fax 020 7229 3215
www.russialink.org.uk

■ **United States**
– 2641 Tunlaw Road NW, Washington, DC 20007
Tel. (202) 939 8907
Email: waconsru@prodigy.net
– 9 East 91st St.
New York, NY 10128
Tel. (212) 348 0926
Email: nymail@ruscon.com
– 2790 Green Street
San Francisco, CA 94123
Tel. (415) 928 6878
www.consulsf@netcom.com

→ TOURIST OFFICES

■ **United Kingdom**
– Russian National Tourist Office
70 Piccadilly
London W1J 8HP
Tel. 020 7495 7555
Fax 020 7495 8555
www.travel-guide/data/rus/
– Intourist Travel Ltd
7 Wellington Terrace
London
W2 4LW
Tel. 020 7727 4100
Fax 020 7727 8090
www.intourist.co.uk

■ **United States**
Russian National Tourist Office
130 W. 42nd St., Suite 412
New York, NY 10036
Tel. (212) 575 3431
Tollfree (US):
Tel. 877 221 7120
Fax (212) 575 3434
www.russia-travel.com

→ RUSSIA ON THE NET

Travel information on St Petersburg:
www.travel.spb.ru
www.infoservices.com/stpete
Travelers' Yellow Pages online
http://petersburgcity.com
Travel information on the Russian Federation:
www.geographia.com/russia
www.russia-travel.com
www.russian-tours.spb.ru

FORMALITIES

→ VISAS

Aren't really straightforward. Contact your nearest consulate or consult the following very helpful website where you can download a visa application form, get the necessary "invitation" you need to enter the Russian Federation and where all other formalities are clearly explained.
www.russianvisas.org
Tariffs vary a lot. Tourist visas cost beetween US$70 and US$80 and take at least eight working days to be processed. The price for a business visa varies on the length of stay and the speed at which you need your visa. Business visas cost from US$110 to US$300, for a same-day visa and/or a year-long stay.
www.russianvisas.org
www.traveldocs.com/ru/

■ **Passport**
Must be valid for six months beyond your intended stay.

■ **Travel insurance**
Your insurance policy must cover medical expenses as well as costs of repatriation and funeral expenses in the case of death. It must be issued by an insurance company that has a reinsurance agreement with a Russian equivalent company.

■ **Tourist invitation**
To enter the Russian Federation you must produce an official "invitation" from a business relation or a friend in Russia, or confirmation of your hotel booking in St Petersburg.

■ **Customs**
When entering the Russian Federation you must fill out one of the two copies of the customs declaration form provided, indicating the amount of foreign currency as well as any valuables you are bringing into the country. Be sure to keep this form safe, together with the receipts for all currency exchange transactions and purchases as you may be required to produce these documents upon leaving the country. You must fill out the second copy of the customs form at the end of your stay. The amount declared when you leave the country must not be superior to the amount declared when you arrived.

→ DRIVING LICENSE

An international driving license is strongly recommended.

TELEPHONE

→ FROM UK

Dial 00 + 7 + 812 (area code for St Petersburg), followed by the 7-digit number.

→ FROM THE US

Dial 011 + 7 + 812, followed by the 7-digit number.

TIME DIFFERENCE

GMT + 3.
St Petersburg is eight hours ahead of Eastern Standard (New York) time and three hours ahead of London all year round.

TRAVEL

→ BY AIR

From the UK, Aeroflot and British Airways operate direct flights to St Petersburg.
In the USA, Continental offer direct flights to St Petersburg from Los Angeles. Other major airlines offer connecting flights. Check with the following companies for details of fares and conditions:

■ **From the UK**
AEROFLOT
Tel. 020 7355 2233
www.aeroflot.co.uk
www.aeroflot.org
AUSTRIAN AIRLINES
Tel. 0845 601 0948
www.aua.com
BRITISH AIRWAYS
Tel. 0345 222 111
www.britishairways.com
FINNAIR
Tel. 0870 241 4411
www.finnair.com
LUFTHANSA
Tel. 0845 773 7747
www.lufthansa.co.uk

■ **From the US**
AEROFLOT
Tel. 1 888 340 6400
www.aeroflot.com
www.aeroflot.org
BRITISH AIRWAYS
Tel. 1 800 AIRWAYS
www.ba.com
CONTINENTAL
Tel. 1 800 525 0280 or 1 800 231 0856
www.continental.com
DELTA
Tel. 1 800 241 4141
www.delta.com
LUFTHANSA
Tel. 1 800 645 3880
www.lufthansa.com/us

→ BY ROAD FROM THE UK

Traveling to St Petersburg by road is not

recommended. Russian authorities cannot guarantee any back-up services in the case of breakdown and other eventualities, and only certain through routes are advised.

→ BY TRAIN AND SEA FROM THE UK

■ **By train**
Eurostar from London Waterloo to Brussels, then another train to Berlin. From Berlin the 'Moskva Express' travels direct to St Petersburg (journey time about one and a half days). Trains leave daily (except Sat.) June–Sep.; Tue., Thur. and Sun. only Oct.–May. A Belarus transit visa is required, as well as your Russian visa.

Information
EUROSTAR (London)
Tel. 0870 160 6600
www.eurostar.com
For train information throughout Europe:
www.seat61.com

■ **By sea**
There are sea links between London, Göteborg, Oslo and Helsinki, and numerous cruises in the Baltic Sea that include St Petersburg on their route. Contact the Russian National Tourist Office or Intourist Travel Ltd (see *Useful addresses* above), or a specialized tour operator.

MONEY

→ CURRENCY
The ruble.
Warning: Rubles issued before 1993 are no longer valid.

■ **Coins**
1, 2, 5 rubles and kopecks (1 r = 100 k)

■ **Bills**
10, 50, 100, 500, and 1,000 rubles.

→ EXCHANGE
Rubles cannot be converted. Exchange can only take place in the Russian Federation.

US$1 = 31.85 rubles, CA$1 = 20.38 rubles, £1 = 51.30 rubles (at time of research).
More on money p279.

CLIMATE

→ GEOGRAPHY
St Petersburg is the most northerly of the world's large metropolises. Its geographical location – at the mouth of the Gulf Stream, close to the Arctic Circle – is the reason for the extreme changes and capricious variations of its continental climate.

→ TEMPERATURES AND RAINFALL
Winters at this latitude are extremely hard, and the short springs and falls are often wet and rainy. Summers are usually mild. The following chart gives the average mimimum and maximum temperatures (in °F), and average rainfall in St Petersburg (in inches).

	Jan.	Feb.	Mar.
T	9	10	18
	19	23	32
R	1½	1¼	1
	Apr.	**May**	**June**
T	32	43	52
	46	59	68
R	1⅓	1½	2
	July	**Aug.**	**Sep.**
T	55	55	48
	70	68	59
R	2¾	3	2¼
	Oct.	**Nov.**	**Dec.**
T	39	28	18
	48	36	27
R	2	1¾	1½

WHEN TO GO

The best months to visit St Petersburg are May, June, July, September, October, December and January.

■ **March to April**
The city is quieter, with fewer visitors, and prices are not as high, especially for accommodation.

■ **Mid-May to mid-July**
Days seem never-ending during the city's "white nights" that occur around the summer solstice (June 11 to early July). This is the perfect time for romantic night-time walks along the Neva. It is also the festival season, see *Celebrations and Festivals* p302.

■ **September to October**
In fall visitors can enjoy in peace the lovely colors of St Petersburg's numerous parks and gardens, as well as cruise down the Neva before it becomes solid ice.

■ **December to January**
There are barely five hours of sunlight a day in December. But it is also the time of the true Russian winter. With luck you may see the Neva frozen over and may be able to walk on the icy solid Gulf of Finland. The Russians hold four end-of-year celebrations: on December 25 and 31 and on January 6 and 13 (Roman Catholic and Orthodox Christmasses and New Year's Days, respectively). Various public events take place (see p308*)*, and major hotels and restaurants also organize end-of-year parties.

HEALTH

→ FIRST-AID KIT
Take your usual medicines with you, such as antibiotics and anti-diarrhea tablets, but make sure all packages are intact in order to avoid trouble at customs when entering the country. If you are undergoing a course of treatment, keep a prescription with you bearing the generic names of the drugs you need.

→ VACCINATIONS
None required from European or American visitors, however DT polyo, typhoid, and hepatitis A and B inoculations are recommended. Any visitor intending to stay in the Russian Federation for more than three months must produce a certificate confirming that they are not HIV-positive. This certificate must mention their passport number and be signed by a doctor. It remains valid for three months.

VOLTAGE

220 Volts.
Plugs are similar to continental European ones. Adapters and power converters are recommended for all American appliances.

PHOTOGRAPHY AND VIDEO

Film, tapes, batteries available from specialized stores, but make sure you take enough equipment with you. In most national museums you can take photographs without a flash for a nominal fee. Never take pictures in theaters or circuses.

When in St Petersburg you do not need to dial the city code 812 before the seven-digit phone number.

ACCOMMODATION

→ CLASSIFICATION AND RATES

The number of foreign visitors to St Petersburg has been growing steadily in recent years, unfortunately the Russian hotel infrastructure has not been able to keep up with the demand. It is still undergoing major transformation, and prices vary greatly according to the season (they actually double during the "white nights" period from mid-May to mid-July). Hotels under 3 stars are practically non-existent in the city center.

■ Hotels

Double room, excluding breakfast:
★★★ US$45–110
★★★★ US$120–380
★★★★★
from US$300

Half-board

★★★ US$ 55–120
★★★★ US$140–400
★★★★★
over US$390

■ Staying with a Russian family

US$20–50 per room
Email: homestays@nb.spb.ru

■ Reservations

See *Useful addresses* p282.

■ Youth Hostels

US$15–35
per person.
www.ryh.ru

■ Apartments

US$30–150 per night for the apartment (may vary according to the size of the apartment and to the distance from the city center).

■ Rental agencies

Adveks
Nevsky Pr. 32–34
Open 9am–9pm.
Closed Sun.

Bekar
Bolshoy Sampsonievsky Pr. 61
Business-center Bekar
Open 9am–10pm,
Sat.–Sun. 10am–8pm

Itaka
Bolshoy Pr. VO 36
Tel. 812 325 8020
or 812 327 9800
Open 10am–7pm,
Closed Sat.–Sun.

ARRIVALS AND DEPARTURES

→ BY AIR

■ Pulkovo 2 International Airport

Located 10 miles south of the city center, on Startovaya Ul.

International flights
Tel. 812 104 3444

Tourist Information Bureau
Arrival hall, or:
Nevsky Pr. 41
Tel. 812 311 2843
Fax 812 311 2943

■ Pulkovo 1 International Airport

Located 10½ miles south of the city center, on Pulkovsky Road.

Domestic flights (C.E.I.)
Tel. 812 104 3822

■ Airport links

From Pulkovo 1
Express bus no. 39 (departure every hour) to Moskovskaya Metro station (15–20 mins); tickets sold on the bus (under US$1). Change at Moskovskaya for Nevsky Pr. station (or other destinations), duration: 15–20 mins.

From Pulkovo 2
Express bus no. 13 or shared taxi (*marshrutnoye taksy*) to Moskovskaya station, from 7am–10pm. Tickets from the bus driver (under US$1).

Taxis
Taxi rank outside the terminal; fares go from US$20–50, according to the length of the journey. Many private cab drivers will offer you their services inside the airport arrival hall; agree on the fare before starting your journey. (See *Transport, city* p281).

■ Airlines

AEROFLOT
Nevsky Pr. 7/9
Tel. 812 314 6959
Pulkovo Airport
Tel. 812 104 3444

BRITISH AIRWAYS
Sweden House
Malaya Konyushennaya Ul. 1/3A, Office B23
Tel. 812 329 2565
Pulkovo Airport
Tel. 812 346 8146

FINNAIR
Kazanskaya Ul. 44
Tel. 812 326 1870
Pulkovo Airport
Tel. 812 324 3249

LUFTHANSA
Nevsky Pr. 32 (2nd Fl.)
Tel. 812 320 1000
Pulkovo Airport
Tel. 812 324 3244

PULKOVO AIRLINES
Pervaya Krasnoarmeyskaya Ul. 4
Tel. 812 303 9268
or 812 303 9267

CENTRAL TICKETING OFFICE
Nevsky Pr. 7/9
Tel. 812 311 80 93
or 812 315 00 72
Open 8am–8pm,
Sat.–Sun. 8am–6pm.

→ BY BOAT

Passenger maritime port (*Morskoy Passajirsky Port*)
Morskoy Slavy Pl. 1
Tel. 812 355 13 10.
Also known as Gavan (harbor), it is located at the end of Great Prospekt (Bolshoy Pr.) on Vasilyevsky Island, on the Gulf of Finland. It is the port of call of all Northern European cruises. The only regular crossing currently operating is between Stockholm and St Petersburg.

→ BY TRAIN

(See *Transport, regional* p282).

BRIDGES

St Petersburg's 300 or so bridges form an intergal part of its architectural heritage. Between them they link the 42 islands that make up the city. Between April and November – when the rivers are not frozen – the swing bridges (20 in total) stay raised for part of the night in order to let commercial vessels through. You are advised to be aware of the bridge opening and closing times in order to avoid being stranded on the wrong island.

→ SWING BRIDGE LIFTING TIMES

■ Alexandra Nevskogo
1.30–5.05am

■ Birzhevoy
2.10–4.50am

■ Bolsheokhtinsky
2–5am

■ Bolshoy Krestovsky
2.05–3.55am and 4.40–5.20am

■ Bolshoy Petrovsky
1.25–2am and 5–5.45am

■ Dvortsovy
1.50-2.55am and 3.15–4.50am

■ Elagin I
by special order

■ Elagin II
by special order

■ Elagin III
by special order

■ Grenadersky
2.45–3.45am and 4.20–4.50am

■ Kamennoostrovsky
2.15–3am and 4.05–4.55am

■ Kantemirovsky
2.45–3.45 am and 4.20–4.50am

■ Lazarevsky
1.55–2.35am and 4.45–5.20am

■ Leitenanta Schmidta
1.40-4.55am

■ Liteiny
1.50–4.40am

■ Sampsonievsky
2.10–2.45am and 3.20–4.25am

■ Troitsky
1.50–4.50am
■ Tuchkov
2.10–3.05am and
3.35–4.45am
■ Ushakovsky
2.15–2.55am and
3.55–4.30am
■ Volodarsky
2–3.45am and
4.15–5.45am

CHILDREN

If your children are accompanying you, take them to:

■ **Central Leisure Park** (Elagin Island): giant wheel, rowing boats...
■ **Victory Park "Primorsky"** (Krestovsky Island): tennis courts, rollerskating rink, dolphins, poneys.
■ **Zoo** and other attractions in Alexandrovsky Park.
■ **Zoological Museum**
One of the largest natural history museums in the world.

COST OF LIVING

Prices are volatile and inflation is rife. The tariffs applied to foreign visitors in tourist areas are those of Western Europe. Admission fees to sites and museums are higher than those charged to Russians in order to finance the restoration of the national heritage, while allowing local people access to their own culture.

■ **Cup of coffee:** US$1.50
■ **Pint of beer:** From US$1
■ **Bottle of wine:** From US$10
■ **Lunch:** From US$3
■ **Dinner in a restaurant:** From US$15 per person
■ **Museum admission fee:** From US$5–10
■ **Theater ticket:** From US$25
■ **Single room in a hotel:** From US$45

DRIVING

→ CARS

■ **Driving license**
You are advised to carry an international driving license.

■ **Highway code**
Roundabouts: cars entering the roundabout have right of way over those already engaged.

■ **Speed limits**
In built-up areas: 37 miles/hr (60km/hr)
On the road: 56 miles/hr (90km/hr)

■ **Alcohol levels in the blood**
Zero tolerance.

■ **Parking**
Parking in the city center is unmarked and free of charge. There are some attended parking lots, charged by the hour, near the major hotels and tourist sites.

■ **Rescue service**
Tel. 320 9000

BOAT CRUISE

HELICOPTER TRIP ABOVE THE NEVA

■ **Gasoline**
Prices (at the time of printing):
Super plus 98: US$1.90/US gallon
Super 95: US$1.50/US gallon
Normal 92: US$1.13/US gallon
Diesel: US$0.95/US gallon
In 2003, the price of gasoline in Russia may rise by 20% to 30%.

■ **Traffic jams**
Traffic and congestion are severe, especially in the city center in the rush hours, between 8am–10am and 5pm–8pm.

→ CAR RENTAL

Not necessary if you're planning to stay in the city.

■ **Conditions**
You must be over 21 and have held a driving license for at least a year.

■ **Payment**
By credit card (Amex, Visa, DC, Mc/Ec, JCB, Hertz Charge Card).

■ **Car rental agencies**
Prices average US$90–120 per day. Make sure you have full insurance.

ASTORIA-SERVICE
Borovaya Ul. 11/13
Tel. 812 112 1583

AVIS
Konnogvardesysky Bul. 4
Tel. 812 312 6312

EXECUTIVE CAR
2 linia 35
Tel. 812 213 1121

HERTZ
Nekrasova Ul. 40
Tel. 812 272 5045

EMERGENCIES

■ **Emergencies, ambulances**
Tel. 03
■ **Fire brigade**
Tel. 01
■ **Gas**
Tel. 04
■ **Loss or theft**
Go to the police station nearest to the place of loss or theft in order to make a declaration and obtain an official police report (Tel. 02) which you will need to submit to your consulate for lost documents, or to your insurance company.
Loss of luggage:
Luggage retrieval service
Pulkovo 2 Airport, open 24 hours
Tel. 812 324 3787
■ **Police**
Tel. 02
■ **Special police service for foreigners**
Tel. 164 9787
■ **SOS on the road**
Tel. 320 9000
■ **Night drugstore (9pm–8pm)**
Tel. 812 311 2077

FINDING YOUR WAY

Nothing could be simpler than finding your way around the center of St Petersburg, where the main tourist attractions (the Admiralty, Peter and Paul Fortress, St Isaac's Cathedral) and the canals provide you with clear landmarks. Out of the center, it is a little more difficult to find your bearings and you need to pay more attention.

→ TOPOGRAPHY

In the heart of St Petersburg (the oldest part of the city), the streets are laid out in a radial system, the main arteries fanning out from a central point while the canals curve around them. Later, more outlying areas were constructed mainly to an orthogonal design, dividing the whole area into a network of streets running at right angles to each other and forming "microdistricts" bound by the main arteries radiating out from the center.

→ SIGNPOSTS
Although the city has readopted many of the pre-revolutionary streetnames, the streets still tend to be known by both their Soviet and post-Soviet names. Newly installed signs are now often sponsored by commercial companies; don't be surprised to find the trademark of a distinctly Western company displayed under the name of the street.

→ STREET NUMBERING
In theory, all streets are numbered starting from the Neva. In practice, in the majority of cases, the direction of street numbering varies from area to area. Guidelines are as follows:
- in the mainland area of the city (south of the Neva): from north to south and from west to east;
- on Vasilyevsky Island: from south to north and from east to west;
- on Petersburg Island (also known as Petrograd Side): from south to north and from west to east.

FOOD AND DRINK

→ BISTROTS
You will find several cheap bistrot and fast-food chains.

→ BRASSERIES AND BREWERIES
There are a great number of brasseries in the city, and several brands of beer are produced in St Petersburg (Baltika, Nevskoye, Stepan Razin).

→ CAFÉS
The number of cafés in the city center is growing rapidly, and many now offer a fine selection of coffees, teas and cakes.

→ RESTAURANTS
Wide range of cuisine: Russian, Georgian (most common), Korean, Chinese and Latin-American.

→ RUSSIAN CUISINE
"Russian cuisine," writes travel journalist Jo Durden Smith, "is a mixture of elements of various origins: its starters (*zakusky*) come from a German and Scandinavian tradition imported by Peter the Great. Its noodles, ravioli (*pelmeny*) and tea derive from the Mongols; its buckwheat *kasha* from central Asia; its shish kebab (*shashlyk*) from the Caucasus; its *borshch* from central Europe – with the whole mix made more sophisticated and various by imported 19th-century French chefs.
Ice-cold vodka is traditionally drunk with *zakuski* (and often throughout the meal). Local beers are now excellent (try, for instance, Baltika no. 7). Georgian red wines are rather sweet to the Western palate, but you could try *kinsmarauli*, Stalin's favorite wine, as well as a dry white called *tsinandali*. Of Russian champagnes, the best is brut (the dryest); it's an agreeable alternative to its distant French cousin which, like all imported wines in Russia, is very expensive. French wines, for all this, are part of the old Russian tradition. Both Ivan the Terrible and Peter the Great had a fondness for Burgundy; and the Hotel Grand Europe, before the Revolution, is said to have had the finest champagne cellar in the world."

→ GLOSSARY
Bitky: meatballs.
Borshch: beetroot soup, potatoes, cabbage and meat.
Goluptsy: small meat-stuffed cabbage.
Kulibiak: salmon or meat pie.
Okhroshka: cold soup.
Pelmeny: a type of ravioli.
Pirozhky: small meat or cabbage pies.
Po-Pojarsky: poultry meat in flat pies).
Shashlyk: meat kebab.
Shchy: cabbage soup.
Ukha: fish soup.
Zakusky: varied hors d'œuvres.

HEALTH

→ PREVENTION
Avoid drinking tap water and bathing in lakes or pools (risk of leptospirosis, or Weil's disease).
Be aware of the expiry dates on food packages (especially frozen food) and avoid "home-made" vodka and other spirits sold at kiosks and street stalls.

→ MEDICAL CENTERS FOR FOREIGN VISITORS
- **American Medical Center**
Serpukhovskaya Ul. 10
Tel. 812 326 1730
www.amcenters.com
Email: stpetersburg@amcenters.com
Open 24 hours daily (office Mon.–Fri. 9am–6pm)
Metro Teknologitchesky Institut
- **British-American Family Practice**
Grafsky Per. 7
el: 812 327 6030
www.british-americanclinic.com
Email: info@british-americanclinic.com
Open 24 hours daily
Metro Dostoevskaya
- **Euromed Clinique**
Suvorovsky Pr. 60
Tel. 812 327 0301

LANGUAGE

English is the foreign language most widely spoken by the population, especially by young people and staff in tourist locations. Russian is the official language, so if you want to be able to find your way around easily you will need to become familiar with the Cyrillic alphabet and its English phonetic transcription (see table, opposite).

MAIL

→ POST OFFICES
There are many post offices throughout the city. They can also be found in major hotels.
Usually open 9am–8pm, closed one day a week.
- **Central post office**
(Glavpotchtamt)
Potchtamtskaya 9 (in the St Isaac's Cathedral district)
Tel. 312 8302 and 312 8039
- **Stamps**
US$0.50 for Europe.
US$0.75 for the US.
Sold at post offices.

Upp. case	Low. case	Phon.
А	а	a
Б	б	b
В	в	v
Г	г	g
Д	д	d
Е	е	ié
Ё	ё	io
Ж	ж	j
З	з	z
И	и	i
-	й	ï
К	к	k
Л	л	l
М	м	m
Н	н	n
О	о	o
П	п	p
Р	р	r
С	с	s
Т	т	t
У	у	ou
Ф	ф	f
Х	х	kh
Ц	ц	ts
Ч	ч	tch
Ш	ш	ch
Щ	щ	chtch
-	ъ	-
-	ы	y
-	ь	-
Э	э	è
Ю	ю	iou
Я	я	ia

MARKETS

→ FOOD, FRUIT AND VEGETABLES
Food markets are open daily. The products are generally fresher and cheaper than in stores.
Kuznechny Market
Kuznechny Per. 3, Tel. 312 4161
Open Mon.–Sat. 8am–8pm, Sun. 8am–6pm.
The largest market in the city center.

→ ART AND ANTIQUES
St Petersburg is known as the "antiques capital". There is a market on Konnyushennaya Sq., near the Church of the Resurrection of Christ. There are also many sale-or-return stores, see *Shopping* p294.

→ FLEA MARKETS
The place to find anything from military belt buckles to antique china sets. They are on the outskirts of the city:
– Udelnaya Metro station, next to the railway tracks.
– Avtovo Metro station
Marshala Kazakova Ul. 40 (Yunona Market, mostly for micro-electronics).

MONEY

→ EXCHANGE
Rubles cannot be converted on the open market. Exchange can only take place in Russia at bureaux de change, hotel receptions, in banks and in the larger stores.
***Warning**: Do not take the risk of changing money on the black market, and beware of the numerous conmen operating in the city.*
■ Banks
Usually open Mon.–Fri. 9.30am–1pm and 2–4pm.
ALFA-BANK
Kanala Griboyedova Nab 6/2
AVTOBANK
Kanala Griboyedova Nab. 24
BALTYSKY BANK
Liteyny Pr. 8/21
MENATEP
Nevsky Pr. 1
PROMSTROY BANK
Nevsky Pr. 40
Dumskaya Ul. 7
SBERBANK
Nevsky Pr. 99
6 Italianskaya Ul., Liteyny Pr. 7
Sadovaya Ul. 35
■ Foreign-capital banks
BNP-DRESDNER BANK
Isaakyevskaya Pl. 11
CRÉDIT LYONNAIS RUSBANK SA
Nevsky Pr. 12
■ Bureaux de change
Open daily 10am–8pm

→ AUTO-TELLERS
They are located in the city center, major hotels and banks. The maximum amount you can take out is set by your bank. Commission is 3%–4%.

→ FORMS OF PAYMENT
■ Cash
Although payment is often made in rubles, the US dollar, known as *kapusta* (cabbage), is the preferred local currency; it is a good idea to bring with you dollars in small denominations to use for tips – clean \$1, £5, \$10 bills issued after 1990. As well as US dollars, euros may also be accepted for unofficial transactions such as the purchase of souvenirs.
■ Credit cards
Are accepted in most restaurants, hotels, stores.
***Warning**: Check all bills and receipts, and only use credit cards in reputable establishments. Beware of fraud.*
■ Traveler's checks
Not recommended. They are accepted only by banks and the commission is 5% to 7%, and sometimes more.

NEWSPAPERS

→ LOCAL NEWSPAPERS
■ In English
The *St Petersburg Times*, a weekly publication for foreign residents, gives information on cultural events and is distributed free to hotels, restaurants, cafés.
www.times.spb.ru
■ In Russian
CULTURAL MAGAZINES
Na Nevskom, *Krasny journal*, *Sobaka.ru* (very trendy).
DAILIES
Vecherny Peterburg, *Smena*, *Sankt-Peterburgskiye Vedomosty.*

→ ENGLISH-LANGUAGE NEWSPAPERS
Sold in hotels and at newsagents in the city center.
■ In English and Russian
Pulse St Petersburg is a weekly publication that gives information on life in the city.
■ In English
Neva News and *Estate News* (real estate in the Russian Federation and Eastern Europe) are both published monthly.

NIGHTLIFE

→ ART AND MUSIC
From permanent exhibitions to special events, there is always something to see or do in St Petersburg. Arts and music have always flourished here in the city that was known as the "Rock capital" during the Soviet era. Nightclubs, theaters, opera halls and cultural venues offer a wide range of concerts and shows all year round.
(See *Leisure* p291, *Celebrations, festivals and events* p302..

→ "WHITE NIGHTS"
The widest range of events occurs in the summer, during the period of the "white nights", when nightlife becomes more intense and

the city center is full of local people out on the streets until dawn (Vasilyevsky, Petrograd Side and Nevsky districts).

■ **Information**
Tourist Information Bureau, the Cultural Program Institute, or the local press.

■ **Reservations**
Ask at your hotel or at the venue itself.

OPENING TIMES

Vary greatly, but the standard opening times (with most places closing for lunch between 1–3pm) are:

■ **Banks**
Open Mon.–Fri. 9.30am–1pm and 2–4pm

■ **Bureaux de change**
Open daily 10am–8pm

■ **Department stores**
8am–9pm (some stay open 24 hours)

■ **Food stores**
8am–8pm or 9am–9pm

■ **Other stores**
10am–7pm

■ **Restaurants**
Times may vary, but restaurants usually serve until 10pm or 10.30pm. Russians tend to have lunch around 2pm and dinner between 9pm and 10pm.

■ **Museums**
See *Places to visit* p298.

PUBLIC HOLIDAYS

■ **January 1**
New Year's Day

■ **January 7**
Orthodox Christmas

■ **February 23**
Defenders of the Nation's Day

■ **March 8**
International Woman's Day

■ **May 1 and 2**
Labor Day

■ **May 9**
Victory Day (1945)

■ **June 12**
Russian Independence Day

■ **November 7**
Reconciliation Day

TRINITY BRIDGE

RELIGION

■ **Jewish**
Synagogue
Lermontovsky Pr. 104; Baltiskaya Metro station

■ **Muslim**
Mosque
Kronversky Pr. 7; Gorkovskaya Metro station

■ **Orthodox**
– Cathedral of St Nicholas, Nikolskaya Pl. 1/3; Mira Square Metro station
– Cathedral of the Holy Trinity, Nevsky Monastery; A. Nevsky Square Metro station

■ **Protestant**
Lutheran Church
Saltikov-Shedrine 8; Chernyshevskaya Metro station

■ **Roman catholic**
Our-Lady-of-Lourdes Church,
Kovenski Pr. 7; Ploshchad Vosstanya Metro station

SHOPPING

Make sure you are given receipts. and that you keep them, as you may be required to produce them by the Russian customs when leaving the country.

→ BUYING

■ Wooden objects, Russian dolls (*matryoshkas*), lacquered boxes, sculpted pictures...

■ Furs (*shapkas*), scarves and shawls, natural fabrics wool. silk, etc. from Central Asia.

■ St Petersburg porcelain from the Lomonosov factory (originally the famous imperial works).

■ Records, cassettes and CDs (classical or folk music).

■ Rare books in European languages (especially French) in the numerous second-hand bookstores or stalls.

■ Gold and silver objects, jewelry, and clocks and watches.

■ Antiques, paintings.

Warning: *Taking antiques and works of art out of the country must be authorized by the Russian Ministry of Culture, so only buy them from stores officially authorized to sell goods for export or the items may be seized by the Russian customs when you leave the country. Keep all certificates and receipts as you may be required to produce them.*

■ Vodka and caviar: max. 7oz (200g) of caviar per person allowed through customs.

Warning: *Buying vodka or caviar from street vendors may seem like a smart move because of the lower price, but you will have no guarantee of freshness or quality.*

→ MAIN SHOPPING STREETS

■ Nevsky Prospekt and its commercial galleries, Gostiny Dvor and Passage.

■ Kamennoostrovsky and Bolshoy Prospekt in the Petersburg Island district.

TELEPHONE

■ **International calls**
To the UK Dial 8 + 10 + 44 + area code (without the initial 0) + number.
To the US and Canada Dial 8 + 10 + 1 + area code + local number.
Mobile phones
Symbol (+) followed by the country code and the number.
International operator
Dial 079 (072 or 073 from your hotel).

■ **Calls within St Petersburg**
When phoning within the city, you do not need to dial the area code 812.

■ **Calls to other Russian cities**
Dial 8 + city code + number, or dial 077 for an operator.
Information for calls outside the city: 070
National city codes:
Moscow: 095
Novgorod: 816
Pskov: 1122

■ **Public telephones**
There are many public phone booths in the streets, in museums and hotels. Various telephone cards are sold at Metro stations and newsagents.

■ **Call Center**
(*Tsentralniye Mejdugorodniye Telefonniye Punkt*)
Bolshaya Morskaya 3/5 (next to Palace Square, by Nevsky Prospekt)
Tel. 812 326 0332 and 812 312 2085
Open 24 hours

■ Business center (located inside the Call Center) for Internet and fax
Open 9am–9pm.

TIPPING

In cafés and restaurants, bills include a 10–15% service charge, but it is customary to leave a tip by rounding up the amount billed. In taxis, tipping is not usual, unless you wish to show special appreciation.

TOURS AND EXCURSIONS

Guided tours are usually in Russian. If you require a tour in English or have any specific request (expect to pay a lot more), contact the Tourist Information Bureau or one of the tour operators (see *Useful addresses* p282)

→ BOAT TOURS

Many different itineraries and types of boats. Trips run Apr.–Nov.

■ **Boat trips by night**
During the "white nights" period. Moyka landing stage (corner of Nevsky Prospekt).

■ **Canal trips by water-taxi**
On the Griboedov, Kriukov and Moyka canals, through the Kolomna (Griboedov Canal landing stage).

■ **Cruises down the Neva**
The Neva and Moscow liners are very comfortable. Departures from Dvortsovaya landing stage, opposite the Hermitage (lower pier).

■ **Trips to Peterhof**
Liners offer cafés, restaurants and banqueting rooms... Decembrists Square. *Meteor* boats, Dvortsovaya landing stage, opposite the Hermitage (upper pier). Duration: 30–35 mins.
Tel. 812 311 9506.

■ **Excursions to Kronstadt**
Meteor boats
Tuchkov Bridge, near Peterhof Hotel
Tel. 812 328 2223

■ **Lastochka omnibus-boat**
Cruise in style in 19th-century interiors, by reservation (Kronversky Bridge, near the Peter and Paul Fortress)
Tel. 812 325 2954

■ **River and canal trips**
Departures from Anichkov Bridge.

→ COACH TOURS

Operators offer many itineraries and thematic tours. Information, reservations and departures from one of the following three stations in the city center: Palace Square, Kazan Square or near the Ruska Portik (next to Gostiny Dvor).

→ TRAMWAY TOURS

You can visit St Petersburg in one of the streetcars that have served the city faithfully for over a century.
Reservations: St Petersburg Tramway Museum
Sredny Pr. 77
Tel. 812 321 5405

VASILYEVSKY ISLAND

AVTOVO METRO STATION

→ HELICOPTER TOURS

■ **Baltic Airlines (Baltyskye Avialiny)**
Nevsky Pr. 7/9
Office no. 12
Tel. 812 311 0084
15-min flight in a MI-8. Departures from the strip situated between the Peter and Paul Fortress and Kronverk; Apr.–Nov., Sat.–Sun. and public hols., around US$17.

TRANSPORT, CITY

→ BUS, TRAMS AND METRO

St Peterburg has over 290 bus, trolleybus and tramway routes, 4 Metro lines and 57 stations, each reflecting the spirit of the time when it was built (do not miss Ploshchad and Vostanya at Avtovo).

■ **Map of the Metro**
(See *Map G* p336)
Maps are displayed at the entrance of every Metro station (all of these are in Russian only). Bilingual city and transport maps are available from some kiosks in the city center, hotels, bookstores and the Tourist Information Bureau.

■ **Tickets**
You must buy Metro tickets at station ticket offices, and bus and tramway tickets when boarding.
Fares: around US$0.15 at time of printing but inflation goes up quickly. Various special passes are also available.

■ **Operating times**
Buses and tramways run between 6am and midnight. The Metro operates between 5.45am and 0.15am, roughly every 1–5 minutes.

→ PRIVATE SHUTTLES

The numerous *marshrutnoye* taxis, indicated by an "express" sign, are just as convenient to get to the surrounding area: shuttles for Petrodvorets (Peterhof) depart from Baltyskaya Metro station; shuttles for Pushkin (Tsarskoe Selo) depart from Moskovskaya Metro station.

→ **TAXIS**
"Official" taxis carry a meter with a black and white checkered band.
■ **Fares**
US$1.30 per mile.
■ **Calling a taxi**
There is an additional charge for reserving a taxi. Tel. 1 000 000 or 068
City center:
Tel. 812 271 88 88

→ **HITCHIKING**
Citizens looking for extra income will stop their car and offer rides to hitchhikers. It's naturally cheaper than official taxis, but agree on the price before getting into the car.

TRANSPORT, REGIONAL

→ **RAIL**
The Russian railway network is very efficient but journeys tend to be very long.
■ **Schedules**
Are based on Moscow time (same as St Peterburg)
■ **Information**
There is one single information line for all stations (calls are only in Russian and there is a charge):
Tel. 055
■ **Reservation and ticket office**
Griboedov Canal 24
Open Mon.–Sat. 8am–8pm,
Sun. 8am–4pm
Tel. 812 162 3344
BALTIC STATION
Obvodny Canal 120
Baltyskaya Metro station
FINLAND STATION
Lenin 6
Ploshchad Lenina Metro station
MOSCOW STATION
Nevsky Pr. 85
Ploshchad Vostanya and Mayakovskaya Metro stations
VITEBSK STATION
Zagorodny Pr. 52, Pushkinskaya Metro station
WARSAW STATION
Obvodny Canal 118
Baltyskaya or Frunzenskaya Metro stations

→ **COACH**
The coach network is very efficient and links the major Russian cities.
■ **Terminal No.1**
(*Avtovokzal*)
Obvodny Canal 36
Tel. 812 166 5777, Ligovskaya Metro station, and a 20-minute walk
■ **Terminal No. 2**
(*Avtovokzal*)
Obvodni Canal 36
Tel. 812 166 5777

→ **BOAT**
Boat terminal
(*Retchnoy vokzal*)
Obukhovskoy Oborony Pr. 195
Tel. 812 262 0239
Proletarskaya Metro station, and a 10-minute walk.
The *Meteor* boats serve Petrodvorets. (See *Tours and Excursions* p281).

USEFUL ADDRESSES

→ **CONSULATES**
■ **Canada**
Malodetskoselsky Prospekt 32
198013 St Petersburg
Tel. 812 325 8448
Fax 812 325 8393
Email: spurb@dfait-maeci.gc.ca
■ **UK**
Proletarskoy Diktatury Pl. 5
193124 St Petersburg
Tel. 812 320 3200
Fax 812 320 3211
www.britemb.spb.ru
Email: bcgspb@peterlink.ru
■ **US**
Furshtatskaya Ul. 15
191028 St Petersburg
Tel. 812 331 2600
Fax 812 331 2852

→ **TOURIST OFFICES**
■ **Tourist Information Bureau**
Pulkovo 2 Airport
Arrival hall, or:
Sadovaya Ul. 14
Tel. 812 311 28 43
Fax 812 311 29 43
Open Mon.–Fri. 10am–6pm.
■ **Cultural Programs Institute**
Rubinchteyna Ul. 8
Tel. 812 164 75 96
Open Mon.–Fri. 10am–6pm
www.300.spb.ru

→ **TOUR OPERATORS**
For accommodation, hotel reservations, tour arrangements, excursions, etc.:
■ **Inexco Voyages**
Nevsky Pr. 30
Tel. 812 318 92 28
Open Mon.–Fri. 10am–7pm.
www.inexco-voyages.com
■ **CGTT St Petersburg**
Bolchaya Morskaya Ul. 42
Tel. 812 311 89 10
Open Mon.–Fri. 9.30am–5.30pm.
www.cgtt-voyages.fr/english
■ **Date-St Petersburg**
Kanal Griboyedova 5
Tel. 812 312 40 59
Open Mon.–Fri. 11am–6pm.

→ **INTERNET CAFÉ**
SOFIT
Mira Ul. 10
Tel. 812 232 9360
Nevsky Pr. 88
Tel. 279 0931
www.sofitspb.ru

Addresses

- Credit cards accepted
- Central
- Animals not accepted
- Air conditioning
- Swimming pool
- Television
- Telephone
- Music
- Quiet
- Terrace
- Views
- Park or garden
- Parking
- Supervized parking

◆ HOTELS

Hotels are listed alphabetically within each district. The ◆ symbol indicates the relevant map reference in the map section at the end of the guide. For a list of symbols, see page 283. Unless otherwise noted, all hotels accept credit cards.

HOTELS

Angleterre

◆ **D** F2
Bolchaya Morskaya Ulitsa 39
Tel. 812 313 56 66
Fax 812 313 51 24
Metro Nevsky Prospekt

The rooms here are cheaper and plainer than those in the Astoria next door (see below)*, but are still to a high standard. They are air conditioned and many have views over St Isaac's Cathedral. A few minutes' walk from Nevsky Prospekt and the Hermitage. The two hotels' public areas interconnect, giving Angleterre guests the run of the Astoria too. Facilities include gym, health club and swimming pool.*
194 rooms.

Astoria

◆ **D** F2
Bolchaya Morskaya Ulitsa 39
Tel. 812 313 57 57
Fax 812 313 50 59
www.astoria.spb.ru
Metro Nevsky Prospekt

Beautiful building, cozy rooms, luxurious touches such as embroidered Russian linen sheets: this is the best hotel in the city, a few minutes' walk from the market at Nevsky Prospekt and the Hermitage. Designed by Fedor Lidval in 1812, the Astoria is grand without being ostentatious. It is also a friendlier place since it was taken over by Rocco Forte Hotels. Gym. Afternoon tea. Ask for a room with a view onto St Isaac's Cathedral.
215 rooooms and suites

Deson-Ladoga

◆ OUTSIDE MAP AREA
Shaumyana Prospekt 26
Tel. 812 528 52 02
Fax 812 528 52 20
www.deson.lek.ru
Metro Novocherkasskaya

Do not judge this hotel by its plain concrete facade. The interior is a totally different and thoroughly modern story. The rooms are light, large, and comfortable, with pastel décor, and the bathrooms are well equipped. The hotel is slightly east of the city center, but close to the metro station and a five-minute bus ride away from the Alexander Nevsky Monastery.
96 rooms

ASTORIA HOTEL

ASTORIA HOTEL

Corinthia Nevsky Palace Hotel

◆ **E** C4
Nevsky Prospekt 57
Tel. 812 380 20 01
Fax 812 380 19 37
www.corinthiahotels.com
Metro Mayakovskaya

This used to be the Sheraton, and seems to have survived the transition to new management more or less intact. Behind the 19th-century neoclassical façade, the interior is modern, characterless and comfortable. Outstanding breakfast buffet – you could spend all day here. The hotel's proximity to the railway station and the cheap winter packages it offers make it a favorite weekend base for Muscovites.
256 rooms

Grand Hotel Europe

◆ **A** D5
Mikhailovskaya Ulitsa 1/7
Tel. 812 329 60 00
Fax 812 329 60 01
www.grand-hotel-europe.com
Metro Gostiny Dvor

Built in 1824 with a baroque façade designed by Italian architect Carlo Rossi, the present Grand Hotel Europe opened its door in 1875. Tchaikovsky, Turgenev, Prokofiev and George Bernard Shaw stayed here. So did, more recently, Elton John. Less flamboyant visitors may find the extravagant interiors, insistent service and lurking security guards a bit exhausting. Fine air-conditioned rooms, big bathrooms, magnificent city views. But beware of the clumsy and overpriced restaurants (Chopsticks, Sadko, Rossi's) on the ground floor. A couple of minutes' walk from the Russian Museum, the Philharmonic Society and the Mussorgsky Opera and Ballet Theater, and near the Hermitage. Services include arranging sightseeing tours and theater and opera tickets.
301 rooms

Holiday Hostel

◆ **C** F5
Arsenalnaya Nab. 9
Tel. 812 327 10 70
Fax 812 327 10 33
www.hostel.ru
Metro Ploshchad Lenina

A youth hostel located on the banks of the Neva, just a few minutes' walk from the metro. Small, tastefully renovated rooms, with showers upstairs and washing machines for the use of guests. US$15–35 per night.
130 rooms

Hotel German Club

◆ OUTSIDE MAP AREA
Ulitsa Gastello 20
Tel. 812 448 51 94
Fax 812 448 56 90
www.germanclub.narod.ru
Metro Moskovskaya

The hotel's website summarizes the place as "Russian hospitality meets German order".

HOTELS
⚀ < US$100
⚁ US$100–250
⚂ > US$250

The German Club is rather out of the city center but in a lively and interesting district. It occupies the third and fourth floors of a tall building typical of the monumental Muscovite architectural style of the Stalin era. The sixteen rooms are plain, spotlessly clean, light, with a lot of pine woodwork and high ceilings. All in all, it's a cozy place to stay, worth the extra journey.
16 rooms
⚀

Korona
◆ **E** A3
Malaya Koniuchennaya Ulitsa 7
Tel. 812 311 00 86
Fax 812 314 38 65
Metro Nevsky Prospekt
This centrally located but quiet hotel, which opened in 2001, occupies the second floor of an 18th-century building. There are only eight rooms and they are will equipped, with air conditioning, safe and hairdryer.
⚁ C

LDM
◆ **C** B3
Ulitsa Profesora Popova 47
Tel. 812 234 32 78
Fax 812 234 23 61
www.ldm.ru
Metro Petrogradskaya
This (very ugly) hotel stands next to the LDM (Leningradsky Dvorets Molodioy – Leningrad Youth Center). Built in 1975, it contains leisure and sports centers, conference rooms and concert halls where music festivals are held. The picturesque view over the Malaya Nevka and the islands compensates for the fact that the nearest metro station is a good 15 minutes' walk away.
201 rooms
⚀

Marshal
◆ **E** D1
Chpalernaya Ulitsa 41
Tel. 812 279 99 55
Fax 812 279 75 00
www.marshal-hotel.spb.ru
Metro Chernychevskaya

PETER AND PAUL FORTRESS

Near Smolny, the Tauride Palace and the botanical gardens, but also a mere 20 minutes' walk from Nevsky Prospekt, the Marshal is located in a former military garrison built in 1802. The rooms have computers connected to the internet. There is also a conference room and sauna.
17 rooms
⚀

Matisov Domik
◆ **D** D3
Reky Priajky Nab. 3/1
Tel. 812 318 54 62
Fax 812 318 74 19
www.matisov.spb.ru
Metro Sennaya Ploshchad
Located on Matisov Island, in the Kolomna district, a quiet, picturesque and historic quarter cut through by canals. This small hotel is recommended both for its cozy family atmosphere and for its standards of service. Guests here include many people from the arts world, from Moscow and the wider world. The only disadvantage of the Matisov is its location relatively far from the public transport network. However, for those who enjoy opera and ballet, it is near the Mariinsky Theater.
25 rooms
⚀

Mercury
◆ **E** E2
Tavricheskaya Ulitsa 39
Tel. 812 325 64 44
Fax 812 276 19 77
Metro Chernychevskaya
Built in 1980 to accommodate official guests, the small but comfortable hotel Mercury is used mostly by visiting state officials and members of parliament. It is also available to foreign visitors, although reservations should be made well in advance.
16 rooms
⚀

Moskva Hotel
◆ **E** E5
Pl. Aleksandra Nevskovo 2
Tel. 812 274 30 01
Fax 812 274 21 30
Metro Ploshchad Aleksandra or Nevskovo
Located opposite the Alexander Nevsky Monastery, and within easy reach of the city center. The building's style reflects the architecture of the Soviet era, with an adequate but plain décor. Facilities include two restaurants, a blinis bar, a casino and a billiard room.
777 rooms
⚁

Neptun
◆ **E** B6
Obvodnogo Kanala Nab. 93a
Tel. 812 324 46 10
Fax 812 324 46 11
Metro Pushkinskaya
Part of the new Neptun business center. Although near the city center this hotel is not very conveniently located: the nearest metro station is 10–15 minutes' walk away. However, with a tennis court, gym, bowling alley, billiard room, squash court, swimming pool and golf simulator, it has much to

HOTELS
< US$100
US$100–250
> US$250

please those who like their hotel to offer more than just a bed.
69 rooms

Neva
◆ **E** C2
Ulitsa Tchaikovskogo 17
Tel. 812 278 05 04
Fax 812 273 25 93
Metro Chernychevskaya
This is a rare instance of an inexpensive hotel right in the center of the city, and in a pleasant location amid several museums and foreign consulates.
133 rooms

Pribaltiyskaya
◆ **B** A6
Korablestroiteley Ulitsa 14
Tel. 812 356 30 01
Fax 812 356 00 94
www.pribaltiyskaya.ru
Email: pribaltiyskaya@travel.spb.ru
Metro Primorkskaya
This typical Soviet-era concrete structure is the biggest hotel in the city, and it was considered the best when built in 1980. The Pribaltiyskaya is well maintained inside, but it is distant from the historic center and rates are steep. Half the rooms though have striking sea views since it stands right on the edge of the gulf, high on a promontory. The restaurants serve Russian and Western European food, and in one, Neva, there is live music every evening. Hotel facilities include sauna, pool, gym, massage, beauty salon, bowling and billiard hall, night club.
1200 rooms

Pulkovskaya
◆ OUTSIDE MAP AREA
Pobedy Ploshchad 1
Tel. 812 123 58 56
Fax 812 123 51 16
www.pulkovskaya.ru
Email: pulkovskaya@travel.spb.ru
Metro Moskovskaya
Though it's located at the end of Moskovsky Prospekt, away from the city center, it's still quite handy for getting in and out of town: the Pulkovskaya is on a direct metro line to the heart of the city: Nevsky Prospekt station is no more than a 20-minute ride away. The hotel is also just 10–15 minutes away from Pulkovo airport by taxi. Built in the 1970's, this is again a charmless establishment, but the rooms are adequate, well equipped and inexpensive. The hotel's lobby is impressive and facilities include two restaurants, two saunas, a tennis court and a health club.
840 rooms

PRIBALTIYSKAYA HOTEL

SANKT PETERSBURG HOTEL

Oktiabrskaya
◆ **E** D4
Ligovsky Prospekt 10
Tel. 812 277 63 30
Fax 812 315 75 01
Metro Ploshchad Vosstaniya
The Oktiabrskaya Hotel stands on the Nevsky Prospekt, midway between the Admiralty and the Alexander Nevsky Monastery. True, it is very central, but its proximity to Moscow Station means noisy crowds and traffic, and this will be for many a disadvantage. The historic 19th-century building, in pure Soviet style, is somewhat charmless but the rooms are being renovated.
Over 500 rooms

Radisson SAS Royal
◆ **E** C4
Nevsky Prospekt 49
Tel. 812 322 50 00
Fax 812 322 50 01
www.radissonsas.com
Metro Mayakovskaya
Medium-sized Scandinavian-run chain hotel in a well-located 18th-century building. The modern, simply furnished rooms are well equipped with such conveniences as air conditioning, trouser press, hairdryer, safe and cable television. Facilities include a gym. Mainly geared to business travelers, this is a good alternative to the Nevsky Palace hotel when the latter is fully booked.
164 rooms

Saint Petersburg
◆ **C** E5
Pirogovskaya Nab. 5/2
Tel. 812 380 19 11
Fax 812 380 19 20
www.hotel-spb.ru
Metro Ploshchad Lenina
At least half the rooms of the Saint Petersburg are newly redecorated. Those at the front offer beautiful views of the river and the city, but you will have to bear the traffic noise. Those at the back are usually quiet, but at the time of writing look onto a building site. Competent service and good buffet breakfast.
410 rooms.

RESTAURANTS

1913 God (Year 1913)
◆ **A** A6
Voznesensky Prospekt 13/2
Tel. 812 315 51 48
Metro Nevsky Prospekt
Open noon–1am
With a classic interior, a relaxed, comfortable atmosphere and high-quality service, this place offers Western European cuisine and a range of very rich and varied Russian dishes.

ESTAURANTS
< US$25
US$25–40
US$40–55
> US$55

Prices are sometimes given as 'y.e.': eg 25 y. e.
y. e. is a conventional monetary unit equivalent to US$1.

–40
◆ C D1-2
olshoy
ampsonievsky Pr. 108
el. 812 246 34 44
letro Lesnaya or
hyornaya Rechka
pen Mon. 3pm–
1pm, Tue.–Sun.
oon–11pm
xceptionally good ewish cuisine, with wide selection of raditionial dishes, ncluding tsimes *and* orchmak. *The food s served on clay rockery painted in he style of Chagall. ive violin music.*

dmiralteistvo Admiralty)
◆ E C4
levsky Palace Hotel
levsky Prospekt 57
el. 812 380 20 01
pen Tue–Sat.
am–10.30pm
letro
layakovskaya
ig, bustling hotel-estaurant where he maritime theme xtends to the décor nd menu. It is trongest on fish but he reliable menu overs Russian and oviet classics ncluding caviar, tolichny *salad meat, hard-boiled ggs, gherkins, peas, otato and onion, vith mayonnaise),* orschch *and* olyanka *(a sharp oup of vegetables nd meat or fish). he Georgian fillet f lamb with garlic nd coriander sauce s particularly good. ackground Russian olk and "urban omance" music.*

kvarel
◆ A A2
irjevoy Most
el. 812 320 86 00
letro Sportivnaya
pen noon–11pm
'Fusion" cooking vith strong Thai nd Japanese ccents, to a high tandard. Modern, light interior. Akvarel occupies a moored boat, with spectacular views of the city. Café above, restaurant below. Bar and dance floor, with DJs on Fridays and Saturdays, add to the lively atmosphere of this trendy new venue.

Austeria
◆ C C6
Peter and Paul Fortress
Tel. 812 238 42 62
Metro Gorkovskaya
Open noon–midnight

RESTAURANT OF THE GRAND HOTEL EUROPE

At the time of Peter the Great "austeria" meant "inn", and the restaurant's interior re-creates a 17th-century Dutch inn. The menu, with a strong emphasis on vodka, caviar and blinis, is typically Russian.

Caviar bar
◆ A D5
Grand Hotel Europe
Mikhailovskaya Ulitsa 1/7
Tel. 812 329 60 00
Open 6am–11pm
Metro Gostiny Dvor
The Caviar Bar's posh, expensive menu is of course strong on caviar dishes but also includes other favorites of wealthy Russians such as crab, sturgeon, pirozhky *(pastry parcels stuffed with meat or cabbage) cooked in champagne. Regular customers here recommend the trout marinated in vodka. Tea is served in samovars, as Russian and gypsy music plays in the background.*

Dvorianskoye Gnezdo (the Nobles' Nest)
◆ A A5
Dekabristov Pl. 21
Tel. 812 312 32 05
Metro Gostiny Dvor
Open noon–midnight
Two elegant, high-ceilinged, candlelit rooms (and an upstairs bar with excellent classical music) in a pavilion of the Yusupov Palace. The atmosphere is both cozy and imperial; the excellent menu, original and imaginative, includes dishes taken from the cookbooks of the Yusupov princes. Classical music is performed in the small rotunda. Wide selection of high-quality wines.

Europa
◆ A D5
Grand Hotel Europe
Mikhailovskaya Ulitsa 1/7
Tel. 812 329 60 00
Metro Gostiny Dvor
Open Mon.–Sat. 7am–11pm; brunch Sun noon–4pm
Russian and Western European cuisine, excellent choice of wines and cigars. Recommended for the lavish Sunday brunch, to be taken lazily with plenty of semi-sweet Russian champagne. But even then, dress at the smart end of casual to feel at ease in this soaring grand, glass-ceilinged Art Deco dining room, where you can expect to see everyone who is anyone in St Petersburg (tie required in the evening).

Federico Fellini
◆ A C4
Malaya Koniuchennaya Ulitsa 4/2
Tel. 812 311 50 78
Metro Nevsky Prospekt
Open noon–1am
The décor of the Fellini's dining rooms re-creates various film studios, with beach, prison and hotel-room sets. Movie paraphernalia can be seen everywhere; even the menus are brought to you in spool cans. Western European cuisine with a strong Italian accent.

RESTAURANTS
< US$25
US$25–40
US$40–55
> US$55

Flora
◆ **A** C1
Kamennoostrovsky Prospekt 5
Tel 812 232 34 00
Metro Gorkovskaya
Open noon–11pm
The dismaying modern exterior conceals a delicate Art Nouveau interior where Ilya Lazerson, one of the city's great chefs, holds court. French and Russian dishes. The flower-filled "tropical" setting, complete with little bridge and live parrot, make this a fun place to escape on a freezing day. With live ballet shows on Fridays and Saturdays, Flora is one of St Petersburg's most entertaining restaurants. Note also the related café and shop nearby, at Malaya Posadskaya ulitsa 18.

Gorny Oriol
◆ **C** B5
Alexander Park
Tel. 812 232 32 82
Metro Gorkovskaya
Open noon–midnight
This family restaurant located opposite the zoo is a good place to come to sample a wide variety of Georgian dishes. Especially recommended are the famous shashlyk *(skewered meat). House wine is served in pitchers. The terrace, open in summer, looks onto the zoo.*

Kamelot
◆ **A** C4
Bolshaya Koniuchennaya Ul. 14
Tel. 812 325 99 06
Metro Nevsky Prospekt
Open noon–midnight
As the restaurant's name suggests, the décor here is inspired by Arthurian legend. Beneath the Gothic vaulting are tables spread with cloths illustrating the adventures of the Knights of the Round Table. Excellent European cuisine, with unusual and generous dishes.

Karavan
◆ **A** A6
Voznesensky Pr. 46
Tel. 812 310 56 78
Metro Sadovaya
Open noon–2am
Traditional Caucasian and Central Asian cuisine served in an Oriental atmosphere. Dishes include Georgian shashlyk *(skewered meat), Azerbaijani* lulia-kebab *(minced meat) and* plov *uzbek (pilau rice).*

Kolkhida
◆ **E** E5
Nevsky Prospekt 176
Tel. 812 274 25 14
Metro Ploshchad Alexandra or Nevskovo
Open noon until the last customer leaves
The Kolkhida offers a traditional Georgian atmosphere, with staff dressed in national costumes. A wide selection of high-quality Georgian wines.

Landscrona
◆ **E** C4
Nevsky Palace Hotel
Nevsky Prospekt 57
Tel. 812 380 20 01
Metro Mayakovskaya
Open 6.30pm–midnight
A well-regarded gourmet restaurant serving a wide range of Mediterranean dishes with an Italian touch but also offering some more unusual dishes, such as oysters with caviar cooked in champagne. The game (shot by a professional hunter on the hotel's staff) is particularly recommended. The restaurant, on the eighth floor, offers fine views over the rooftops of St Petersburg. Live vocal music.

VALHALL RESTAURANT ON NEVSKY PROSPEKT

VALHALL RESTAURANT

Masha i Medvyed
◆ **A** D6
Malaya Sadovaya Ulitsa 1
Tel. 812 310 46 31
Metro Gostiny Dvor
Open 11am–11pm
Plain, simple basement restaurant with plain, simple cooking. Its chief boast is pike caviar with onion. Also serves pirozhky *(pastry parcels stuffed with meat or cabbage) prepared with beer, onion soup and* kasha *(grilled millet) with mushrooms.*

Matrosskaya Tichina (Seaman's Silence)
◆ **E** C4-5
Ulitsa Marata 54/34
Tel. 812 164 44 13
Metro Ligovsky Prospekt
Open noon–midnight
Exceptionally good fish dishes prepared by a highly regarded French chef. The atmosphere here evokes the sea: the sound of waves whispers in the background, waitresses are dressed as sailors, and there is a large aquarium from which you may select your fish.

Na Zdorovye
◆ **D** A5
Bolshoy Prospekt 13
Tel. 812 232 40 39
Metro Sportivanaya
Open noon–11pm
Exceptional kitchen. "The utopia of Russian cooking" says one Russian critic. The décor is a mix of Soviet retro and old Russian. The menu likewise, but with a few dishes betraying a French influence. Duck breast and fried goat's cheese jostle with the salted salmon and the pork

marinated in kvass (a popular Russian drink made from fermented bread). A cheerful atmosphere, with gypsy entertainment.

New Island
◆ D E1
Universitetskaya Nab. (level with 1 Linia)
Tel. 812 963 67 65
Metro Vasileostrovskaya
A restaurant on a boat moored near Rumiantsevsky ramp on University Embankment. Enjoy Russian and Western European cuisine as the boat makes its way along the Neva, passing a succession of magnificent riverside palaces. The boat trips take place only between April and November, when the river is navigable; New Island is ice-bound in winter. Trips along the Neva cost US$8, and dinner about US$35.

Podvorie
◆ OUTSIDE MAP AREA
Flitrovskoye Chosse 16
Tel. 812 465 13 99
www.podvorye.ru
Open noon–11pm
Well-known country-style restaurant at the entrance to Pavlovsk park. A favorite spot for company junkets and the banqueting of visiting VIPs – Vladimir Putin once celebrated a birthday here. Standard Russian dishes, good choice of Crimean wines. Live music. Cossack and gypsy shows. A Russian bear at the entrance offering visitors a shot of vodka sets the tone for a fun place.

Restoran
◆ D F1
Tamozhenny Per. 2
Tel. 812 327 89 79
Metro Vasileostrovskaya
Open noon–11pm
Opposite the entrance to Peter the Great's Kunstkammer on Vasilyevsky Island. Smart, restrained interior by Andrei Dmitriev, the most original young designer in the city – he also designed the Mariinsky Theater's restaurant; spacious space, with a menu printed on recycled banknotes, that will suit all budgets. Good service, excellent atmosphere. The kitchen attracts mixed reports for its fancier dishes, but the open fire makes this a good place to retreat for blinis and dumplings with tea on a cold day.

PAVLOSK PALACE
PAVLOSK GARDENS

Russkaya Rybalka (Russian Fishing)
◆ B B2
Iujnaya Doroga 11
Primorsky Victory Park
Tel. 812 323 98 13
www.russian-fishing.com
Metro Krestovsky Ostrov
Open noon–9pm
Set amid greenery, this restaurant stands on stilts at the edge of a lake filled with trout and sturgeon. Fishing tackle can be hired on site and guests may catch their own fish, which are then prepared – smoked, grilled or baked in foil – according to individual taste. Guests have included Russian president Vladimir Putin, who has entertained foreign leaders here. Prices are based on the weight of the fish caught: about US$7 per lb for trout and US$9 for sturgeon. There is no additional charge for cooking the fish.

Russkiy Kitsch
◆ D E1
Universitetskaya Nab. 25
Tel. 812 325 11 22
Open noon–2am
Metro Vasileostrovskaya
The décor is everything the name suggests – a parody of nouveau-riche bad taste. Some of the joke carries over into the food: blinis with asparagus, for example. But the French-influenced cooking is fundamentally serious, and for this city is by no means overpriced. Six rooms, two galleries behind glass, dance hall.

Senat-bar
◆ D E2
Galernaya Ulitsa 1
Tel. 812 314 92 53
Open noon–2am
Metro Nevsky Prospekt
A restautant in the cellars of the Senate where the imperial archives were stored before the Russian Revolution. Spacious interiors with décor with depictions of archivists, and busts and frescoes in the Empire style. Russian and Western European cuisine. Some of the dishes are cooked in front of diners. A very good place for lunch.

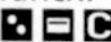

Staraya Tamozhnaya (Old Customs House)
◆ D F1
Tamojenny Per. 1
Tel. 812 327 89 80
Metro Vasileostrovskaya
Open 1pm–1am
Exceptional kitchen. Grand food, even grander wine list, high prices, French chef. The mainly French menu also salutes some Russian classics, including blinis with black caviar. Historical touches to the décor help to create the sense of tradition in this red-brick vaulted chamber, a customs point in the 18th century. Two

RESTAURANTS
< US$25
US$25–40
US$40–55
> US$55

bars, jazz in the evening. An institution.

La Strada
◆ A C4
Bolshaya Koniuchennaya 27
Tel. 812 312 47 00
Metro Nevsky Prospekt
Open noon–11pm
A glass-walled gallery in a picturesque courtyard set out in the style of an Italian street. The specialty here is pizza cooked in front of customers. This is also a good place for families: there is special children's menu, and a children's room with toys and a nanny.

Stroganovsky Dvor
◆ A B4
Nevsky Prospekt 17
Tel. 812 315 23 15
Metro Nevsky Prospekt
Open noon–midnight
A café-restaurant in the glass-roofed courtyard of the Stroganovsky Palace. Noted for its buffet, a touch simple and stodgy but one of the bargains of the city when you happen to be very hungry. Buffet US$5 (open until 10pm).

Valhall
◆ A B4
Nevsky Pr. 22/24
Tel. 812 311 00 24
www.valhall.ru
Metro Nevsky Prospekt
Open 10am–3am
Recently opened in the city center, opposite the Cathedral of Our Lady of Kazan, Valhall has quickly become popular. Russian, Western European and Scandinavian cuisine, in which northern dishes feature prominently: Norwegian salmon, Greenland prawns, steaks served 'on a Viking shield'. The décor features 9th-century armory, and the waitresses are dressed as Valkyries.

U Gorchakova
◆ C C4
Bolchaya Monetnaya Ulitsa 19
Tel. 812 233 92 72
Metro Gorkovskaya
Open noon–midnight

VIEW OF VASILYEVSKY ISLAND

GRIBOIEDOV CANAL

The Gorchakova is ocated in the fine residence of Prince Gorchakov, the eminent 19th-century Russian diplomat and chancellor. However, neither the unusual and eclectic décor nor the menu match the atmosphere of the state rooms. Worth a visit.

Za Stsenoy (Behind the Scenes)
◆ D F3
Teatralnaya Ploshchad 18/10
Tel. 812 327 06 84
Metro Sennaya Ploshchad or Sadovaya
Open noon–2am
This is the restaurant of the Mariinsky Theater, whose very first guest was Placido Domingo. It has a bohemian atmosphere, and the dining room is pleasingly decorated with theatrical paraphernalia – curtains, mirrors and pointed shoes. Russian and Western European cuisine.

Zolotoi Ostap
◆ A D4
Italianskaya Ulitsa 4
Tel. 812 303 88 22
Metro Gostiny Dvor
Open noon–midnight
The entrance to the Zolotoi Ostap, located beside Arts Square, is guarded by a bronze statue of Ostap Bender, the hero of Soviet satyrical literature. Within is a suite of dining rooms decorated in the Art Nouveau style. The menu features not only Russian and Western European dishes but Caucasian and Chinese specialties as well. Zolotoy ostap, the house specialty – veal steak stuffed with smoked salmon – is recommended.

CAFÉS

Bistro le Français
◆ D E2
Galernaya Ulitsa 20
Tel. 812 315 24 65
Open 11am–1am
Traditional French cuisine. Bar with movie theater and videos of French movies for hire.

Coffee-Break
◆ A C5
Kanala Griboyedova Nab. 22
Tel. 812 314 67 29
Open 7.30am–11pm
A café with a fine view of the Cathedral of Our Lady of Kazan. Wide selection of coffees, and black, green and red tea; delicious desserts. Exhibitions of contemporary painting.

Idiot
◆ A A6
Nab. Reky Moyky 82
Tel. 812 315 16 75
Open 11am–1am
Vegetarian cuisine. Cluster of noisy, cosily furnished basement rooms, a popular refuge for students and foreigners. Overflowing bookshelves and bizarre ornaments help to create the wonderfully eclectic atmosphere. The food is mainly but not solely vegetarian. Complimentary shot of vodka provided with each alcoholic drink. The full bar, which serves cocktails, makes this an excellent place for a late drink as well as for a leisurely lunch.

Literaturnoye Kafe (Literary Café)
◆ A B4
Nevsky Prospekt 18
Tel. 812 312 60 57
Open 11am–1am
This café, of the famous Wolf and Béranger patisserie, was a meeting place for writers and the venue of public debates in the 19th century. Traditional Russian cuisine. Concerts of classical music and readings of Russian romances (8.30pm–1am daily).

Publika (The Public)
◆ C B4
Gachinskaya Ul. 2
Tel. 812 232 99 81
Open daily from noon until the last customer leaves.
Unusual décor and impeccable service. A wide choice of desserts.

PUBS AND BARS

Mollie's Irish Bar
◆ A F6
Ulitsa Rubinstein 36
Tel. 812 319 97 68
Open noon–2am
An off-the-shelf Irish pub, and none the worse for that. Guinness, some 20 types of beer and a wide range of cocktails on offer. Some hot food, and hardwood stools. Friendly atmosphere. Popular with foreigners.

Shamrock
◆ A A6
Ulitsa Dekabristov 27
Tel. 812 318 46 25
Open noon–2am
Another Irish pub, located opposite the Mariinsky Theater, and again a fashionable place with a bohemian atmosphere. Beer from US$2.

Sunduk (the Trunk)
◆ E D2
Furchtatskaya Ulitsa 42
Tel. 812 272 31 00
Open 10am–10pm
Three small rooms, one with a stage where jazz, blues and rock bands perform. Friendly, relaxed atmosphere. Beer from US$2.50; snacks from US$1 (cover charge US$1).

Tinkoff
◆ A C5
Kazanskaya Ulitsa 7
Tel. 812 314 84 85
www.tinkoff.ru
Open noon–2am
Microbrewery (the modern interior with a glass partition allows customers to watch the brewing in action) with fine beer and fair food, including a sushi bar. A St Petersburg institution. Big and often noisy (quieter at lunch), with live music and giant television screen. A trendy, vibrant place, popular with students.

NEVSKY PROSPEKT

JAZZ PHILHARMONIA

LEISURE

JAZZ CLUBS

Filarmonia Djazovoy Muzyki (Jazz Philharmonia)
◆ E B5
Zagorodny Pr. 27
Tel. 812 164 85 65
www.jazz-hall.spb.ru
Open: *Great Room* Tue.–Sun. 7–11pm; *Ellington Room* Tue., Fri., Sat. 8–11pm
Established in the 1980's by David Golochtchekin, the renowned jazz musician, this is the oldest jazz club in St Petersburg. Performers from all over the world are invited here, notably for the annual Swing on Summer Nights festival in June. Smart dress required.

JFC Jazz Club
◆ E C1
Chpalernaya Ul. 33
Tel. 812 272 98 50
www.jfc.spb.ru
Open daily 7–10pm
One of the best jazz clubs in the city, where international musicians perform all types of jazz. Knowledgeable audience. Drinks at reasonable prices.

Neo Jazz Club
◆ A E3
Solianoy Per. 14
Tel. 812 273 38 30
Open noon–11.40pm; concerts at 8pm
Soft jazz, duos and trios. Western European and Armenian cuisine.

NIGHTCLUBS

Club Fakultet
◆ A A1
Dobrolubova Pr. 6
Tel. 812 233 06 72
Open Wed.–Sun. 6pm–6am
A wide range of musical styles. Located in the university's halls of residence, the club has a clientele consisting largely of students and lecturers. The books lining the walls are for patrons' use. There is also a mail box that clubbers can use to leave messages for their friends.

Decadence
◆ A A4
Admiralteyskaya Naberejnaya 12
Tel. 812 312 39 44
www.decadence.spb.ru
Open noon–6am, concerts at 9pm (Fri.–Sat. at 10pm); dancing from midnight.
Located on the banks of the Neva, this trendy jazz club has counted stars such as Sting among its patrons. Drinks are relatively expensive and the bar staff are dwarves. Russians must show their membership card.

Fish Fabrique
◆ E C5
Ligovsky Prospekt 53
Tel. 812 164 48 57
www.fishfabrique.spb.ru
Open 4pm–5.30am; concerts start around 10pm
All styles of music.

One of the oldest-established underground clubs in St Petersburg, with a bohemian atmosphere. Table soccer and terrace open in summer.

Griboyedov Club
◆ **E** C6
Voronejskaya Ul. 2a
Tel. 812 164 43 55
Open 6pm–6am (Fri., Sat., till 7am) concerts at 10pm
A fashionable venue located in a disused air-raid shelter hung with Persian carpets. DJ.

Hollywood Nights
◆ **A** E5
Nevsky Prospekt 46
Tel. 812 311 60 77 or 812 325 74 74
Open 10pm–6am; concerts at 1am
A wide range of entertainment, including famous rock bands, DJs and dancing, women's mud wrestling, fashion parades and erotic shows. Restaurant.

Jimi Hendrix Jazz Club
◆ **A** F4
Liteiny Prospekt 33
Tel. 812 279 88 13
Open 24 hours daily
A club by night and a café by day. Blues, Latino and rock'n'roll evenings. A pleasant place for dinner with friends. Affordable prices. As space is limited, reservations must be made.

Luna (the Moon)
◆ **A** A6
Voznessensky Pr. 46
Tel. 812 310 16 16
Open 6pm–6am
Two levels, three rooms, restaurants, casino, bars and a dance floor. A varied range of evening performances, with high-class professional choreography. Smart dress required.

OSTROVSKY SQUARE

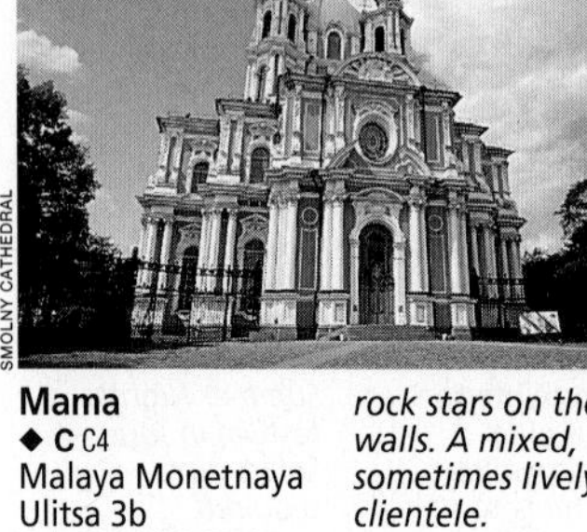
SMOLNY CATHEDRAL

Mama
◆ **C** C4
Malaya Monetnaya Ulitsa 3b
Tel. 812 232 31 37
Open Fri.–Sat. midnight–10am
House, drum'n'bass, trip-hop, acid-jazz, with European DJs and a young, loud atmosphere. Many people come here after other nightclubs have closed.

Manhattan
◆ **E** B5
Reky Fontanky Nab. 90
Tel. 812 113 19 45
www.manhattan.by.ru
Open 2pm–5am; concerts at 9pm (except Mon.)
Rock, blues and jazz. Internet café and billiards.

Money Honey and City Club
◆ **A** E4
Sadovaya Ulitsa 13
Tel. 812 310 05 49
www.moneyhoney.org
Open 11am–6am; concerts at 8pm
Rock music. A club on two floors, with two dance areas and two bars. It has a "saloon" feel, with fireplaces and photographs of rock stars on the walls. A mixed, sometimes lively clientele.

Ostrov
◆ **D** D2
Letenanta Shmidta Nab. 37
Tel. 812 328 46 49
Open Wed.–Sun. 10pm–6am
Located in a fine restored residence. Unusual décor and a rotating dance floor with special effects. DJ, erotic shows. A relatively wealthy clientele.

Plaza
◆ **C** B6
Nab. Makarova 2
Tel. 812 323 90 90
Open 24 hours daily
Located in a beautiful old building. Huge dance floor, restaurant, casino and other facilities. Tue.: karaoke. Wed.: erotic shows, fashion parades, games, etc. Fri.–Sat.: concerts. Sun.: DJ.

Port
◆ **A** B6
Antonenko Per. 2
Tel. 812 314 26 09
www.clubport.spb.ru
Open Wed.–Sat. 10pm–6am
Located next to St Isaac's Square, opposite the Mariinsky Palace. The venue has a high-tech feel. There is a billiard room, several bars and dance floors, including an outsize one. A very mixed clientele and special student evenings.

Red Club
◆ **E** D5
Poltavskaya Ulitsa 7
Tel. 812 277 13 66
www.redclubonline.com
Open noon–6am; concerts at 8pm
A varied program, with an orientation toward young rockers. Excellent acoustics. Two floors, with two bars, two stages and a billiard room. A quieter atmosphere than elsewhere.

CONCERT HALLS

Bielosselskikh-Bielozerskikh Dvorets
◆ **A** E5
Nevsky Pr. 41
Tel. 812 315 52 36
Chamber music performed in the oak Room and Mirror Room of the Beloselsky-Belozersky Palace.

Filarmonia Dmitria Shostakovicha
◆ **A** D5
Home of the fine St Petersburg Philharmonic and of the smaller Glinka recital hall.
SHOSTAKOVICH (LARGE) PHILHARMONIC HALL (Bolshoy Zal):
Mikhailovskaya Ul. 2
Tel. 812 110 42 57
Ticket office open 11am–3pm, 4–7.30pm
GLINKA (SMALL) PHILHARMONIC CHAMBER HALL (Maly Zal):
Nevsky Pr. 30
Tel. 812 311 83 33
Ticket office open

11am–3pm, 4–7pm
The Shostakovich Philharmonia's distinguished concert hall has an excellent orchestra. Major international musicians perform here. The Glinka Philharmonia also hosts several festivals, including an early music festival performed on period instruments.

Hermitage Theater (Ermitazny Teatr)
Dvortsovaya Nab. 34
Metro Nevsky Prospekt or Gostiny Dvor
Tel. 812 311 34 65
Performances begin at 7pm unless announced otherwise

Kapella
◆ **A** C3
Reky Moiky Nab. 20
Tel. 812 314 11 53
or 812 314 10 58 (ticket office)
Ticket office open noon–3pm, 4–6.30pm
An architectural jewel, St Petersburg's State Capella is now a concert hall with a wide-ranging musical program.

Oktiabrsky
◆ **E** D3
Ligovsky Prospekt 6
Tel. 812 275 12 73
Ticket office open 11am–8pm
The largest concert hall in St Petersburg, with a wide-ranging program.

Smolny Sobor (Smolny Cathedral)
◆ **E** F1
Rastrelli Pl. 3/1
Tel. 812 271 76 32
Concerts of Russian church music.

THEATERS

Aleksandrinsky Theater
◆ **A** E6
Ostrovskogo Pl. 2
Tel. 812 110 41 03
Ticket office open 11am–3pm, Sat.–Sun. 4–6pm
A classical repertoire of plays performed in the fine setting of a theater designed by the great Carlo Rossi.

Baltisky Dom (Baltic house)
◆ **C** C5
Alexander Park
Tel. 812 232 62 44
Ticket office open noon–3pm, 4–7pm
Having evolved from TRAM (Young Workers' Theater) and LenKom (Komsomol Leninist Theater), this theater is now the home of several small companies that are known for their experimental productions. It also hosts the annual Baltic House international festival in October.

STAGE AT THE MARINSKY THEATER

AUDITORIUM OF THE MARINSKY THEATER

G. Tovstonogov's BDT (Grand Dramatic Theater)
◆ **A** B4
Fontanky Nab. 65 .
Tel. 812 310 92 42
Ticket office open 1–3pm, 4–7pm.
This theater was revived by the eminent director G. Tovstonogov, who brought together the best actors of the Soviet era. The company's repertoire covers the major works of the Russian theater.

Konservatori Rimskogo-Korsakova
◆ **D** E3
Teatralnaya Pl. 3
Tel. 812 312 25 07
Ticket office open 11am–7pm
The Rimsky-Korsakov Conservatoire's opera and ballet theater is a showcase for its students and teachers. The theater also organizes various Russian and international festivals and competitions.

Maly (Mussorgsky Opera and Ballet Theater)
◆ **A** D4
Iskusstv Pl. 1 (Arts Square)
Tel. 812 595 42 84
or 812 595 43 05 (ticket office)
Ticket office open 11am–3pm, 4–6pm (6–7pm for that day's performance only)
The former Mikhailovsky Theater is St Petersburg's second most important center of opera and ballet. It was once used only by foreign companies, particularly from Italy and France, but now puts on a range of classic works performed by Russian singers and dancers. Worth a visit for the architecture and décor alone.

Maly Dramatichesky Teatr (Theater of Europe)
◆ **A** F6
Ulitsa Rubinstein 18
Tel.812 113 20 28
or 812 113 20 78 (ticket office)
Ticket office noon–3pm, 4–7pm.
This theater's artistic achievements and innovative productions have won it a reputation of European stature. Its artistic leader, Lev Dodin, was voted Europe's most outstanding director three years ago. The company goes on frequent foreign tours.

Mariinsky Opera and Ballet Theater
◆ **D** E3
Teatralnaya Pl. 1 (Theater Square)
Tel. 812 114 43 44
or 812 114 12 11
Ticket office open 11am–2pm, 3–7pm.
Performances 7pm, matinees 11.30am.
The history of this theater is closely linked to Russian musical culture. Formerly known as the Kirov Theater, it has reverted to its original name and continues to attract the most highly talented actors and directors.

CIRCUS, FILM, CASINOS, ENTERTAINMENT CENTERS, SHOPPING

With one of the best orchestras in the world, new productions of the great classical operas and ballets are particularly worth seeing. As the main companies have gained such an international reputation they are more likely to be away touring in spring and summer. Winter is a better time to find them in St Petersburg. The annual White Nights festival (June) regularly offers a highly innovative program. Note, however, that ticket prices are higher at this time of year, the high tourist season.

St Petersburg Opera
◆ **D** E2
Galernaya Ulitsa 33
Tel. 812 312 39 82
or 812 315 67 69
This young opera company has already won several awards. Shows take place at the Yusupov Palace (Reky Moiky Nab. 94) or at the Hermitage Theater (Dvortsovaya Nab. 34). Its productions have won praise for their avant-garde, nonconformist spirit.

Teatr Muzikalnoy Komedy (Musical Comedy Theater)
◆ **A** E5
Italianskaya Ul. 13
Tel. 812 313 43 16
or 812 313 48 68
Ticket office open 11am–3pm, 4–7pm
This theater, specializing in operetta, puts on magical productions performed by a company long recognized as distinctive masters of the genre. The theater has a sumptuous interior.

ARTS SQUARE

VIEW OF VASILYEVSKY ISLAND

Zazerkalie (Children's musical theater)
◆ **A** F6
Ulitsa Rubinstein 13
Tel. 812 112 51 35
Ticket office open noon–3pm, 4–7pm
Although most of the repertoire consists of tales and fables, the musical shows put on here appeal to both children and adults.

CIRCUS

Sankt Peterburgsky Tsirk
◆ **A** E2
Reky Fontanky Naberejnaya 3
Tel. 812 314 84 78
Ticket office open 11am–7pm
One of the oldest Russian circuses. Traditional performances.

FILM

Dom Kino (the Movie House)
◆ **A** E5
Karavannaya Ul. 12
Tel. 812 314 80 36
Open exclusively to members of the film-directors' union during the Soviet era, the Movie House is now a center for cinema enthusiasts. Events include screenings of European movies, retrospectives and film festivals.

CASINOS

Premier Casino Club
◆ **A** F5
Nevsky Pr. 47
Tel. 812 315 78 93
Open 24 hours
Bars and Palkin restaurant: cozy atmosphere and good-quality Western European cuisine.

Taléon Casino Club
◆ **A** B5
Reky Moiky Nab. 59
Tel. 812 315 76 45
Open noon–6am
Located in the former residence of the Russian merchant Eliseev, with many rooms and a strong gambling atmosphere. Restaurants and concerts. Private functions some evenings.

ENTERTAINMENT CENTERS

Carnaval
◆ **A** E5
Anichkov Palace
Nevsky Prospekt 39
Tel. 812 310 99 88
Russian folk music and dance performed by top professional companies.

Sankt Petersburg
◆ **C** E5
Lenina Pl. 1
Tel. 812 542 15 25
or 812 542 09 44
Ticket office open 1–3pm, 4–7pm
Concerts, shows and other entertainments. Wide-ranging program.

SHOPPING

ARMY ACCESSORIES

Soldat Udatchi (Soldier of Fortune)
◆ **E** D3
Nekrassova Ulitsa 37
Tel. 812 272 39 78
Open daily 11am–8pm
Army equipment, military decorations and accessories. Large selection of knives.

ART AND ANTIQUES

Antikvarnitsentr
◆ **D** A2
Nalitchnaya Ul. 21
Tel. 812 355 10 10
Open daily 11am–7pm
One of the oldest-established antique shops in the city. Large showroom with a wide variety of pieces.

Lavka Stariovchtchika (Bric-a-brac)
◆ **D** D1
9 Linia 26
Tel. 812 328 56 37
Open Mon.–Fri.11am–6pm (3pm Sat.)
All kinds of old utilitarian objects, including dinner services and flatware, samovars, coffee mills and furniture. Affordable prices.

Panteleimonovsky
◆ **A** F3
Pestelia Ulitsa 13/15
Tel. 812 279 72 35

Open Mon.–Sat.
11am–7pm
A wealth of beautiful old decorative objects and fine porcelain. Knowledgeable staff.

Petersburg
◆ **A** F5
Nevsky Prospekt 54
Tel. 812 311 40 20
Open daily
10am–8pm
A variety of objects at reasonable prices.

Rapsodia
◆ **A** C4
Bolshaya Koniuchennaya Ulitsa 13
Tel. 812 314 48 01
Open daily
11am–8pm (Sun. from noon)
Well-known for its collection of icons chosen by experts. Many silver and crystal pieces.

Renaissance
◆ **A** F3
Pestelia Ulitsa 8
Tel. 812 273 54 04
Open daily
11am–8pm
Decorative objects, porcelain and bronze, and a wide selection of Empire furniture.

BOOKS

ABOOK
◆ **A** B4
Nevsky Prospekt 18
Tel. 812 312 20 81
Open Mon.–Sat.
10am–8pm,
Sun. noon–6pm
Antiquarian books, engravings, prints, collectors' pieces.

Bukinist
◆ **E** C3
Liteiny Pr. 59
Tel. 812 273 25 04
Open daily
10am–2pm, 3–7pm
Wide range of antiquarian and art books. A browser's paradise.

Dom Knigi (the Book House)
◆ **A** C5
Nevsky Prospekt 28
Tel. 812 318 65 46
Open daily
9am–10pm (9pm Sun.)
The largest bookstore in the city, stocking all kinds of books, including illustrated books, postcards, and many books on St Petersburg.

Iskusstvo (Art)
◆ **A** B4
Nevsky Prospekt 16
Tel. 812 311 54 73
Open daily
10am–8pm
Art books, including illustrated books.

FABRICS

Dom Tkanei (the Fabric House)
◆ **E** D1
Komsomola Ul. 45
Tel. 812 542 43 43
Open Mon.–Sat.
10am–7pm
Wide selection of European and Central Asian fabrics, as well as good-quality, inexpensive Russian linen and lace and bedlinen.

FASHION AND FURS

Lena, Torgovy Dom
◆ **A** F5
Nevsky Prospekt 50
Tel. 812 311 71 69
Open daily
10am–9pm
Wide range of "exotic" furs from various countries, including Scandinavia.

Rot-Front
◆ **D** F2
Bolshaya Morskaya Ulitsa 34
Tel. 812 311 73 57
Open Mon.–Fri.
10am–7pm (6pm Sat.)
The city's other leading fur house.

Salon de Tatiana Kotegova
◆ **C** C4
Kamennoostrovsky Prospekt 34
Tel. 812 346 34 67
Open Mon.–Fri.
noon–8pm
Classic clothes with simple outlines, in plain colors (white, black and brown) and natural fabrics such as fine linen, cashmere and taffeta.

Tatiana Parfionova's Fashion House
◆ **A** F5
Nevsky Prospekt 51
Tel. 812 113 36 69
Open Mon.–Fri.
noon–8pm,
Sat.–Sun. 11am–9pm
One of the city's most prestigious fashion houses, with distinctive collections of clothes with a retro touch. Fine fabrics and a wide selection of scarves and embroidered chiffon shawls.

NEVSKY PROSPEKT

FOOD AND DRINK

Belotchka (Little Squirrel)
◆ **D** D1
Sredny Pr. 28
Tel. 812 323 17 63
Open Mon.–Fri.
9am–8.30pm
(7pm Sat.)
Lovely confectionery shop. It takes its name from the famous nut candy.

Liviz
◆ **E** A5
– Sadovaya Ulitsa 53
Tel. 812 310 45 58
Open daily
10am–10pm
(8pm Mon.)
– Marata Ulitsa 54
Tel. 162 59 37
Open 24 hours daily
A chain of shops specializing in vodka and other alcoholic drinks.

Sever
◆ **A** E5
Nevsky Prospekt 44
Tel. 812 311 25 89
Open Mon.–Fri.
10am–9pm,
Sat.–Sun. 10am–8pm
An historic institution: all the best Russian chocolate and candy.

Zhar-Ptitsa (Firebird)
◆ **E** B5
Marata Ulitsa 70b
Tel. 812 315 26 87
Open Mon.–Sat.
10am–8pm
The retail outlet of the great Russian confectioners, the Krupskaya. Huge choice of delicious eastern European confectionery.

Supermarkets
(All open daily)
AYAKS ◆ **D** A1
Nalitchnaya Ul. 32

Open 9am–1am
KALINKA STOCKMANN ◆ C D5
Finliandsky Pr. 1
Open 9am–10pm
MAGASIN ELISSEIEV ◆ A F5
Nevsky Prospekt 56
Open 9am–9pm
A notable example of modern architecture, with an Art Nouveau interior.
PASSAGE ◆ A F5
Nevsky Prospekt 48
Open 10am–11pm
PRIMA ◆ D F2
26 Bolshaya Morskaya Ulitsa
Open 24 hours
SUPER-BABYLON ◆ C B4
Maly Pr. 54/56, PS
Tel. 812 233 88 92
Open 24 hours

GIFTS AND SOUVENIRS

Art-Boutique
◆ D F3
Mariinsky Teatralnaya Pl. 18
Tel. 812 326 41 96
Open Tue.–Sun. 11am–7pm
Souvenirs of the Mariinsky Theater, unusual decorative pieces and theatrical objects, illustrated books, postcards, CDs and DVDs.

Red October
◆ C B5
Ulitsa Blokhina 8
Tel. 812 232 65 19
Open daily 10am–6pm
Palekh lacquered boxes, Russian dolls, shawls, Gjel crockery, and amber and malachite objects.

Stroganoff
◆ A B4
Nevsky Prospekt 17
Open daily 11am–8pm
Contemporary art, art glass and handicrafts.

Vasilyevsky Ostrov
◆ D D1
Sredny Prospekt 31
Tel. 812 323 28 35
Open Mon.–Fri. 11am–2pm, 2.30–7pm, Sat. 11am–4pm.
Souvenirs, handcrafted boxes and Russian lace.

JEWELRY

Ananov Jewelry Showroom
◆ A C5
Nevsky Prospekt 31
Tel. 812 110 55 92
Open daily 10am–7pm
Large showroom with jewelry representing the major periods and styles of the Russian jeweler's art, including that of Fabergé.

Belage
◆ A F5
Nevsky Prospekt 57
Tel. 812 310 66 88
Open daily 11am–8pm
Upmarket jewelry.

Luvelirtorg
◆ B A5
Flagship shop: Novosmolenskaya Nab. 1
Tel. 812 355 58 61
Open Mon.–Sat. 10am–2pm, 3–7pm, Sun. 11am–6pm
A major chain of jewelry shops with branches in several dsitricts of the city.

Salon Bouré
◆ A C5
Nevsky Prospekt 23
Tel.812 311 75 34
Open daily 10am–8pm
High-quality jewelry, clocks and watches.

MUSIC

Klassika
◆ A D5
Mikhailovskaya Ul. 2
Tel. 812 110 44 28
Open Mon.–Sat. 11am–3pm, 4–7.30pm, Sun. noon–3pm, 4pm–7.30pm
Located in the Philharmonia's ticket office, the shop specializes in classical music, including secondhand CDs, cassettes, vinyl records and old musical scores. Mail order.

Otkryty Mir (Open World)
◆ A A5
Isaakievskaya Pl. 5
Tel. 812 311 59 76
Open Mon.–Sat. 11am–8pm, Sun. noon–7pm.
Wide choice of classical music. Mail order.

Rock Island
◆ E C2
Kirochnaya Ulitsa 8
Tel. 812 273 07 22
Open Mon.–Sat. 11am–7pm, Sun. till 6pm
Rock music. The secondhand section has a large collection of vinyl records and original recordings of Soviet-era rock.

Severnaya Lira (the Northern Lyre)
◆ A C5
Nevsky Prospekt 26
Tel. 812 312 07 96
Open Mon.–Sat. 10am–8pm, Sun. 11am–7pm
Musical instruments scores, accessories and CDs.

PORCELAIN

Lomonosov Porcelain Shops
◆ E E4
– Nevsky Pr. 160
Tel. 812 277 48 38
Open daily 10am–8pm
– Vladimirsky Pr. 7
Tel. 812 113 15 13
Open daily 10am–8pm
– Obukhovskoy Oborony Pr. 151
Tel. 812 560 85 44
Open Mon.–Sat. 10am–7pm, Sun. 11am–5pm
Descended from the imperial porcelain factory established in 1744, Lomonosov still produces high-quality porcelain today.

SHOPPING ARCADES

Dom Leningradskoy Torgovly (DLT)
◆ E A3
Bolshaya Koniuchennaya Ul. 21/23
Tel. 812 312 26 27
Open Mon.–Sat. 10am–9pm, Sun. 11am–7pm.
St Petersburg's third great historic arcade.

Gostiny Dvor
◆ A D5
Nevsky Prospekt 35
Tel. 812 110 54 08
Open daily 9am–10pm
One of St Petersburg's oldest shopping arcades.

Passage
◆ A F5
Nevsky Prospekt 48
Tel. 812 311 70 84
Open Mon.–Sat. 10am–9pm, Sun. 11am–7pm
Designed as a promenade, the arcade links Nevsky Prospekt and Italianskaya Ulitsa.

SPORT AND LEISURE

Medved (the Bear)
◆ E A5
Sadovaya Ul. 55/57
Tel. 812 310 83 77
Open Mon.–Sat. 10am–7pm (5pm Sun)
Everything for hiking, shooting and fishing, which, particularly in the case of fishing through the ice in winter, are all popular leisure activities in Russia. High quality and inexpensive.

VIDEOS

Na Lenfilme
◆ C C5
Kamennoostrovsky Prospekt 10
Tel. 812 232 28 40
Open daily 11am–11pm
For the widest choice of Russian and Soviet films (over 1,000 titles).

Directory

◆ PLACES TO VISIT

Places to visit are listed alphabetically.
The symbol ▲ refers to a page number in the Itineraries, the ◆ refers to the Map section.

ST PETERSBURG		
ACADEMY OF ARTS Universitetskaya Nab. 17 Tel. 812 323 3578/812 323 6496	*Open Wed.–Sun. 11am–6pm.*	▲ *162* ◆ **D** E1-2
AKHMATOVA MUSEUM Fontanka Nab. 34 (entrance on Liteiny Pr. 53 or through the Sheremetev Palace) Tel. 812 272 2211/812 272 5758	*Open Tue.–Sun. 10.30am–5.30pm.* *Closed last Wed. of the month.*	▲ *237* ◆ **A** F4-5
ALEXANDER NEVSKY MONASTERY (SCULPTURE MUSEUM) Nevsky Pr. 179/2 Tel. 812 274 2635/812 277 1716	*Open Apr.–Sep.: Fri.–Wed. 9.30am–7pm;* *Oct.–Mar.: Fri.–Wed. 9.30am–5pm.*	▲ *253* ◆ **E** E5
APARTMENT OF ALEXANDER BLOK Dekabristov Ul. 57, Apartment 21, 23 Tel. 812 113 8627/812 113 8633	*Open Thur.–Mon. 11am–5pm* *and Tue. 11am–6pm.* *Closed last Tue. of the month.*	▲ *199* ◆ **D** E3
BELOSELSKY-BELOZERSKY PALACE Nevsky Pr. 41 Tel. 812 319 99 90	*Open daily noon–6pm.* *Guided tours only (Tel. for info 812 315 5636).* *Musical evenings (Tel. 812 315 5236).* *Wax museum (History of Russia from the 11th to the 20th century) open daily 11am–6pm).*	▲ *238* ◆ **A** F5
BOTANICAL GARDENS AND MUSEUM Professora Popova Ul. 2 Tel. 812 234 1764	*Open 11am–4pm.* *Closed Fri.*	▲ *153* ◆ **C** C3
BREAD MUSEUM Ligovsky Per. 73 Tel. 812 164 1110	*Open Tue.–Sat. 10am–5pm.* *Closed last Tue. of the month.*	▲ *244* ◆ **E** D4
CABIN OF PETER THE GREAT Petrovskaya Nab. 6 Tel. 812 232 4576	*Open Wed.–Sun. 10am–4pm.*	▲ *151* ◆ **C** D5
CATHEDRAL OF OUR LADY OF KAZAN Kazanskaya Pl. 2	*Open daily noon–6pm.*	▲ *217* ◆ **A** C5
CHURCH OF THE RESURRECTION Kanala Griboiedova Nab. 2a Tel. 812 315 1636	*Open 11am–6.30pm.* *Closed Wed.*	▲ *228* ◆ **A** D4
CRUISER *AURORA* Petrogradskaya Nab. 4 Tel. 812 230 8440	*Open Tue.–Thur. and Sat.–Sun. 10.30am–4pm.* *Free.*	▲ *152* ◆ **C** D5
DOSTOEVSKY MUSEUM Kuznechny Per. 5 Tel. 812 311 4031/812 164 6950	*Open Tue.–Sun. 11am–6pm.* *Closed last Wed. of the month.*	▲ *240* ◆ **E** C4
ELAGIN PALACE – MUSEUM OF DECORATIVE ARTS (18th and beg. 19th centuries) Elagin Island Tel. 812 430 1131	*Open Wed.–Sun. 10am–6pm.*	▲ *154* ◆ **B** E1
ENGINEERS' CASTLE Sadovaya Ul. 4 Tel. 812 313 4173	*Open Mon. 10am–5pm* *and Wed.–Sun. 10am–6pm.*	▲ *229* ◆ **A** E3-4
ETHNOGRAPHIC MUSEUM Ingenernaya Ul. 4 Tel. 812 313 4421	*Open Tue.–Sun. 10am–6pm.* *Closed last Fri. of the month.*	▲ *228* ◆ **A** D4

THE HERMITAGE MUSEUM (also known as WINTER PALACE) Dvortsovaya Nab. 36 Tel. 812 311 2420/812 311 3465 *www.hermitagemuseum.og*	*Open Tue.–Sat. 10.30am–6pm, and Sun. 10.30am–5pm.*	▲ *168* ◆ **A** B3
KUNSTKAMMER Universitetskaya Nab. 3 Tel. 812 328 1412/812 328 0118	*Open Tue.–Sun. 11am–5.45pm. Closed last Tue. of the month.*	▲ *160* ◆ **A** A3
LOMONOSOV MUSEUM Universitetskaya Nab. 3 Tel. 812 328 1011	*Open Tue.–Sun. 11am–5.30pm.*	▲ *160* ◆ **A** A3
MARBLE PALACE Millionaya Ul. 5 Tel. 812 312 9196	*Open Mon. 10am–4pm, Wed.–Sun. 10am–5pm.*	▲ *184* ◆ **A** D2
MENDELEEV MUSEUM (THE TWELVE COLLEGES) Mendeleevskaya Linya 2 Tel. 812 328 9744	*Open Mon.–Fri. 11am–4pm.*	▲ *159* ◆ **C** E1
MENSHIKOV PALACE Universitetskaya Nab. 15 Tel. 812 323 1112	*Open Tue.–Sun. 10.30am–4.30pm. Guided tours only (call for information).*	▲ *161* ◆ **D** E1
MUSEUM OF DECORATIVE AND APPLIED ARTS Solianoi Per. 15 Tel. 812 273 3258	*Open Tue.–Sun. 11am–5pm.*	▲ *188* ◆ **A** E3
MUSEUM OF LITERATURE (PUSHKIN HOUSE) Naverejnaya Makarova 4 Tel. 812 328 0502	*Open Mon.–Fri. 10.30am–4.30pm. Guided tours only, by appointment (Tel. 812 108 4761). A must for Russian literature aficionados.*	▲ *158* ◆ **B** F6
MUSEUM OF THEATER AND MUSIC – FOUNTAINS HOUSE Fontanki Nab. 34 Tel. 812 272 44 41	*Open Wed.–Sun. noon–5pm. Closed last Wed. of the month.*	▲ *236* ◆ **A** F4-5
MUSEUM OF POLITICAL HISTORY Kubysheva Ul. 2–4 Tel. 812 233 7113/812 233 7052	*Open 10am–6pm. Closed Thur.*	▲ *150* ◆ **C** D5
MUSEUM OF THE ARCTIC AND ANTARCTIC Marata Ul. 24a Tel. 812 311 2549	*Open Wed.–Sun 10am–6pm. Closed last Sat. of the month.*	▲ *241* ◆ **E** C4
NABOKOV'S HOUSE AND MUSEUM Bolshaya Morskaya Ul. 47 Tel. 812 315 4713	*Open Mon.–Thur. 11am–6pm. Fri. 11am–5pm, Sat. and Sun. noon–5pm.*	▲ *198* ◆ **D** F2
NAVAL MUSEUM Birgevaya Pl. 4 Tel. 812 328 2502	*Open Wed.–Sun. 11am–6pm. Closed last Thur. of the month.*	▲ *157* ◆ **A** A3
PETER AND PAUL FORTRESS Revolyutsy Pl. Tel. 812 238 4540/812 238 4511	*Open 11am–5pm. Closed Wed. and last Tue. of the month.*	▲ *144* ◆ **A** B-C1
PUSHKIN MUSEUM AND HOUSE Reki Moiky Nab. 12 Tel. 812 311 3531/812 311 3801	*Open Wed.–Mon. 11am–5pm. Closed last Fri. of the month.*	▲ *182* ◆ **A** C3
THE RIDING SCHOOL Isaakievskaya Pl. 1 Tel. 812 314 8253	*Open Fri.–Wed. 11am–7pm.*	▲ *194* ◆ **A** A5

◆ PLACES TO VISIT

RIMSKY-KORSAKOV MUSEUM Zagorodny Pr. 28 Tel. 812 113 3202/812 315 3975	*Open Wed.–Sun. 11am–6pm.* *Closed last Fri. of the month.*	▲ *239* ◆ **E** C4-5
RUSSIAN MUSEUM Ingenernaya Ul. 2 Tel. 812 314 3448	*Open Mon. 10am–5pm, Wed.–Sun. 10am–6pm.* *Closed Tue.*	▲ *225* ◆ **A** D4
RUSSIAN VODKA MUSEUM Konnogvardeisky Bl. 5 Tel. 812 311 7247	*Open daily 11am–10pm.*	◆ **D** F2
ST ISAAC'S CATHEDRAL Isaakievskaya Pl. 1 Tel. 812 315 9732	*Museum open Thur.–Tue. 11am–6pm.* *Panoramic visit 11am–5pm.*	▲ *195* ◆ **A** A5
ST NICHOLAS' CATHEDRAL Nikolskaya Pl. 1/3	*Open daily 7am–7.30pm.*	▲ *204* ◆ **D** F4
ST PETERSBURG HISTORY MUSEUM (ARTILLERY/ENGINEERS) Alexandrovsky Park 7 Tel. 812 232 0296	*Open Wed.–Sun. 11am–5pm.* *Closed last Thur. of the month.*	▲ *149* ◆ **C** C5
SHALYAPIN HOUSE (MUSEUM OF RUSSIAN OPERA) Graftio Ul. 26 Tel. 812 234 1056	*Open Wed.–Sun. noon–6pm.* *Closed last Fri. of the month.*	▲ *153* ◆ **C** B2
SMOLNY CHURCH AND MONASTERY Rastelli Pl. 3/1 Tel. 812 271 9182	*Open Fri.–Wed. 11am–5pm.* *Guided tours by appointment (Tel. 812 271 9421).* *Concerts (Tel. 812 271 7632).*	▲ *246* ◆ **E** F1-2
SMOLNY INSTITUTE Proletarskoy Diktatury Pl. Tel. 812 276 1461	*Open Mon.–Fri. 10am–4pm.* *Guided tours only, by appointment.*	▲ *250* ◆ **E** F2
STROGANOV PALACE 17 Nevsky Pr. Tel. 812 311 2360	*Open Mon. 10am–5pm, Wed.–Sun. 10am–6pm.* *Waxworks exhibition: the Romanov family, open Mon.–Fri. 11am–8pm, Sat.–Sun. 11am–9pm; guided tours (Tel. 812 311 3944).*	▲ *215* ◆ **A** C5
SUMMER GARDEN Kutuzova Nab. 2 Tel. 812 314 0374/812 314 0456	*Open May–Oct.: 10am–9pm; Nov.–Mar: 10am–6pm.* *Closed Tue., last Mon. of the month and part of April.*	▲ *186* ◆ **A** E3
SUMMER PALACE Kutuzova Nab. Tel. 812 314 0456	*Open Wed.–Mon. 10am–5pm. Closed last Mon. of the month and Nov.–early May.*	▲ *187* ◆ **A** E2
SUVOROV MUSEUM Kirochnaya Ul. 43 Tel. 812 279 3914	*Open Mon. 10am–4.15pm, Tue. and Fri. 10am–5.15pm, Sat.–Sun. 10am–6.15pm. Closed Wed, Thur and last Monday of the month.*	▲ *252* ◆ **E** E2
THEATER MUSEUM Ostrovsky Pl. 6 Tel. 812 311 2195	*Open Thur.–Mon. 11am–6pm, Wed. 1–7pm.* *Closed last Fri. of the month.*	▲ *231* ◆ **A** E6
WINTER PALACE see HERMITAGE		
WRITERS' WALKWAYS MAUSOLEUM (LITERATORSKIYE MOSTKI) Rastannya Ul. 30 Tel. 812 166 2383	*Open Apr.–Oct.: Fri.–Wed. 11am–7pm;* *Nov.–Mar.: Fri.–Tue. 11am–5pm.*	▲ *244* OFF MAP
YUSUPOV PALACE Reki Moiki Nab. 94 Tel. 812 314 9883	*Open Tue.–Sun. noon–5pm.* *Guided tours only, by appointment (Tel. 812 314 8893).*	▲ *202* ◆ **D** E-F3
ZOOLOGICAL GARDENS Alexandrovsky Park 1 Tel. 812 232 4828/812 232 8260	*Open Tue.–Sun. 10am–5pm.*	▲ *151* ◆ **C** C5
ZOOLOGICAL MUSEUM Universitetskaya Nab. 1 Tel. 812 328 0112	*Open Sat.–Thur. 11am–6pm.*	▲ *158* ◆ **D** F1

AROUND ST PETERSBURG

OFF MAPS

Place	Opening times	Page
GATCHINA		
GATCHINA PALACE Tel. (271) 1 34 92	*Museum open Tue.–Sun. 10am–5pm. Closed last Tue. of the month.*	▲ 272
ORANIENBAUM		
CHINESE PALACE Tel. 812 422 8016 or 422 3753	*Open Apr.–Oct.: Mon. 11am–4pm, Wed.–Sun. 11am–5pm; Nov.–Mar.: daily 11am–4pm. Closed last Mon. of the month. (The Chinese Kitchen is currently being refurbished.)*	▲ 262
JAPANESE PAVILION (GREAT PALACE) Tel. 812 423 1639	*Open Apr.–Oct.: Mon. 11am–4pm, Wed.–Sun. 11am–5pm; Nov.–Mar.: daily 11am–4pm. Closed last Mon. of the month.*	▲ 262
ORANIENBAUM ESTATE (MENSHIKOV PALACE) Tel. 812 423 1627	*Open Apr.–Oct.: Mon. 11am–4pm, Wed.–Sun. 11am–5pm; Nov.–Mar.: daily 11am–4pm. Closed last Mon. of the month.*	▲ 262
PETER III'S PALACE Tel. 812 422 3756	*Open Apr.–Oct.: Mon. 11am–4pm, Wed.–Sun. 11am–5pm; Nov.–Mar.: daily 11am–4pm. Closed last Mon. of the month.*	▲ 263
"SLIDING HILL" (KATALNOY GORKY PAVILION) Tel. 812 422 3758	*Closed in 2003 for renovation.*	▲ 263
PAVLOVSK		
PALACE Tel. 812 470 2156	*Open Sat.–Thur. 10am–6pm. Closed Fri.*	▲ 268
PETERHOF		
BENOIS MUSEUM Dvortsovaya Plochtchad 8 (Bus 351, 356, 359)	*Open Sat. and Sun. 10am–4.30pm.*	▲ 261
CATHERINE WING Nijny Park Tel. 812 427 9129	*Open May–Oct.: Fri.–Wed. 10.30am–5pm; Nov.–Apr.: Sat.–Sun. 10.30am–4pm.*	▲ 261
COTTAGE Alexandria Park (Buses 351, 356, 359) Tel. 812 427 9953	*Open June.–Sep.: Tue.–Sun. 10.30am–5pm. Closed last Tue. of the month. Open Oct.–May: Sat.–Sun. 10.30am–5pm.*	▲ 261
GREAT PALACE Razvodnaya Ul. 2 (Buses 351, 356) Tel. 812 427 9527	*Open Tue.–Sun. 10.30am–4pm.*	▲ 257
HERMITAGE PAVILION Nijny Park Tel. 812 427 5325	*Open May–Oct.: Tue.–Sun. 10.30am–5pm; Nov.–Mar.: Sat.–Sun. 10.30am–4pm.*	▲ 260
MARLY PALACE Nijny Park (West side) Tel. 812 427 7729	*Open May–Oct.: Tue.–Sun. 10.30am–5pm; Nov.–Apr.: Sat.–Sun. 10.30am–4pm.*	▲ 260
MONPLAISIR Nijny Park Tel. 812 427 9129	*Open Sat.–Sun. 10.30am–4pm. Closed Oct.–end May. The Imperial spa and its Chinese garden, the Assembly Room, the offices, the kitchen and the bedroom have been open to the public since 2001.*	▲ 260
TSARSKOE SELO		
CATHERINE PALACE Sadovaya Ul. 7 Tel. 812 466 6669	*Open Apr.–Oct.: Wed.–Mon. 10am–5pm; Nov.–Mar.: Wed.–Mon. 10am–4pm. Closed last Mon. of the month. Guided tours (Tel. 812 465 5308 for information).*	▲ 264
PUSHKIN LYCEUM Tel. 812 476 6411	*Open Wed.–Mon. 10.30am–4.30pm. Closed last Fri. of the month. Visits by appointment only.*	▲ 267

LEBRATIONS, FESTIVALS AND EVENTS

CELEBRATIONS AND FESTIVALS

DECEMBER–JANUARY	ARTS SQUARE	ARTS SQUARE INTERNATIONAL FESTIVAL *Concerts, exhibitions, competitions*
	CITY PALACES	CHRISTMAS ENCOUNTERS IN THE PALMYRA OF THE NORTH *Christmas and New Year's balls (Roman Catholic and Orthodox) in the city palaces*
FEBRUARY	PETER AND PAUL FORTRESS	ICE SCULPTURE FESTIVAL *On Fortress beach*
	THE CAPELLA	VIVA LA MUSICA ANTIQUA! *Early music festival*
	MARIINSKY THEATER	INTERNATIONAL BALLET FESTIVAL *Participants of the third International Ballet Festival (2003) included dancers from the American Ballet Theater, the Royal Ballet of Great Britain and Moscow Bolshoi, as well as Mariinsky's own ballet troupe*
MARCH	MUSEUMS, GALLERIES	FROM AVANT-GARDE TO THE PRESENT *International arts festival*
APRIL	CONCERT HALLS	SERGEI KURIOKHIN INTERNATIONAL FESTIVAL *Contemporary music festival*
MAY	PETERHOF	FOUNTAIN OPENING FESTIVAL *In Peterhof gardens*
	VARIOUS VENUES	INTERNATIONAL MUSICAL SPRING *Two weeks of contemporary academic music by leading Russian and international composers of the 20th century*
MAY 27	HISTORICAL SQUARES AND MONUMENTS	CITY CELEBRATIONS AND BRASS BAND FESTIVAL *Entertainment, concerts, etc.*
END MAY-EARLY JUNE	PETERHOF PALACE, PAVLOVSK, TSARSKOE SELO	MUSICAL OLYMPUS *One week. Gala parade of the winners of the world's most prestigious classical competition.*
MAY 31– JUNE 30	MARIINSKY THEATER	STARS OF THE WHITE NIGHTS *World-famous international festival of classic arts. Organized by the Mariinsky Theater, much attention is given to Russian opera*
JUNE	ST PETERSBURG MUSEUMS	CONTEMPORARY ART IN TRADITIONAL MUSEUMS *Exhibitions in several small museums*
JUNE 15–22	JAZZ PHILHARMONIA, MIKHAIL PALACE GARDENS	SWING ON SUMMER NIGHTS *International jazz festival*
	HOME OF THE MOVIES	MESSAGE TO MANKIND *International documentaries and short films*
JUNE 1–30	HERMITAGE THEATER AND CITY PALACES	ST PETERSBURG'S PALACES *International chamber music festival at Mikhail, Yusupov, Sheremetev, Menshikov and other palaces*
	HOME OF THE MOVIES	FESTIVAL OF ALL FESTIVALS! *International movie festival*
JULY	CLUBS, CAFÉS, ETC.	OPEN YOUR WINDOWS! *Rock festival*
OCTOBER	CAPELLA, PAVLOSK, PETERHOFF, MENSHIKOV, PHILHARMONIA HALL	INTERNATIONAL EARLY MUSIC FESTIVAL *Founded in 1998 as a joint initiative between the British Council and the emsemble Musica Petropolitana to celebrate the 300th anniversary of Peter I's "Great Embassy" to England. The Festival draws on the musical traditions of Western Europe, Russia and the East, and strives for the greatest possible degree of historical accuracy*
	THEATER BALTIC HOUSE	BALTIC HOUSE *International theater festival*

OTHER EVENTS

AUGUST	ON THE NEVA	REGATTA (SAILBOATS)
SEPTEMBER	GALLERIES, EXHIBITIONS HALLS	FALL PHOTO-MARATHON *Photography exhibitions*

ST PETERSBURG'S TRICENTENARY

THROUGHOUT 2003		REGULAR EVENTS
	Program listings in the local press, at hotel receptions and in tourist offices (see Useful addresses p282)	
MAY 24–JUNE 1, 2003		JUBILEE WEEK
	Entertainment in public squares and gardens, science festival, city festival, sports festival, theater festival, "Open Museums", special exhibitions, international events, children's festival, processions and parades	

URBAN VOCABULARY

Avenue: *prospekt*
Bridge: *most*
Bus: *avtobus*
Car: *mashina*
Canal: *kanal*
Cathedral: *sobor*
Courtyard: *dvor*
District: *rayon*
Garden: *sard*
House: *dom*
Left: *nalevo*
Palace: *dvorets*
Passage: *proyezd*
Pedestrian crossing: *perekhod*
Quay: *naberezhnaya*
Right: *napravo*
River: *reka*
Square: *ploshchad*
Station: *vokzal*
Stop (bus, etc.): *ostanovka*
Street: *ulitsa* (small street: *pereulok*)
Suburbs: *prigorod*
Taxi rank: *stoyanka taxi*
Terminal (bus, etc.): *stantsiya*
Ticket: *bilet*
Train: *poyezd*
Tramway: *tramvay*
Trolley-bus: *troleybus*
"Watch out!": *ostorojno!*
Where is ...?: *gde nakhoditsa*

TRADES/ STORES

Baker's: *bulochnaya*
Bank: *bank*
Café: *kafe*
Closed: *zakryto*
Delicatessen: *gastronom*
Department store: *univermag*
Food store: *producty*
Gas station: *stantsiya tekhnicheskogo obslujivanya*
Gasoline: *benzin*
Hospital: *bolnitsa*
Jeweler: *yuvelirniye izdeliya*
Market: *rynok*
Open: *otkryto*
Patisserie: *konditerskaya*
Pharmacy: *apteka*
Post office: *pochta*
Restaurant: *restoran*
Souvenirs: *souveniry*
Stamp: *marka*
Telephone: *telefon*
Tobacco, cigarettes: *tabak, sigarety*

NIGHTLIFE

Chamber music: *kamernaya muzyka*
Club: *klub*
Concert: *kontsert*
Evening: *vecher*
Exhibition: *vystavka*
Go to the theater (to a concert): *poyty v teatr (na kontsert)*
Guide: *ekskursovod*
Movies: *kino*
Nightclub: *nochnoy klub*
Museum: *muzey*
Music: *muzyka*
Program: *programma*
Theater: *teatr*
Ticket: *bilet*
Visit: *poseshcheniye* (or *vizit*)

FOOD

"The bill, please": *schet, pojaylusta*
Beef: *goviadina*
Beer: *pivo*
Bread: *khleb*
Breakfast: *zavtrak*
Cheese: *syr*
Cold: *kholodnyï*
Cool: *svejiye*
Dinner: *ujin*
Drink: *oit*
Eat: *yest*
Fish: *ryba*
Fruit juice: *sok*
Ham: *vechina*
Hot: *goriashiye*
Lunch: *Obed*
Menu: *menu*
Mineral water: *mineralnaya voda*
Pork: *svinina*
Potatos: *kartofel*
Rice: *ris*
Salt: *sol*
Sugar: *sakhar*
Veal: *teliatina*
Waiter: *ofitsiant*
Wine: *vino* (white wine: *bieloye vino*, red wine: *krasnoye vino)*

CAFÉS

Café: *kafe*
Cake: *pirog, pirojnoye, tort*
Capuccino: *kapuchino*
Coffee: *kofe* (large black/small black coffee: *bolchoy/malenkiye kofe*, strong coffee: *krepkiye kofe)*
Dessert: *dessert*
Expresso: *espresso*
Green tea: *zelioniye tchay)*
Lemon tea: *tchaye s limonom*
Sweet: *sladkiye*
Tea: *tchaye*
Turkish coffee: *kofe po vostochnomu*
White coffee: *kofe s molokom*
Without sugar: *bez sakhara*

MONEY

Autoteller: *bankomat*
Bureau de change: *obmen valuty*
Buy: *kupit'*
Car rental: *prokat mashin*
Cheap: *dioshevo*
Convertible currencies: *SKV (CKB)*
Credit card: *kreditnaya kartochka*
Expensive: *dorogo*
How much is ...?: *skolko stoyt?*
Make a reservation: *zakazat'*
Money: *dengui*
Rent (to): *sniat*

ACCOMMODATION

Cleaning lady: *gornichnaya*
Day: *dien*
Double bedroom (two beds): *nomer*
Hotel: *gostinitsa*
Rent an apartment (a room): *sniat kvartiru (komnatu)*
Night: *notch*
Single room (one bed): *odnomestniye nomer dvukh-mestniye*
What's the price for one night?: *skolko stoyt odna notch?*
Youth hostel: *obshchejitiye, hostel*

CONVERSATION

Do you speak English?: *vy govorite po anglisky?*
Good-bye: *do svidanya (poka,* fam.)
Good evening: *dobriye vetcher!*
Hello!: *dobryï dien* (Hi!: *privet!*, between friends only)
I don't understand: *ya ne ponimayu*
I'd like ...: *ya khotel by*
Madam/Sir: Madam/Sir (or start the sentence with the phrase "Please")
No: *niet*
Please: *pojaylusta*
Please excuse me: *izvinite*
Thank you: *spassibo*
Yes: *da*

DAYS

Monday: *ponedelnik*
Tuesday: *vtornik*
Wednesday: *sreda*
Thursday: *chetverg*
Friday: *piatnitsa*
Saturday: *subota*
Sunday: *voskresseniye*
Holiday: *vykhodnoy dien*
Week: *nedelia*
Weekend: *vykhodniye (or weekend)*

MONTHS

January: *yanvar*
February: *fevral*
March: *mart*
April: *aprel*
May: *may*
June: *iyun*
July: *iyul*
August: *avgust*
September: *sentiabr*
October: *oktiabr*
November: *noyabr*
December: *dekabr*

COUNTING

1: *odin*
2: *dva*
3: *trY*
4: *chetyry*
5: *piat*
6: *shest*
7: *sem*
8: *vosem*
9: *deviat*
10: *desiat*
20: *dvadtsat*
21: *dvadtsat odin*
30: *tridtsat*
50: *piatdesiat*
100: *sto*
1000: *tysiacha*

◆ BIBLIOGRAPHY

ESSENTIAL READING

◆ Dostoevsky (F.): *Crime and Punishment*, trans. Pevear (R.) and Volokhonsky (L.), Everyman's Library, London and Alfred A. Knopf, New York, 1993

◆ Kelly (L.) ed.: *St Petersburg – a travellers' companion*, Constable, London, 1981

◆ Kroptopkin (Prince Piotr): *Memoirs of a revolutionist*, Dover Publications Inc., New York, 1971

◆ Ometev (B.) and Stuart (J.): *St Petersburg: portrait of an Imperial city*, Cassell, London, 1990

◆ Pipes (R.): *Russia before the revolution*, Weidenfeld & Nicolson, London and Alfred A. Knopf, New York, 1934

◆ Pushkin (A.): *The Captain's Daughter and other stories*, trans. Debreczeny (P.) and Volokhonsky (L.), Everyman's Library, London and Alfred A Knopf, New York, 1994.

◆ Wilmot (M.) and (C.): *The Russian Journals of Martha and Catherine Wilmot*, ed. M. of Londonderry and Hyde (H.M.), Macmillan & Co., London, 1934

GENERAL INTEREST

◆ Clarkson (J.D.): *A History of Russia from the Ninth Century*, Longmans, London, 1961

◆ Fallowel (D.): *One hot summer in St Petersburg*, J. Cape, London, 1994.

◆ Gunter (J.): *Inside Russia Today*, Hamish Hamilton, London, 1958

◆ Hingley (R.F.): *A Concise History of Russia*, Thames & Hudson, London, 1972

◆ Marsden (C.A.): *Palmyra of the North. The first days of St Petersburg*, Faber & Faber, London, 1942

◆ Miller (W.M.): *Russians as People*, Dutton, NY, 1961

◆ Reed (J.): *Ten Days that Shook the World*, Modern Books, London, 1928

◆ Simpson (C.): *This is Russia*, Hodder and Stoughton, London 1965

◆ Wiltshire (S.): *Floating cities: Venice, Amsterdam, Leningrad – and Moscow*, M. Joseph, London, 1991

HISTORICAL ACCOUNTS

◆ Coxe (W.): *Travels into Poland, Russia, Sweden and Denmark, interspersed with historical relations and political inquiries*, S. Price et al., Dublin, 1784

◆ Custine (Marquis A.L.L. de): *Letters from Russia*, trans. and ed. Buss (R.), Penguin Books, Harmondsworth, 1991

◆ Herzen (A.): *My Past and Thoughts*, trans. Garnett (C). and Higgens (H.), Chatto & Windus, London, 1968

◆ Masson (C.F.P.): *Secret Memoirs of the Court of Petersburg*, P. Wogan, Dublin, 1801

◆ Paléologue (M.): *An Ambassador's Memoirs 1914–1917*, trans. F.A. Holt, London 1924–5

◆ Parkinson (J.): *A Tour of Russia, Siberia and the Crimea, 1792–1794*, London, 1971

◆ Van der Post (L.): *Journey into Russia*, Penguin Books, Harmondsworth, 1965

IMPERIAL RUSSIA

◆ Baddeley (J.F.): *Russia in the Eighties*, Longman & Co., London, 1921

◆ Barrow (Sir J.): *The Life of Peter the Great*, William Tegg, L, 1874

◆ Anthony (K.): *Memoirs of Catherine the Great*, Alfred A. Knopf, New York and London, 1927

◆ Grey (I.): *Peter the Great, Emperor of all Russia*, J.B. Lippincott & Co., PA and NY, 1960

◆ Hingley (R.F.): *The Tsars*, Corgi, London, 1973

◆ Massie (R.K.): *Peter the Great, his Life and World*, Phoenix Press, London, 2001

◆ Mazour (A.): *The First Russian Revolution, 1825*, University of California Press, Berkeley, 1937

◆ Mosse (W.E.): *Alexander II and the Modernisation of Russia*, Collier, NY, 1962

◆ Oldenbourg (Z.): *Catherine de Russie*, trans. Carter (A.), Heinemann, London, 1965

◆ Schuyler (E.): *Passages from the life of Peter the Great*, Sampson, Low & Co., London, 1881

◆ Troyat (H.): *Catherine the Great*, Phoenix Press, London, 2000; *Ivan the Terrible*, Phoenix Press, London, 2001

THE REVOLUTION

◆ Carr (E.H.): *The Bolshevik Revolution*, 3 vols., Macmillan, New York, 1951–3

◆ Conquest (R.): *The Great Terror: Stalin's Purges in the Thirties*, Macmillan, London, 1968

◆ Deutscher (J.): *Stalin*, Penguin Books, Harmondsworth, 1966 *The Unfinished Revolution. Russia 1917–1967*, George Macauley Trevelyan Lectures, OUP, Oxford, 1967

◆ Hingley (R.F.): *Russian Revolution*, Bodley Head, London, 1970

◆ Lukacs (J.): *A History of the Cold War*, Doubleday, New York, 1962

◆ McKean (R.B.): *St Petersburg between the revolutions: workers and revolutionaries*, Yale University Press, New Haven (Conn.), 1989

◆ Mandel (D.): *The Petrograd Workers and the Soviet Seizure of Power*, Macmillan, London, 1984

◆ Philby (K.): *My Silent War*, MacGibbon & Kee, London, 1968

◆ Trotsky (L.): *My Life*, Grosset & Dunlap, NY, 1960

◆ Salisbury (H.E.): *The 900 Days: The Siege of Leningrad*, Harper & Row, New York, 1969

◆ Wade (R.A): *Red Guards and workers' militias in the Russian Revolution*, Stanford UP, Stanford, 1984

◆ Wolfe (B.D.): *Three Who made a revolution, Lenin, Trotsky, Stalin*, Dial Press, New York, 1961

SOCIETY

◆ Bach (M.): *God and the Soviets*, Thomas Y. Crowell, New York, 1958

◆ Bater (J.H.): *St Petersburg: Industrialisation and Change*, Edward Arnold, London, 1976

◆ Bourdeaux (M.): *Religious Ferment in Russia. Protestant Opposition to Soviet Religious Policy*, Macmillan, London, 1968

◆ Neuberger (J.): *Hooliganism: crime, culture and power in St Petersburg*, UCP, Berkeley, c. 1993

ART AND ARCHITECTURE

◆ Billington (J.H.): *The Icon and the Axe: an interpretive history of Russian culture*, Alfred A. Knopf, NY, 1967

◆ Cooke (C.): *Architectural Drawings of the Russian Avant-Garde*, Museum of Modern Art, New York, 1990

◆ Descargues (P.): *The Hermitage*, trans. Delavenay (K), Thames & Hudson, London, 1961

◆ Elliott (D.): *New Worlds: Russian Art and Society 1900–1937*, Thames & Hudson, London, 1989 *Photography in Russia 1840–1940*, Thames & Hudson, London, 1992

◆ Kahn-Magomedov (S.O.): *Pioneers of Soviet Architecture, the Search for new Solutions in the 1920's and 1930's*, Thames & Hudson, London, 1987

◆ Opolovnikov (A.) and (Y.), Buxton (D.) *ed.*: *The Wooden Architecture of Russia*, Thames & Hudson, London, 1989

◆ Rice (T.T.): *A Concise History of Russian Art*, Thames & Hudson, London, 1963

◆ Salmina-Haskell (L.): *Panoramic Views of St Petersburg, 1716–1835* Ashmolean Museum, Oxford, 1993

◆ Strizhenova (T.): *Soviet Costume and Textiles 1917–1945*, Thames & Hudson, London, 1991

◆ Tolstoy (V.), Bibikova (I.) and Cooke (C.) eds.: *Street Art of the Revolution*, Thames & Hudson, London, 1990

LITERATURE

◆ Biely (A.): *St Petersburg*, trans. Cournos (J.), Grove Press Inc., New York, 1959

◆ Brodsky (J.): *Less than One: Selected Essays*, Farrar, Strauss & Giroux, NY, 1986

◆ Chekhov (A.): *The Lady with the Dog*, trans. Pevea (R.) and Volkokhonsky (L.), Everyman's Library, Londor and Alfred A. Knopf, New York, 1993

◆ Dostoevsky (F.): *the Best Short Stories of Dostoevsky*, trans. Magarshack (D.), the Modern Library, NY, 1955

◆ Gogol (N.): *The Overcoa and Other Stories*, trans. Garnett (C.), Chatto & Windus, London, 1923 *Tales of Good and Evil*, trans. Duddingion (N.), Everyman's Library, Londor and Alfred A. Knopf, New York, 1992

◆ Goncharov (I.): *Oblomov*, trans. Duddington (N.), Everyman's Library, Londor Alfred A. Knopf, NY, 1992

◆ Ignatieff (M.): *The Russian Album, Chatto & Windus*, London, 1987

◆ Miller (J. and K) eds.: *St Petersburg: Chronicles Abroad*; Chronicle Books, San Francisco, 1995

◆ Nabokov (V.) trans.: *Eugene Onegin: a novel in verse by Alexander Pushkin*, trans. Nabokov (V.), Routledge & Kegan Paul, London, 1964 *Speak Memory – an Autobiography Revisited*, Weidenfeld and Nicolson, London, 1960

◆ Pushkin (A.): *Selected Poems*, trans. Thomas (D.M.), Secker & Warburg, London, 1982 *The Letters of Alexander Pushkin*, trans. Shaw (J.T.), Wisconsin, 1967

◆ Sitwell (S.): *Valse des Fleurs, a Day in St Petersburg and a Ball at the Winter Palace*, Faber and Faber, London

◆ Tolstoy (L.N.): *Anna Karenina*, trans. Maude (L.) and (A.) Everyman's Library, London and Alfred A. Knopf, New York, 1992 *War and Peace*, trans. Maude (L.) and (A.) Everyman's Library, London and Alfred A. Knopf, New York, 1992

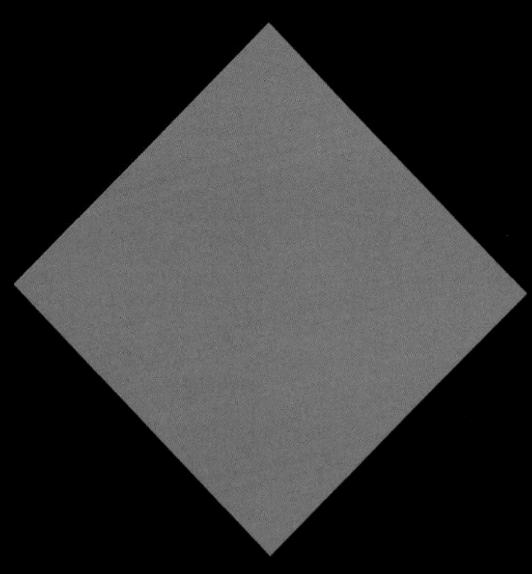

◆ LIST OF ILLUSTRATIONS

◆ LIST OF ILLUSTRATIONS

LIST OF ILLUSTRATIONS

In some cases, we have been unable to trace the owners and publishers of some of the photographs and illustrations used. We will be happy to acknowledge them if they make themselves known to us.

Acknowledgements

Grateful acknowledgment is made to the following for permission to reprint previously published material:

◆ Associated University Presses: Excerpt from "Tristia" #88 page 77, from Poems of Mandelstam by Osip Mandelstam, translated by R.H. Morrison © 1990 by The Associated University Presses. Reprinted by permission

◆ Farrar, Straus & Giroux, Inc.: Excerpt from "Less Than One" from Less Than One by Joseph Brodsky, © 1986 by Joseph Brodsky; excerpt from Turgenev's Literary Reminiscences, translated by David Magarshack, © 1958 by Farrar, Straus & Cudahy, Inc., copyright renewed 1986 by Elsie D. Magarshack. Reprinted by permission of Farrar, Straus & Giroux, Inc.

◆ Grove/Atlantic, Inc.: Excerpt from St. Petersburg by Andrei Biely, translated by John Cournos, © 1959 by Grove Press, Inc. Reprinted by permission of Grove/Atlantic, Inc.

◆ John Johnson (Authors' Agent) Limited: Excerpt from "The Bronze Horseman" from Selected Poems by Alexander Pushkin, translated by D.M. Thomas, translation © 1982 by D.M. Thomas (London: Secker & Warburg Ltd). Reprinted by permission of John Johnson (Authors' Agent) Limited.

◆ New Directions Publishing Corp.: Excerpt fom Futility by William Gerhardie, © 1971 by The Estate of William Gerhardie. Reprinted by permission of New Directions Publishing Corp.

◆ Princeton University Press: Excerpt from "Travels in Russia" by William Coxe from Seven Britons in Imperial Russia 1698–1812, edited by Peter Putnam, © 1952 by Princeton U. Press, copyright renewed 1980 by Princeton U. Press. Reprinted by permission of Princeton U. Press.

◆ Random House, Inc.: Excerpt from "White Nights" from The Best Short Stories of Fyodor Dostoyevsky by Fyodor Dostoyevsky, translated by David Margarshack, translation © 1955 by Random House, Inc. Reprinted by permission of Random House, Inc.

◆ Viking Penguin: Letter to M.P. Chekhova, Petersburg, Jan. 14, 1891, from The Letters of Anton Chekhov by Anton Chekhov, translated by Avrahm Yarmolinsky, translation copyright © 1947, 1968 by The Viking Press, Inc., © 1973 by Avrahm Yarmolinsky. Reprinted by permission of Viking Penguin, a division of Penguin books USA Inc.

◆ Vintage Books: Excerpt from Speak Memory by Vladimir Nabokov, © 1989 by The Estate of Vladimir Nabokov. Reprinted by permission of Vintage Books, a division of Random House, Inc.

◆ A.P. Watt Ltd and Chatto & Windus: Excerpt from "The Nevsky Prospect" from The Overcoat and Other Stories by Nikolai Gogol, translated by Constance Garnett, © 1923 by Mrs Edward Garnett. Reprinted by permission of A.P. Watt Ltd and Chatto & Windus on behalf of The Executors of The Estate of Constance Garnett.

◆ INDEX

T

U/V

W/Y/Z

◆ NOTES

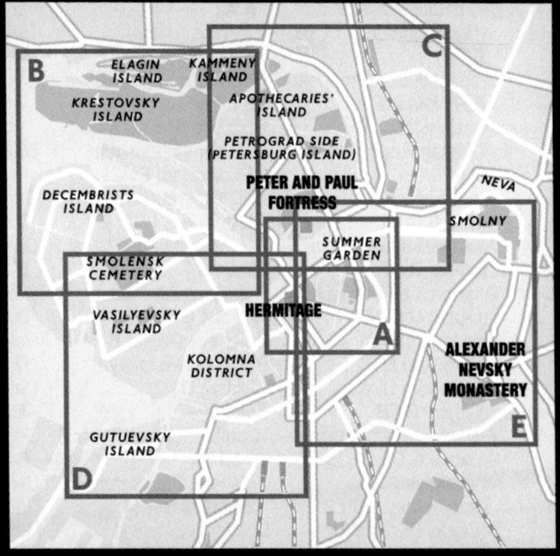
B
ELAGIN ISLAND
KAMMENY ISLAND
C
KRESTOVSKY ISLAND
APOTHECARIES' ISLAND
PETROGRAD SIDE (PETERSBURG ISLAND)
PETER AND PAUL FORTRESS
NEVA
DECEMBRISTS ISLAND
SMOLNY
SUMMER GARDEN
SMOLENSK CEMETERY
HERMITAGE
VASILYEVSKY ISLAND
A
ALEXANDER NEVSKY MONASTERY
KOLOMNA DISTRICT
E
GUTUEVSKY ISLAND
D

Map section

CENTER

A

A B C

ULITSA IABLOTCHKOVA
MYTNINSKY PER.
KRONVERKSKAYA NABEREJNAYA
KRONVERKSKY STRAIT
PETER AND PAUL CATHEDRAL
PR. DOBROLUBOVA
PETROGRAD SIDE (PETERSBURG ISLAND)
PETER AND PAUL FORTRESS
BIRJEVOY MOST
NEVA
ROSTRAL COLUMNS
Birzevaya Ploshchad
DVORTSOVAYA NABEREJNAYA
MOCHKOV PER.
HERMITAGE THEATER
LARGE HERMITAGE
MILLIONNAYA
BIRJEVOY PROIEZD
ACADEMY OF SCIENCES
UNIVERSITETSKAYA NAB.
DVORTSOVY MOST
SMALL HERMITAGE
WINTER PALACE
ALEXANDER COLUMN
MOIKA
NABEREJNAYA ADMIRALTEISKAYA
Dvortsovata Ploshchad
ADMIRALTY
NABEREJNAYA REKY MOIKY
BOL. KONIUCHENNAYA
MONUMENT TO PETER I
ALEXANDER GARDEN
ADMIRALTEISKY PROSPEKT
NEVSKY PROSPEKT
Ploshchad Dekabristov
KIRPITCHNY PER.
MALAYA MORSKAYA ULITSA
ST ISAAC'S CATHEDRAL
STROGANOV PALACE
GOROKHOVAYA ULITSA
ASTORIA & ANGLETERRE HOTELS
MORSKAYA
POCHTAMTSKAYA ULITSA
Isaakievskaya Ploshchad
RAZUMOVSKY PALACE
NABEREJNAYA REKI MOIKY
FONARNY
BOLCHAYA
MONUMENT TO NICHOLAS I
PEREULOK ANTONENKO
PEREULOK GRIVTSOVA
NABEREJNAYA KANALA
KAZANSKAYA ULITSA
NABEREJNAYA REKY MOYKY
PEREULOK
VOZNESENSKY PR.
MARIINSKY PALACE
GRIBOYEDOV CANAL
MOSKATELNY PER.
MUTCHNOY PER.
PIROGOVA
PEREULOK
PRATCHETCHNY PEREULOK
KAZANSKY ISLAND
UL. DEKABRISTOV
SPASSKY PER.
GRAJDANSKAYA UL.
0 330 100 660 ft 200 m

1 2 3 4 5 6

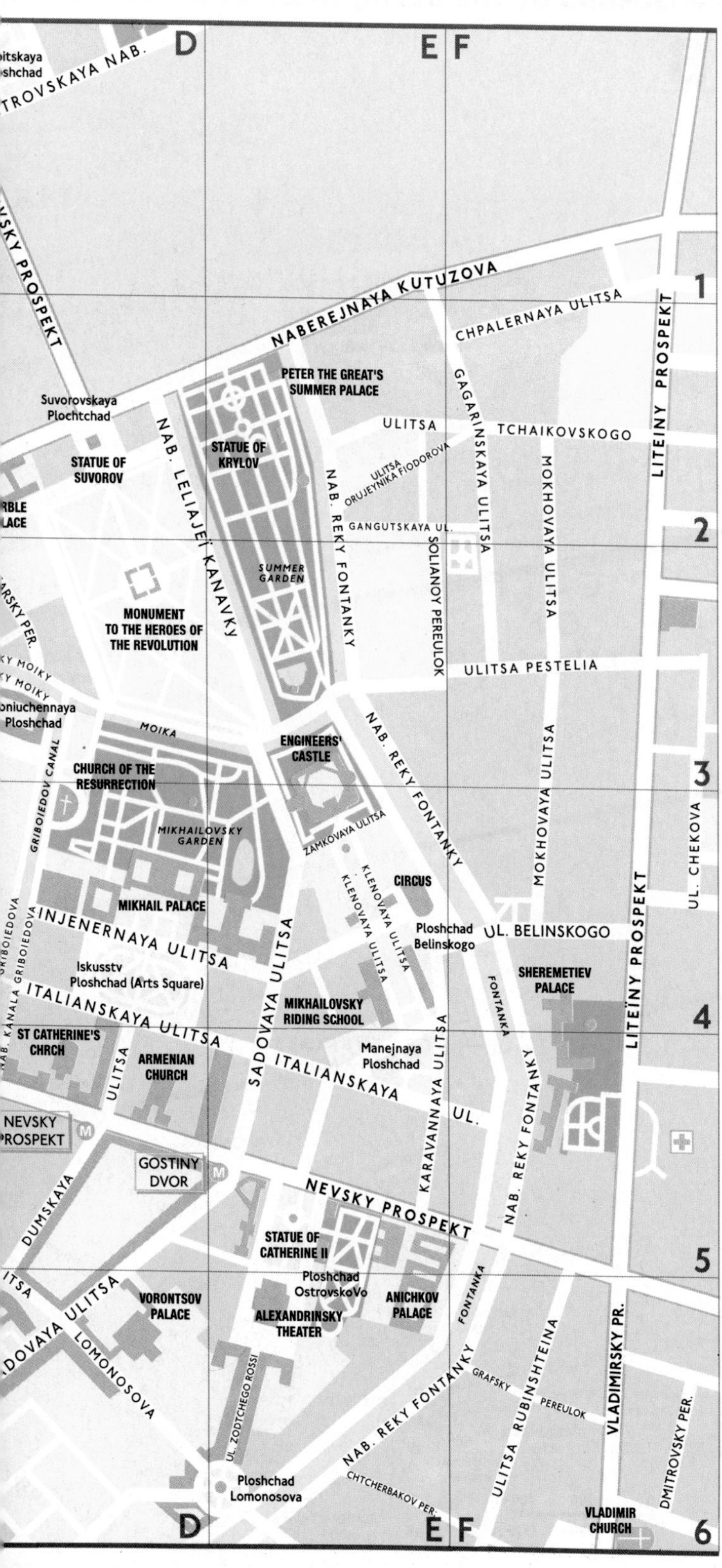

D
E
F
1
2
3
4
5
6
NABEREJNAYA KUTUZOVA
CHPALERNAYA ULITSA
LITEINY PROSPEKT
PETER THE GREAT'S SUMMER PALACE
Suvorovskaya Plochtchad
STATUE OF SUVOROV
NAB. LELIAJEÏ KANAVKY
STATUE OF KRYLOV
ULITSA
TCHAIKOVSKOGO
ULITSA ORUJEYNIKA FIODOROVA
NAB. REKY FONTANKY
GAGARINSKAYA ULITSA
MOKHOVAYA ULITSA
GANGUTSKAYA UL.
SOLIANOY PEREULOK
SUMMER GARDEN
MONUMENT TO THE HEROES OF THE REVOLUTION
ULITSA PESTELIA
MOIKA
Ploshchad
ENGINEERS' CASTLE
CHURCH OF THE RESURRECTION
GRIBOIEDOV CANAL
MIKHAILOVSKY GARDEN
ZAMKOVAYA ULITSA
CIRCUS
KLENOVAYA ULITSA
UL. CHEKOVA
MIKHAIL PALACE
INJENERNAYA ULITSA
Ploshchad Belinskogo
UL. BELINSKOGO
Iskusstv Ploshchad (Arts Square)
SHEREMETIEV PALACE
ITALIANSKAYA ULITSA
SADOVAYA ULITSA
MIKHAILOVSKY RIDING SCHOOL
FONTANKA
ST CATHERINE'S CHRCH
ARMENIAN CHURCH
Manejnaya Ploshchad
ITALIANSKAYA
UL.
KARAVANNAYA ULITSA
NEVSKY PROSPEKT
GOSTINY DVOR
DUMSKAYA
NEVSKY PROSPEKT
STATUE OF CATHERINE II
Ploshchad OstrovskoVo
VORONTSOV PALACE
ALEXANDRINSKY THEATER
ANICHKOV PALACE
SADOVAYA ULITSA
LOMONOSOVA
UL. ZODTCHEGO ROSSI
NAB. REKY FONTANKY
GRAFSKY PEREULOK
ULITSA RUBINSHTEINA
VLADIMIRSKY PR.
DMITROVSKY PER.
Ploshchad Lomonosova
CHTCHERBAKOV PER.
VLADIMIR CHURCH

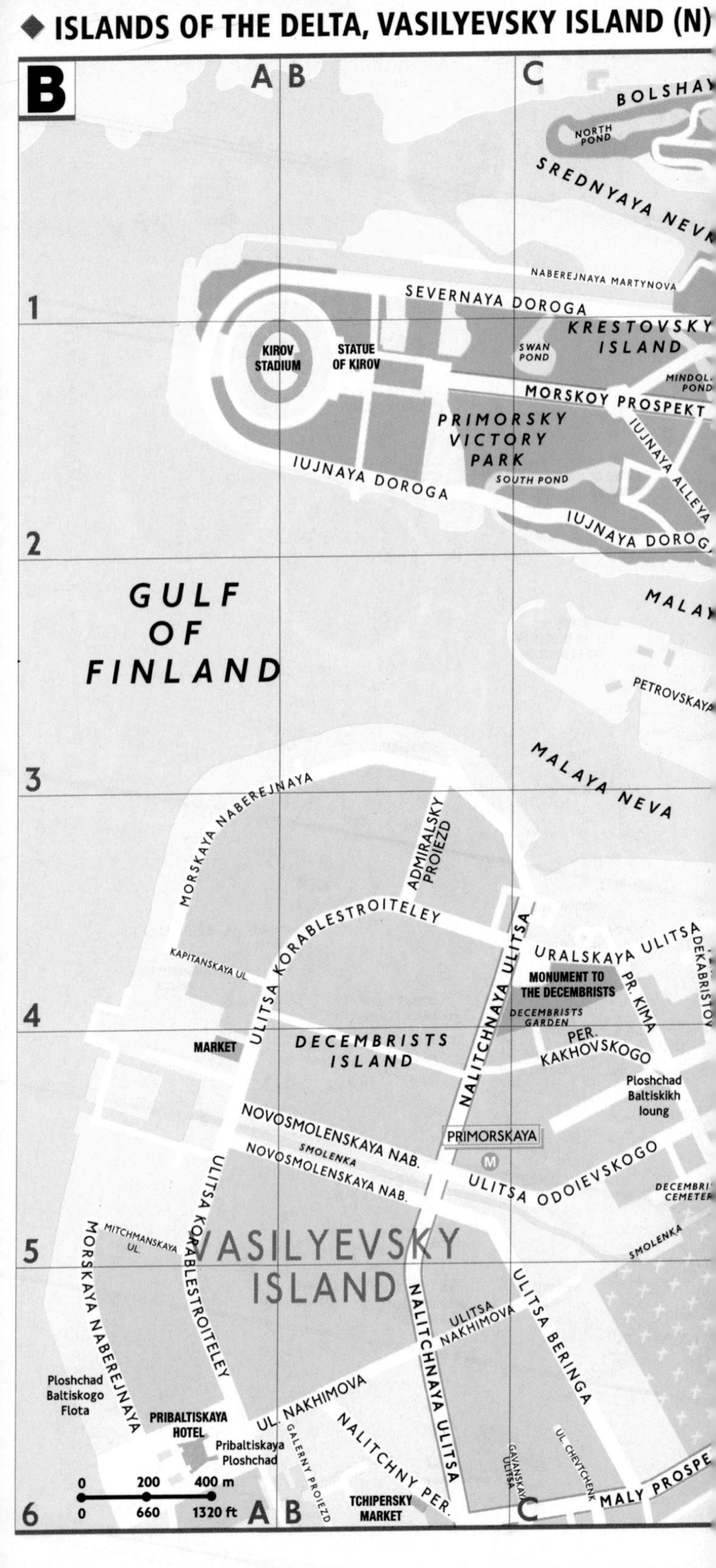
B
A B
C
1
2
3
4
5
6
BOLSHAY
NORTH POND
SREDNYAYA NEV
NABEREJNAYA MARTYNOVA
SEVERNAYA DOROGA
KRESTOVSKY ISLAND
KIROV STADIUM
STATUE OF KIROV
SWAN POND
MINDOL. POND
MORSKOY PROSPEKT
PRIMORSKY VICTORY PARK
IUJNAYA ALLEYA
SOUTH POND
IUJNAYA DOROGA
IUJNAYA DOROG
GULF OF FINLAND
MALAY
PETROVSKAYA
MALAYA NEVA
MORSKAYA NABEREJNAYA
ADMIRALSKY PROIEZD
ULITSA KORABLESTROITELEY
KAPITANSKAYA UL.
NALITCHNAYA ULITSA
URALSKAYA ULITSA
DEKABRISTOV
MONUMENT TO THE DECEMBRISTS
PR. KIMA
DECEMBRISTS GARDEN
MARKET
DECEMBRISTS ISLAND
PER. KAKHOVSKOGO
Ploshchad Baltiskikh Ioung
NOVOSMOLENSKAYA NAB.
PRIMORSKAYA
SMOLENKA
NOVOSMOLENSKAYA NAB.
ULITSA ODOIEVSKOGO
DECEMBRI CEMETER
MITCHMANSKAYA UL.
VASILYEVSKY ISLAND
SMOLENKA
ULITSA NAKHIMOVA
ULITSA BERINGA
Ploshchad Baltiskogo Flota
PRIBALTISKAYA HOTEL
UL. NAKHIMOVA
GALERNY PROIEZD
NALITCHNY PER.
GAVANSKAYA ULITSA
UL. CHEVTCHENK
Pribaltiskaya Ploshchad
0 200 400 m
0 660 1320 ft
TCHIPERSKY MARKET
MALY PROSPE

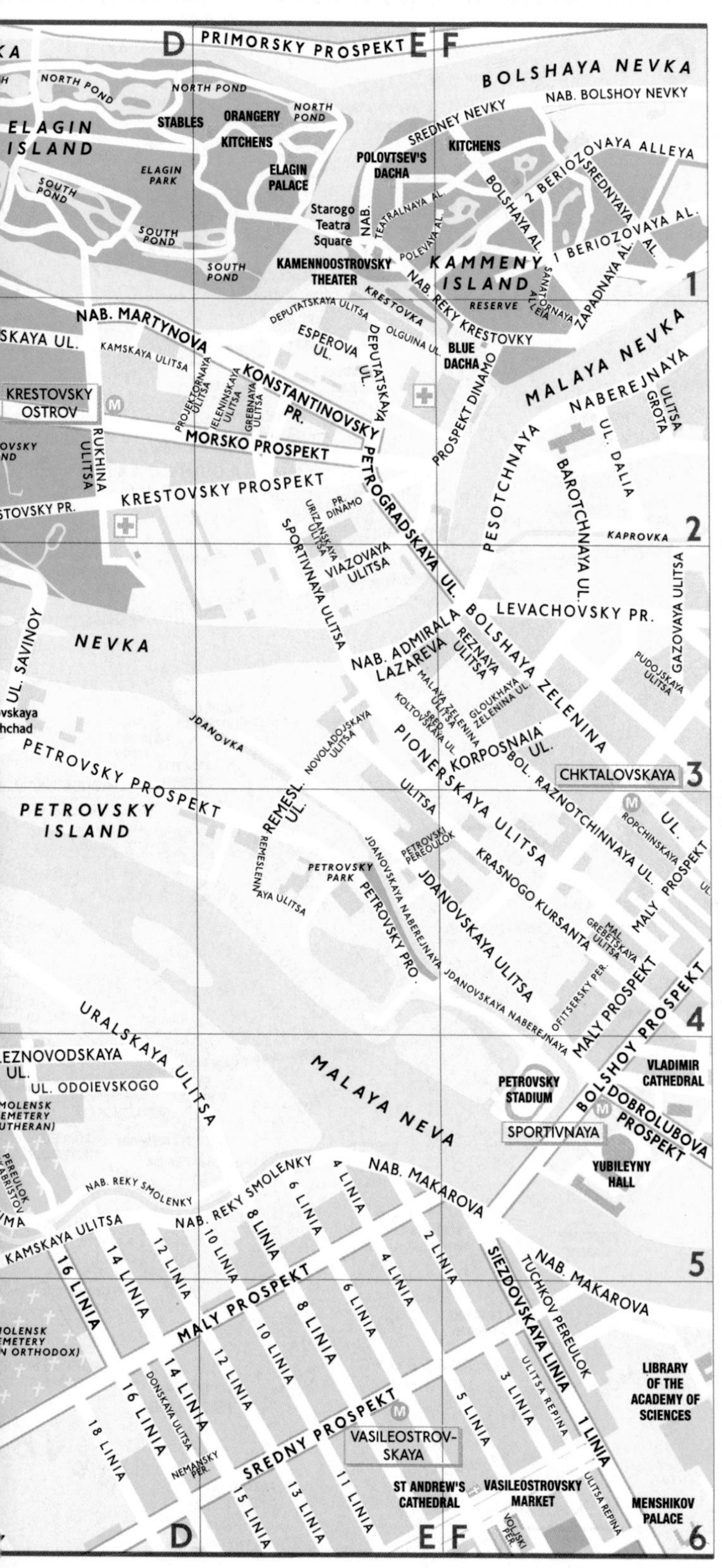

PRIMORSKY PROSPEKT
BOLSHAYA NEVKA
NAB. BOLSHOY NEVKY
NORTH POND
ELAGIN ISLAND
STABLES
ORANGERY
KITCHENS
ELAGIN PARK
ELAGIN PALACE
SOUTH POND
SREDNEY NEVKY
POLOVTSEV'S DACHA
Starogo Teatra Square
KAMENNOOSTROVSKY THEATER
BERIOZOVAYA ALLEYA
KAMMENY ISLAND
RESERVE
NAB. REKY KRESTOVKY
NAB. MARTYNOVA
KAMSKAYA ULITSA
KRESTOVSKY OSTROV
KONSTANTINOVSKY PR.
MORSKO PROSPEKT
KRESTOVSKY PROSPEKT
RUKHINA ULITSA
ESPEROVA UL.
DEPUTATSKAYA UL.
BLUE DACHA
PROSPEKT DINAMO
MALAYA NEVKA
NABEREJNAYA
ULITSA GROTA
UL. DALIA
PESOTCHNAYA
BAROTCHNAYA UL.
KAPROVKA
PETROGRADSKAYA UL.
SPORTIVNAYA ULITSA
VIAZOVAYA ULITSA
LEVACHOVSKY PR.
GAZOVAYA ULITSA
NEVKA
UL. SAVINOY
NAB. ADMIRALA LAZAREVA
BOLSHAYA ZELENINA
KORPOSNAIA UL.
CHKTALOVSKAYA
PETROVSKY PROSPEKT
PETROVSKY ISLAND
JDANOVKA
PIONERSKAYA ULITSA
BOL. RAZNOTCHINNAYA UL.
KRASNOGO KURSANTA
PETROVSKY PARK
JDANOVSKAYA ULITSA
JDANOVSKAYA NABEREJNAYA
MALY PROSPEKT
BOLSHOY PROSPEKT
URALSKAYA ULITSA
MALAYA NEVA
PETROVSKY STADIUM
VLADIMIR CATHEDRAL
DOBROLUBOVA PROSPEKT
SPORTIVNAYA
YUBILEYNY HALL
NAB. REKY SMOLENKY
NAB. MAKAROVA
KAMSKAYA ULITSA
SIEZDOVSKAYA LINIA
TUCHKOV PEREULOK
MALY PROSPEKT
SREDNY PROSPEKT
VASILEOSTROVSKAYA
LIBRARY OF THE ACADEMY OF SCIENCES
ST ANDREW'S CATHEDRAL
VASILEOSTROVSKY MARKET
MENSHIKOV PALACE
D
E
F
1
2
3
4
5
6

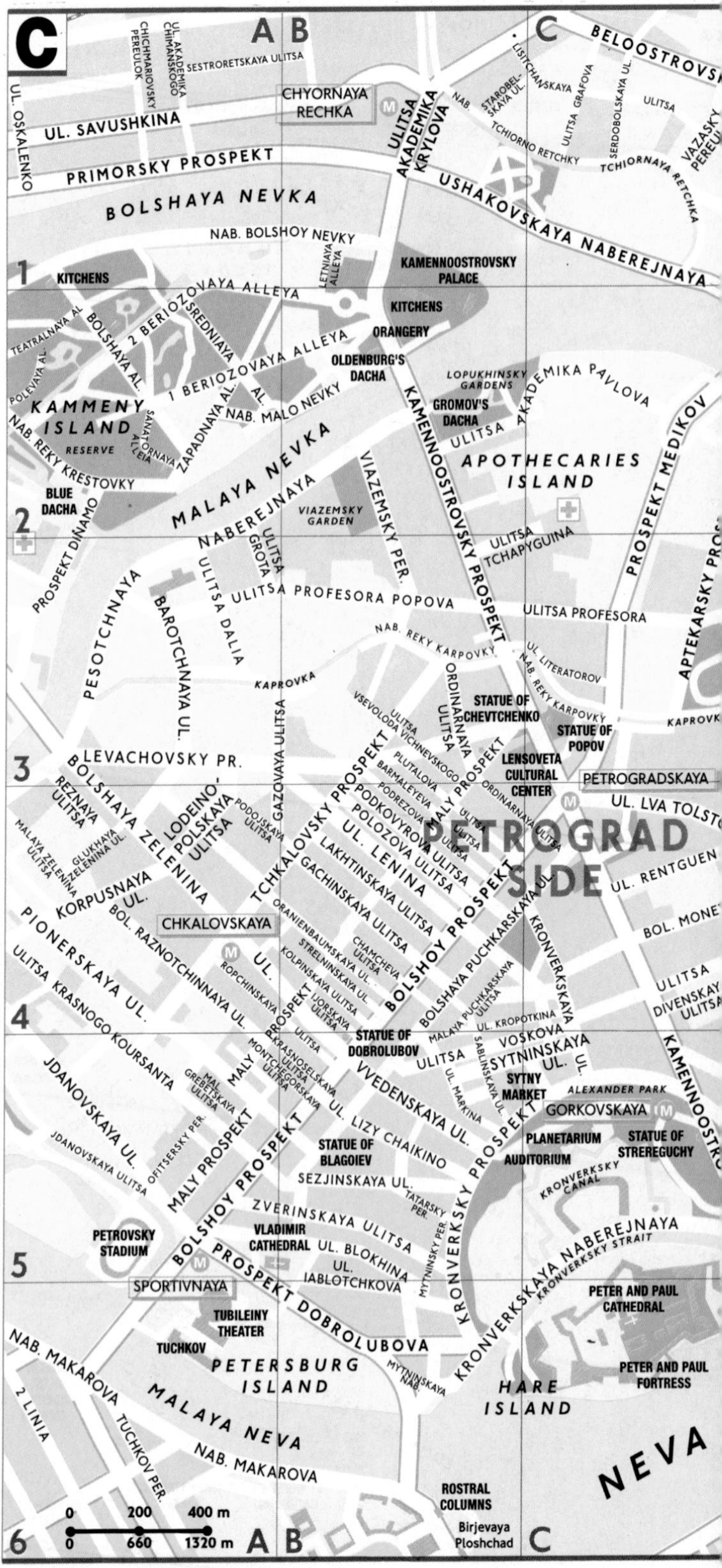

C

A B C

CHICHMARIOVSKY PEREULOK
UL. AKADEMIKA CHIMANSKOGO
SESTRORETSKAYA ULITSA
CHYORNAYA RECHKA
UL. OSKALENKO
UL. SAVUSHKINA
PRIMORSKY PROSPEKT
BOLSHAYA NEVKA
NAB. BOLSHOY NEVKY
ULITSA AKADEMIKA KRYLOVA
NAB.
LISITCHANSKAYA
STAROBELSKAYA UL.
ULITSA GRAFOVA
SERDOBOLSKAYA UL.
ULITSA
BELOOSTROVSK
VAZASKY PEREUL
TCHIORNO RETCHKY
TCHIORNAYA RETCHKA
USHAKOVSKAYA NABEREJNAYA
1
KITCHENS
LETNIAIYA ALLEYA
KAMENNOOSTROVSKY PALACE
KITCHENS
ORANGERY
2 BERIOZOVAYA ALLEYA
TEATRALNAYA AL.
BOLSHAYA AL.
SREDNIAIYA
POLEVAYA AL.
1 BERIOZOVAYA ALLEYA
OLDENBURG'S DACHA
LOPUKHINSKY GARDENS
AKADEMIKA PAVLOVA
KAMMENY ISLAND
RESERVE
SANATORNAYA ALLEIA
ZAPADNAYA AL.
AL.
NAB. MALO NEVKY
GROMOV'S DACHA
ULITSA
NAB. REKY KRESTOVKY
MALAYA NEVKA
KAMENNOOSTROVSKY PROSPEKT
APOTHECARIES ISLAND
PROSPEKT MEDIKOV
BLUE DACHA
2
PROSPEKT DINAMO
NABEREJNAYA
VIAZEMSKY GARDEN
VIAZEMSKY PER.
ULITSA GROTA
ULITSA TCHAPYGUINA
APTEKARSKY PROS
PESOTCHNAYA
BAROTCHNAYA UL.
ULITSA DALIA
ULITSA PROFESORA POPOVA
ULITSA PROFESORA
NAB. REKY KARPOVKY
UL. LITERATOROV
NAB. REKY KARPOVKY
KAPROVKA
KAPROVK
ORDINARNAYA ULITSA
STATUE OF CHEVTCHENKO
STATUE OF POPOV
GAZOVAYA ULITSA
ULITSA VSEVOLODA VICHNEVSKOGO
3
LEVACHOVSKY PR.
BOLSHAYA ZELENINA
TCHKALOVSKY PROSPEKT
PLUTALOVA
BARMALEYEVA
MALY PROSPEKT
ORDINARNAYA ULITSA
LENSOVETA CULTURAL CENTER
PETROGRADSKAYA
UL. LVA TOLSTO
REZNAYA ULITSA
LODEINO-POLSKAYA ULITSA
PODOJSKAYA ULITSA
PODREZOVA
PODKOVYROVA ULITSA
ULITSA
PETROGRAD SIDE
POLOZOVA ULITSA
UL. LENINA
UL. RENTGUEN
MALAYA ZELENINA ULITSA
GLUKHAYA ZELENINA UL.
LAKHTINSKAYA ULITSA
GACHINSKAYA ULITSA
BOLSHOY PROSPEKT
BOLSHAYA PUCHKARSKAYA UL.
KRONVERKSKAYA
KORPUSNAYA UL.
BOL. RAZNOTCHINNAYA UL.
CHKALOVSKAYA
ORANIENBAUMSKAYA UL.
STRELNINSKAYA UL.
CHAMCHEVA ULITSA
BOL. MONE
PIONERSKAYA UL.
ROPCHINSKAYA
UL.
KOLPINSKAYA ULITSA
IJORSKAYA ULITSA
BOLSHAYA PUCHKARSKAYA ULITSA
MALAYA PUCHKARSKAYA ULITSA
ULITSA DIVENSKAY ULITSA
4
ULITSA KRASNOGO KOURSANTA
PROSPEKT
ULITSA
STATUE OF DOBROLUBOV
UL. KROPOTKINA
VOSKOVA
ULITSA
SYTNINSKAYA UL.
UL.
KAMENNOOSTRO
KRASNOSELSKAYA ULITSA
MONTCHEGORSKAYA ULITSA
MALY
VVEDENSKAYA UL.
UL. MARKINA
SABLINSKAYA UL.
SYTNY MARKET
ALEXANDER PARK
JDANOVSKAYA UL.
MAL. GREBETSKAYA ULITSA
UL. LIZY CHAIKINO
GORKOVSKAYA
PLANETARIUM
STATUE OF STREREGUCHY
JDANOVSKAYA ULITSA
OFITSERSKY PER.
MALY PROSPEKT
STATUE OF BLAGOIEV
AUDITORIUM
KRONVERKSKY PROSPEKT
KRONVERKSKY CANAL
SEZJINSKAYA UL.
TATARSKY PER.
BOLSHOY PROSPEKT
ZVERINSKAYA ULITSA
PETROVSKY STADIUM
VLADIMIR CATHEDRAL
UL. BLOKHINA
MYTNINSKY PER.
KRONVERKSKAYA NABEREJNAYA
KRONVERKSKY STRAIT
5
UL. IABLOTCHKOVA
SPORTIVNAYA
PROSPEKT DOBROLUBOVA
PETER AND PAUL CATHEDRAL
TUBILEINY THEATER
TUCHKOV
PETERSBURG ISLAND
MYTNINSKAYA NAB.
PETER AND PAUL FORTRESS
NAB. MAKAROVA
HARE ISLAND
MALAYA NEVA
2 LINIA
TUCHKOV PER.
NAB. MAKAROVA
NEVA
ROSTRAL COLUMNS
0 200 400 m
0 660 1320 m
Birjevaya Ploshchad
6
A B C

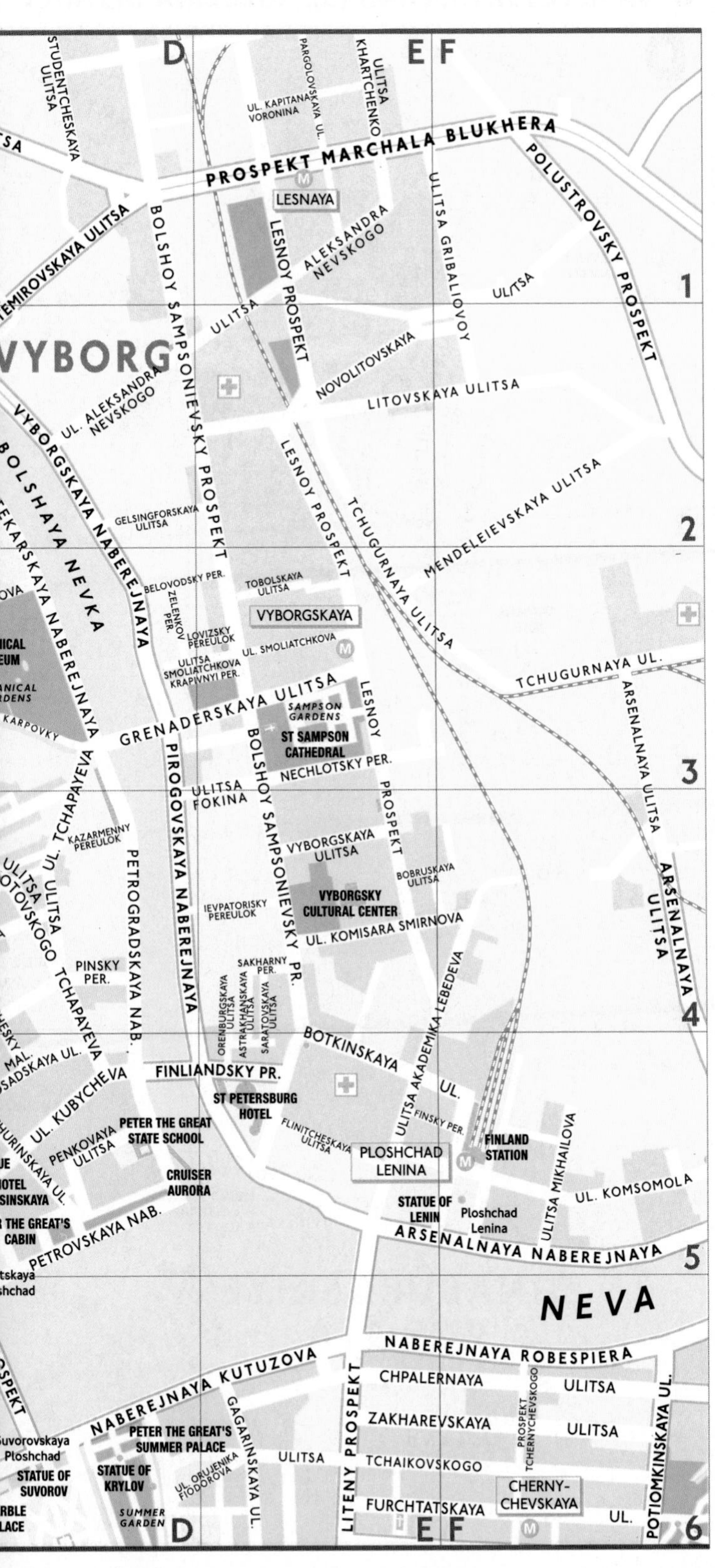

D
E F
1
2
3
4
5
6
VYBORG
PROSPEKT MARCHALA BLUKHERA
LESNAYA
POLUSTROVSKY PROSPEKT
BOLSHOY SAMPSONIEVSKY PROSPEKT
LESNOY PROSPEKT
ULITSA GRIBALIOVOY
LITOVSKAYA ULITSA
NOVOLITOVSKAYA
MENDELEIEVSKAYA ULITSA
TCHUGURNAYA ULITSA
TCHUGURNAYA UL.
ARSENALNAYA ULITSA
VYBORGSKAYA
VYBORGSKAYA NABEREJNAYA
BOLSHAYA NEVKA
GRENADERSKAYA ULITSA
ST SAMPSON CATHEDRAL
SAMPSON GARDENS
NECHLOTSKY PER.
ULITSA FOKINA
VYBORGSKAYA ULITSA
VYBORGSKY CULTURAL CENTER
UL. KOMISARA SMIRNOVA
PIROGOVSKAYA NABEREJNAYA
PETROGRADSKAYA NAB.
BOTKINSKAYA UL.
FINLIANDSKY PR.
ST PETERSBURG HOTEL
PETER THE GREAT STATE SCHOOL
CRUISER AURORA
PLOSHCHAD LENINA
FINLAND STATION
STATUE OF LENIN
Ploshchad Lenina
ULITSA MIKHAILOVA
UL. KOMSOMOLA
ARSENALNAYA NABEREJNAYA
NEVA
NABEREJNAYA ROBESPIERA
NABEREJNAYA KUTUZOVA
LITENY PROSPEKT
CHPALERNAYA ULITSA
ZAKHAREVSKAYA ULITSA
TCHAIKOVSKOGO
FURCHTATSKAYA UL.
CHERNYCHEVSKAYA
POTIOMKINSKAYA UL.
PETER THE GREAT'S SUMMER PALACE
STATUE OF KRYLOV
SUMMER GARDEN
GAGARINSKAYA UL.
STATUE OF SUVOROV
Suvorovskaya Ploshchad
PETROVSKAYA NAB.
UL. KUBYCHEVA
PENKOVAYA ULITSA
UL. TCHAPAYEVA
KAZARMENNY PEREULOK
PINSKY PER.

D
A B C
1 2 3 4 5 6
ULITSA NAKHIMOVA
UL. NAKHIMOVA
NALITCHNAYA UL.
NALITCHNY PER.
GALERNY PROJEZD
CHKIPERSKY MARKET
SMOLENSK CEMETERY (RUSSIAN ORTHODOX)
ULITSA BERINGA
ULITSA CHEVTCHENKO
GAVANSKAYA ULITSA
MALY PROSPEKT
OSTUMOVA ULITSA
24 LINIA
18 LINIA
16 LINIA
14 LI
DONSKAYA ULITSA
NEMA
19 LINIA
20 LINIA
22 LINIA
SREDNY PROSPEKT
ULITSA BERINGA
ULITSA CHEVTCHENKO
KARTACHIKHINA ULITSA
CHKIPERSKY PROTO
GAVANSKAYA ULITSA
OPOTCHININA ULITSA
NALITCHNAYA ULITSA
VIOSSELNAYA ULITSA
28 & 29 LINIA
KIROV ARTS CENTER
KLUBNY PEREULOK
26 LINIA
24 LINIA
VASILEOSTROVETS GARDENS
BOL
23 LINIA
25 LINIA
DETSKAYA ULITSA
KANAREYETCHNAYA ULITSA
SREDNEGAVANSKY PR.
BOLSHOY PROSPEKT
MORSKAYA HOTEL
Ploshchad Morskoy Slavy
KOSAYA LINIA
27 LINIA
KAN
MASLIANY
KOJEVENNAYA LINIA
BOLSHAYA NEVA
GALL ISLAN
RIJSKY PRO
GAPSALSKAYA ULITSA
ULITSA STEPANA RAZINA
MEJEVOY KANAL
SEAMEN'S CULTURAL INSTITUTE
DVINSKAYA ULITSA
CHOTLANDSKAYA ULITSA
DINABURGSKIYE VOROTA
DVINSKAYA ULITSA
NAB. REKY IEKATERINGOFKY
IEKATERINGOFKA
LIFLIANDSKAYA ULITSA
NEVELSKAYA UL
GUTUEVSKY ISLAND
MALY REZVY ISLAND
IEKATERINGOF PARK
NAB. REKY IEKATERINGOFKY
BUMAJNY CANAL

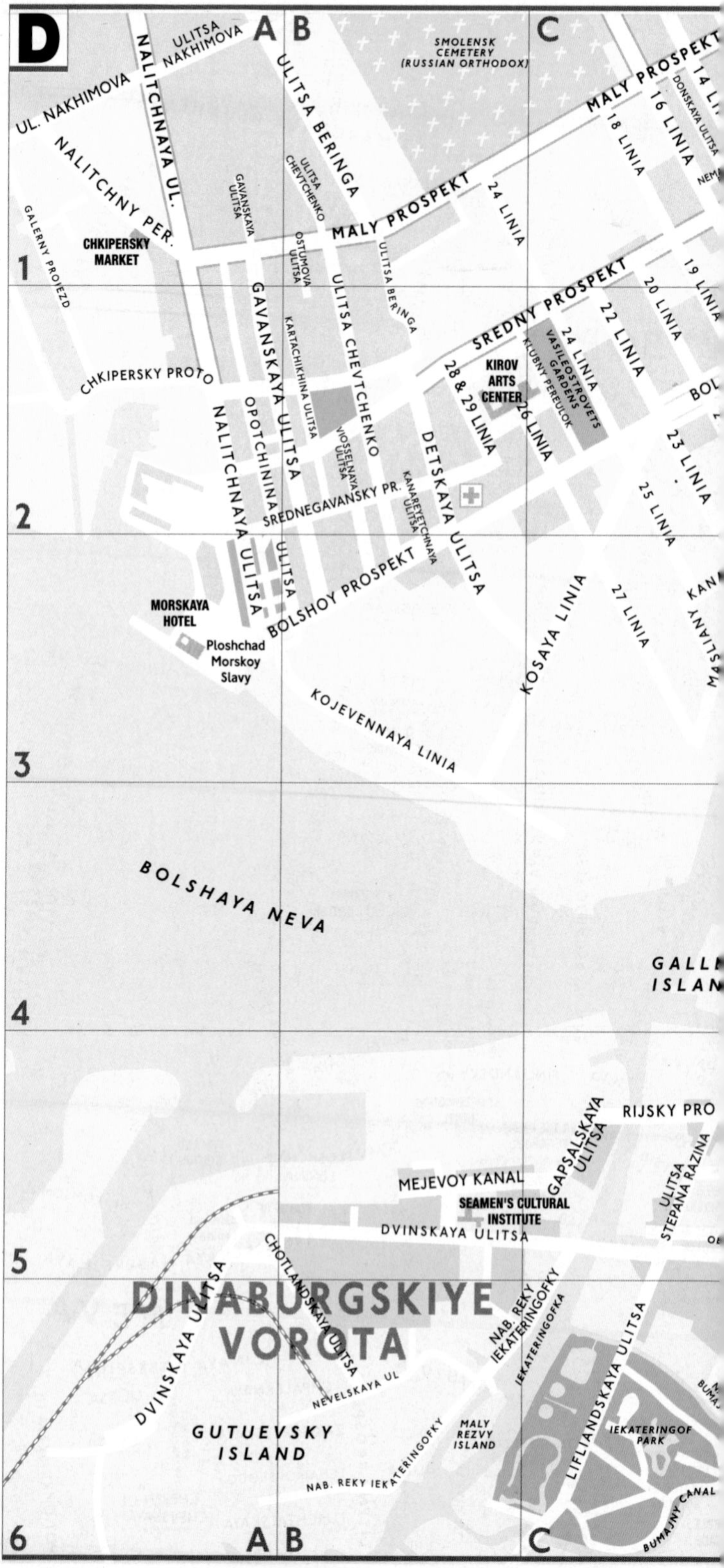

D
E
F
ROSTRAL COLUMNS
Birjevaya Ploshchad
LIBRARY OF THE ACADEMY OF SCIENCES
PEREULOK TUTCHKOV
SEZDOVSKAYA LINIA
ULITSA REPINA
3 LINIA
4 LINIA
6 LINIA
8 LINIA
5 LINIA
DNY PROSPEKT
VASILEOSTROVSKAYA
11 LINIA
LINIA
ST ANDREW'S CATHEDRAL
VASILEOSTROVSKY MARKET
1 LINIA
MENDELEIEVSKAYA LINIA
BIRJEVOY
PROIEZD
FILOLOGUITCHESKY PEREULOK
ACADEMY OF SCIENCES
SMALL HERMITAGE
WINTER PALACE
Dvortsovaya Ploshchad
ST ANDREW'S MARKET
VOLJSKY PER.
ULITSA REPINA
MENSHIKOV PALACE
UNIVERSITETSKAYA NAB.
Ploshchad Chevtchenko
9 LINIA
DNEPROVSKY PER.
7 LINIA
NAB. ADMIRALTEISKAYA
ADMIRALTY
1
OSPEKT
13 LINIA
11 LINIA
SEZDOVSKY PER.
AKADEMITCHESKY PEREULOK
ACADEMY OF ARTS
ALEKSANDROVSKY GARDENS
STATUE OF PETER THE GREAT
ADMIRALTEISKI PR.
15 LINIA
INOSTRANNY PER.
ADMIRALTY ISLAND
MALAYA MORSKAYA ULITSA
ENANTA SHMIDTA
STATUE OF KRUSENSTERN
ZAMIATIN PER.
KONOGVARDESKY BULVAR
IAKUBOVITCHA
ST ISAAC'S CATHEDRAL
ASTORIA & ANGLETERRE HOTELS
BOLSHAYA NEVA
ANGLISKAYA NAB.
NIKOLAEVSKY PALACE
Pl. Trouda
CENTRAL POST OFFICE
POTCHTAMTSKAYA UL.
NAB. REKY MOIKY
ULITSA
GALERNAYA ULITSA
BOLSHAYA MORSKAYA ULITSA
STATUE OF NICHOLAS I
PER. GRIVTSOVA
2
NEW ADMIRALTY ISLAND
BOBRINSKY PALACE
NEW HOLLAND
NAB. KRIUKOVA KANALA
ULITSA TRUDA
MARIINSKY PALACE
PER. ANTONENKO
PRATCHETCHNYI PER.
FONARNY PER.
PIROGOVA
PER.
NAB. REKY MOIKY
YUSUPOV PALACE
PALACE OF THE GRAND DUKE ALEXEI ALEXANDROVICH
NAB. REKY MOIKY
KOLOMENSKY ISLAND
UL. GLINKI
UL. DEKABRISTOV
KAZANSKY ISLAND
MOIKA
ANGLISKY
ULITSA PISSAREVA
PER. MATVEYEVA
THE CONSERVATOIRE
PODIATCH. UL.
SREDNAYA PODIATCH. UL.
NAB. KANALA GRIBOYEDOVA
KOLOMNA
ATISOV ISLAND
NAB. REKY
DEKABRISTOV
MARIINSKY THEATER
MINSKY PER.
Teatralnaya Ploshchad
UL. ALEKSANDRA BLOKA
PRIAJKY
MATISSOV PER.
ULITSA
CENTRAL SYNAGOGUE
PECHATNIKOV
PEREVOZNAYA ULITSA
ST NICHOLAS' CATHEDRAL
BOLSHAYA PODATCHESKAYA UL.
VOZNESSENSKY PR.
SADOVAYA ULITSA
3
YUSUPOV GARDENS
UL. SUZA
PROSPEKT
LERMONTOVSKY PROSPEKT
NAB. KRIUKOVA KANALA
NAB. REKY
DROVIANOY PER.
ULITSA VOLODY YERMAKA
PER. BOTSOVA
NIKOLSKY PER.
GRIBOEDOV CANAL
PR. RIMSKOGO-KORSAKOVA
VITEBSKAYA UL.
NAB. KANALA GRIBOIEDOVA
PSKOVSKAYA UL.
KANONERSKAYA UL.
MAKARENKO PER.
NAB. REKY FONTANKY
ISMAILOVSKY GARDENS
LOTSMANSKAYA ULITSA
POKROVSKY ISLAND
Ploshchad Turgueneva
Ploshchad Repina
ULITSA LABUTINA
KLIMOV PER.
PRIADILNY PER.
LIUBLINSKY PER.
FONTANKA
TROTSKY MARKET
PROSPEKT
POLISH GARDENS
DERJAVINSKY PER.
NAB. REKY FONTANKY
ISMAILOVSKY REGIMENT CATHEDRAL
4
NTANKA
REKY FONTANKY
ULITSA TSIOLKOVSKOGO
TROTSKY PR.
1 KRASNOAR. UL.
SOVETSKAYA HOTEL
13 KRASNOAR. ULITSA
2 KRASNOAR. UL.
LIBAVSKY
8 KRASNOAR. ULITSA
3 KRASNOAR. UL.
RIJSKY PROSPEKT
9 KRASNOAR. ULITSA
4 KRASNOAR. UL.
DERPTSKI PER.
PER. LODYGUINA
REVELSKY PER.
10 KRASNOAR. UL.
5 KRASNOAR. UL.
KURLANDSKAYA ULITSA
DROVIANAYA ULITSA
11 KRASNOARMESKAYA ULITSA
6 KRASNOAR. UL.
12 KRASNOAR. UL.
7 KRASNOAR. UL.
STATUE OF LERMONTOV
IZMAILOVS
ULITSA YEGOROVA
STARO-PETERGOFSKY PROSPEKT
NAB. OBVODNOGO KANALA
LERMONTOVSKY PROSPEKT
NAB. OBVODNOGO KANALA
5
BALTISKAYA
BALTIC STATION
WARSAW STATION
ULITSA ROZENCHTEINA
ULITSA CHKAPINA
FRUNZENSKAYA
MITROFANIEVSKOYE CHOSE
NARVSKY PR.
UL. IVANA TCHERNYKH
ULITSA METROSTROEVTSEV
ULITSA CHKAPINA
ULITSA KRASUTSKOGO
BALTISKAYA ULITSA
0
200
400 m
0
660
1320 ft
6
ARVSKAYA
D
E
F

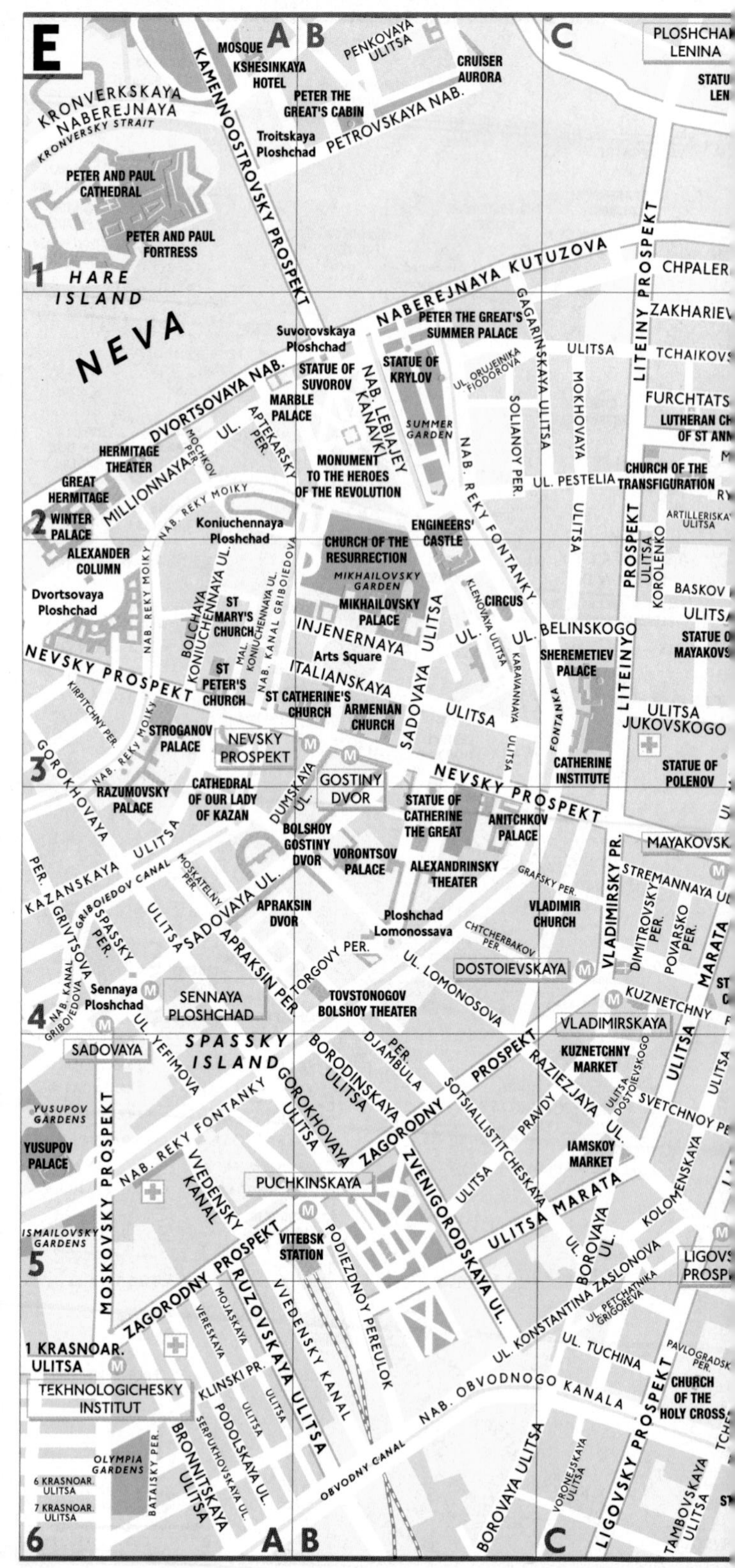
E
MOSQUE
KSHESINKAYA HOTEL
PENKOVAYA ULITSA
CRUISER AURORA
PLOSHCHAD LENINA
KRONVERKSKAYA NABEREJNAYA
KRONVERSKY STRAIT
PETER THE GREAT'S CABIN
PETROVSKAYA NAB.
Troitskaya Ploshchad
KAMENNOOSTROVSKY PROSPEKT
PETER AND PAUL CATHEDRAL
PETER AND PAUL FORTRESS
HARE ISLAND
NEVA
NABEREJNAYA KUTUZOVA
LITEINY PROSPEKT
CHPALER
ZAKHARIEV
Suvorovskaya Ploshchad
PETER THE GREAT'S SUMMER PALACE
GAGARINSKAYA ULITSA
STATUE OF SUVOROV
STATUE OF KRYLOV
UL. ORUJEINIKA FIODOROVA
ULITSA
TCHAIKOVS
DVORTSOVAYA NAB.
MARBLE PALACE
NAB. LEBIAJEY KANAVKI
SOLIANOY PER.
MOKHOVAYA
FURCHTATS
LUTHERAN CH OF ST ANN
SUMMER GARDEN
HERMITAGE THEATER
MOCHKOV PER.
UL.
APTEKARSKY PER.
MONUMENT TO THE HEROES OF THE REVOLUTION
NAB. REKY FONTANKY
GREAT HERMITAGE
MILLIONNAYA
NAB. REKY MOIKY
UL. PESTELIA
CHURCH OF THE TRANSFIGURATION
WINTER PALACE
Koniuchennaya Ploshchad
ENGINEERS' CASTLE
ARTILLERISKAYA ULITSA
ALEXANDER COLUMN
CHURCH OF THE RESURRECTION
MIKHAILOVSKY GARDEN
ULITSA
PROSPEKT
ULITSA KOROLENKO
Dvortsovaya Ploshchad
BOLCHAYA KONIUCHENNAYA UL.
ST MARY'S CHURCH
MAL. KONIUCHENNAYA UL.
NAB. KANAL GRIBOIEDOVA
MIKHAILOVSKY PALACE
CIRCUS
KLENOVAYA ULITSA
BASKOV
ULITSA
INJENERNAYA
UL.
UL. BELINSKOGO
STATUE OF MAYAKOVS
Arts Square
KARAVANNAYA
SHEREMETIEV PALACE
NEVSKY PROSPEKT
ST PETER'S CHURCH
ITALIANSKAYA
ST CATHERINE'S CHURCH
ARMENIAN CHURCH
SADOVAYA ULITSA
ULITSA
LITEINY
KIRPITCHNY PER.
FONTANKA
ULITSA JUKOVSKOGO
STROGANOV PALACE
NEVSKY PROSPEKT
GOROKHOVAYA
NAB. REKY MOIKY
GOSTINY DVOR
CATHERINE INSTITUTE
STATUE OF POLENOV
RAZUMOVSKY PALACE
CATHEDRAL OF OUR LADY OF KAZAN
DUMSKAYA UL.
STATUE OF CATHERINE THE GREAT
ANITCHKOV PALACE
ULITSA
BOLSHOY GOSTINY DVOR
MAYAKOVSK
PER.
KAZANSKAYA
GRIBOIEDOV CANAL
MOSKATELNY PER.
VORONTSOV PALACE
ALEXANDRINSKY THEATER
GRAFSKY PER.
VLADIMIRSKY PR.
STREMANNAYA UL
GRIVTSOVA
SPASSKY PER.
ULITSA
SADOVAYA UL.
APRAKSIN DVOR
VLADIMIR CHURCH
DIMITROVSKY PER.
POVARSKO PER.
MARATA
Ploshchad Lomonossava
CHTCHERBAKOV PER.
APRAKSIN PER.
TORGOVY PER.
UL. LOMONOSOVA
DOSTOIEVSKAYA
NAB. KANAL GRIBOIEDOVA
Sennaya Ploshchad
SENNAYA PLOSHCHAD
TOVSTONOGOV BOLSHOY THEATER
KUZNETCHNY
VLADIMIRSKAYA
SADOVAYA
UL. YEFIMOVA
SPASSKY ISLAND
BORODINSKAYA ULITSA
PER. DJAMBULA
PROSPEKT
RAZIEZJAYA UL.
KUZNETCHNY MARKET
ULITSA DOSTOIEVSKOGO
ULITSA
YUSUPOV GARDENS
YUSUPOV PALACE
NAB. REKY FONTANKY
GOROKHOVAYA ULITSA
ZAGORODNY
SOTSIALLISTITCHESKAYA
PRAVDY
SVETCHNOY PE
MOSKOVSKY PROSPEKT
VVEDENSKY KANAL
PUCHKINSKAYA
ZVENIGORODSKAYA UL.
ULITSA
IAMSKOY MARKET
KOLOMENSKAYA
ULITSA MARATA
ISMAILOVSKY GARDENS
VITEBSK STATION
PODIEZDNOY PEREULOK
UL. BOROVAYA
LIGOVS PROSP
ZAGORODNY PROSPEKT
RUZOVSKAYA ULITSA
VVEDENSKY KANAL
MOJASKAYA
VERESKAYA
UL. KONSTANTINA ZASLONOVA
UL. PETCHATNIKA GRIGOREVA
1 KRASNOAR. ULITSA
UL. TUCHINA
PAVLOGRADSK PER.
TEKHNOLOGICHESKY INSTITUT
KLINSKI PR.
ULITSA
NAB. OBVODNOGO KANALA
CHURCH OF THE HOLY CROSS
LIGOVSKY PROSPEKT
PODOLSKAYA ULITSA
SERPUKHOVSKAYA UL.
BRONNITSKAYA ULITSA
OLYMPIA GARDENS
BATAISKY PER.
OBVODNY CANAL
BOROVAYA ULITSA
VORONEJSKAYA ULITSA
TAMBOVSKAYA ULITSA
6 KRASNOAR. ULITSA
7 KRASNOAR. ULITSA
A B C
1 2 3 4 5 6

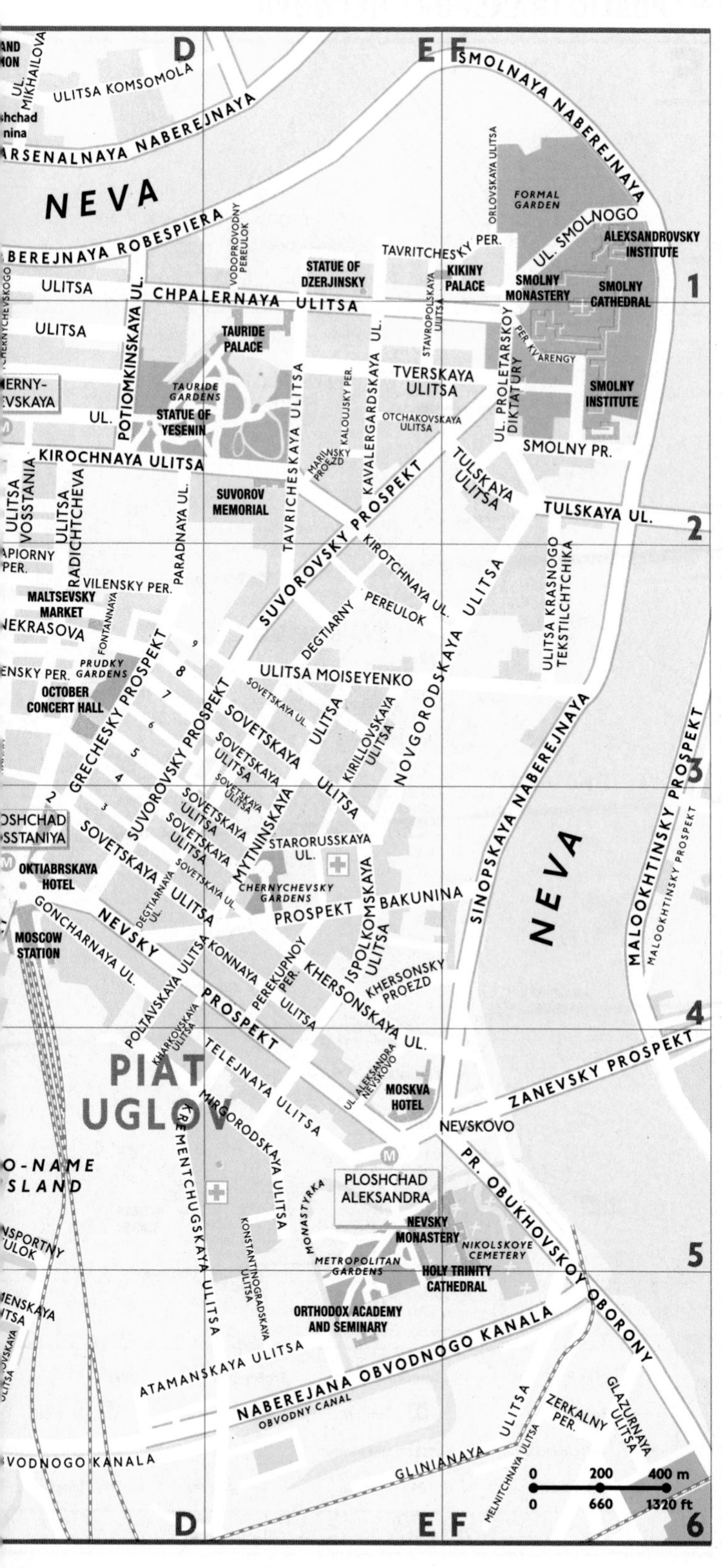

D
E
F
1
2
3
4
5
6
NEVA
ULITSA KOMSOMOLA
UL. MIKHAILOVA
ARSENALNAYA NABEREJNAYA
SMOLNAYA NABEREJNAYA
ORLOVSKAYA ULITSA
FORMAL GARDEN
UL. SMOLNOGO
ALEXSANDROVSKY INSTITUTE
SMOLNY MONASTERY
SMOLNY CATHEDRAL
SMOLNY INSTITUTE
TAVRITCHESKY PER.
KIKINY PALACE
STATUE OF DZERJINSKY
VODOPROVODNY PEREULOK
NABEREJNAYA ROBESPIERA
CHPALERNAYA ULITSA
ULITSA
POTIOMKINSKAYA UL.
TAURIDE PALACE
TAURIDE GARDENS
STATUE OF YESENIN
STAVROPOLSKAYA ULITSA
TVERSKAYA ULITSA
KAVALERGARDSKAYA UL.
KALOUJSKY PER.
OTCHAKOVSKAYA ULITSA
PER. KVARENGY
UL. PROLETARSKOY DIKTATURY
SMOLNY PR.
KIROCHNAYA ULITSA
ULITSA VOSSTANIA
ULITSA RADICHTCHEVA
PARADNAYA UL.
SUVOROV MEMORIAL
TAVRICHESKAYA ULITSA
MARIINSKY PROEZD
SUVOROVSKY PROSPEKT
TULSKAYA ULITSA
TULSKAYA UL.
KIROTCHNAYA UL.
PEREULOK
ULITSA KRASNOGO TEKSTILCHTCHIKA
VILENSKY PER.
MALTSEVSKY MARKET
FONTANNAYA
NEKRASOVA
PRUDKY GARDENS
OCTOBER CONCERT HALL
GRECHESKY PROSPEKT
DEGTIARNY
ULITSA MOISEYENKO
NOVGORODSKAYA ULITSA
SOVETSKAYA UL.
SOVETSKAYA ULITSA
KIRILLOVSKAYA ULITSA
SINOPSKAYA NABEREJNAYA
MALOOKHTINSKY PROSPEKT
MYTNINSKAYA
STARORUSSKAYA UL.
PLOSHCHAD VOSSTANIYA
OKTIABRSKAYA HOTEL
CHERNYCHEVSKY GARDENS
PROSPEKT BAKUNINA
ISPOLKOMSKAYA ULITSA
DEGTIARNAYA UL.
MOSCOW STATION
GONCHARNAYA UL.
NEVSKY PROSPEKT
KONNAYA ULITSA
PEREKUPNOY PER.
KHERSONSKAYA UL.
KHERSONSKY PROEZD
POLTAVSKAYA ULITSA
KHARKOVSKAYA ULITSA
PIAT UGLOV
TELEJNAYA ULITSA
UL. ALEKSANDRA NEVSKOVO
MOSKVA HOTEL
NEVSKOVO
ZANEVSKY PROSPEKT
MIRGORODSKAYA ULITSA
KREMENTCHUGSKAYA ULITSA
PLOSHCHAD ALEKSANDRA
PR. OBUKHOVSKOY OBORONY
MONASTYRKA
KONSTANTINOGRADSKAYA ULITSA
NEVSKY MONASTERY
NIKOLSKOYE CEMETERY
METROPOLITAN GARDENS
HOLY TRINITY CATHEDRAL
ORTHODOX ACADEMY AND SEMINARY
ATAMANSKAYA ULITSA
NABEREJANA OBVODNOGO KANALA
OBVODNY CANAL
GLINIANAYA ULITSA
MELNITCHNAYA ULITSA
ZERKALNY PER.
GLAZURNAYA ULITSA
0 200 400 m
0 660 1320 ft

PUBLIC TRANSPORT NETWORK

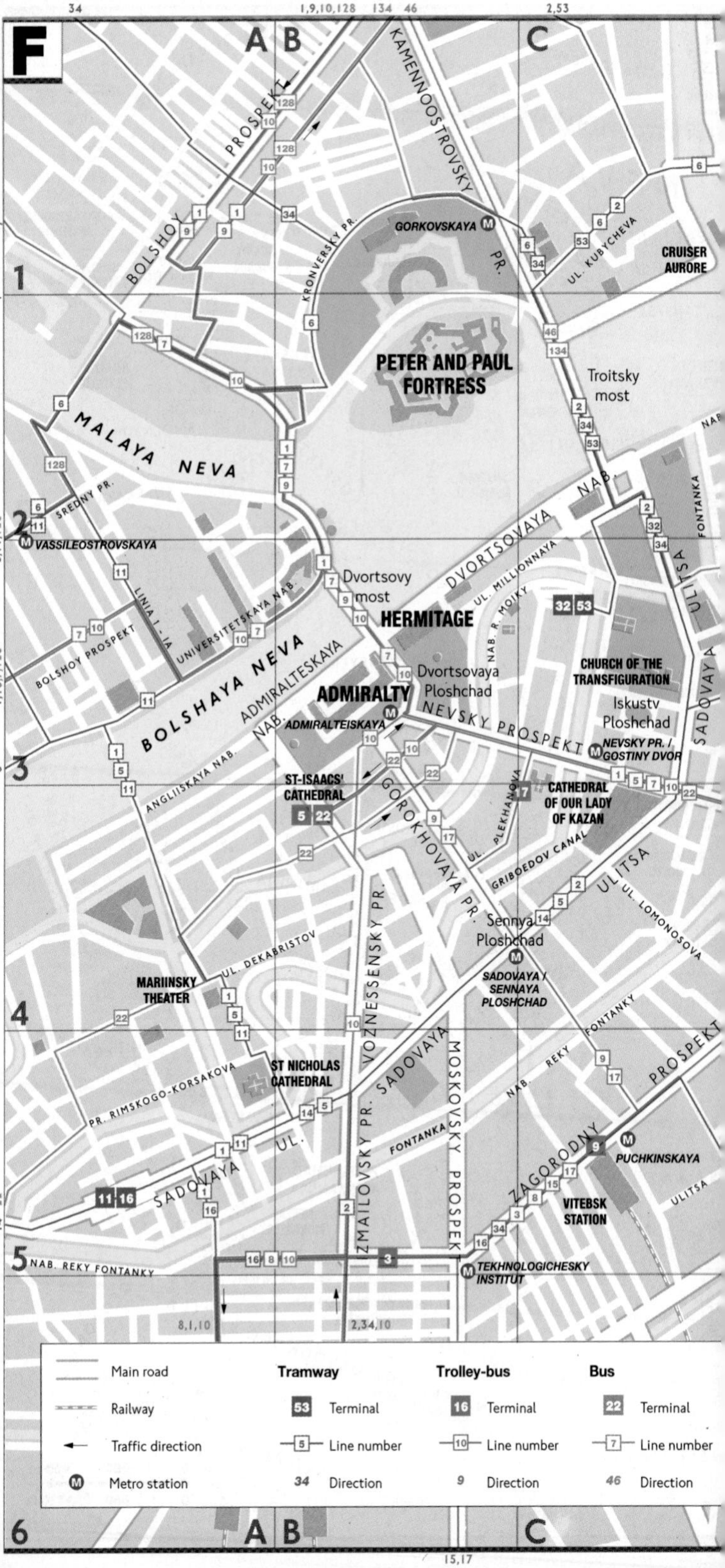

Main road

Railway

Traffic direction

Metro station

Tramway

53 Terminal

5 Line number

34 Direction

Trolley-bus

16 Terminal

10 Line number

9 Direction

Bus

22 Terminal

7 Line number

46 Direction

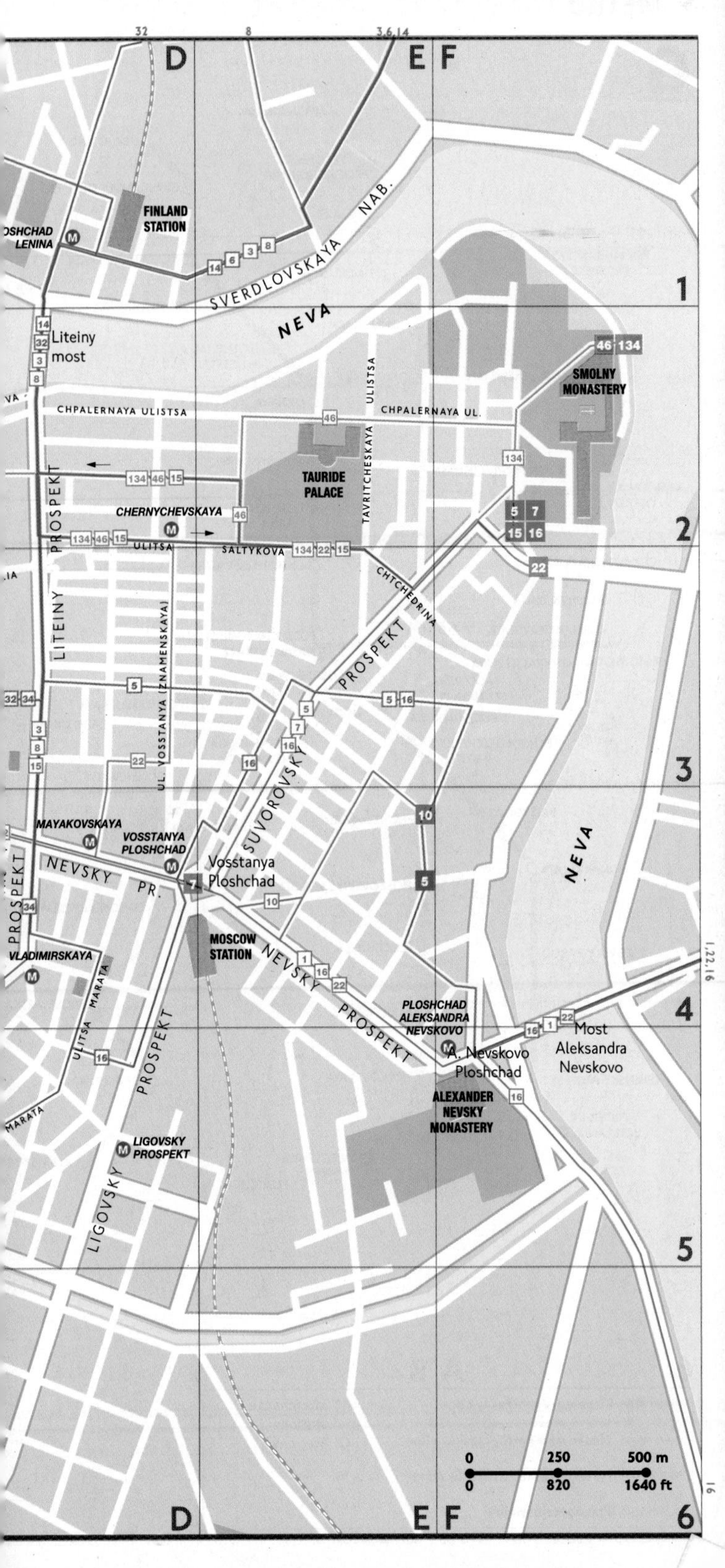
FINLAND STATION
PLOSHCHAD LENINA
SVERDLOVSKAYA NAB.
NEVA
Liteiny most
CHPALERNAYA ULISTSA
CHPALERNAYA UL.
TAVRITCHESKAYA ULISTSA
SMOLNY MONASTERY
TAURIDE PALACE
CHERNYCHEVSKAYA
SALTYKOVA
ULITSA
CHTCHEDRINA
LITEINY PROSPEKT
UL. VOSSTANYA (ZNAMENSKAYA)
SUVOROVSKY PROSPEKT
MAYAKOVSKAYA
VOSSTANYA PLOSHCHAD
Vosstanya Ploshchad
NEVSKY PR.
MOSCOW STATION
NEVSKY PROSPEKT
VLADIMIRSKAYA
ULITSA MARATA
MARATA
PLOSHCHAD ALEKSANDRA NEVSKOVO
A. Nevskovo Ploshchad
Most Aleksandra Nevskovo
ALEXANDER NEVSKY MONASTERY
LIGOVSKY PROSPEKT
LIGOVSKY PROSPEKT
0 250 500 m
0 820 1640 ft

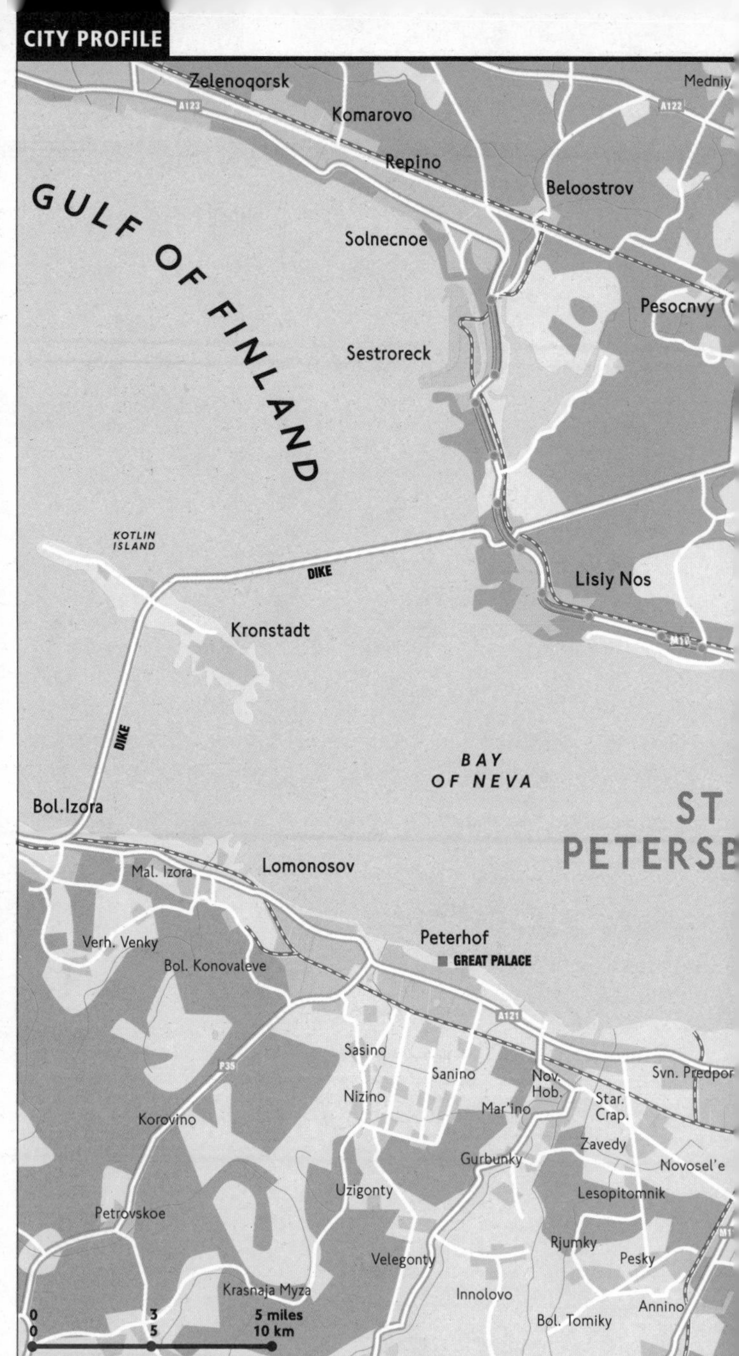

ST PETERSBURG IN FIGURES
The cultural and tourist capital of Russia and the country's second-largest city after Moscow. Built on the Neva delta, the city consists of 42 islands linked by some 300 bridges.

LATITUDE
Lying at 60°, it is the largest megalopolis at this latitude.

SURFACE AREA
540 square miles.
Administrative subdivision (*oblast*): 772 square miles.
20 districts (*raion*):

- Admiralteisky
- Vasileostrovsky
- Vyborgsky
- Kalininsky
- Kirovsky
- Krasnogvardeisky
- Krasnoselsky
- Moskovsky
- Nevsky
- Petrogradsky
- Primorsky
- Frunzensky
- Tsentralnyy
- Puchkinsky
- Pavlovsky
- Lomonosovsky
- Petrodvortsovy
- Kronchtadsky